Whales, Dolphins, and Porpoises of the Eastern North Pacific and Adjacent Arctic Waters

A Guide to Their Identification

Stephen Leatherwood, Randall R. Reeves,
William F. Perrin, and William E. Evans

Appendix A by Larry Hobbs
Foreword by Victor B. Scheffer, Ph.D.

DOVER PUBLICATIONS, INC., NEW YORK

The National Marine Fisheries Service (NMFS) does not approve, recommend or endorse any proprietary product or proprietary material mentioned in this publication. No reference shall be made to NMFS, or to this publication furnished by NMFS, in any advertising or sales promotion which would indicate or imply that NMFS approves, recommends or endorses any proprietary product or proprietary material mentioned herein, or which has as its purpose an intent to cause directly or indirectly the advertised product to be used or purchased because of this NMFS publication.

Dover Publications would like to thank the Scientific Publications Office, National Marine Fisheries Service, Seattle, Washington, for their help in preparing the Dover reprint of this book.

Published in Canada by General Publishing Company, Ltd., 30 Lesmill Road, Don Mills, Toronto, Ontario.

Published in the United Kingdom by Constable and Company, Ltd., 10 Orange Street, London WC2H 7EG.

This Dover edition, first published in 1988, is a corrected and slightly revised republication of the work originally published by the National Marine Fisheries Service (National Oceanic and Atmospheric Administration, United States Department of Commerce), Seattle, Washington, July 1982, as NOAA Technical Report NMFS Circular 444. A new Foreword has been written for the Dover edition by Victor B. Scheffer, and the authors have added a new Preface and made a few corrections, alterations, and additions to the original text.

Manufactured in the United States of America
Dover Publications, Inc., 31 East 2nd Street, Mineola, N.Y. 11501

Library of Congress Cataloging-in-Publication Data

Whales, dolphins, and porpoises of the eastern North Pacific and adjacent Arctic waters : a guide to their identification / by Stephen Leatherwood . . . [et al.] ; appendix A by Larry Hobbs ; foreword by Victor B. Scheffer.
p. cm.
"Corrected and slightly revised republication of the work originally published by the National Marine Fisheries Service"—CIP t.p. verso.
Bibliography: p.
ISBN 0-486-25651-0 (pbk.)
1. Cetacea—North Pacific Ocean—Identification. 2. Cetacea—Arctic Ocean—Identification. 3. Mammals—North Pacific Ocean—Identification. 4. Mammals—Arctic Ocean—Identification. I. Leatherwood, Stephen. II. Hobbs, Larry J.
QL737.C4W443 1988
559.5'09164'3—dc19 88-16159
CIP

FOREWORD TO THE DOVER EDITION

Cetophilia, or love of whales, is a curious thing. It was seldom professed until the early 1970s, when environmentalism won a place in Western thought, when men and women in all ranks of society began looking anew at "man's place in nature." Suddenly whales and their smaller kin became symbolic of the many wildlife forms that were disappearing as a result of ignorance, indifference, and greed. Although the world population of hunted whales still remained at about one-half its prehunting level, the populations of four highly prized species had been reduced to one-tenth or less, an alarming low. Considerate persons campaigned—successfully, it now seems—for laws to protect whales. One important impetus to legislation was the startling revelation that commercial fishermen in the tropical East Pacific were accidentally killing about a half-million dolphins a year in nets set for tuna. Meanwhile the public manifested a surprising desire to learn more about the mysterious lives of animals that, to many, were merely images on Save the Whale posters. Scores of books about cetaceans, inspired by the curiosity of both amateurs and professionals, were published after 1970.

Responding to this new interest, Steve Leatherwood and two professional colleagues published in 1972 a looseleaf guide to the identification of whales in the water. What made it unique among whale books was its rich display of photographs and its ready-identification keys. The conventional way of portraying whales had been to sketch them from dead, distorted subjects lying on the beach or on the deck of some grimy whaling vessel. Witness the 1940 *National Geographic* story "Whales—Giants of the Sea," illustrated by watercolors. Ironically, the few persons most likely to know the true shapes and patterns of whales were the whalers. With the notable exception of Charles M. Scammon,[1] whalers evidently showed little interest in sketching the animals they hunted. When modern scuba and free-diving gear, underwater cameras, and fast color emulsions became available to wildlife photographers, they began to show us images of whales undistorted, moving freely in their undersea domain. Careful observations from boats and aircraft clarified our understanding of whales in motion. Rippling muscles, gaping blowholes and jaws, and dripping baleen plates came sharply into focus. In 1976 a second *National Geographic* feature, "Whales of the World," employed photographs as well as paintings. The book you are now about to read is a completely new successor to the Leatherwood team's 1972 work, enriched with over 500 photographs.

While technically explicit, this book is addressed primarily to lay readers: to those of you who are pleasure boaters, fisherfolk, commercial and military sailors, coastal aircraft pilots, and others who often scan the sea for spouts or hike along its borders in search of stranded curios. You are naturalists of a sort, and you share the human craving to know the *names* of living things, as well as to gain insight into their ways of life. (I have sometimes wondered, is putting a name to an object a subconscious way of capturing it? A flickering instinct from primitive times?)

Anyway, this book is basically a field guide to the identification of forty species. It is written by experts who know which features of cetacean anatomy and behavior are specific, or diagnostic, and which ones are shared by many species. It is organized not by taxonomic but by practical groups. That is, whales are separated by size and by the presence or absence of a dorsal fin. To get the most out of the field-guide aspects of this book, when you are looking at a cetacean in the water, observe its size, color, fin (if present), tail flukes, and flippers; then its behavior in swimming, blowing, and diving. If you are looking at one on the beach, observe also details such as ventral grooves, baleen plates, and teeth. (Be aware that no one species has all three of these features.)

Or you can simply take pleasure in reading the Natural History Notes that are part of each Species Account and in studying the action photos. Here you will be introduced to cetaceans leaping high in the air; engaging in "synchronous swimming," as in water follies; following cracks through polar ice to their feeding and calving grounds; racing in groups of a hundred or more to compose a pattern of dark-and-light like the burst of a skyrocket; mating and giving birth; "smiling" at visitors through aquarium glass; wearing radio transmitters for science; receiving first aid; struggling to escape from a tuna net; and being butchered by the long knives of the whalemen.

You will see images of fetal cetaceans and of a hybrid between two species; whale teeth the size of carrots and larger; and whale "lice" and whale barnacles, both peculiar to cetaceans. You will see baleen plates that filter up to eight tons of plankton food per day. A photo from an airplane shows a "bubble net" in the shape of the Greek letter *alpha,* blown by a feeding humpback whale to trap (so it is believed) small schooling prey for easier capture.

In the final pages you will learn how scientists track the movements of cetaceans after attaching to their bodies numbered tags or radio transmitters, or by capitalizing on the fact that, like Moby Dick, most individuals sport distinctive patterns. About 30,000 killer-whale "mug shots" are now on file in research centers from Alaska to California. For those of you who wish to contribute new cetological data from the field, this book tells how to describe, in standard terminology, sightings at sea and key anatomical features of stranded carcasses.

In its original edition, this book, the work of four senior members of the marine-mammal research community, has been widely used by professionals. Thanks to Dover Publications, it is now available to nonprofessionals as well. You will find it fact-filled and stimulating. It invites you to visit the whales, dolphins, and porpoises in their own world. And perhaps what you learn will enable you to add to the fund of knowledge of a group of animals so very far removed from, and yet so near, humankind. "There is no proper place for them in a *scala naturae,*" wrote George Gaylord Simpson of the American Museum of Natural History as he struggled years ago to classify the cetaceans. "They may be imagined as extending into a different dimension from any of the surrounding orders or cohorts."[2]

Victor Scheffer, Ph.D.
Biologist (Retired), U.S. Fish and Wildlife Service
Chairman (Retired), Marine Mammal Commission

[1]Author of *The Marine Mammals of the North-western Coast of North America Described and Illustrated,* 1874 (Dover reprint, 0-486-21976-3).
[2]"The Principles of Classification and a Classification of Mammals," *Bull. Amer. Mus. Nat. Hist.,* vol. 85 (1945), pp. 213–214.

PREFACE TO THE FIRST EDITION

In March 1972, the Naval Undersea Center (NUC), San Diego, Calif., in cooperation with the National Marine Fisheries Service (NMFS), Tiburon, Calif., published a photographic field guide—*The Whales, Dolphins and Porpoises of the Eastern North Pacific; A Guide to Their Identification in the Water*, by S. Leatherwood, W. E. Evans, and D. W. Rice (NUC TP 282). This guide was designed to assist laymen in identifying cetaceans encountered in that area and was intended for use in two ongoing cetacean-observer programs, NUC's Whale Watch and NMFS's Platforms of Opportunity Program. These programs relied on observations by oceanographers, commercial and sport fishermen, naval personnel, commercial seamen, pleasure boaters, and coastal aircraft pilots, who together canvas large areas of the oceans which scientists specializing in whale research (cetologists) have time and funds to survey only occasionally. By training nonspecialists in species identification and asking them to report their sightings to data centers, scientists stand to gain otherwise unavailable insights into distribution, migration, and seasonal variations in abundance of cetaceans. For such a cooperative program to work, a usable field guide is essential. Because many of the publications on whales, dolphins, and porpoises of this region were either too technical in content or too limited in scope, and because conventional scientific or taxonomic groupings of the animals are often not helpful in field identification, the photographic field guide took a new approach. Instead of being arranged on the basis of their taxonomic relationships, species were grouped according to similarities in appearance during the brief encounters typical at sea. Photographs of the animals in their natural environment, supplemented by drawings, descriptions, and tables distinguishing the most similar species, formed the core of the guide.

Despite deficiencies in the first effort and the inherent difficulties of positively identifying many cetacean species at sea, results obtained from the programs were encouraging. Many seafarers who had previously looked with indifference or ignorance on the animals they encountered became good critical observers and found pleasure in the contribution they were making.

Interest in a similar guide to cetaceans of the western North Atlantic was spurred by the appearance of the Pacific Guide. *Whales, Dolphins, and Porpoises of the Western North Atlantic; a Guide to Their Identification* by S. Leatherwood, D. K. Caldwell, and H. E. Winn was published in August 1976 as NOAA Technical Report NMFS CIRC-396. In it, many of the errors and inadequacies of the Pacific Guide were remedied. A section on the identification and reporting of stranded cetaceans was included, and it has proven to be one of the most valued parts of the Atlantic Guide. We therefore include aids to the identification of stranded cetaceans in this much-revised version of the Pacific Guide. In addition, we have included, as available, aerial and underwater photographs of each species. Aerial surveys have become a widely accepted technique for assessing distribution of marine mammals, and more and more pilots who fly for business or pleasure have expressed an interest in learning how to identify whales, dolphins, and porpoises from the air. Also, divers increasingly seek out cetaceans and enjoy viewing the animals in their own fluid, multidimensional world. We are indebted to several pilots and divers for providing new perspectives on the subjects of this book.

We are convinced that this, the third, photograph-laden guide to cetacean identification off North American coasts, is an improvement on the previous two. Like them, however, it will start to become out-of-date even before it reaches you, the reader. We therefore ask for your indulgence and, more importantly, for your cooperation in letting us know what we have said poorly, incorrectly, or not at all. Suggestions for this book's improvement are at all times welcome.

Funds for the preparation of this guide were provided by a grant to Randall R. Reeves from the Northwest and Alaska Fisheries Center National Marine Mammal Laboratory, National Marine Fisheries Service, National Oceanic and Atmospheric Administration, Seattle, Wash.

PREFACE TO THE DOVER EDITION

In the years since 1982, when this book was first published, there has been an enormous amount of research on cetaceans of the world, resulting in a great increase in information available about many species. It would have been a significant task for us to revise this book to reflect all those findings, and we have elected not to do so. Instead, we have simply corrected errors detected in the original version, convinced that the book's usefulness as a field guide has not been compromised by leaving the text and figures basically as originally printed. The one exception is that we have corrected our description of the external appearance of the vaquita (previously known as the "cochito"), which, in 1982, had not yet been adequately described, and we have added two illustrations of that species.

We are pleased that this publication has been so well received and widely used. The Government Printing Office has distributed over 17,000 copies in English, and the Inter-American Tropical Tuna Commission has recently completed a Spanish edition for use in its research and fishing-observer programs. We thank Dover Publications for making the book more generally and widely available, and we sincerely hope that it continues to stimulate interest in cetaceans and their conservation.

CONTENTS

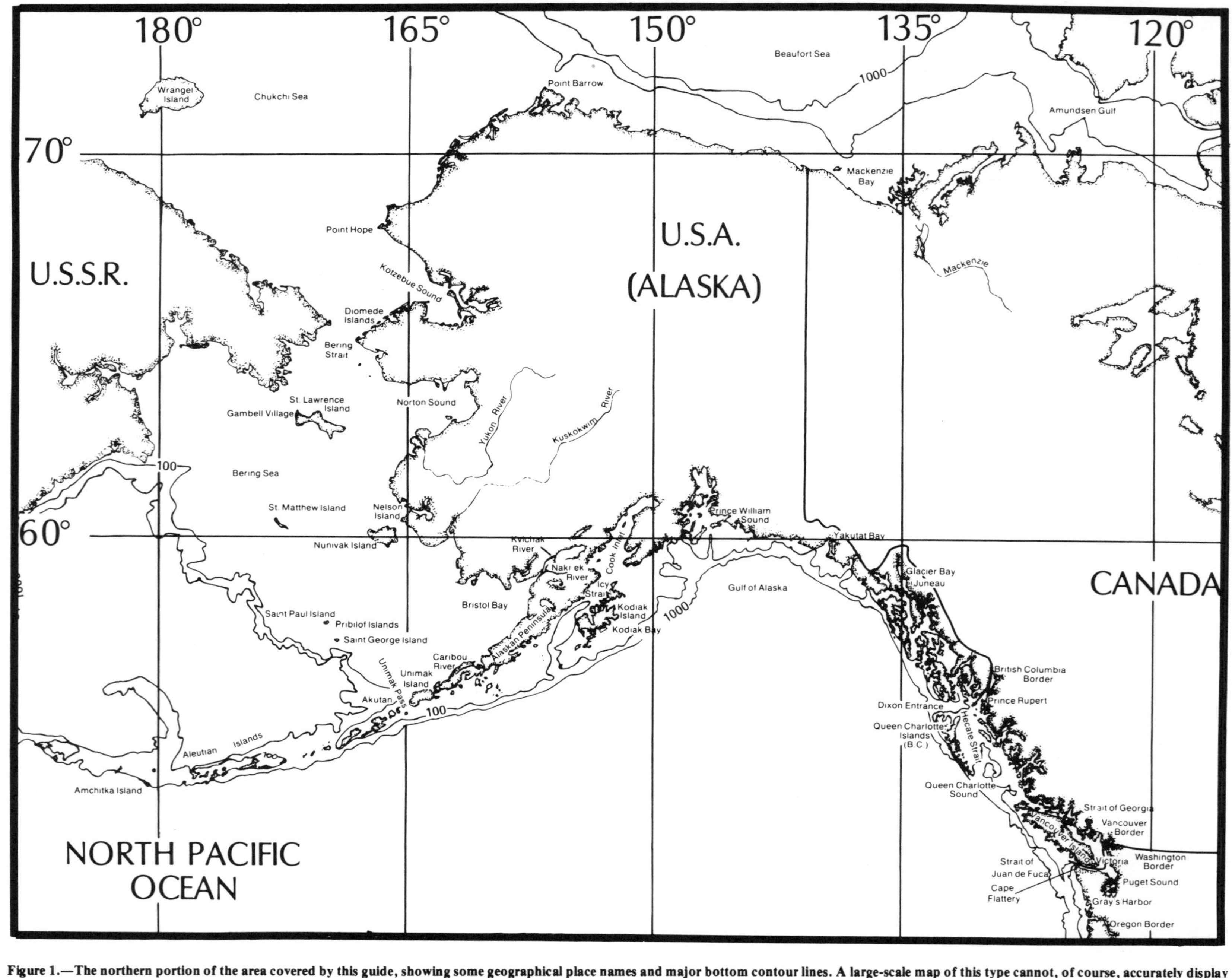

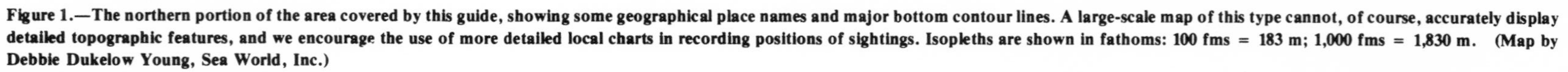

Figure 1.—The northern portion of the area covered by this guide, showing some geographical place names and major bottom contour lines. A large-scale map of this type cannot, of course, accurately display detailed topographic features, and we encourage the use of more detailed local charts in recording positions of sightings. Isopleths are shown in fathoms: 100 fms = 183 m; 1,000 fms = 1,830 m. (Map by Debbie Dukelow Young, Sea World, Inc.)

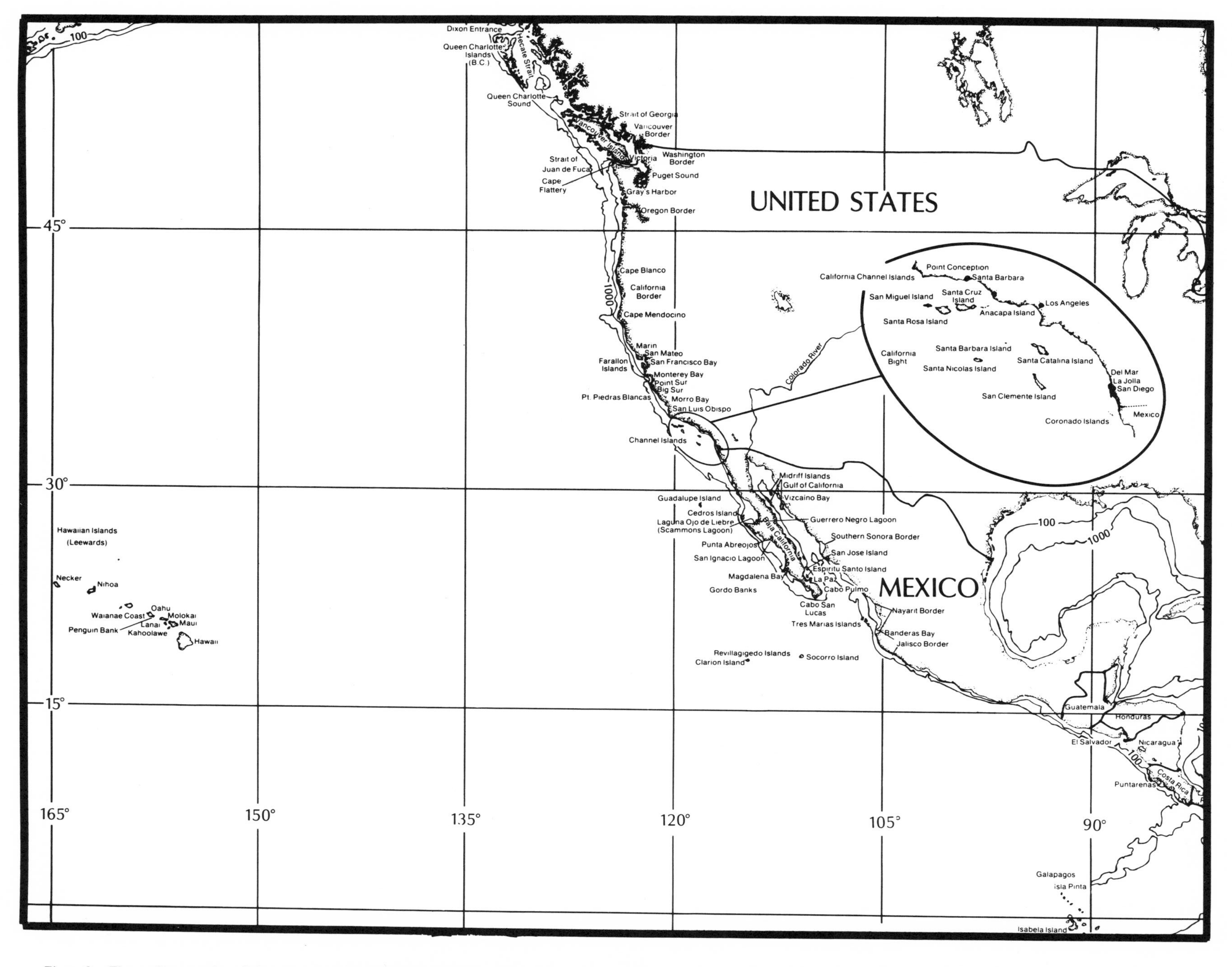

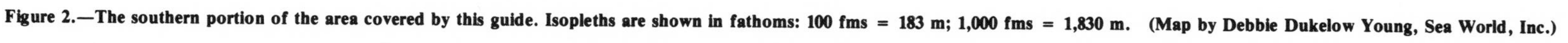

Figure 2.—The southern portion of the area covered by this guide. Isopleths are shown in fathoms: 100 fms = 183 m; 1,000 fms = 1,830 m. (Map by Debbie Dukelow Young, Sea World, Inc.)

Whales, Dolphins, and Porpoises of the Eastern North Pacific and Adjacent Arctic Waters

A Guide to Their Identification

STEPHEN LEATHERWOOD,[1] RANDALL R. REEVES,[2] WILLIAM F. PERRIN,[3] and WILLIAM E. EVANS[1]

with Appendix A on Tagging by Larry Hobbs[4]

ABSTRACT

This field guide is designed to permit observers to identify the cetaceans (whales, dolphins, and porpoises) they see in the waters of the eastern North Pacific, including the Gulf of California, Hawaii, and the western Arctic of North America. The animals described are grouped not by scientific relationships but by similarities in appearance in the field. Photographs of the animals in their natural environment are the main aids to identification.

Appendices describe how and to whom to report data on live and dead cetaceans and provide information to aid in identification of stranded cetaceans.

INTRODUCTION

All whales, dolphins, and porpoises belong to an order or major scientific group called the Cetacea. They are mammals (air-breathing animals which have hair in at least some stage of their development, maintain a constant body temperature, bear their young live, and suckle them) whose body form (anatomy) and functions (physiology) have been drastically modified to cope with a life spent entirely in water. The breathing apparatus, a blowhole or pair of blowholes, has migrated to the top of the head to facilitate breathing while swimming; the forward appendages have become flippers; the hind appendages have nearly disappeared, remaining only as small bones deeply imbedded in the muscles. Propulsion is provided by fibrous, horizontally flattened tail flukes.

Scientists recognize two suborders of living cetaceans: the whalebone (baleen) whales or mysticetes, suborder Mysticeti; and the toothed whales or odontocetes, suborder Odontoceti. The two groups are distinguished in the following ways:

BALEEN OR WHALEBONE WHALES. Instead of teeth these whales possess up to 800 or more plates of baleen or whalebone, rooted in the gums of the upper jaw. They use these plates to strain their food, which consists of zooplankton and small schooling fish. Water is taken into the mouth and forced out through the overlapping fringes of the baleen plates. Some species feed by skimming, passing slowly through swarms of relatively passive prey, engulfing them in a smooth and deliberate fashion. Others feed by gulping, distending the throat to take in huge quantities of water and the food organisms it contains, in a far more dramatic process. Baleen whales are externally distinguishable from toothed whales by having paired blowholes. There are nine species of baleen whales in the eastern North Pacific, ranging in maximum size from the 10 m minke whale to the 26 m blue whale.

TOOTHED WHALES. Unlike the baleen whales, the toothed whales have teeth after birth. The teeth vary in number from 2 to over 250, and in females of some species they remain concealed in the gum throughout life. Toothed whales have a single blowhole. Included in this group are animals commonly called dolphins or porpoises as well as many of the whales (e.g., the sperm whale and the killer whale). There are currently about 30 species of toothed whales known from the eastern North Pacific, ranging in maximum adult size from the 1.5 m harbor porpoise to the 21 m male sperm whale.

CLASSIFICATION OF CETACEANS

In addition to the two suborders (Mysticeti and Odontoceti), the order Cetacea is subdivided into numerous families, genera, and species. Each of these groupings represents a progressively more specialized division on the basis of similarities in skull, postcranial skeleton, and external characteristics. The discipline which concerns itself with naming plants and animals and assigning appropriate scientific categories is known as taxonomy. An example of the classification of a cetacean species is shown in the following:

[1]Hubbs/Sea World Research Institute, 1700 South Shores Road, San Diego, CA 92109.

[2]National Fish and Wildlife Laboratory, Smithsonian Institution, U.S. National Museum, Washington, DC 20560.

[3]Southwest Fisheries Center La Jolla Laboratory, National Marine Fisheries Service, NOAA, P.O. Box 271, La Jolla, CA 92037.

[4]Northwest and Alaska Fisheries Center National Marine Mammal Laboratory, National Marine Fisheries Service, NOAA, 7600 Sand Point Way N.E., Seattle, WA 98115.

Figure 3 (opposite page, top).—A humpback whale with paired blowholes opened during respiration. The paired blowholes distinguish this whale as a baleen whale. The splash guards (raised, fleshy prominences surrounding the blowholes—exaggerated during exhalation and relatively flattened following) are common to rorquals. (Photo from Newfoundland by J. C. Norris.)

Figure 4 (opposite page, bottom).—A right whale on the deck of a whaling station in British Columbia. Note the plates of baleen (often called whalebone) suspended from the roof of the mouth. The baleen is much longer in the right whales (the right and the bowhead) than in other species. (Photo by G. C. Pike, courtesy I. A. MacAskie.)

Figure 5 (above).—A mother bottlenose dolphin and her calf. The single blowhole identifies them as toothed whales. (Photo from Sea Life Park, Hawaii, by S. Leatherwood.)

Figure 6 (right).—The open mouth of a bottlenose dolphin. Like other toothed whales, these dolphins use their teeth primarily for seizing prey rather than for chewing. The teeth of toothed whales vary in number among species from 2 to over 250 and vary greatly in form. (Photo courtesy of Wometco Miami Seaquarium.)

SCIENTIFIC CLASSIFICATION OF THE NORTHERN·RIGHT WHALE DOLPHIN

Kingdom:	Animalia	all animals
Phylum:	Chordata	having at some stage a notochord, the precursor of the backbone
Subphylum:	Vertebrata	animals with backbones—fishes, amphibians, reptiles, birds, and mammals
Class:	Mammalia	animals that have hair and nurse their young
Order:	Cetacea	carnivorous, wholly aquatic mammals: whales, including dolphins and porpoises
Suborder:	Odontoceti	toothed whales as distinguished from Mysticeti, the baleen whales
Family:	Delphinidae	dolphins and some small whales
Genus:	*Lissodelphis*	right whale dolphins
Species:	*Lissodelphis borealis*	northern right whale dolphin

Modern taxonomy originated with the Swedish naturalist Linnaeus, whose 10th edition of the *Systema Naturae* in 1758 forms the official starting point for the current application of scientific names of species. Following Linnaeus, modern scientific names of cetaceans consist of two words, a generic name, which is capitalized, and a trivial name, which is not. Both names are usually of Latin origin (sometimes Greek, English, or other languages) and are italicized or underlined. The scientific name is often accompanied by the name of the scientist (author) who first described the species and the year when he described it. If the author and date of description are in parentheses, it means that the species was originally described under a different genus than the one to which it is presently assigned. These scientific names are of particular importance because, although common names of species often vary by country or region, scientific names remain standard throughout the world. For example, the bowhead whale is universally known as *Balaena mysticetus* though its common names include (or have included) Arctic right whale, Greenland whale, Greenland right whale, great polar whale, and sometimes just the whale. Nonstandard nomenclature is particularly troublesome in the older whaling literature; it is sometimes impossible to know what species is being discussed in a given logbook or journal entry.

Although classification of many species is still tentative, we have chosen the following provisional classification and nomenclature for eastern North Pacific cetaceans:

			Page no.
Order Cetacea			
Suborder Mysticeti—Baleen whales			
Family Balaenopteridae—Rorquals			
Balaenoptera acutorostrata	Lacépède, 1804	Minke whale	80
Balaenoptera physalus	(Linnaeus, 1758)	Fin whale	23
Balaenoptera musculus	(Linnaeus, 1758)	Blue whale	13
Balaenoptera borealis	Lesson, 1828	Sei whale	29
Balaenoptera edeni	Anderson, 1878	Bryde's whale	34
Megaptera novaeangliae	(Borowski, 1781)	Humpback whale	39
Family Balaenidae—Right whales			
Balaena mysticetus	Linnaeus, 1758	Bowhead whale	60
Eubalaena glacialis	(Borowski, 1781)	Right whale	67
Family Eschrichtidae—Gray whales			
Eschrichtius robustus	Lilljeborg, 1861	Gray whale	72
Suborder Odontoceti—Toothed whales			
Family Ziphiidae			
Mesoplodon stejnegeri	True, 1885	Stejneger's beaked whale	102
Mesoplodon densirostris	(Blainville in Desmarest, 1817)	Blainville's beaked whale	103
Mesoplodon carlhubbsi	Moore, 1963	Hubbs' beaked whale	99
Mesoplodon ginkgodens	Nishiwaki and Kamiya, 1958	Ginkgo-toothed beaked whale	107
Mesoplodon hectori	(Gray, 1871)	Hector's beaked whale	110
Ziphius cavirostris	G. Cuvier, 1823	Cuvier's beaked whale	94
Hyperoodon sp.		(Southern ?) bottlenose whale	92
Berardius bairdii	Stejneger, 1883	Baird's beaked whale	88
Family Physeteridae			
Physeter macrocephalus	Linnaeus, 1758	Sperm whale	51
Kogia breviceps	(Blainville, 1838)	Pygmy sperm whale	193
Kogia simus	(Owen, 1866)	Dwarf sperm whale	198
Family Monodontidae			
Monodon monoceros	Linnaeus, 1758	Narwhal	137
Delphinapterus leucas	(Pallas, 1776)	White whale	134
Family Delphinidae			
Steno bredanensis	(G. Cuvier in Lesson, 1828)	Rough-toothed dolphin	178
Peponocephala electra	(Gray, 1846)	Melon-headed whale	188
Feresa attenuata	Gray, 1874	Pygmy killer whale	184
Pseudorca crassidens	(Owen, 1846)	False killer whale	118
Globicephala macrorhynchus	Gray, 1846	Short-finned pilot whale	123
Orcinus orca	(Linnaeus, 1758)	Killer whale	113
Lagenorhynchus obliquidens	Gill, 1865	Pacific white-sided dolphin	168

Lagenodelphis hosei	Fraser, 1956	Fraser's dolphin	166
Tursiops truncatus	(Montagu, 1821)	Bottlenose dolphin	173
Grampus griseus	(G. Cuvier, 1812)	Risso's dolphin	129
Stenella attenuata	(Gray, 1846)	Spotted dolphin	141
Stenella longirostris	(Gray, 1828)	Spinner dolphin	148
Stenella coeruleoalba	(Meyen, 1833)	Striped dolphin	155
Delphinus delphis	Linnaeus, 1758	Common dolphin	160
Lissodelphis borealis	(Peale, 1848)	Northern right whale dolphin	209
Family Phocoenidae			
Phocoena phocoena	(Linnaeus, 1758)	Harbor porpoise	205
Phocoena sinus	Norris and McFarland, 1958	Vaquita	208
Phocoenoides dalli	(True, 1885)	Dall's porpoise	200

The names we have used for the large whales follow long-standing usage by the International Whaling Commission (IWC), except that the name for the sperm whale used by the IWC has recently been changed from *Physeter catodon* to *P. macrocephalus*. The scientific and common names we have used for the smaller cetaceans follow a list published in 1977 by the IWC. Because the species are not arranged in taxonomic order in this field guide, the page of the synoptic account of each is provided in the column to the right.

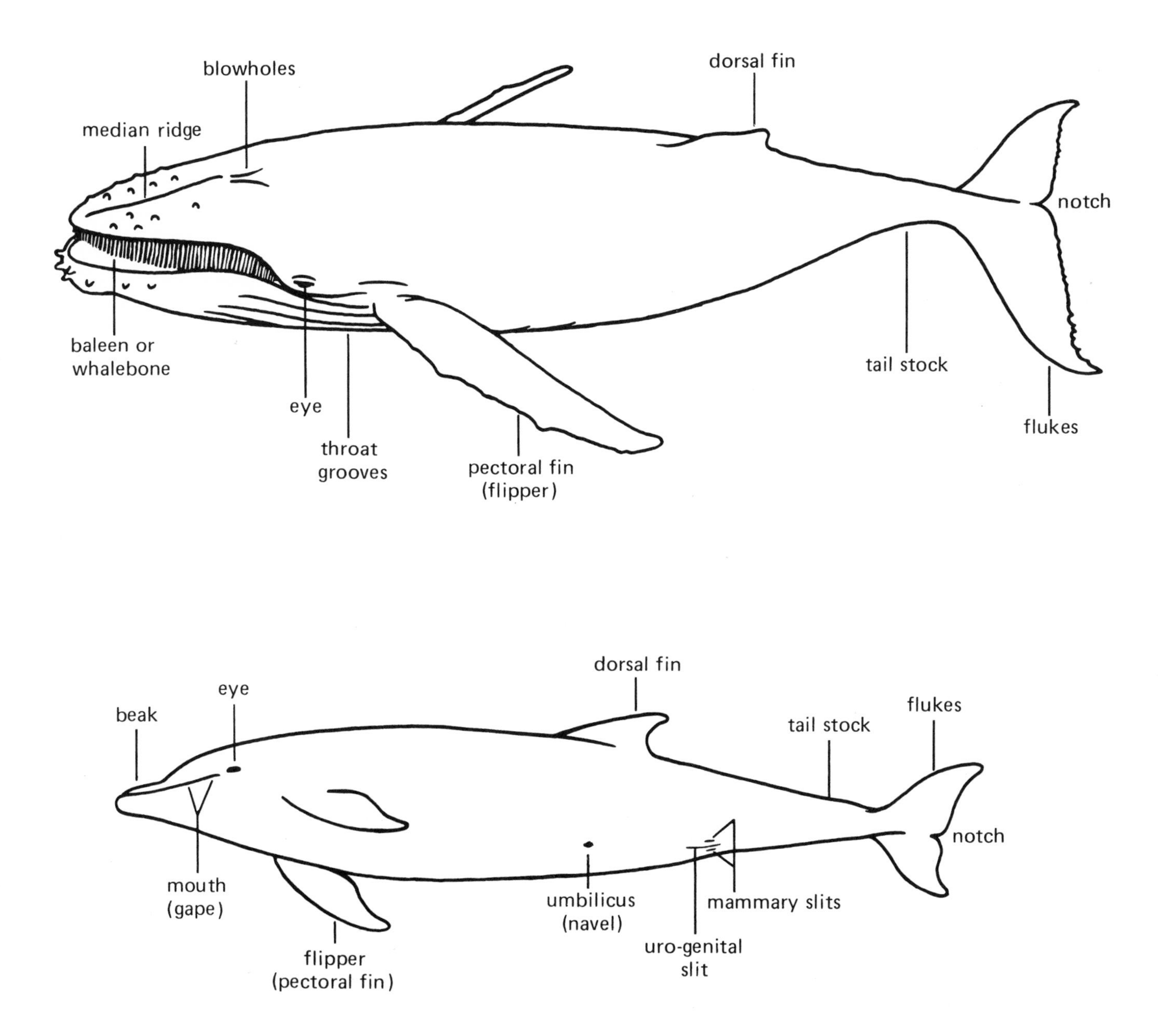

Figure 7.—A baleen whale (humpback whale), top, and a toothed whale (bottlenose dolphin), bottom, showing the primary body parts referred to in the text. (Drawings by Larry Foster, courtesy of General Whale.)

DOLPHIN, PORPOISE, OR WHALE?

There is still some controversy and misunderstanding about the correct usage of the terms dolphin and porpoise. As mentioned in the preceding section, common names of any species may vary from locale to locale and even from individual to individual. Some persons, especially seagoing people such as fishermen and including some U.S. scientists, use the term porpoise for all small cetaceans. Others, especially those associated with oceanaria and conservation organizations and including most non-American English-speaking peoples, call most members of the family Delphinidae dolphins and members of the family Phocoenidae porpoises. As with all vernacular language there is no universally correct terminology, and usage is a matter of personal preference and the need to communicate. We see no satisfactory resolution to this problem in terminology. For convenience only, we refer to many members of the family Delphinidae as dolphins, and to the three local members of the family Phocoenidae—*Phocoena phocoena*, *P. sinus*, and *Phocoenoides dalli*—as porpoises. Although all cetaceans may be regarded as whales, the term "whale" most commonly is applied only to the larger species. There are, of course, many common names for most species, including several in English; we use here the standard common names used by the IWC, the U.S. Marine Mammal Commission, the National Marine Fisheries Service, and several international conservation organizations. We also list some other widely used common names.

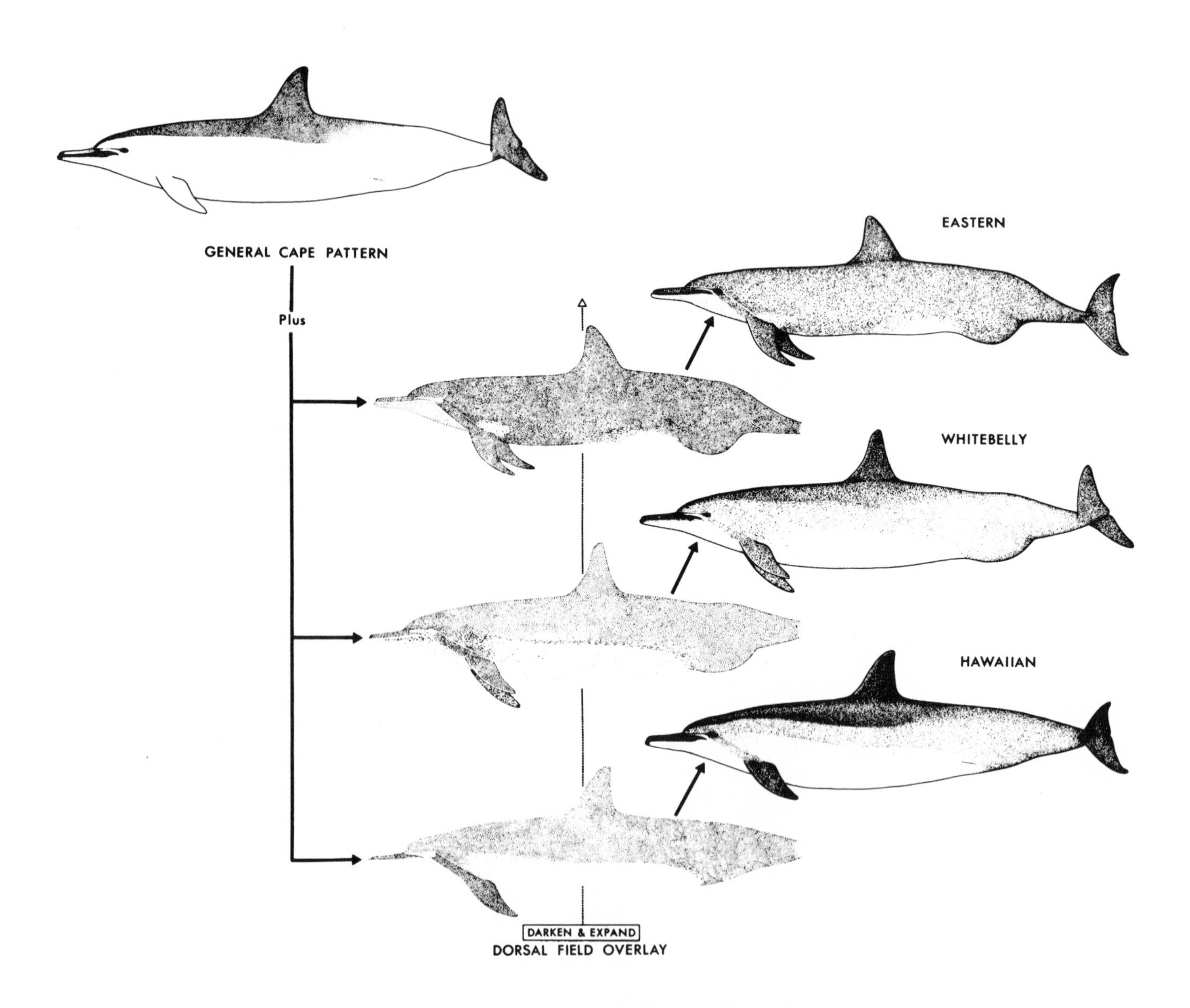

Figure 8.—Scheme for analyzing pigmentation patterns of spinner dolphins, showing how discrete components of varying strength combine to produce the pattern. (From Perrin 1972.)

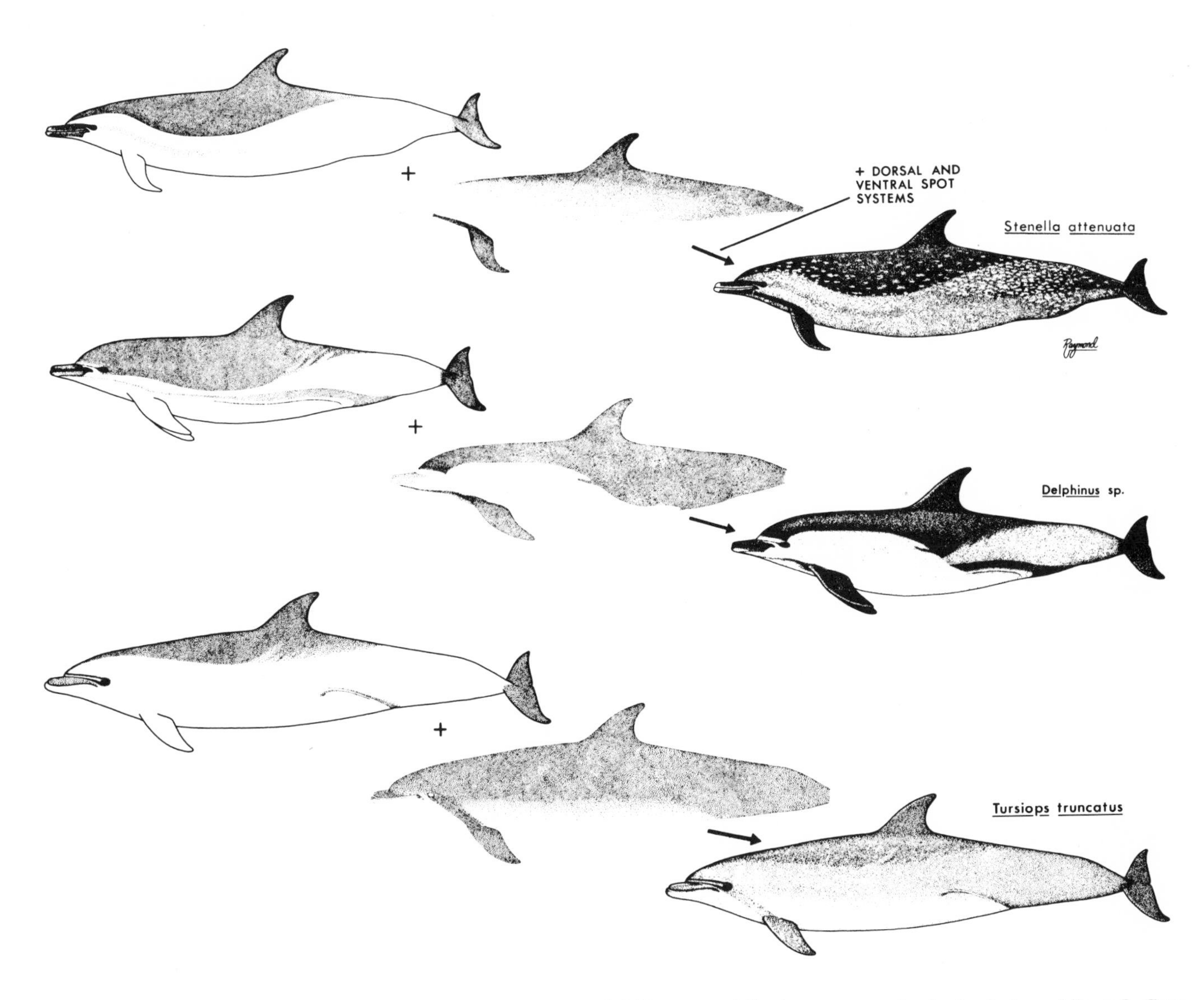

Figure 9.—Component analysis of pigmentation patterns of *Stenella attenuata, Delphinus* sp., and *Tursiops truncatus* using the terminology of Figure 8. (From Perrin 1972.)

ORGANIZATION OF THE GUIDE

The differences between baleen whales and toothed whales are easily distinguishable in stranded or captive animals. But since an animal at sea can seldom be examined closely, its most obvious characteristics may be overall size, the presence or absence of a dorsal fin, and swimming, blowing, and diving behavior. For that reason, regardless of their scientific relationships, all the whales, dolphins, and porpoises covered in the main text of this guide are divided into three groups. Those over 12 m long are discussed in the section on Large Whales, those from 4 m to 12 m with the Medium-Sized Whales, and those less than 4 m in the section on Small Whales, Dolphins, and Porpoises. Each section is further divided into sections on animals with a dorsal fin and animals without. Animals likely to be confused in the field are grouped together and the important differences among them are discussed.

The synoptic accounts of the species are followed by five appendices. Appendix A discusses and illustrates man-made and applied tags and natural markings on cetaceans, and their importance in studies of natural history. Appendix B discusses the data which are most important to record in observations of cetaceans at sea, gives examples, and provides blank sighting forms. Appendix C discusses possible causes of cetacean strandings and the manner in which stranded animals should be handled; it includes tables to aid in identifying stranded cetaceans. Appendix D provides guidelines for collecting data on stranded cetaceans and provides forms and specific instructions for taking standard measurements. Appendix E lists institutions to be contacted in the event of a cetacean stranding. Appendix F tabularizes cetacean names in Japanese and Russian.

A bibliography of useful references on cetaceans in general and cetaceans of this region in particular is provided.

HOW TO USE THE GUIDE

To Identify Animals at Sea

To use the guide to identify living animals observed at sea, the observer should:

1. First estimate the animal's size and determine whether or not it has a dorsal fin.
2. Note any distinctive features of body shape and coloration and observe its general behavior, including swimming, blowing, and diving characteristics. Coloration may vary somewhat at sea, depending on light conditions and water clarity. For example, animals which appear dark gray or black at the surface or when dead may appear brown in good light or when submerged. Making a brief sketch at this point may aid in identifying the animal or in recalling its distinctive features later. Photographs can be invaluable in this regard.
3. Consult the appropriate section. Examine the photographs and read the discussion of the animal's size, geographic range, and distinctive characteristics. Be careful to note the brief discussion of species with which it is likely to be confused in the field.

The information on distribution and movements of most species is presented in narrative form. Inherent in this approach is our recognition that maps cannot fairly represent the actual range of mobile, pelagic species whose survival strategies are tied, in ways we only poorly understand, to oceanographic conditions that vary within and among seasons and years. Maps have been provided only for species for which distribution is well known because of indirect exploitation in high-profile fisheries (i.e., spinner dolphin, spotted dolphin, common dolphin, striped dolphin). Most place names used in the narrative accounts have been included on the maps for the areas (Figs. 1, 2).

As noted in the Preface and Acknowledgments, there are an increasing number of research programs that depend heavily on low-altitude aerial surveys. In such surveys, cetaceans are identified and enumerated along a flight path of predetermined or measured width. Observed densities may be extrapolated, using various techniques, to densities or population estimates for a larger area. With this new (aerial) perspective on cetaceans come slightly different requirements for identification. Some species, particularly the large whales, are easier to identify from the air than from shipboard. Others, like most of the beaked dolphins, are very difficult to identify from the air. Several passes over a group of dolphins is often necessary before an opportune view of lateral pigmentation or dorsal fin shape and appearance leads to a reliable identification.

This guide will probably work best if, before attempting to use it in the field, you become familiar with the general outline, with characters and behavior to note, and with the locations of the various species accounts. The observer should school himself to ask a series of questions about the animal(s) at the time of the encounter rather than depending on recall at a later time (see p. 231). As we emphasize several times in this guide, positive identification of cetaceans at sea, whether from boat or aircraft, can only occasionally be made on the basis of a single characteristic. Therefore, the greater the amount of pertinent evidence an observer obtains, the greater the likelihood of making a reliable identification. It should also be remembered that a bad identification is worse than no identification at all. Even highly experienced observers collect many, and in some cases mostly, "unidentified" sightings during a cruise.

Throughout, we have sought to describe normal or average appearances and behavior. We recognize that much variability around these norms or averages will be encountered in the field. It is also important to stress that careful and thorough descriptions of what was actually seen are often of greater value to scientists than a mere assumption about species identification. Admission of one's inability to make a positive identification should be seen as a testimony not to the observer's incompetence but to his/her respect for a genuinely difficult art.

To Identify Stranded Animals

Stranded animals can best be identified by referring to Appendix C and its associated tables, making a preliminary determination, and then consulting the species accounts in the main body of the book for verification of the identification. As noted in that appendix, if the animal is recently stranded, identification can be made using any of the externally visible characteristics described for the living species at sea. But even if the animal is in an advanced stage of decomposition, it can usually be identified by referring to 1) the number and description of baleen plates for all baleen whales (Table 1, p. 216), 2) the number and relative length of ventral grooves for all balaenopterid whales (Table 1), or 3) the number and description of teeth for toothed whales (Table 2, p. 217).[5]

To Record and Report Information

Though learning to identify the whales, dolphins, and porpoises one sees can be rewarding in itself, many persons may want to go farther by passing on their observations to scientists who may be able to make use of the information.

Sample data forms and suggestions for making and recording observations of cetaceans at sea are included in Appendix B. Similar suggestions for work with stranded cetaceans are included in Appendix D. For both types of data, blank data forms located after the appendices may be photocopied for use in the field.

Completed data forms and all associated information for sightings at sea should be forwarded to the Platforms of Opportunity Program, Northwest and Alaska Fisheries Center National Marine Mammal Laboratory, National Marine Fisheries Service, NOAA, 7600 Sand Point Way N.E., Bldg. 32, Seattle, WA 98115, or to one of the authors of this guide. From there, they will be made available to scientists actively studying a given species or geographical area.

Completed data forms and all associated information for observations of stranded cetaceans should be forwarded to the Division of Mammals, U.S. National Museum, Washington, D.C. 20560, to one of the authors of this guide, or to one of the regional laboratories listed in Appendix E.

[5]For well-studied species, particularly those involved in extensive fisheries from which large samples have been taken, tooth and baleen counts and ventral groove counts and descriptions may be accurate. But it is extremely important to keep in mind that many of the numbers in the text and tables are based on only a few specimens and may not accurately reflect the range of characters for the entire species.

SPECIES ACCOUNTS

LARGE WHALES WITH A DORSAL FIN

(12–26 m maximum length)

There are six species of large whales with a dorsal fin in the eastern North Pacific. Five of them belong to the same major baleen whale group, the balaenopterid whales or rorquals, and the sixth is the largest of the toothed whales, the sperm whale.

All of the rorquals have a series of ventral grooves usually visible on stranded specimens. The length and number of these grooves are diagnostic for some species. In addition, all species have at least one distinct, though often not prominent, ridge along the head from just in front of the blowholes to near the tip of the snout. The humpback whale's median rostral ridge is obscured by numerous knobs scattered about the head, some of which are located along the midline. In Bryde's whale, the single head ridge characteristic of the other rorquals is supplemented by two auxiliary ridges, one on each side of the main ridge. Faint auxiliary ridges can sometimes be detected on the heads of fin and blue whales. Recent studies have revealed intergradation of a number of features of this group (e.g., ridges and baleen characteristics), which sometimes confound identification even when fragments of a specimen are in hand. Because of its small adult size, usually less than 9 m, the sixth member of the rorqual family, the minke whale, is included with the medium-sized whales in this guide.

At sea, these whales often appear similar and must be examined carefully before they can be identified with confidence. Observers should not feel overly disappointed about not being able to make a reliable identification. There is enough overlap in the behavior of these whales and in the appearance of their surfacing profiles to dictate caution in using any single characteristic for positive identification. Depending on the animal's activities, the following features may be useful in distinguishing the balaenopterids from one another: 1) the size, shape, and position of the dorsal fin and the timing of its appearance on the surface relative to the animal's blow (in general, the larger the whale, the smaller the dorsal fin, the farther back its position, and the later its appearance on the surface after the animal's blow); 2) the height of body in the area of the dorsal fin which is exposed as the animal sounds, relative to the size of the dorsal fin; 3) sometimes the blow rate and movement patterns; and 4) the shape and color of the head.

The sixth species, the sperm whale, is a toothed whale. It has a low, humplike dorsal ridge which, from certain views, particularly when the animal is humping up to begin a dive, may be clearly visible and look similar to a dorsal fin. At other times, particularly on some individuals, it is more indistinct. Because the profile of its hump and the knuckles along its spine are often prominent, the sperm whale has been classified with the large whales possessing a dorsal fin.

The sperm whale has a huge head in relation to body size, and perhaps the most distinctive blow of all cetaceans, emanating as it does from a blowhole that is displaced to the left of the head near the front. The blow projects obliquely forward and to the animal's left. This blow seen under calm conditions positively distinguishes a large whale as a sperm whale. However, wind conditions may affect the disposition and duration of the blow of any species, and a single character alone is seldom sufficient to permit positive identification.

Behavior by members of the same species often varies from one encounter to the next. An observer can greatly increase the reliability of his identification by forming the habit of working systematically through a set of characteristics for the species rather than depending on any single characteristic.

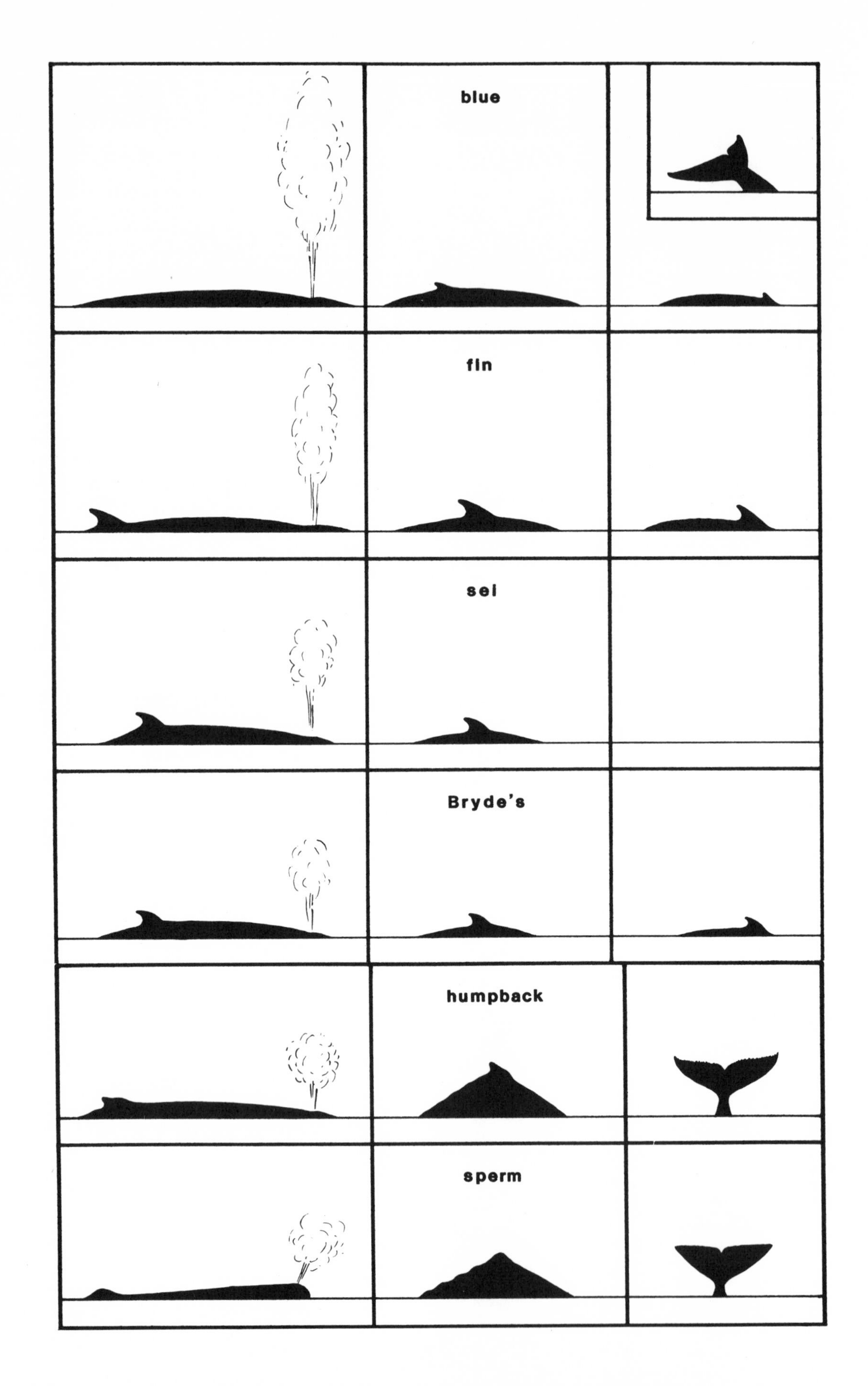

Figure 10.—Surfacing characteristics of "Large Whales With a Dorsal Fin." These are typical appearances and patterns which in nature may vary considerably about the norms for each species. (Drawings by Larry Foster, courtesy of General Whale.)

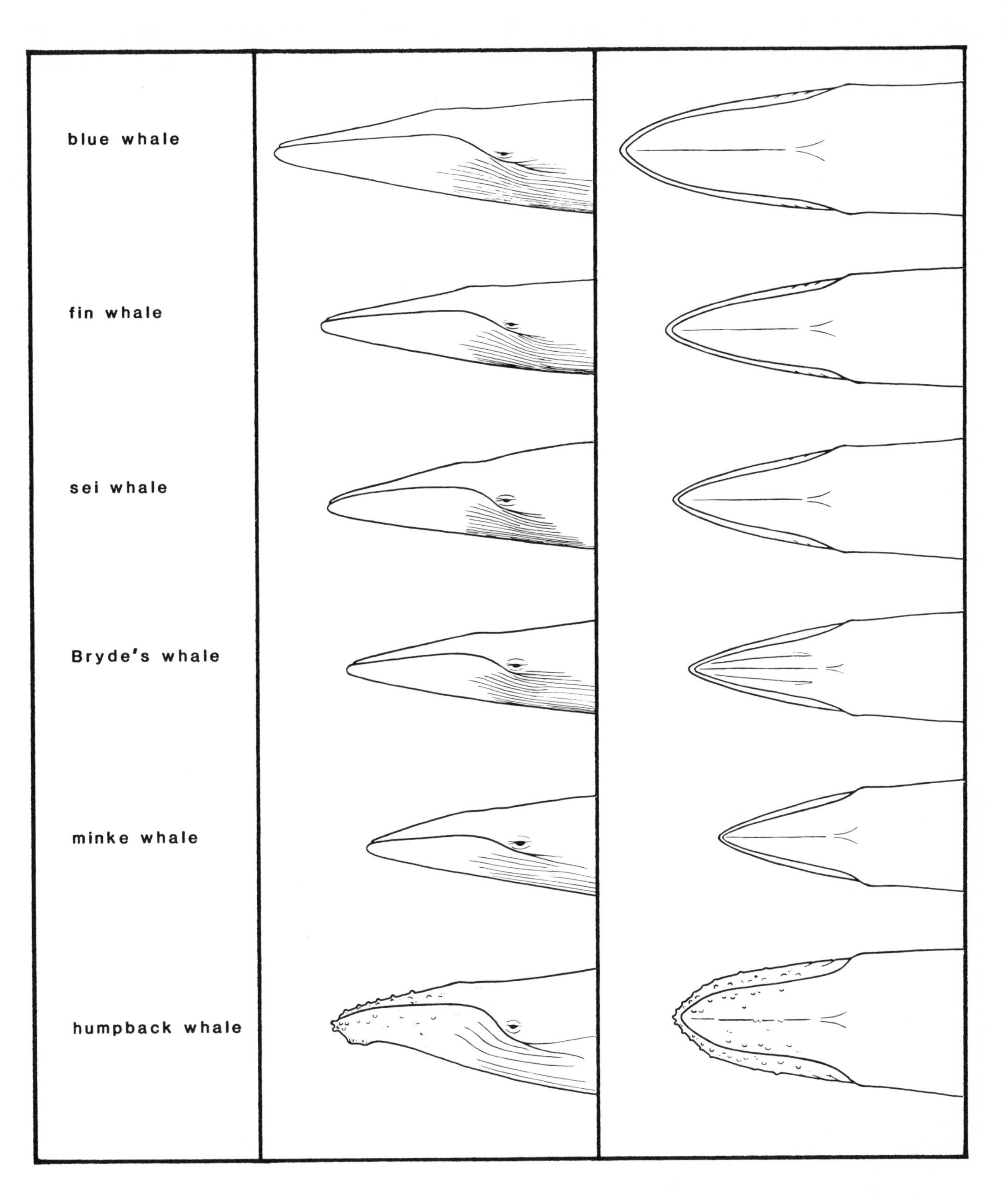

Figure 11.—Comparative dorsal and lateral views of the heads of the 11 largest whale species known to occur in eastern North Pacific and western Arctic waters. (Drawings by Larry Foster, courtesy of General Whale.)

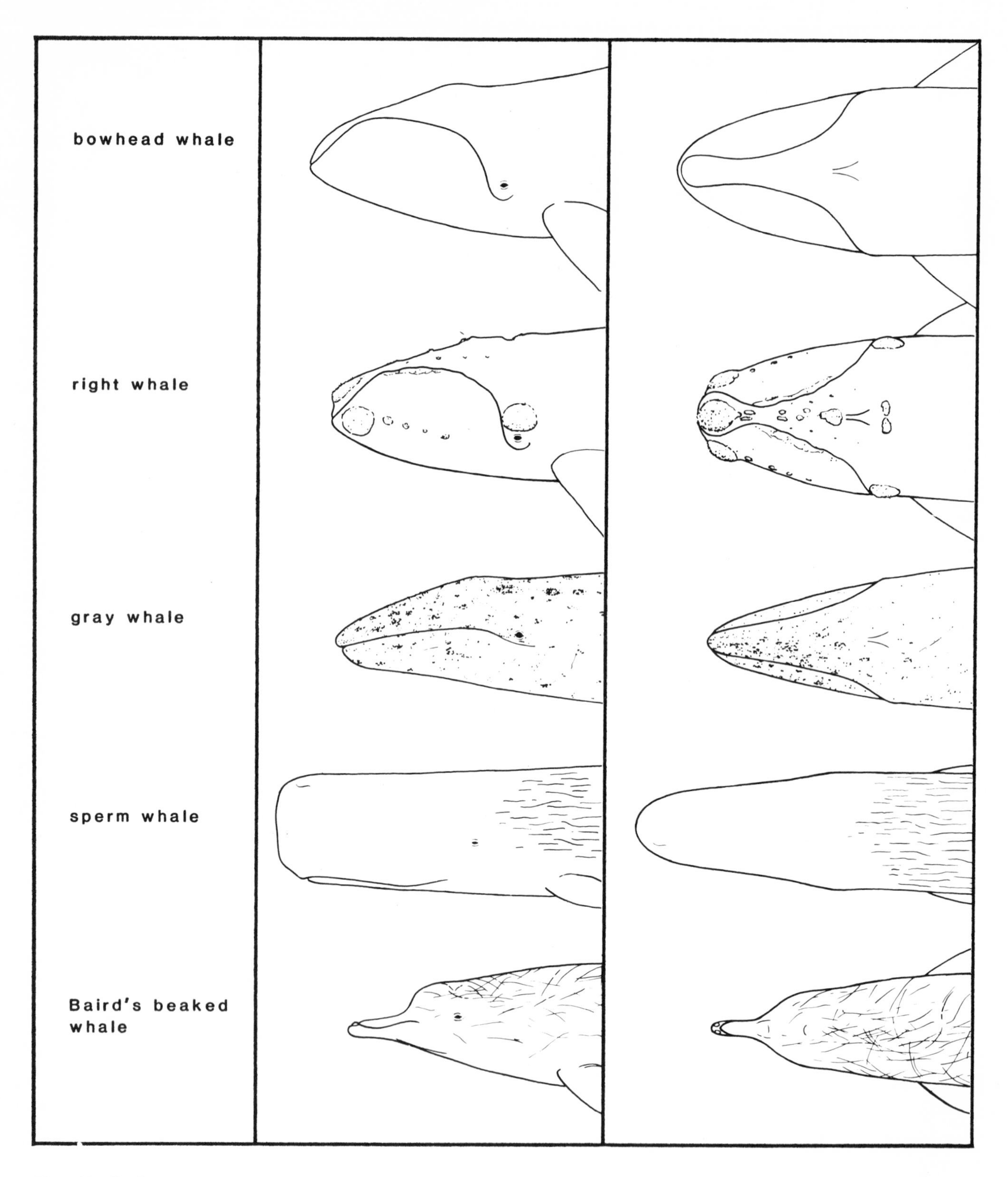

Figure 11.—*Continued.*

BLUE WHALE (B)[6]

Balaenoptera musculus **(Linnaeus, 1758)**

Figure 12.—Much sleeker than might be expected for the largest animals in the world, blue whales are awesome power and bulk combined with streamlined grace and beauty. (From a painting by Larry Foster, courtesy of General Whale.)

Other Common Names

Sulphurbottom; ballena azul (Latin America)[7]; shiro nagasu kujira (Japanese); takerrkak (Alaska Eskimo Yupik); blyuval, goluboy kit (Russian).

Description

This whale is not only the largest of the cetaceans, but also the largest living animal. The maximum size of blue whales, attained by individuals living in the Antarctic, is about 30 m and 160 t.[8] In the North Pacific few grow larger than about 26 m and perhaps 125 t. Females are larger than males. Newborn blue whales are generally about 7–8 m long and weigh about 2–3 t.

Viewed from above, the blue whale's rostrum is broad, flat, and shaped like a Gothic arch, slightly flattened at the tip. A single ridge extends from the raised area just ahead of the blowholes toward the tip of the rostrum.

The paired blowholes are protected anteriorly and laterally by prominent, fleshy crests, sometimes called splash guards. The blow is tall, slender, and vertical (perhaps 9 m high), neither bushy as in the humpback nor V-shaped as in the right whale and bowhead whale.

The dorsal fin is small—to only about ⅓ m high—and variable in shape, from triangular and pointed to falcate and rounded at the tip. It is placed so far back on the animal—about three-fourths of the body length—that it is rarely seen until just before the whale submerges following a blow.

The blue whale's flukes are broad—up to one-fourth of body length—with a straight or slightly concave trailing edge and a median notch. The flukes are sometimes lifted slightly as the animal dives following the last of a series of blows. The flippers are long—to 14% of body length—and pointed, with a convex leading edge.

[6]The letters in parentheses indicate whether the species is a baleen (B) or a toothed (T) whale.

[7]Common names in Spanish are available for many of the species seen regularly off Latin American shores. For rarer species and ones not known to range into Latin American waters, English common names have been translated literally.

[8]Although greater sizes have been reported, the largest blue whale measured in the scientifically accepted manner, in a straight line from the tip of the snout to the notch between the tail flukes, was 29.4 m long. The largest weighed specimen, a 26.7 m female, was 145 t. The confusion in reported lengths of this and other species stems largely from differences in measurement technique.

Figure 13.—Blue whales off British Columbia (top) and Baja California (bottom). Note the broad, rounded appearance of the head and the flattened rostrum with a single, prominent median ridge (top). In the animal on the top, note also the black baleen plates, barely visible at the front of the slightly open mouth. In the animal at the bottom, note the raised areas around the blowholes and the light grayish-white mottling on the back. (Photos by R. M. Gilmore [top]; K. C. Balcomb [bottom].)

a

b

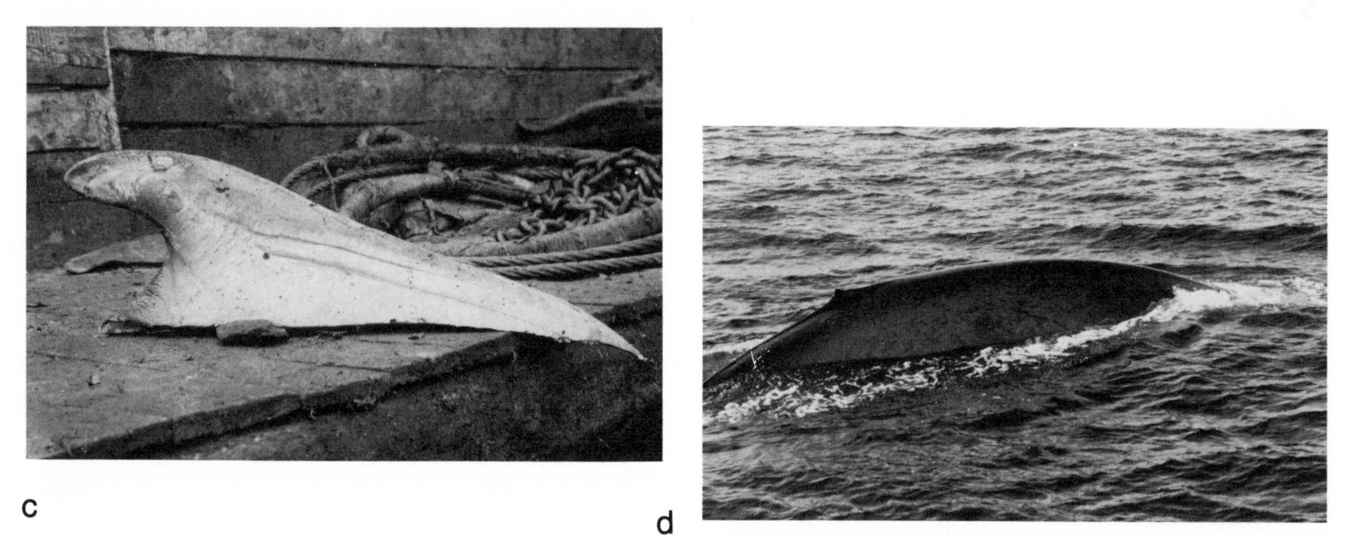

Figure 14.—The dorsal fin of the blue whale varies from distinctly triangular (a), to broadly rounded (b), to smoothly falcate (c), to little more than a pointed nubbin (d). Regardless of its shape, however, the fin is always located well back on the body and does not usually become visible until after the animal's blow has dispersed. (Photos by Japanese Whales Research Institute, (mid-Pacific,) courtesy of H. Omura [a]; S. Leatherwood, southern California [b]; F. W. True, western North Atlantic, courtesy of U.S. National Museum [c]; J. F. Fish, Patton Escarpment, courtesy of NOSC [d].)

The chest and belly have 55–88 parallel, longitudinal grooves, the longest of which reach from the chin to or slightly past the navel.

The body is light bluish-gray overall broken by a distinctive gray to grayish-white mottling effect. The undersides of the flippers are light grayish blue to white. The skin of some individuals has a yellowish or mustard cast, especially on the belly. This color is due to the presence of diatoms, which accumulate on the whales in the colder waters where they feed in summer.

The blue whale's tongue, palate, and baleen are uniformly inky black. There are 270–395 baleen plates on each side, and the longest of these are usually less than 1 m long. The plates are wide relative to their length.

Natural History Notes

Blue whales are usually encountered alone or in pairs. However, concentrations of food, often found on shallow

Figure 15.—Two views of slow-moving blue whales: (top) an animal swimming leisurely at the surface off San Clemente Island, Calif., and (bottom) a harpooned animal in tow by a whaling boat from a shore station (now closed) in western Canada. Note in the top photo that the blowholes, marked by the raised areas on top of the head, are still exposed after the doral fin has become visible during the roll. In the lower photo the animal's head is twisted slightly to the left, and the median head ridge is visible just to the right of the cannon barrel. In both photos note also the very small size and shape of the doral fin, and its position well aft on the body. (Photos by S. Leatherwood [top]; R. M. Gilmore [bottom].)

banks, may attract numerous single whales or pairs to the same general area.

Most young are born in late fall and winter, after the whales have left their high latitude summer feeding grounds. Gestation is believed to last somewhat less than a year, and calves are weaned at about 7 months of age, having doubled their length and increased their weight an average of ninefold on milk that can be up to 50% fat. The interbirth interval is usually 2 or 3 years. Blue whales live to ages in excess of 25 years.

Blue whales prey almost exclusively on small, shrimplike crustaceans known as krill, most of which are found at depths of less than 100 m. Off Baja California they also eat red crabs, a form of decapod crustacean that occurs there in dense swarms.

There is a well-documented attack on a blue whale by killer whales off Cabo San Lucas in Baja California.

Distribution

Movement patterns of baleen whales generally consist of poleward shifts in spring/summer and shifts toward the equator in fall/winter. Unfortunately, however, neither the seasonal distribution nor the routes traveled by blue whales in the eastern North Pacific are well mapped. Whaling records indicate that some degree of north-south movement takes place, but in parts of the species' range individuals are present in unlikely months. There may be geographically separate stocks whose wanderings, viewed collectively, defy recognition of a neat migratory pattern for the species in the eastern North Pacific.

Blue whales are distributed from the southern Chukchi Sea south at least to waters off Panama. Recently, substantial numbers have been seen at distances of 1,300–2,800 km off Central

Figure 16.—A fast-swimming blue whale off southern California. The animal rises rather steeply to the surface (a), emits a tall, vertical blow (b, c), shows its broad bluish back mottled with grayish white, and its small dorsal fin (d, e), and then dives (f). (Photos by J. F. Fish.)

Figure 17.—Raised tail flukes of a diving blue whale. Flukes of blue whales are straight on the rear margin, broad relative to body width, and preceded by a tail stock which is thickened dorsoventrally. The only other large whale whose tail flukes have such a straight rear edge is the sperm whale, readily distinguishable from the blue in a number of ways. (Photo from the North Atlantic by K. C. Balcomb.)

America at lat. 7°–9°N in February, March, and June. These individuals may belong to a year-round tropical stock.

In most years, blue whales are first seen off Baja California and the Mexican mainland in February. Their density at the mouth of the Gulf of California and along the entire west coast of Baja California apparently peaks in April. Some are still present there until early July. They appear again briefly in October but seem to be absent between November and January. Blue whales have been seen in the Gulf of California in fall/spring, ranging north at least to the Midriff Islands. Nearly 1,000 blue whales were killed along the west coast of Baja California by Norwegian whalers in the 1920's and 1930's. Winter/spring was the primary catching period, and effort was focused on the west coast between Cabo San Lucas and Cedros Island.

In southern California, sightings are fairly regular from July through October, often just outside the Channel Islands along the edge of Patton Escarpment. Blue whales, thought to be the same individuals, have been reported around San Miguel Island for several weeks at a time during these months. This may mean that some whales, in some years, venture little farther north than Point Conception. Catches off San Francisco in the 1950's and 1960's occurred primarily in September and October and were presumably of southward migrating animals. Blue whales recently have been seen in Monterey Bay in December. Peaks in blue whale catches at British Columbia shore stations were in June and September, suggesting a northward movement past Vancouver Island in spring and a southward shift in autumn.

Three major northern summer grounds have been identified: 1) the eastern Gulf of Alaska, between long. 130°W and 140°W; 2) the area south of the eastern Aleutians, between long. 140°W and 180°; and 3) the area from the far western Aleutians to Kamchatka, between long. 170°E and 160°E. Catches in the first area peaked in July; in the second, in June. Tagged whales were found to move freely among the three areas.

Recent observations in the northern portions of the range consist primarily of midsummer sightings off the southern side of the Aleutians. Eskimos at Gambell Village on St. Lawrence Island report that blue whales, absent from those waters for some 30 years, are again being seen in small numbers in late summer.

It should be noted that blue whales have been seen far off the coast of northern California (at lat. 41°–42°N, long. 130°W) in May. At least some of their movements, then, must occur along pelagic routes.

The blue whale was badly overexploited throughout much of its range, including the eastern North Pacific, and it has become a symbol of the need for restraint by the whaling industry. Happily, the population of blue whales in the eastern North Pacific seems to have recovered much of the ground it lost during the first two-thirds of this century. Several thousand are believed to survive.

Can Be Confused With

At sea blue whales can be confused with fin whales (p. 23). Though the two can be difficult to distinguish from a distance, the following comparison should be helpful:

Blue Whale	**Fin Whale**
Coloration	
Mottled bluish gray above and below.	Dark gray above, white below; frequently grayish-white chevron behind head.
Baleen	
All black.	Bluish gray with yellowish-white stripes; front fifth to third of baleen on right side white.
Head	
Broad and nearly U-shaped; uniformly gray.	Narrower, more V-shaped; right lower lip white.
Dorsal Fin	
Strikingly small in proportion to entire animal (to only 1/3 m high); triangular or falcate; located about one-fourth forward from tail; visible well after blow.	Prominent and more erect (to 5/8 m high); falcate; located about one-third forward from tail; usually visible shortly after blow.
Surfacing and Diving	
Often shows head and blowholes, then broad expanse of back, and much later the dorsal fin.	Usually rolls higher out of water, particularly before long dive, presenting a "wheellike" silhouette; dorsal fin visible soon after blow.
Diving	
Sometimes raises flukes slightly on last dive.	Does not show flukes when diving.

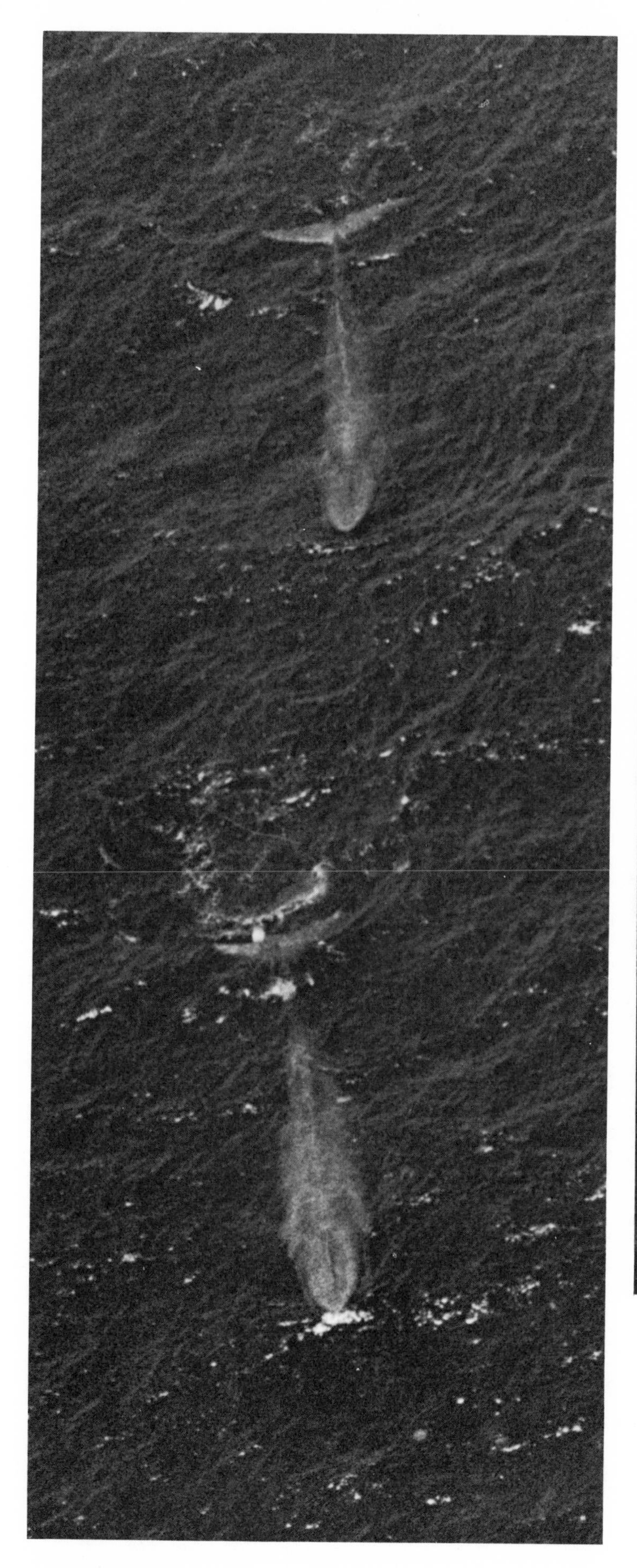

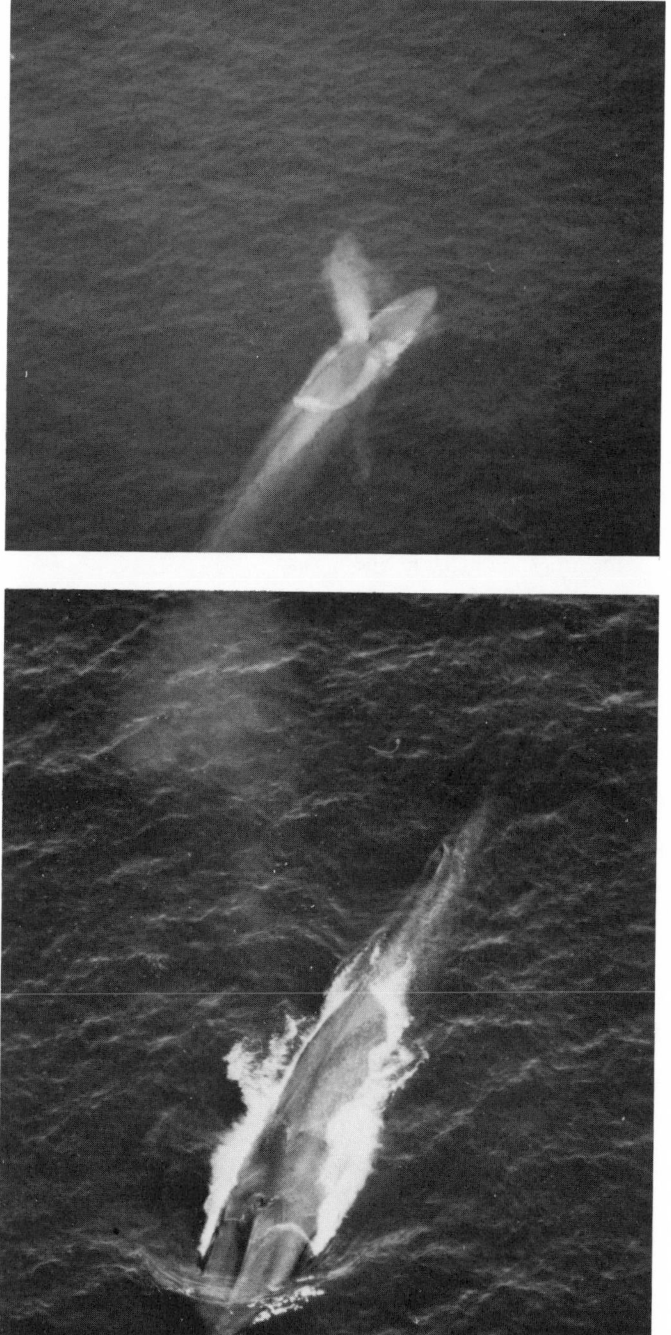

Figure 18.—Three aerial views of blue whales, in the Gulf of California (left), off San Nicholas Island (top right), and in the Gulf of St. Lawrence (bottom right). Note the broad "Gothic arch" shape of the head, the prominent central head ridge, the raised area along the spine behind the head, the broad flukes (left), and the mottling behind the head (bottom right). (Photos courtesy of Sea World, Inc. [left]; by J. D. Hall [top right]; by Russ Kinne, copyrighted [bottom right].)

Grouping

Usually found singly or in pairs.	Occasionally found singly or in pairs, but more often in pods of 6 or 7.

See also comparison of fin whale and sei whale (p. 27).

Viewed from the air, only two large whales appear lightly mottled to powdery blue when at the surface—blue whales and sei whales. Seis do not exceed 16 m; blues often do. The sei whale's head is long and pointed, with the rostrum slightly arched, while the blue whale's head is broader, more rounded, and flattened—almost shelflike. In good light, the blue whale's head may appear uniformly dark blue, while the rest of the body is mottled. The region of the lungs, viewed from an aerial perspective, may be slightly indented and appear to collapse substantially upon exhalation.

Identification of Dead Specimens

Dead blue whales can be readily identified by 1) the large body size (any whale longer than 24 m is almost certainly a blue whale); 2) the broad, flat head; 3) the inky tongue and palate and the all-black baleen plates, which are usually barely more than twice as long as they are wide; and 4) the 55–88 ventral grooves which extend to the navel at the midline and become progressively shorter toward the flippers.

Figure 19.—Normally slim of chin, like all rorqual whales, this feeding blue whale takes on an unexpected "guppy" or "tadpolelike" appearance when seen from the air. The distortion is due to expansion of the throat as the mouth cavity is filled with water. Similar changes in appearance are observed in other large rorquals as they feed. (Photo from the Gulf of California by R. Storro-Patterson.)

Figure 20.—A young (18 m) blue whale under attack by killer whales off Cabo San Lucas, Baja California. Attacks by killer whales on a number of large whales have been reported, and though the extent of predation is unknown, this dramatic instance graphically demonstrates the vulnerability of even the sea's largest animals to this supreme predator. (Photo courtesy of Sea World, Inc.)

Figure 21.—Two views of blue whales on the ramps of whaling stations, in Japan (top) and at Hermitage Bay, Newfoundland (bottom). Note the broad, flattened head, the prominent central head ridge, and the dark bluish-gray coloration, interrupted only by grayish-white mottling behind the head. (Photos by Japanese Whales Research Institute, courtesy of H. Omura [top]; F. W. True, courtesy of U.S. National Museun [bottom].)

Figure 22.—Dead blue whales, harpooned and afloat off the stern of a factoryship in the Antarctic (top) and on the deck of a whaling station in western Canada (bottom). Note the numerous narrow ventral grooves (from 55 to 88 or more) extending to the region of the navel and sometimes beyond, and the light coloration of the undersides of the flippers. (Photos by Japanese Whales Research Institute, courtesy of H. Omura [top]; G. C. Pike, courtesy of I. A. MacAskie [bottom].)

FIN WHALE (B)

Balaenoptera physalus **(Linnaeus, 1758)**

Other Common Names

Finback, razorback, finner, common rorqual; ballena (or rorcual) de aleta or rorcual cummun (Latin America); nagasu kujira (Japanese); finval (Russian).

Description

Fin whales in the North Pacific are very rarely 24 m long; a 22 m female would be exceptionally large. Females are slightly larger than males. Newborn are usually about 6 m long and may weigh close to 2 t.

The head of the fin whale is V-shaped, the rostrum narrow. The splash guards are prominent and there is a single median head ridge. The rostrum is otherwise flat, though less so than that of the blue whale. The fin whale's cone-shaped blow ascends vertically for 6 m or more.

Figure 23.—Surfacing fin whales off Newfoundland (top), Monterey, Calif., (middle), and northwestern Baja California (bottom). When approached from the right side or viewed head on, fin whales can be distinguished from other large balaenopterids by the white right lower lip and the flat, narrow head with a single prominent ridge originating in front of the blowholes and extending toward but usually not reaching the tip of the rostrum. (Photos by K. C. Balcomb [top]; D. Lewis [middle]; R. L. Pitman, courtesy of NMFS [bottom].)

The fin whale is a slender, streamlined animal, with a sharp ridge along the spine, hence the name "razorback."

The prominent, falcate dorsal fin can be ⅔ m tall. The angle formed by the back and forward margin of the dorsal fin usually is less than 40°. The fin is situated about two-thirds of the way back on the animal's body and usually emerges shortly after the blow. The breadth of the flukes, tip to tip, is one-fifth to one-fourth of body length. The trailing edge is slightly concave, and a deep notch separates the flukes. The flippers are similar to those of the blue whale but proportionately smaller.

The 56–100 ventral grooves extend at least as far back as the navel.

Fin whales are a uniform dark gray to brownish black on the back and sides. There is none of the mottling characteristic of

Figure 24.—A group of at least five fin whales surfacing together in waters off British Columbia. In the North Pacific numbers of these pods often congregate to form loose herds of 50 or more animals on the northern feeding grounds. (Photo by G. C. Pike, courtesy of I. A. MacAskie.)

blue whales, nor is scarring usually as extensive as on sei whales. There often is a grayish-white chevron on the back, with its apex at the midline and arms oriented posteriorly. This muted marking, most easily seen when viewing the animal from the air, is not always apparent. The undersides, including those of the flukes and flippers, are white. The right lower lip, including the mouth cavity, is white, and the white to light gray area can extend onto the upper lip and right side of the neck in some individuals. This feature—asymmetric head coloration—is a reliable key for distinguishing the fin whale from other balaenopterids. The flippers may appear light blue when seen through the water, inviting confusion with the humpback.

Most of a fin whale's baleen is striped with alternate bands of yellow-white and dark bluish gray. However, the baleen in the right front one-fifth to one-third of the upper jaw is evenly white or slightly yellowish. The bristles of the baleen are finer than the blue whale's, and they are brownish gray to grayish white. Maximum length of fin whale baleen is about 70 cm, exclusive of the 7–9 cm buried in the gum, and the width of the longest plates is about one-fourth to two-fifths the length. The number of plates per side ranges from 262 to 473.

Natural History Notes

Before the era of modern whaling, the cosmopolitan fin whale was one of the most abundant baleen whales. Its swimming speed, with bursts of up to 20 knots, kept it safe from most whalers until steam-propelled catcher boats were used.

Though fin whales are sometimes found alone or in pairs, they more often occur in pods of 6 or 7 individuals. Feeding concentrations may consist of numerous pods, with as many as 50 whales gathered in a small area.

Winter is the reproductive season for this species, with a breeding peak in January and February. Young are born after a gestation period of about 11 months, and they nurse for about half a year. Although females may be capable of calving every other year, many have a resting year between pregnancies, giving birth at 3-year intervals.

In spring most fin whales leave the temperate waters in which they breed and move to richer feeding grounds at higher latitudes. The fin whale is one of the more versatile feeders among the baleen whales, preying on krill, fishes such as herring, pollock, capelin, and lanternfish, and occasionally squid.

Fin whales dive to depths of at least 230 m. This is deeper than either blue or sei whales usually dive and helps explain differences in surfacing, blowing, and diving characteristics among the three species. When moving leisurely at the surface, fin whales expose the dorsal fin soon after the appearance of the blowholes. After a deep dive they surface at a steeper angle, blow, submerge the blowholes, and then arch the back and dorsal fin high into the air before beginning another long dive. They almost never lift their flukes above the surface when diving.

Unlike blue or sei whales, fin whales do leap clear of the water occasionally. When they breach, they usually reenter with a resounding splash, unlike minke whales, which often reenter smoothly and headfirst.

Distribution

The winter distribution of fin whales in the eastern North Pacific extends at least from the Big Sur area off central California (lat. 35°30′N) south to Cabo San Lucas, Baja California (lat. 22°50′N). Within this range they are most frequently observed just outside the Channel Islands. Much of the population is believed to winter far offshore, as sightings have been reported in May south of Hawaii, in February in Kanai Channel, Hawaii, and in February at long. 138°W directly west of central California.

In summer fin whales range throughout most of the Bering Sea, as well as in the immediate offshore waters of North America as far south as southern California or central Baja California. They are fairly common in outer Prince William Sound (Hinchinbrook Entrance—Montague Island to Middleton Island) along the convoluted south coasts of the Alaska Peninsula, near the Aleutian Islands, and along the continental slope in the Bering Sea, especially near the Pribilof Islands. Tag-

Figure 25.—Fin whales off Isla Angel de la Guardia (middle) and Isla Raza (top, bottom) in the Gulf of California, showing the raised splash guards during respiration, the long back, and the slightly falcate, blunt-tipped dorsal fin placed far back on the body. These whales were all traveling slowly. (Photos by P. R. Kelly [top, bottom]; D. W. Anderson [middle].)

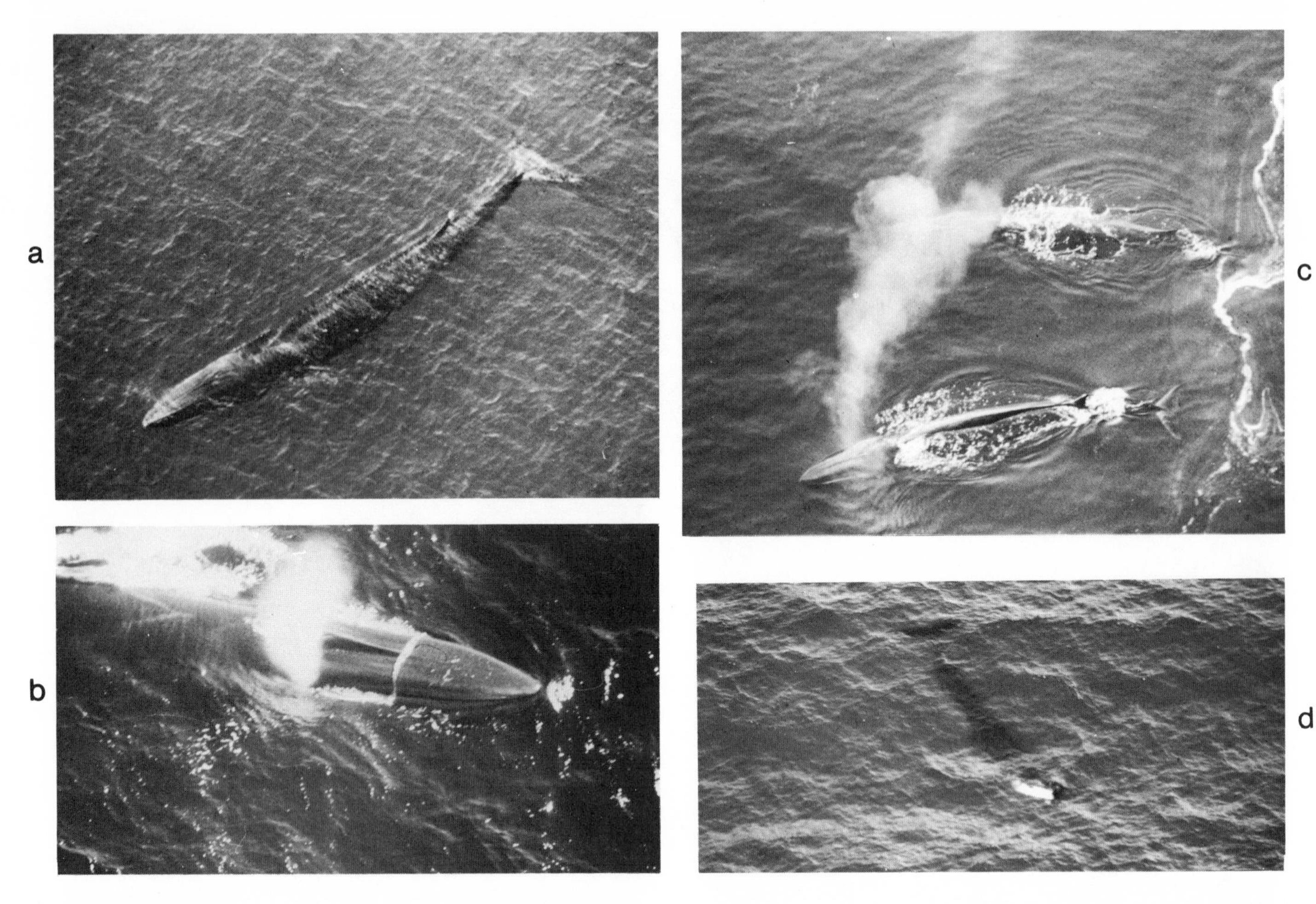

Figure 26.—Four aerial views of fin whales, three off California (a, b, c) and one in Gonzaga Bay in the northern Gulf of California (d). Notice how long and streamlined the bodies are and how smoothly the head tapers toward the end of the rostrum. In two of the photos a distinct white chevron can be seen on the back well behind the blowholes (a, b). Many fin whales have such a chevron. In the animal at the lower right, the white right lower lip is clearly visible, accentuated by the otherwise dark tones of body and water. This feature, variable in its degree of expression, is almost always visible when fin whales are viewed from the air and is the single most reliable key to identification. (Photos by M. Bonnell [a, c] and G. Farrens [b], courtesy of Bureau of Land Management; S. Leatherwood [d].)

ging studies have demonstrated that fin whales move from winter (November–January) grounds off southern California to summer (May–July) grounds off central California, Oregon, and British Columbia, and into the Gulf of Alaska. Based on historical evidence, it was written in the 1960's that the fin whale was once the most abundant large baleen whale off California in spring and summer, with a peak of abundance in May or June. Whaling from California shore stations during the late 1950's and 1960's apparently reduced the fin whale stocks considerably, however, and in extensive research off Baja California and southern and central California during the decade beginning in 1968, fin whales were uncommonly encountered. The species is now protected throughout the eastern North Pacific. The North Pacific population is presently estimated at about 16,000 whales.

Mention should be made of an apparently isolated, year-round fin whale population found inside the Gulf of California and ranging north to the shallow Colorado River Delta. The size of this stock is not known, but fin whales are commonly observed in the upper Gulf, especially in winter. Their scarcity along the outer coast of Baja California suggests that there is lit-

Figure 27.—A breaching balaenopterid, probably a fin whale though possibly a Bryde's whale, in the eastern tropical Pacific. This type of behavior is much more common in humpback and minke whales. The whale is about to land flat on its back. (Photo by K. D. Sexton, courtesy of NMFS.)

Figure 28.—Three views of a small fin whale stranded in New England. The asymmetrical coloration is clearly apparent, the white extending farther onto the right than the left side. The dorsal fin forms an angle of less than 40° with the back, a feature which often helps distinguish fin from sei whales. (Photos courtesy of H. E. Winn.)

tle, if any, interchange between the Gulf population and those in the open ocean.

Can Be Confused With

Fin whales can be confused with blue whales (p. 13), sei whales (p. 29), and in the southernmost portion of their range, Bryde's whales (p. 34). They can be distinguished from blue whales by differences in overall coloration, coloration and shape of the head, and size, shape, position, and time of appearance of the dorsal fin (see p. 18). When seen closely, they can be distinguished from Bryde's whales by the presence of a single prominent head ridge, compared to three in Bryde's whales, and by their larger, less sharply pointed dorsal fin. Fin whales frequently have auxiliary head ridges on either side of the median ridge, but they are generally much less prominent than those of Bryde's whales. Fin whales can be distinguished from sei whales in the following ways:

Fin Whale	Sei Whale
Color of Undersides	
White; extends higher up on right than on left.	Mostly gray, with irregular whitish area on belly.
Color of Lower Lip	
White on right, gray on left.	Gray on both sides.

Baleen

Anterior one-fifth to one-third of right side white; the rest banded with yellowish white and bluish gray; bristles grayish white.	Ash black with a blue tinge; fine grayish bristles.

Dorsal Fin

Falcate; usually forms angle of less than 40° with back; located about one-third forward from flukes.	Sharply pointed and falcate; usually forms angle of greater than 40° with back; located just more than one-third forward from tail.

Surfacing and Preparing to Dive

A gulping feeder that usually rises obliquely so top of head breaks surface first; after blowing, animal arches its back and rolls forward with a wheellike motion, exposing dorsal fin.	Primarily a skimming feeder that usually rises to surface at shallow angle, exposing head and dorsal fin almost simultaneously; usually arches the back less before long dive than does the fin whale.

Diving

Blows 3–7 times or more at intervals of up to several minutes, then dives deeply.	Usually blows at even intervals over long periods of time; often visible just below the surface, even during longer dives, causing a trail of slicks.

The fin whale is one of the easiest of the rorquals to identify from the air because of its strikingly asymmetrical pigmentation. The whiteness of the right lower lip is readily apparent, except when an animal is viewed from a bad angle, i.e., from the left side.

It is important to stress that distinctive features among the large balaenopterids are very difficult to detect in the field and that the characteristics noted above should be used with caution. Identifications based solely on behavioral nuances are unreli-

Figure 29.—Dead fin whales on the deck of a Japanese whaling ship in the North Pacific (top) and at a shore station in Newfoundland (bottom). In the upper photo, note the asymmetrical coloration of the lower jaw, baleen, and roof of the mouth. In the lower, note that the ventral grooves extend past the navel, a feature shared by fin, Bryde's, blue, and humpback whales. (Photos by Japanese Whales Research Institute, courtesy of H. Omura [top]; courtesy of J. G. Mead, U.S. National Museum [bottom].)

able. Of the features described here, only the asymmetrical coloration is diagnostic for recognizing fin whales.

Identification of Dead Specimens

The most useful keys to identifying dead fin whales are 1) the white or yellowish color of the right lower lip, right front baleen, and right side of the palate; 2) the striped gray and white color of the rest of the baleen; 3) the 56-100 ventral grooves, the longest of which reach the navel or beyond; and 4) the broad, flat, sharply pointed head with a single prominent ridge.

Figure 30.—In fin whales, the right front one-third to one-fifth of the baleen, like the right lower jaw and lip, is white. (Photo from New Jersey by R. Reeves.)

SEI WHALE (B)

***Balaenoptera borealis* Lesson, 1828**

Other Common Names

Rudolphi's rorqual; ballena boba, rorcual de rudolphi, ballena boreal, rorcual negro (Latin America); iwashi kujira (Japanese); seyval (Russian).

Description

Sei whales rarely reach lengths in excess of about 16 m in the North Pacific. Physically mature females captured off California averaged 15.0 m; males, 13.7 m. At birth, sei whales are 4.3-5.3 m long.

The head of this species generally is less acutely pointed than that of the fin whale. When viewed from the side it appears slightly arched with the downward turn accentuated at the tip. In dorsal view, the head shape of the sei whale is intermediate between that of the blue whale and that of the fin whale. The elevated forward edges of the blowholes are less prominent than in the fin and blue whales. A pronounced ridge begins at their apex and extends to the tip of the rostrum. The sei whale's blow is not as high as the fin whale's but is similar in shape.

The dorsal fin is ¼-⅔ m high, strongly falcate, and located a little more than one-third of the way from caudal notch to tip of rostrum, slightly farther forward than that of the fin whale. It is generally more erect than the fin whale's dorsal fin, although wide variability in dorsal fin shape for both species makes this character less than absolutely reliable. The width of the flukes is about one-fourth of total body length; their trailing edge is

Figure 31.—In these sei whales from the Antarctic (left) and North Pacific (right), note the single ridge beginning just in front of the blowholes and ending at the tip of the rostrum. Bryde's whales, with which sei whales are likely to be confused in the tropical and subtropical portions of their range, have two auxiliary ridges, one on either side of this central ridge. The angle at which the whale in the right photo is surfacing is much steeper than is usual for sei whales. Note also the slight downward turn to the tip of the rostrum, a distinctive feature of the species. (Photos by Asahi Shinbun Press [left] and Japanese Whales Research Institute [right], both courtesy of H. Omura.)

Figure 32.—This photo of a harpooned North Pacific sei whale demonstrates a key difference between the sei whale and the fin whale. The sei's right lower lip is gray, while the fin's is white. This feature can be discerned on living animals only when they are approached from the right side or viewed from directly overhead. (Photo by Japanese Whales Research Institute, courtesy of H. Omura.)

almost straight, and there is a deep notch separating the flukes. The pointed flippers are similar to those of the fin whale, but relatively shorter.

There are only 32–60 ventral grooves and these terminate about midway between the flippers and the navel. When seen, they provide a very useful feature for distinguishing the sei from fin, blue, and Bryde's whales. Only the minke whale has such short ventral grooves.

Sei whales are dark gray or bluish gray on the back and sides and on the posterior portion of the ventral surface. On the belly, there is a region of grayish white that is almost always confined to the area of the ventral grooves. Neither the flippers nor the flukes are white underneath. The right lower lip and mouth cavity, unlike those of the fin whale, are uniformly gray. The body often has a galvanized appearance due to scars inflicted by either lampreys or parasitic copepods (*Penella* spp.). These scars are gray to white.

Figure 33.—Four views of swimming sei whales. In all, note the tall, falcate dorsal fin. In the top left photo, note that the dorsal fin has appeared on the surface while the blowholes are still open. Sei whales, generally skimmer feeders and shallow divers, often show the dorsal fin and much of the back for relatively long periods as they surface to breathe. (Photos from off central California, courtesy of NMFS [top left]; northeast of Hawaii by S. Ohsumi [top right, bottom right]; off Japan by Whales Research Institute, courtesy of H. Omura [bottom left].)

Figure 34.—Two extraordinary views of a live sei whale under water. These photos were taken off Japan, after the animal had been tethered with a harpoon. The dappling effect is from surface reflection and not part of the animal's pigmentation pattern. (Photos by G. R. Williamson, courtesy of General Whale.)

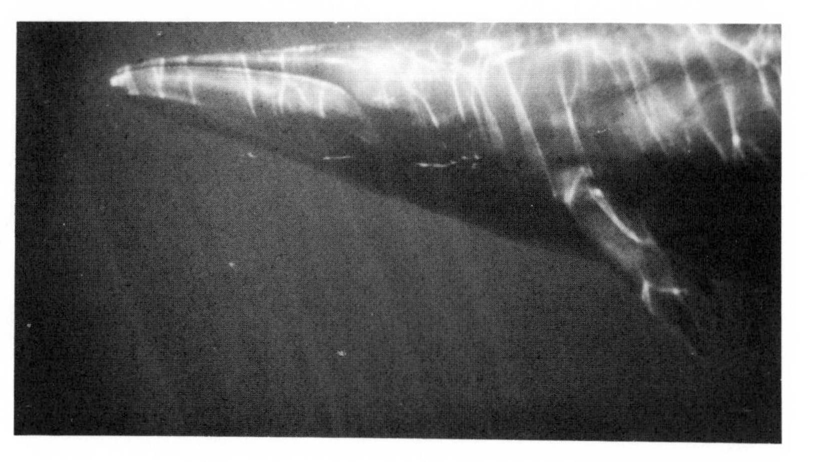

The baleen of sei whales is uniformly grayish black (blue or green tinged) with fine white to grayish-white fringes. Some whales have a few lighter, or white-streaked, plates toward the front of the mouth, and these can cause confusion with fin whales. The longest plates measure 75–80 cm. The width of these plates is one-third to one-half their length. The number of plates on a side ranges from 219 to 402. Sei whale baleen is highly elastic and has fine, hairlike fringes. Its texture is similar to that of right whale baleen.

Natural History Notes

Sei whales are normally found alone or in groups of 2–5 individuals, though larger feeding concentrations are not unusual. They are regarded as the fastest swimmers among the great whales, reaching bursts of speed over 20 knots, though high speed is generally not employed in their skimming mode of feeding.

Sei whales, like other balaenopterids, breed to some extent throughout the year, but there is a clear peak of sexual activity in winter. Most young are also born in this season (September-March), after slightly more than a year of gestation. Lactation may last for up to 9 months. Assuming that each growth layer in the ear plugs of sei whales represents a year, both males and females in the California region attain sexual maturity at an average age of 10 years. The interval between pregnancies is most often 3 years.

In northern latitudes sei whales feed primarily on surface plankton—mainly copepods but also euphausids. Elsewhere small schooling fishes and squid form an important part of their diet. A small percentage of the sei whales taken by the whaling industry off central California during the 1960's suffered from badly diseased baleen; one animal had entirely lost its baleen. Surprisingly, the infected animals were not emaciated and had quantities of anchovies, sauries, or jack mackerel in their stomachs.

Sei whales are generally skimming feeders and do not, as a rule, dive deeply. They tend to surface at a shallower angle than do fin whales. The head rarely emerges at a steep angle, except when the whales are being chased. The blowholes and much of the back, often including the dorsal fin, become visible almost simultaneously and remain visible for relatively long periods.

As sei whales begin a dive, they seldom arch the tail high or expose the flukes. Instead, they usually submerge by slipping quietly below the surface, often remaining in view only a few meters down and leaving a series of swirls or tracks on the surface as they move their flukes. While feeding in this manner, sei whales may exhibit a highly regular blowing and diving pattern over long periods.

Distribution

The sei whale is primarily a pelagic, temperate-water species. In winter (December-March) it is widely but sparsely distributed between Point Piedras Blancas, Calif. (lat. 35°30′N) and the vicinity of the Revillagigedo Islands 600 km off Baja California (lat. 18°30′N). Recently some sei whales were reported during April far offshore in the eastern tropical Pacific. If these were in fact sei whales, their range would overlap that of the Bryde's whale. They also have been sighted near the Galapagos, so the winter range of Northern Hemisphere stocks may extend all the way to the equator. One difficulty in determining the sei whale's southern distribution is the close similarity in appearance between it and the Bryde's whale and the fact that until recently records of the two species were indiscriminately mixed in cruise and whaling logs.

There is a general northward shift of the sei whale population in summer, at which time its range resembles that of the fin whale. Most are found west of California's Channel Islands and farther north throughout the Gulf of Alaska, but generally not north of the Aleutians. Sei whales are usually present off central California in considerable numbers only during late summer and early fall, arriving any time from late May or early June to early

Figure 35.—A freshly dead sei whale from the Pacific (top) and a stranded specimen in an advanced stage of decomposition at Cape Island, S.C. (middle, bottom). Note that even though the distinctive coloration of the fresh specimen has faded on the rotting specimen, the number and length of the ventral grooves (38–56 in number and stopping well short of the navel) still permit the specimen to be distinguished from fin, blue, and Bryde's whales, in all of which grooves extend at least to the navel. (Photos by Japanese Whales Research Institute, courtesy of H. Omura [top]; J. G. Mead [middle, bottom].)

July. A summer sighting at lat. 27°N off Baja California has been reported.

North-south movement along the west coast of North America has been documented by tag returns. An animal tagged off southern California in November was killed off Vancouver Island, British Columbia, almost 4 years later in August. Another whale marked in the same area in June was taken 4 years later off Washington in July.

Due to their depletion by modern commercial whaling, sei whales are currently protected throughout the North Pacific. They declined considerably after scarcely a decade of heavy catching, with no more than about 20,000 (compared to nearly 50,000 in 1963) remaining in the adult population in 1974.

Can Be Confused With

The sei whale's smaller size and taller dorsal fin located just less than two-thirds of the way back from the rostrum tip should help avoid confusion with the blue whale (p. 13). At a distance, however, it is very difficult to distinguish seis from fin (p. 23) and Bryde's whales (p. 34). The asymmetrical coloration of the fin whale's head and baleen is probably the most reliable feature for distinguishing it from the sei whale, particularly in combination with the other features listed on p. 27-28.

Sei whales can be distinguished from Bryde's whales only on close examination. The most reliable character is the single head ridge of the sei whale. The Bryde's whale has two additional ridges—one on each side of the main ridge. Generally speaking, the Bryde's whale has a smaller dorsal fin, up to ½ m high, sharply pointed, and often frayed on the rear margin. Also, the

Figure 36.—Dorsal view of a sei whale on the deck of a whaling ship in the North Pacific. Note the numerous scars on the body and the otherwise dark gray coloration of the back. (Photo by Japanese Whales Research Institute, courtesy of H. Omura.)

Figure 37.—An excellent view of the head of a sei whale stranded in early 1940 at Rio Gallegos, Argentina. The downward turn to the tip of the rostrum is clearly visible, as is the dark gray baleen. The large falcate dorsal fin is visible near the right shoulder of the rightmost person. Note also the thick tail stock. (Photo courtesy of J. G. Mead, U.S. National Museum.)

Figure 38.—The right upper jaw of a sei whale stranded at Cape Island, S.C. The baleen plates, here partly buried in the sand, number from 219 to 402 per side and are uniformly dark gray with fine, lighter gray bristles. They continue to serve as identifying characteristics even on a badly decomposed specimen. (Photo by J. G. Mead.)

Bryde's whale is more piscivorous than the sei whale, so its diving behavior resembles more closely that of the fin whale. Bryde's whales are generally smoky gray, while sei whales are more bluish gray and often mottled.

The minke whale (p. 80) is much smaller than the adult sei whale, reaching 10 m in length only very exceptionally. Its white flipper patches are a distinguishing feature.

From the air, sei whales appear mottled bluish, much like blue whales, darker than gray whales, but considerably lighter than fin or Bryde's whales. They are distinguished from blue whales by their much smaller size, more pointed rostrum, and much more prominent and anteriorly situated dorsal fin.

As in the case of fin whales, field identification of sei whales is a tricky matter. Even experienced observers have been known to mistake sei whales for small blue whales. The generalizations about behavior, especially, tend to break down when the whales are being pursued or when they are preying on fish rather than plankton. Resting blue and fin whales can surface at a shallow angle, exposing the dorsal fin as they blow, then sinking a few meters under the surface—behavior that is generally attributed to sei whales.

Identification of Dead Specimens

Dead sei whales can be confused with young blue whales, fin whales, Bryde's whales, and minke whales. The three head ridges of the Bryde's whale should be adequate for distinguishing it. Features that distinguish sei whales from other rorquals are 1) the color of the baleen—uniformly ash black (blue- or green-tinged) with fine white or light gray fringes; 2) the density of bristles on the baleen plates—sei whales having 35–60 fringes per centimeter, all other rorquals fewer; 3) the relative length of the ventral grooves—those of sei whales and minke whales ending well before the navel; and 4) the relatively small number of ventral grooves (32–60)—blues, fins, and most minkes have more, Bryde's whales about the same number. In addition, the fin whale's white right lower lip and the minke's white flipper bands are distinctive.

If the animal is not in an advanced state of decomposition, the region of white coloration on the sei whale's belly may also be visible and aid in identification.

BRYDE'S WHALE (B)

Balaenoptera edeni **Anderson, 1878**

Other Common Names

Ballena de Bryde[9] (Latin America); nitari kujira (Japanese); kit Brayda (Russian).

Description

Maximum length for Bryde's whales is about 14 m, with females somewhat larger than males.

In overall appearance the Bryde's whale resembles closely the sei whale (p. 29), though the Bryde's whale is dark smoky gray while the sei whale is often a galvanized blue-gray. The most distinctive field character of the Bryde's whale, and the feature which distinguishes it most readily from the sei whale, is the presence of three prominent, parallel ridges anterior to the blowholes. At least in some populations the extent of expression of these ridges is variable. The central ridge extends to the tip of the rostrum. The auxiliary ridges, which begin as slight depressions adjacent to the blowholes, bow along the rostrum almost

[9]A necessary invention of a common name in Spanish. It is only in the last few years that any attempt has been made (in Chile and Peru) to distinguish Bryde's whales from sei whales.

a

Figure 39.—Four views of swimming Bryde's whales that allow positive identification. The presence of prominent auxiliary head ridges can generally be used to identify a whale as a Bryde's whale, though at least in some populations the extent of expression of these ridges is variable. In these photos of Bryde's whales, taken off La Jolla, Calif. (a), and at lat. 22°26'N, long. 111°26'W (b), at least two of the three rostral ridges are clearly visible. In those taken off Hawaii's Leeward Island Chain (c) and off the east coast of Islas Fernandina in the Galapagos (d), the right lateral ridge is barely discernible. (Photos by F. Morejohn [a]; S. Sinclair, courtesy of NMFS [b]; R. L. Brownell, Jr. [c]; G. M. Wellington [d].)

b

c

d

reaching the tip. If the head can be examined at close range, most Bryde's whales can be positively identified by this character alone.

The dorsal fin can be about ½ m high. It is extremely falcate, pointed at the tip, and located about one-third forward from the tail. It is often irregularly notched or frayed on its rear margin.

There are about 40–50 ventral grooves, and these extend posteriorly at least to the navel.

The body is generally smoky gray, with no conspicuous interruptions except in some individuals that have a small region of lighter gray on either side just forward of the dorsal fin.

Bryde's whale baleen is shorter and stiffer than sei whale baleen, with a maximum plate length of about 40 cm. The longest plates are approximately half as wide as they are tall. There is usually a noticeable gap at the tip of the rostrum between the left and right rows of baleen, which number about 255–365 plates each. The baleen is slate gray with coarse, lighter gray bristles.

There may be two kinds of Bryde's whales in the North Pacific, as there are off South Africa. Inadequate sampling of the population(s) in the eastern North Pacific, however, precludes any judgment about inshore-offshore differences here.

Natural History Notes

Bryde's whales do not appear to be gregarious. They are usually alone or in pairs, although loose feeding aggregations of up to seven whales have been reported.

As a primarily tropical species, the Bryde's whale might be expected to have an unrestricted breeding season. Indeed, this has proven true for the relatively sedentary inshore population off South Africa. Offshore animals, however, which presumably undertake seasonal migrations, were found to have a breeding peak in autumn. The reproductive cycle for individual Bryde's whales is believed to be little different from those of other balaenopterids—a year of gestation, half a year of nursing, and half a year of resting.

Bryde's whales have been observed feeding on red crabs, an abundant planktonic crustacean, off Baja California, and probably take anchovies as well. Inshore Bryde's whales off South Africa and Japan subsist almost entirely on epipelagic schooling fishes, while offshore whales consume large quantities of krill as well as mesopelagic fishes.

Figure 40.—Byrde's whales off the Galapagos Islands (top left), at lat. 24°13.5′N, long. 156°25′E (top right), and off Puerto la Cruz, Venezuela (bottom). In all note the tall, falcate dorsal fin, much like that of the sei whale. In many Bryde's whales the rear margin of the dorsal fin is ragged. In the animal on the top right, note also the region of gray on the sides in front of the dorsal fin. (Photos by G. M. Wellington [top left]; S. Ohsumi [top right]; G. di Sciara, courtesy of Hubbs-Sea World Research Institute [bottom].)

The Bryde's whale usually surfaces steeply, much like the fin whale, with the blow occurring well before the dorsal fin is exposed. However, this characteristic is not particularly useful for identification purposes, since individuals have been seen to surface at a much shallower angle reminiscent of the sei whale, exposing the blowholes and dorsal fin almost simultaneously. Bryde's whales are thought to breach more often than the other large balaenopterid whales. When pursued, they generally undertake an evasive swimming course, changing directions underwater frequently. Feeding Bryde's whales move quickly and change direction suddenly.

Distribution

Until very recently, when it became the only remaining large baleen whale in the North Pacific believed abundant enough to exploit, the range of the Bryde's whale was poorly known. Stepped-up whaling activity has begun to clarify the species' distribution. The only record for the west coast of the United States is that of an animal sighted off La Jolla, Calif. For the most part, the species appears to be confined to warm waters south of lat. 30°N. It seems fairly strictly limited by the 20°C isotherm. Its presence has been confirmed from lat. 26°N off western Baja California, south to Cabo San Lucas, into the Gulf of California, and south along the Mexican mainland to the Trés Marías Islands (ca. lat. 21°N). Sightings in the Gulf of Panama, around the Galapagos, and in many equatorial regions far offshore suggest that Bryde's whale may be continuously distributed from Baja California to the equator. It is common around the mouth of the Gulf of California and penetrates the upper reaches of the Gulf at least in summer. There is no evidence that Bryde's whales are strongly migratory.

Bryde's whales are relatively abundant in summer and fall on the Mellish and Miluoki Banks northeast of Hawaii between lat. 31°N and 35°N and near the Midway Islands. They have also been hunted with some success northeast of Hawaii between lat. 24° and 43°N, long. 165°E and 150°W. There is no evidence of their regular occurrence around the main Hawaiian Islands, although they are known to be present near the Leeward Chain.

The current population of Bryde's whales in the western North Pacific is estimated at about 14,500. There is no estimate for the eastern North Pacific.

Can Be Confused With

There is little chance of seeing a Bryde's whale off the west coast of North America north of California. However, there is every possibility that from Mexico south, in tropical and subtropical waters, this whale will be confused with other balaenopterids. At a distance, it is virtually impossible for anyone other than a highly skilled observer, familiar with the region and used to viewing both sei (p. 29) and Bryde's whales, to make a positive identification. The head ridges (one in sei whales, three in Bryde's whales) are the only reliable feature. Generally speaking, Bryde's whales are deeper divers than sei whales, and they are less likely to surface and blow at evenly spaced intervals.

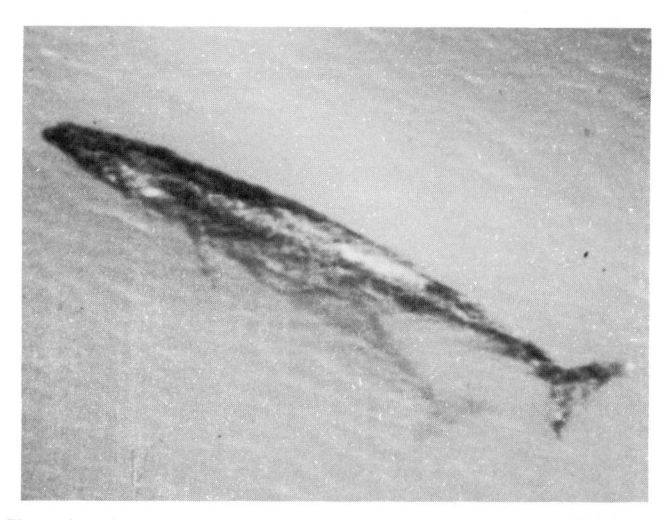

Figure 41.—An adult and calf Bryde's whale off Puerto la Cruz, Venezuela, in 1979. (Photo by G. di Sciara, courtesy of Hubbs-Sea World Research Institute.)

Figure 42.—Stranded Bryde's whales at Ft. George Island, Fla., (above) and Panacea, Fla., Gulf of Mexico (right). In both animals note the head shape, similar to that of the sei whale though lacking the pronounced downward turn to the tip of the rostrum. Note also the three distinct head ridges and, in the animal at the top, the baleen plates, up to at least 300 per side and dark gray with lighter gray bristles. (Photos courtesy of Marineland of Florida [above]; by M. B. Rank, courtesy of Wide World Photos [right].)

Figure 43.—A Bryde's whale stranded in 1972 on a South African beach. Note the head, slim in profile and bearing the diagnostic auxiliary ridge, and the prominent dorsal fin. The mottled, or pock-marked, appearance of the skin is due to scars left by epizoic parasites. (Photo by P. Best, courtesy of General Whale.)

The best feature for distinguishing fin whales (p. 23) from Bryde's whales in, for instance, the Gulf of California, is to note the color of the right lower lip and right front baleen and to compare this to the left side. If the right side is white and the left grayish, the animal is almost certainly a fin whale; if both sides are gray or white, it is probably a sei or Bryde's whale. If the three head ridges are seen, the animal can usually be identified as a Bryde's whale. However, fin whales sometimes have faint auxiliary ridges similar to those found consistently on the head of Bryde's whales. Generally speaking, the Bryde's whale has a smaller, more pointed dorsal fin that is often ragged on the trailing edge. However, in both species there is enough variability in dorsal fin size and shape to make this an inadequate way, by itself, of telling them apart.

Minke whales (p. 80) have an acutely pointed head with a single ridge, and a white band on each flipper. Also, they rarely reach 10 m in length, so only very large individuals are likely to be confused with Bryde's whales.

Of the baleen whales with sharply pointed heads, Bryde's whales viewed from the air can readily be distinguished from fin and minke whales, but not from sei whales. Sei whales are often a mottled bluish gray, while Bryde's whales are usually an even smoky gray except for the light gray zone on the sides behind the flippers in some individuals. The three head ridges are visible from the air only under excellent viewing conditions.

Identification of Dead Specimens

Stranded Bryde's whales can be positively identified by the three ridges along the top of the head from the area of the blowholes to the tip of the rostrum. All the other balaenopterid whales have but a single prominent ridge. If the head of a stranded specimen is buried in sand, is decomposed beyond recognition, or is otherwise inaccessible for identification, Bryde's whales can still be distinguished from sei whales by differences in the relative lengths of the ventral grooves, and from both the fin whale and the sei whale by differences in the characteristics of the baleen plates (Table 2 (p. 217)).

HUMPBACK WHALE (B)

Megaptera novaeangliae **(Borowski, 1781)**

Figure 44.—An excellent view of the head and trunk of a humpback whale in the Antarctic. Note the bumps on the head and the long flippers, in this specimen almost all white, with two prominent bumps and a series of smaller bumps on the forward margin. Note also the small circles on the lip and lower jaw, scars from barnacles which have been shed, and the small number of barnacles still clinging to the upper jaw. (Photo by J. Holbrook, courtesy of Hubbs-Sea World Research Institute.)

Other Common Names

Humpbacked whale, hump; ballena jorobada, yubarta or gubarta (Latin America); zatō kujira (Japanese); aghvesiiq (Alaska Eskimo Yupik); gorbach (Russian).

Description

Female humpback whales grow to lengths of just over 16 m and are somewhat larger than males. Both sexes reach reproductive maturity at about 11-12 m in length. Newborn calves are 4.5-5.0 m long.

The body of this whale is robust, narrowing rapidly behind the dorsal fin. In profile, the head of a nonfeeding whale is sometimes alligatorlike, very slim from the gape forward. In feeding humpbacks, as in many other rorquals, the throat grooves are often greatly distended as the animal gulps water and the food it contains. In dorsal aspect, the head is broad and rounded, like that of the blue whale. The median head ridge is obscured by a string of fleshy knobs. Many more of these knobs are present on top of the head and on the lower jaw. There is a distinctive rounded protuberance near the tip of the lower jaw. Large, conspicuous barnacles are present on the body, as are less noticeable whale lice—small cyamid crustaceans.

The wide ventral grooves, of which there are 14-22, extend to the navel. The most lateral few may take a high turn anteriorly, extending above the eye.

The flippers are a diagnostic feature of humpbacks because they are extremely long—nearly a third as long as the body. They are scalloped along at least the leading edge. This scalloping is dominated by two knobs that are larger than the rest. Though constant, this feature is unlikely to be needed for positive identification inasmuch as a full view of the enormous, winglike flippers will itself obviate the chance of error. The flippers are incredibly flexible and appear to be important tactile organs.

The dorsal fin is situated a little more than two-thirds of the way back on the body. It is variable in shape, from a small, triangular ridge to a more substantial, sharply falcate fin. The dorsal fin often rests on a step or hump, which is especially evident when the animal arches its back to begin a dive and from which the species gets its common name.

Figure 45.—A sequence showing a lateral view of the blow and roll of two humpback whales surfacing off Oregon. Note the knobs on the top of the head (a), the emergence of the dorsal fin while the blowholes are still exposed (b), the hump as the animals arch their backs to dive (c), and the flukes of the animal on the right, about to be lifted from the water (d). (Photos by Clyde Harrison, courtesy of NMFS.)

The flukes are often lifted high into the air as the whale dives, showing the slight S-curve of each fluke's rear margin and the scalloped trailing edge as well as the often white or white-flecked underside. The flukes are so distinctive and so frequently exposed that photos of them are used to identify individual whales—a natural tag.

Humpbacks are basically gray to black. The throat and chest have a variable amount of white spotting, streaking or patching, and there is usually some white along the ventral midline to the anus. The flippers of most whales are white underneath, but the color of the upper surface varies from all black to all white.

The relatively short baleen is all black, with black or olive bristles (infrequently whitish with grayish-white bristles). The longest of the 270–400 baleen plates found on each side of the upper jaw seldom measure more than 80 cm, and they are about one-third as wide as they are long.

Natural History Notes

Humpbacks are gregarious, often found in groups of 7–10 individuals.

Although conception can occur in any season, there is a strong winter–spring peak in reproductive activity. Most calves are born in winter, after slightly less than a year of gestation. They are probably weaned after about 6 months of dependence.

Humpbacks are strongly migratory and appear to follow fairly narrow routes between winter calving areas and summer feeding grounds. They occur very close to shore in some areas and appear to be quite sedentary once they arrive at their northern or southern seasonal destination.

The humpback's blow is generally 2–3 m high and balloon-shaped or bushy. It is wide relative to its height. Occasionally two divergent columns of vapor are apparent, allowing the possibility of confusion with right and bowhead whales. Humpbacks are among the most acrobatic of cetaceans, especially on winter grounds, where they breach repeatedly and slap flippers or flukes on the surface, making loud reports. Humpbacks on the winter grounds are often encountered with one long flipper raised into the air.

An interesting aspect of humpback whale behavior is the complicated repertoire of "songs" sung on the winter grounds (recent evidence suggests some "singing" on the summer grounds as well).

One of the most remarkable forms of behavior is called bubble-net feeding. In this type of feeding a humpback circles a school of fish from below and blows bubbles as it spirals toward the surface. The fish appear to be intimidated by the resultant "bubble net," and they form a tightly packed ball through which the whale swims, mouth agape. The whale's throat becomes enormously distended to contain its giant mouthful of prey, and the lower jaw may move so far as to appear in jeopardy of unhinging. Krill and schooling fishes are the mainstay of the humpback's diet.

Humpbacks are sometimes attacked and killed by killer whales.

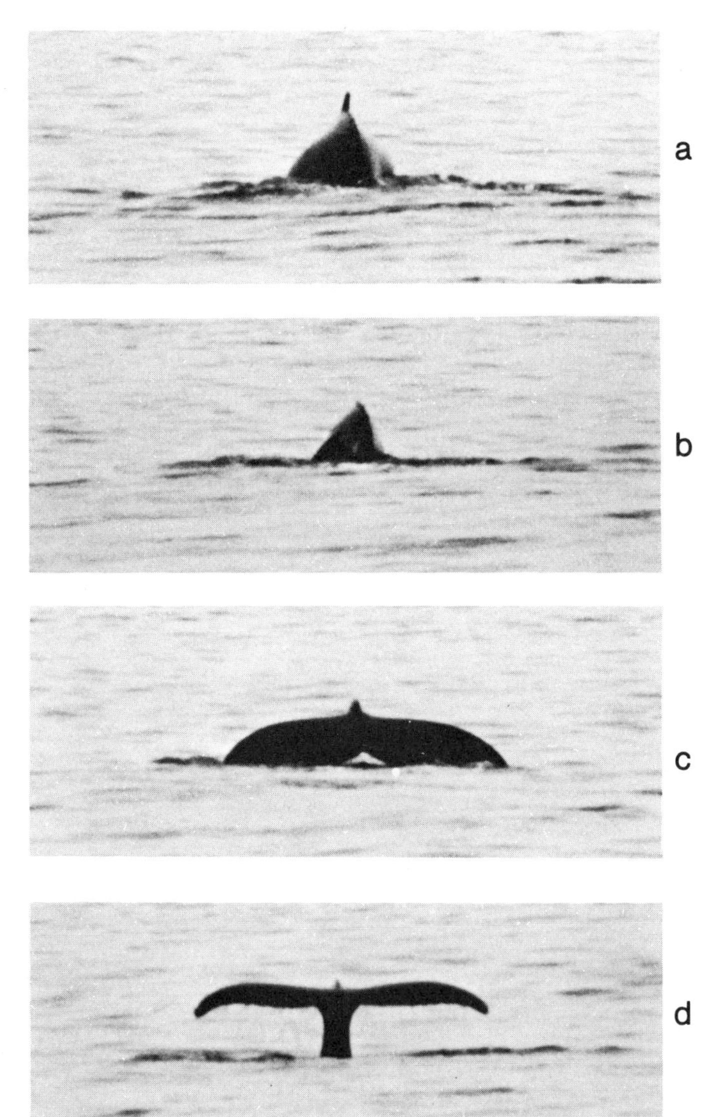

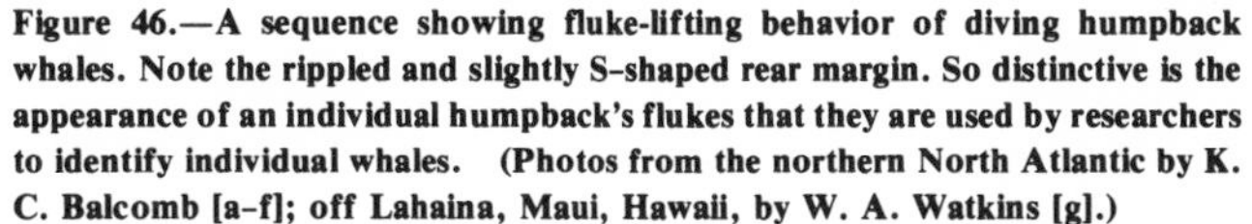

Figure 46.—A sequence showing fluke-lifting behavior of diving humpback whales. Note the rippled and slightly S-shaped rear margin. So distinctive is the appearance of an individual humpback's flukes that they are used by researchers to identify individual whales. (Photos from the northern North Atlantic by K. C. Balcomb [a–f]; off Lahaina, Maui, Hawaii, by W. A. Watkins [g].)

Distribution

The summer grounds of humpback whales include the cool temperate waters of the entire continental shelf of the North Pacific, from Point Conception on the American side and Japan on the Asian side northward as far as Bering Strait. Important feeding areas include Glacier Bay, Stephens Passage, Frederick Sound, and Prince William Sound on the coast of Alaska, and good numbers were found historically near the Aleutian chain.

Three stocks are recognized in the North Pacific, based primarily on the three known wintering areas. Considerable mixing may take place on the northern feeding grounds, but it has been postulated, with some evidence, that individual whales return year after year to the same wintering sites. The Asian stock winters around the Mariana, Bonin, and Ryukyu Islands and Taiwan. Since marked whales from this stock have been captured in the eastern Bering Sea and near the Aleutians, they can be regarded as seasonal inhabitants of eastern North Pacific waters. Humpbacks from the Asian stock were overexploited by commercial whalers for more than half a century and are now seriously depleted.

Another winter concentration of humpbacks begins to arrive in Hawaiian waters in November and remains through March. Penguin Bank and the area bounded by Molokai, Maui, Kahoolawe, and Lanai are pockets of abundance. This Hawaiian stock numbers at least several hundred whales.

The third stock winters along the coast of Baja California, principally around Gorda Bank, northeast of Cabo San Lucas; along mainland Mexico from southern Sonora to Jalisco, especially the vicinity of the Trés Marías Islands, Isabela Island, Nayarit, and Banderas Bay, Jalisco, and around the offshore Revillagigedo Islands. Humpbacks penetrate the Gulf of California at least as far north as San Jose Island. This Mexican population probably includes more than 100 whales.

About 15,000 humpback whales are believed to have been present in the North Pacific prior to 1905. They were heavily hunted from that time on, with about 18,000 killed in the period of 1905–1929 alone. Today there are probably not more than 1,000 humpbacks in the entire North Pacific.

a

b

c

d

e

f

g

Figure 47.—A series showing the extreme variability in dorsal fin shapes of humpback whales: (a) a rounded nubbin, (b) slightly falcate, (c) strongly falcate, (d) hooked with a pronounced hump, (e) rounded with a pronounced hump, (f) triangular with a pronounced hump, and (g) gouged and disfigured. (Photos from off Lahaina, Maui, Hawaii, by S. Leatherwood [a, b, c, f]; from Socorro Island by R. L. Pitman, courtesy of NMFS [d, g]; from Baja California by K. C. Balcomb [e].)

Figure 48.—Humpbacks are easy to identify from the air by the long, winglike flippers, that are usually all or partly white. These are dramatically extended as the animals approach the surface to respire (top) or breach (lower left). Also, the body is more rotund and less streamlined than those of other rorquals. At least in tropical portions of their range, humpbacks are frequently found in the company of small dolphins (lower right). (Photos from Hawaii bv P. H. Forestell [top left], R. C. Antinoja [lower right], and L. M. Herman, all courtesy of L. M. Herman.)

Can Be Confused With

From a distance humpback whales can be confused with any other of the large rorquals—blue (p. 13), fin (p. 23), sei (p. 29), and Bryde's (p. 34). Although it is highly variable, the dorsal fin most closely resembles that of the blue whale. However, it is located further forward on the body, and it generally is proportionately larger. Humpbacks distinguish themselves from the other rorquals by their habit of raising the flukes high when beginning a long dive, although in very shallow water they may not show the flukes at all. The only other rorqual that regularly lifts its flukes clear of the surface is the blue whale, but its tail stock is much thicker than the humpback's and the rear margin of its flukes is smooth and straight, not frayed or scalloped and deeply notched like the humpback's

Under some conditions humpbacks can be confused with sperm whales (p. 51) at a distance. Both may show a distinct dorsal hump when arching the back to begin a long dive. They differ in several ways. The flukes of humpbacks usually have varying amounts of white on the undersides, are tapered at the tips, and are deeply and widely notched with a scalloped rear margin. The sperm whale's flukes are all dark and nearly straight along the trailing edge, although they are divided by a distinct notch. Other differences are tabulated below:

Figure 49.—Humpback whales are well known for their aerial displays. These individuals are about to fall back into the water after breaching. The rounded projection below the tip of the lower jaw, with its clusters of adhering barnacles, is a puzzling and distinctive feature in this species. (Photos from off Baja California by K. C. Balcomb [top]; off Hawaii by D. McSweeney [bottom].)

Figure 50.—A dramatic view of a humpback whale lunging from the waters of Glacier Bay, Alaska, in an almost dolphinlike leap. Humpbacks often lunge in this manner during feeding passes. (Photo by R. Storro-Patterson.)

Figure 51.—Humpback whales often lie on their sides at the surface, one long flipper in the air. They often slap this flexible appendage against the surface, creating a loud report thought to be used for communication. This animal's flipper is black and white, a typical characteristic of humpbacks in the North Pacific. (Photo from Baja California by K. C. Balcomb.)

Figure 52.—A feeding humpback whale in Glacier Bay, Alaska, (top left) demonstrates the remarkable plasticity of its throat, which is distended to contain an enormous load of water and food. Humpbacks frequently rise to the surface, mouth agape, amid a circle of bubbles of their own making (top right), engulfing fish and krill apparently enclosed within the bubble net (bottom). (Photos by A. Wolman, courtesy of NMFS [top left]; from southeastern Alaska by J. Olson [top right]; off San Nicholas Island, Calif., by J. Leckey, courtesy of NMFS [bottom].)

Figure 53.—In their usually clear tropical wintering areas humpback whales have been particularly accommodating to human divers and photographers. Thanks to a flurry of still photos and motion picture films over the past half decade, the appearance of the humpback has become perhaps better known than that of any other of the world's large whales. The underwater perspective has given us a new appreciation for the surprising grace and beauty of the bulky larger whales. The body of the humpback, as well as those of other rorquals, turns out to be considerably slimmer and more streamlined than had been suggested by depictions of dead specimens. (Photos from Hawaii by S. Dillow, courtesy of General Whale.)

Figure 54.—Detail of the head of a humpback whale harpooned off Japan. Note the knobs along the top of the head and on the lower jaw, the rounded projection near the tip of the lower jaw, and the wide ventral grooves. The large mass of tissue to the left of the animal is its tongue. In the top photo from a Canadian whaling station, note the baleen plates, less than 0.9 m long and dark olive green to black in color. (Photos by Japanese Whales Research Institute, courtesy of H. Omura; J. G. Mead [top].)

Humpback Whale	Sperm Whale
Blow	
Projects upward from center of head. Usually blows 4–8 times (2–4 times in tropics) before diving.	Projects obliquely forward from left forward side of head. Usually blows many times (20–50 or more) before diving.
Head	
Raised area around paired blowholes; knobs on surface.	Blunt, long, smooth; single large blowhole at front of head, to left of midline.
Flukes	
Often white underneath; scalloped rear margin; S-shaped from fluke tip to apex of notch.	All dark; smooth, straight, notched rear margin.
Flipper	
Extremely long (to one-third of body length), often white or partly white and knobbed along leading edge.	Short; paddled-shaped; all dark.
Dorsal Fin (or Hump)	
Triangular to falcate fin, including step or hump in front of dorsal fin; followed by smooth or slightly irregular bumpy dorsal ridge.	Low rounded hump or apparent fin; two-thirds of distance from tip of snout to fluke notch; followed by knuckles or crenulations.

When seen at close range, humpbacks are distinguishable from all other whales by the knobs on the head, the long white (or partly white) flippers knobbed on the leading edge, the small dorsal fin, and the distinctively shaped flukes.

From the air, humpbacks are easy to identify. The long flippers may either flash white or, as they are extended and retracted in a sinuous flying motion, provide an unmistakable clue to the identity of the dark broad form below.

Identification of Dead Specimens

The most distinctive features of dead humpback whales are the very wide ventral grooves, 14–22 in number, extending to the navel; the knobs on the head and lower jaw, which are often the sites of numerous barnacle colonies; the long flippers (to nearly a third of total body length); and the distinctive rounded lump near the tip of the lower jaw.

If these characteristics are not adequate, the humpback whale may be identified by the characteristics of its baleen, which numbers 270–400 plates per side. Humpback baleen is ash-black to olive-brown, sometimes whitish, with grayish-white bristles. It is relatively short (about 70 cm or less) and stiff, with coarse fringes.

Figure 55.—A humpback whale on the deck of a whaling station (now closed) in western Canada. All of the species' most distinctive characteristics are evident in this photograph: 1) the hump and the dorsal fin; 2) the knobs on the top of the snout; and 3) the long flipper, with numerous barnacles attached to its leading edge. (Photo by G. C. Pike, courtesy of I. A. MacAskie.)

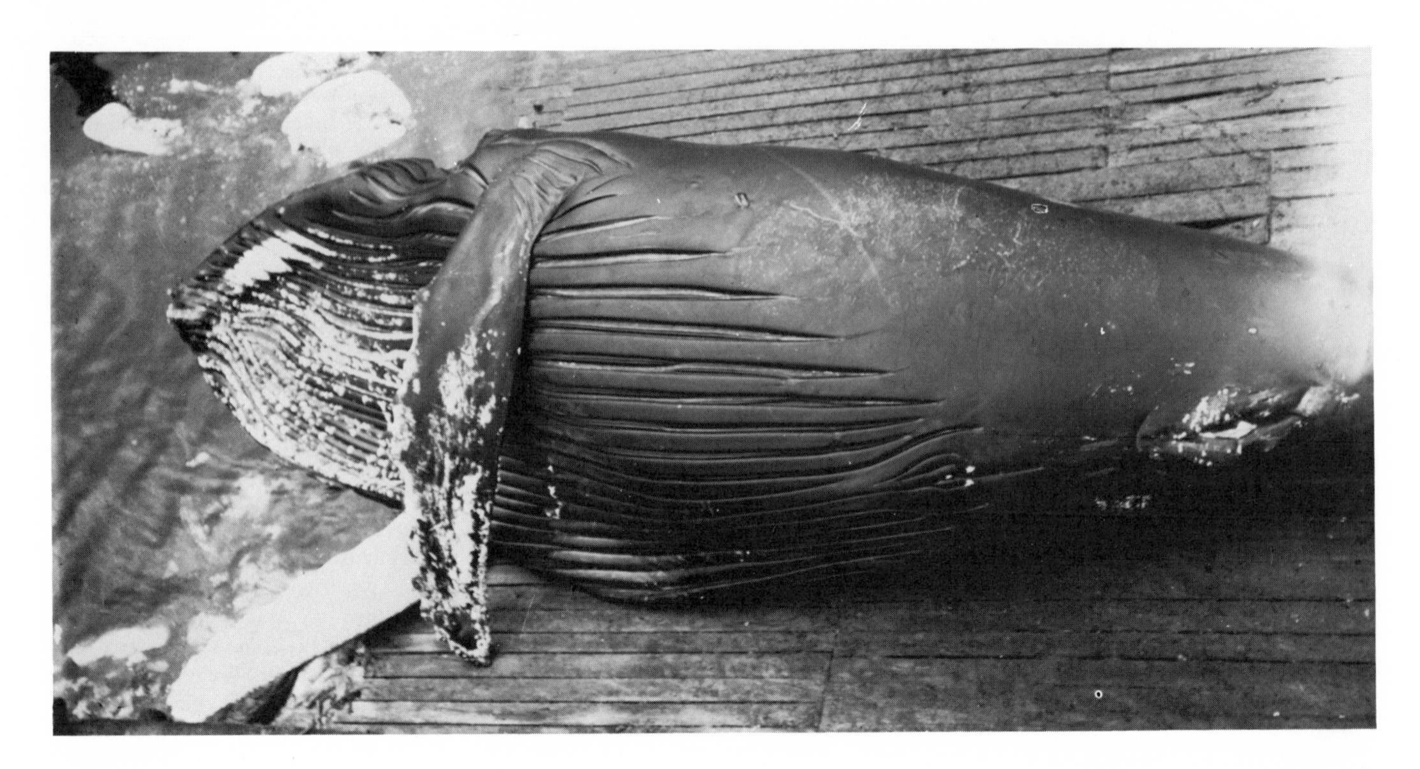

Figure 56.—Humpback whales have 14-20 broad, widely spaced ventral grooves which extend about to the navel. These grooves remain good diagnostic characters for considerable periods after the animal's death, as evidenced in the freshly killed specimen from Newfoundland (top) and the badly decomposed stranded animal from New Jersey (bottom). (Photos from U.S. National Museum, courtesy of J. G. Mead.)

SPERM WHALE (T)

Physeter macrocephalus **Linnaeus, 1758**

Other Common Names

Cachalot, cachalote or ballena esperma (Latin America); makkō kujira (Japanese); kashalot (Russian).

Figure 57.—A side view of a sperm whale near the equator in the eastern Pacific showing the small dorsal fin, the large head, and the distinctive blow (above). In these two photos, note that the spout projects obliquely forward from the blowhole, which is positioned at the left front of the head. (Photos by H. E. Winn, courtesy of NMFS [above]; from the West Indies by K. D. Sexton [left].)

Figure 58.—In this closeup view of two swimming sperm whales off the bow of a research ship note the position of the blowhole. (Photo from the North Pacific by S. Ohsumi.)

Description

Males are much larger than females, occasionally reaching lengths of 17 m but more often about 15 m. Females rarely exceed 12 m. At birth sperm whales are about 3.5–5.0 m long and weigh about 1,000 kg.

A sperm whale is among the easiest of the large whales to identify at sea, even when comparatively little of the animal is seen. It has a huge head, sometimes likened to a boxcar, which comprises one-fourth to one-third of total body length, the proportion being considerably higher for males than females. The blunt, squarish snout may project as much as 1.5 m beyond the tip of the narrow, undershot lower jaw. The head contains the

a

d

b

e

c

f

Figure 59.—Profiles of a sperm whale at the surface, clearly showing the large head (a), the humplike dorsal fin and crenulations (b, c), and the tail flukes, raised high above the surface as the dive begins (d-f). (Photos from the eastern tropical Pacific by G. Friedrichsen, courtesy of NMFS.)

Figure 60.—Profiles of a sperm whale mother and calf off Baja California. Note the generally wrinkled appearance of the body behind the head. (Photo by K. C. Balcomb.)

Figure 61.—Sperm whales often show their broad flukes as they begin long dives, which may last over an hour and take them to depths of 1,000 m or more. Note the smooth rear margin and the nearly triangular shape of the flukes. (Photo from off Point Conception, Calif., by K. C. Balcomb.)

spermaceti organ, a reservoir of high-quality oil like wax for which this whale has been relentlessly hunted. In adults there are numerous short, irregular creases on the throat.

The single blowhole is located well to the left of the midline and far forward on the head. Consequently, the projection of the small bushy blow is forward at a sharp angle and to the left. Under favorable wind conditions this feature alone may permit identification of sperm whales even at a considerable distance.

Sperm whales have a dorsal hump or fin, usually rounded at the peak but sometimes triangular, located about two-thirds of the way back from the front of the head. The hump and crenulations following it are clearly visible when an animal arches its back on diving. Each fluke is in the shape of a right triangle, with the hypotenuse as the leading edge. They are sometimes slightly frayed along the straight rear margin, but not as regularly as in the humpback whale (p. 39, 41). The right and left flukes often overlap slightly at the median notch. The flippers are short and paddle-shaped, tapering only slightly toward their tips.

Sperm whales usually appear dark brownish gray. The skin posterior to the neck often has a shriveled appearance. The belly and front of the head are often light gray to off-white. The skin around the mouth, particularly near the corners, is often white, flecked with gray. The undersides of the flukes and flippers vary in color through numerous shades of brown and brownish gray. Newborn sperm whales are light grayish tan, and they darken in the first few weeks of life.

Natural History Notes

Sperm whales are gregarious, traveling in groups of up to 50 individuals. Such groups are usually composed exclusively of bachelor bulls (males not contributing to reproduction) or of females and young accompanied in some cases by one or several large males. When not associated with a harem, older males are generally solitary. During peak breeding seasons large, loosely associated herds of 50–150 sperm whales are sometimes encountered.

Figure 62.—An aerial view of 21 sperm whales, including two very young calves and several large males, off Japan. Even from an aircraft, the body shape and the position of the blowhole clearly distinguish these animals as sperm whales. (Photos by Suisan Koku Company, courtesy of T. Kasuya.)

Breeding occurs at any time between late winter and late summer. Gestation lasts for 14–15 months and calves are weaned when about 7 m long, or at 1–2 years of age. Females become sexually mature when about 9 m long, at which time they are thought to be 8–11 years of age. Males mature sexually at 12 m and probably about 10 years of age, but they do not become socially mature (participate in reproduction) until they are at least twice as old. The interval between births for a given female is 3–5 years.

The seasonal movements of sperm whales are not as regimented as those of many baleen whales. Males are more mobile than females, traveling much farther poleward in summer. The sperm whale is seldom found in water less than 200 m deep.

Sperm whales dive to depths in excess of 1,000 m and remain submerged for periods of an hour or more. Like other whales, when surfacing from a deep dive they emit a single explosive blow and then, depending on the length of the dive, may remain at the surface for over 60 minutes and blow more than 50 times before diving again. Shorter periods at the surface and fewer blows are more common. Sperm whale calves lying unattended at the surface mark an area below which adults are searching for food. When beginning a dive, sperm whales usually throw their flukes high into the air.

Figure 63.—A small sperm whale as it breaches beside a research vessel in the equatorial Pacific at lat. 1°30′N, long. 88°05′W in January 1979. Sperm whales are often seen breaching. Note the bushy blow, emanating from the front of the squarish head. (Photo by R. L. Pitman, courtesy NMFS.)

Figure 64.—Among the great whales, only sperm whales are known to strand en masse with any regularity. In June 1979 a large herd swam onto Florence Beach, Oreg., where they stirred the participants in a nearby meeting of the American Society of Mammalogists and public sanitation officials. (Photo by J. Larison, courtesy B. Mate.)

Figure 65.—A stranded young male sperm whale at Melbourne Beach, Fla., (top) and a female adult sperm whale on the deck of a whaling ship in the North Pacific (bottom). Note the bulging forehead, the narrow, underslung lower jaw, the white coloration around the mouth, and the wrinkled appearance of the skin. In the bottom photo, note also the whitish region on the belly, the extent of which may be used to distinguish among various regional populations. (Photos by P. Winfield, courtesy of Marineland of Florida [top]; Japanese Whales Research Institute, courtesy of H. Omura [bottom].)

Figure 66.—The throat and lower jaw of a sperm whale on the deck of a Canadian whaling station, showing the numerous short throat creases, which are most clearly evident on adult animals. Though often deemed vestigial in sperm whales, these grooves may yet prove to be functional. In recent underwater photos there have been bulges in the area of the grooves, suggesting a use of some sort. (Photo by J. G. Mead.)

As deep divers, sperm whales feed primarily on squid but also eat octopuses and a variety of fishes. Killer whales attack sperm whales occasionally. Sperm whales probably live for at least 45-60 years. Mass strandings, such as the recent widely publicized strandings in the Gulf of California and Oregon, happen occasionally throughout the species' range.

Distribution

Sperm whales are very widely distributed in the eastern North Pacific. During winter they are mostly found anywhere south of lat. 40°N. They are known to be fairly common over the continental slope off central California from November to April. Important winter sperm whaling grounds existed during the 19th century off southern Baja California and off the west coast of southern Mexico.

Sperm whaling occurred year-round "On the Line" (along the equator), on the "Panama Bay Ground," the "Galapogos Ground," and the "Offshore Ground." It appears, then, that there may be a discrete stock (or stocks) in the eastern tropical Pacific. The "Hawaiian Ground" was another popular year-round sperm whaling area. Sperm whales are seen infrequently today near the main Hawaiian Islands but are considered common in the vicinity of the Leeward Chain.

During summer sperm whales can be found anywhere in the North Pacific. In recent years large catches in spring, summer, and autumn were made off British Columbia, within 400 km of shore. Some sperm whales are found inshore, e.g., in Hecate Strait, Dixon Entrance, and Queen Charlotte Sound. Females generally do not venture north of lat. 50°N, though in warm-water years they may reach the Aleutians. Males enter the Bering Sea, where they generally are encountered singly or in pairs. A major summer hunting area during the 19th century was the "Kodiak" or "Northwest Ground," which formed a broad band beginning in the southwestern Bering Sea, continuing along the Aleutians, throughout much of the Gulf of Alaska

Figure 67.—The narrow lower jaw of a sperm whale contains 18–25 large functional teeth, which fit into sockets in the upper jaw. The upper jaw also contains some teeth, but they are imbedded and nonfunctional. (Photos from the North Pacific by Japanese Whales Research Institute, courtesy of H. Omura [left]; from La Jolla, Calif., courtesy NMFS [right].)

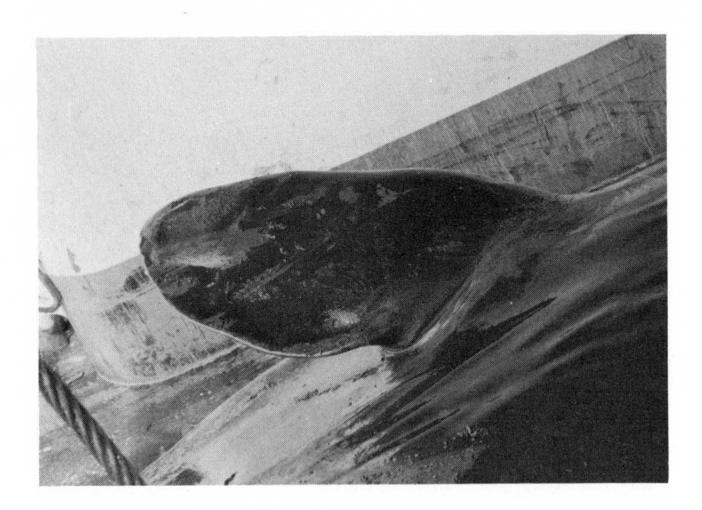

Figure 68.—The paddle-shaped flipper of a sperm whale from the North Pacific. (Photo from Japanese Whales Research Institute, courtesy of H. Omura.)

north to lat. 50°N, and extending below lat. 40°N along the American coast.

Movements of a few individuals have been inferred from tag-recapture studies. Three animals were marked off southern California in January. Of these, a male was killed off northern California in June, one was taken off Washington in June, and a female was captured in the western Gulf of Alaska in April.

Can Be Confused With

Sperm whales are so distinctive, particularly in head shape, and in the appearance and trajectory of their blow, that they should not be confused with other whales. However, there is some possibility of confusing them with humpback whales (p. 39), which can have a sperm whalelike hump. Both species arch their backs when beginning a long dive, raising the fin or hump, and both throw the tail flukes high. The most distinctive differences are tabularized on p. 43, 49.

There is some possibility of confusing the sperm whale with Baird's beaked whale (p. 88). The latter has a dorsal fin, but it is located far back on the body and is generally more prominent than the hump of the sperm whale. In addition, Baird's beaked whale has a long, cylindrical beak, and smooth but heavily scarred skin.

When clearly seen from the air, sperm whales are easily identified, particularly when they raft in tight resting groups, catching their breath in preparation for another long dive. Their deep-diving regimen usually ensures that you will see them well, or not at all. The blow projects forward, and the extreme anterior position of the gaping blowhole is usually evident. The lower jaw usually looks stark white under the surface. The flukes are broad relative to the body and straight on the rear margin. From the tail stock forward the body broadens, then tapers from the neck forward.

Identification of Dead Specimens

Dead sperm whales are unmistakable. The only other whales with narrow underslung lower jaws are the dwarf (p. 198) and pygmy (p. 193) sperm whales, both of which have dorsal fins and both of which are smaller as adults than even newborn sperms. The sperm whale's teeth are also distinctive. They are massive, bluntly conical, and only slightly curved. There are 18–25 functional teeth in each lower jaw, and these fit into sockets in the upper jaw. The huge head and the position of the blowhole are also unmistakable.

LARGE WHALES WITHOUT A DORSAL FIN

(12–16 m maximum length)

There are three species of large whale without a dorsal fin in eastern North Pacific and western Arctic waters. All are baleen whales. The first two, the bowhead and right whales, have enormous heads and smooth backs with no dorsal fin (see Figs. 11, 69). The third, the gray whale, has a head which is triangular in lateral or dorsal aspect, and a distinct dorsal ridge with 6–12 bumps that give the back a knuckled appearance as the animal humps up to begin a dive. In the bowhead and right whales, the projection of the blow upward from two widely separated blowholes assumes a V-shape with two distinct columns, evident when the animal is viewed from front or back. Though other baleen whales may exhibit a V-shaped blow under ideal conditions, this feature is exaggerated and consistent in the bowhead and right whales and may be used as a key to their identification. In calm conditions the gray whale's low, bushy blow can appear heart-shaped.

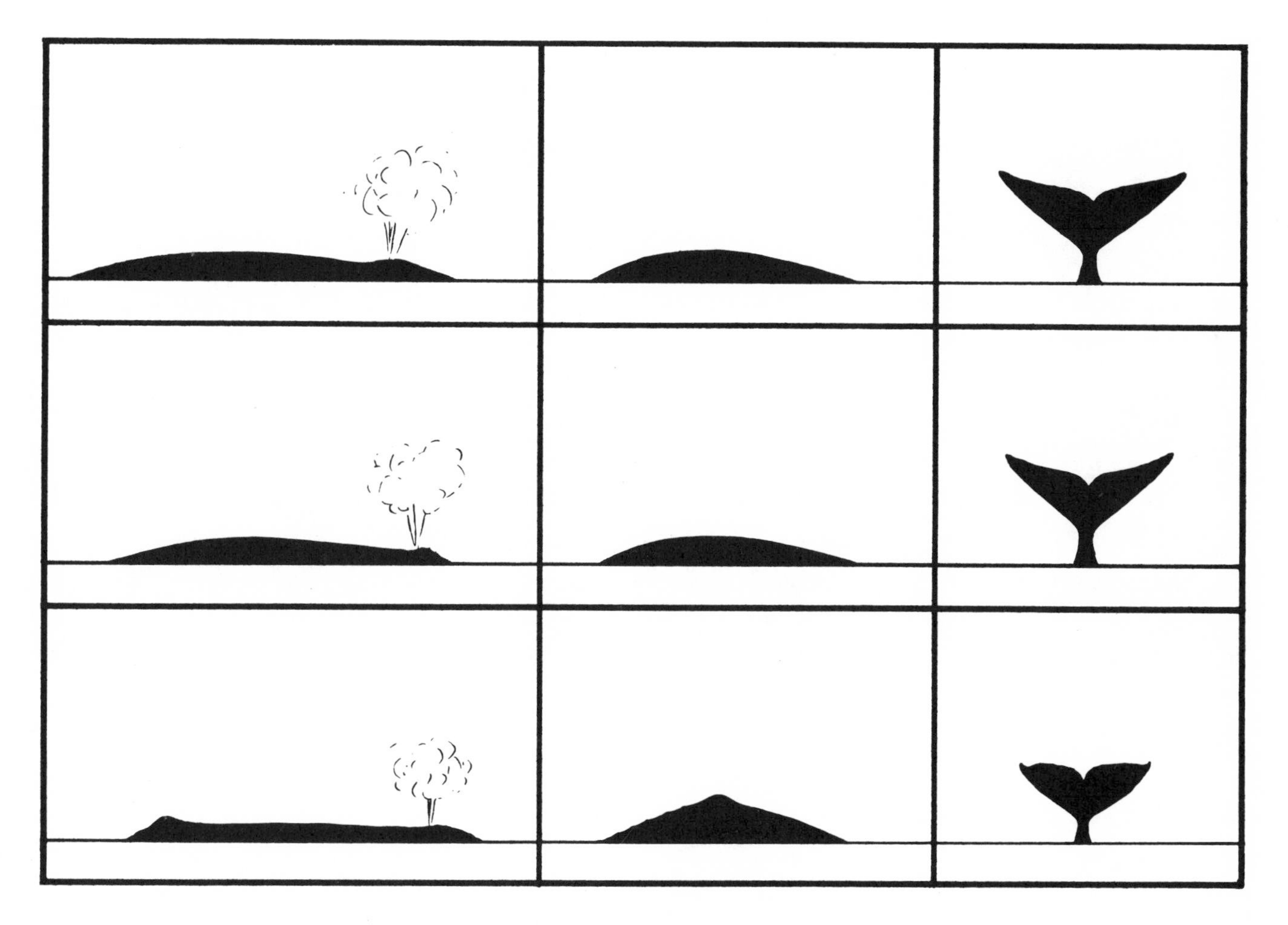

Figure 69.—Surfacing characteristics of "Large Whales Without a Dorsal Fin." (Drawings by Larry Foster, courtesy of General Whale.)

BOWHEAD WHALE (B)

Balaena mysticetus Linnaeus, 1758

Figure 70.—A bowhead blowing in the eastern Beaufort Sea. The two-pronged or V-shaped spout distinguishes bowhead and right whales from all other species, though under calm conditions the blows of humpback and gray whales may have two separate elements. (Photo by W. Hoek.)

Figure 71.—The bowhead whale's white chin, interrupted in most cases by a string of black spots, is evident in the surfacing individual (left) and in both members of the pair (right). (Photos from off Point Hope, Alaska, bv J. Lentfer.)

Other Common Names

Greenland whale, Greenland right whale, Arctic right whale, great polar whale, kiralick (plus special words for age and sex classes, used only by the northern Alaska Eskimos); hokkyoku kujira (Japanese); grenlandskiy, polyarnyy kit (Russian).

Description

The bowhead whale grows to 18 m long and can weigh upwards of 50 t. Sexually mature females are at least 12.2 m long; males, 11.6 m. Newborn bowheads are 3-4.5 m long.

The most conspicuous feature of this whale is its enormous head, often a third as long as the entire body. The lower jaws are strongly bowed. The top of the head is smooth, black, and without the bonnet or "rock garden" characteristic of the right whale (p. 67). The blowholes are widely separated, and the blow projects upwards in two distinct columns. Though the blows of other mysticetes may be similar under calm conditions this feature is exaggerated and highly characteristic in the bowhead and right whales.

When viewed from the side, some swimming bowhead whales show a classic Loch Ness monster profile, with two curves to the back—one forming a triangular hillock between the tip of the snout and the neck, the other encompassing the entire back from the neck to the tail. This description may apply only to adults. Other bowheads, usually smaller individuals, lack the indentation behind the head, having instead a single smooth contour from snout to tail. In all animals, the back is smooth, lacking any trace of a dorsal fin or ridge.

The flukes, which are frequently lifted clear of the surface as the whale begins a long dive, are broad, tapered at the tips, and concave along the rear margin with a deep median notch. The flippers have an almost rectangular shape, unlike those of rorquals.

Figure 72.—A surfacing bowhead whale off Point Barrow, Alaska, in April 1978, showing its "Loch Ness monster" profile. (Photo by S. Leatherwood.)

Figure 73.—Bowhead whales have no dorsal fin. The back is smooth and black, though often irregularly spaced white or grayish scars of unknown origin appear. (Photos from off Barrow, Alaska, by J. Lentfer.)

Figure 74.—The flukes of a young male bowhead whale captured in Osaka Bay, Japan. The flukes of bowheads are slightly sinusoidal on the rear margin and pointed at the tip. (Photo courtesy Yomiuri, Osaka, Japan.)

Figure 75.—Aerial views of bowhead whales in the Bering and Chukchi Seas: two animals resting near Wainwright Village (left) and a single individual in a hole in new sheet-ice off Diomede Islands (right). In the animals on the left, note the smooth finless back and the white chin; in the animal on the right, the double curve to the back and the arcuate contour of the mouth line. (Photos by S. Leatherwood.)

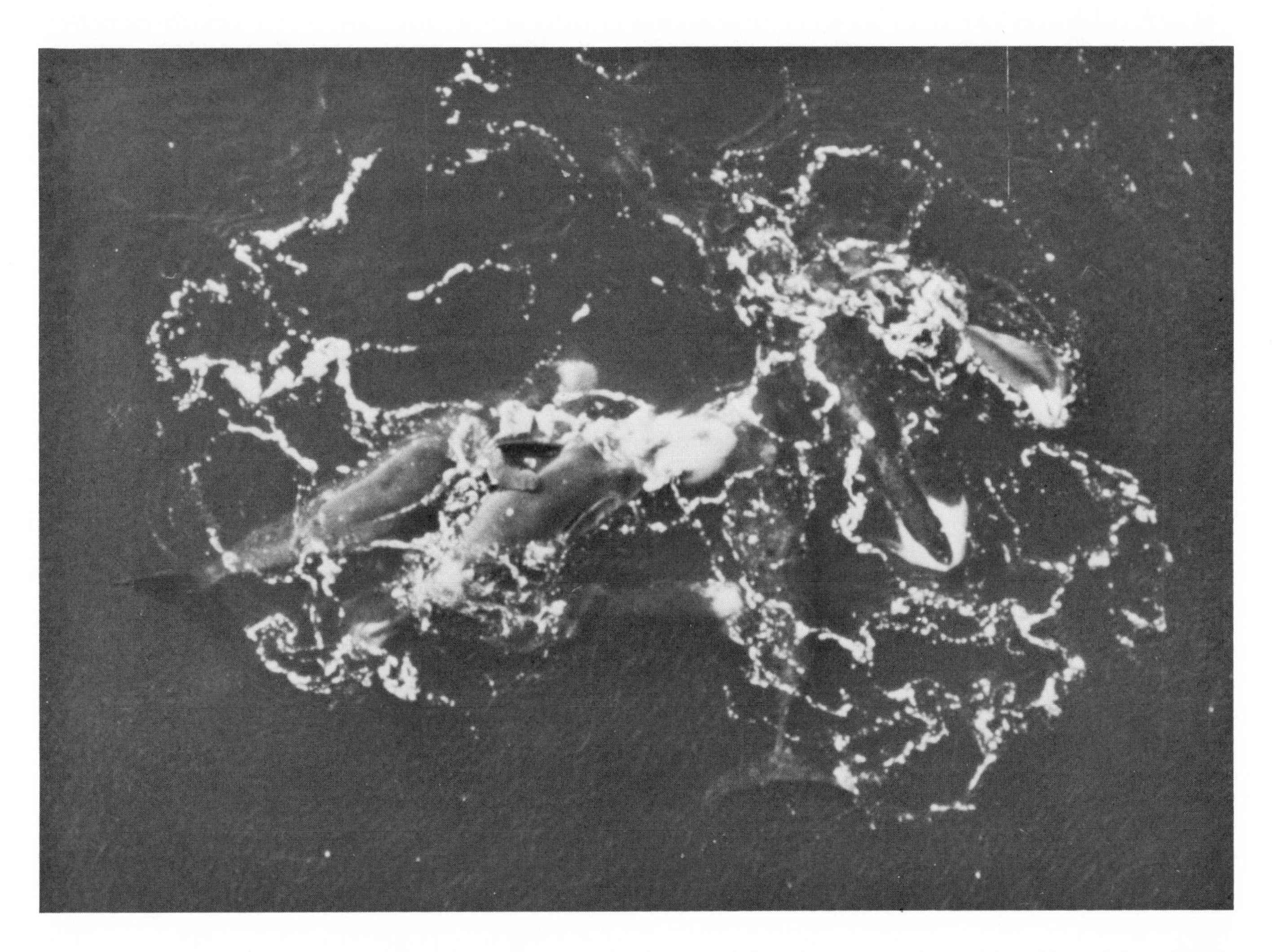

Figure 76.—A remarkable photo of a group of courting bowhead whales in the Beaufort Sea, including at least one copulating pair. Many of the species' most distinctive features are clearly evident. (Photo by B. Krogman, courtesy of NMFS.)

Figure 77.—A female bowhead whale and her calf near Diomede Islands in spring of 1978. Calves like this are the hope for the future of bowhead whales and for the Eskimo culture which has depended on them for centuries. There is grave concern that the low population size, the low productivity (approximately 1% per year verified), and continued harvest may prevent recovery and even lead to extinction of this last sizable stock of bowhead whales. (Photo by S. Leatherwood.)

Bowheads are almost completely black, except for a white chin patch. A string of gray or black spots often extends along the chin toward the tip of the lower jaw and stands out like a string of beads against the white chin patch. Also, there frequently is a white or light gray stripe around the narrowest portion of the tail stock.

Bowhead baleen is long and springy, reaching lengths of up to 4.3 m. The length of the longest plate is well over 10 times its width. The baleen is uniformly dark gray to black, with the fringes slightly lighter. There are 230–360 plates per row.

Natural History Notes

Bowheads are found in loose herds of a few dozen on feeding grounds, but while traveling they show little evidence of strong social ties among adults. A feeding concentration of over 60 individuals was seen near St. Matthew Island in the Bering Sea, March 1979.

Reproductive data on bowhead whales are sketchy despite the fact that hundreds of thousands of them have been killed by commercial whalers. Most calves apparently are born in April or May, after a gestation period believed to be a year or slightly longer. Age at sexual maturity and the calving interval are not

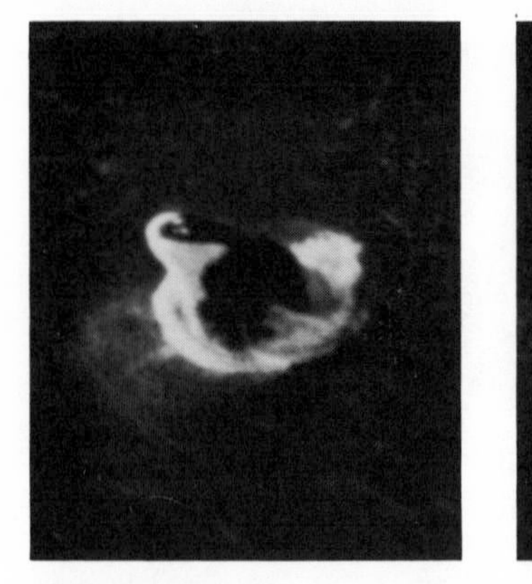

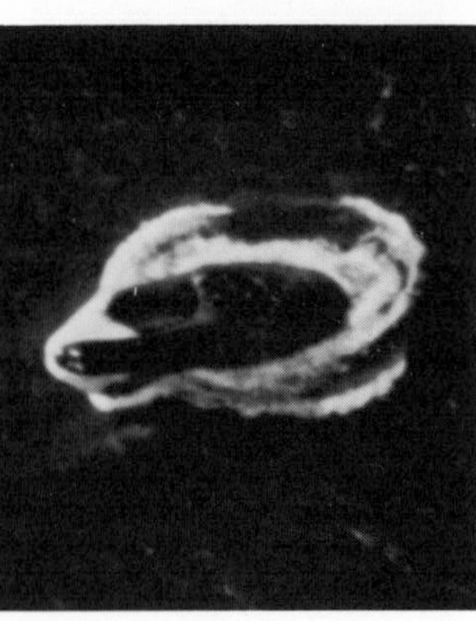

Figure 78.—Views of breaching bowhead whales, including aerial views taken off Diomede Island, (top photos) and an ice-level view (bottom) from near Barrow, Alaska. Migrating bowheads frequently breach, taillob, and lie on their sides slapping their flippers against the water surface. (Photos by S. Leatherwood [top photos]; G. Carroll, courtesy of NMFS [bottom].)

known, but the latter is at least 2 years. Because of the failure of bowhead stocks to recover after being badly depleted, there is reason to believe that their productivity, at present, is very low. In fact, in recent research cruises and flights through much of the bowhead's range, only about 1% of the animals seen were calves of the year.

The most obvious thing about bowhead ecology is the whale's close association with pack ice. Its seasonal movements can be explained primarily on the basis of changes in ice conditions.

Bowheads are slow swimmers and can be approached very closely. However, they are strongly allergic to noise during their spring migration. Behaviorally, bowheads seem much like right whales, assuming many different postures at the surface and breaching occasionally, sometimes many times in succession. Bowheads are not thought to be deep divers, although they can remain underwater for at least 42 minutes. This capability is useful during migration when the distance between breathing spaces in the ice may be considerable.

Swarms of small to medium-size zooplankton, including euphausiids, amphipods, copepods, mysids, and pteropods, are favored by bowheads. Though basically skimmers, bowheads are known to feed at or near the bottom in shallow areas, sometimes emerging from a dive with sand and detritus streaming from both sides of the mouth. Killer whales are probably the bowhead's only natural enemy. Its close association with ice makes the bowhead susceptible to accidental entrapment, crushing, or stranding.

Distribution

Bowhead whales are found in the Bering, Chukchi, and Beaufort Seas, where their precisely timed seasonal migrations are in concert with the retreat and advance of arctic ice. Though once much more abundant (perhaps 18,000 or more in 1842) and more wide-ranging (with catches as far southeast as the Pribilof Islands), the estimated 1,000-3,000 remaining bowheads in the western Arctic apparently winter in the southwestern Bering Sea along and south of the pack ice edge and in a few polynyas, areas of permanently open water in the otherwise solid pack.

In early spring, the bowheads begin to move north, passing St. Lawrence Island and Diomede Islands, primarily on their western sides, in three or four waves of abundance between late March and late May. Recent evidence suggests that at least part of the migrating population congregates near St. Matthew Island in early spring, beginning their northward movements as ice conditions permit. Once through Bering Strait, most appear to veer toward the northeast, follow the most easterly leads in the ice of the Chukchi Sea, round Point Barrow in April or May, and continue along the nearshore leads to Banks Island and Prince Patrick Island. As the ice recedes in summer, they spread south and east into Amundsen Gulf. As ice begins to re-form and advance in fall, they move westward, most apparently moving close alongshore or along the ice edge, some reaching the northeast Siberian coast near Wrangel Island, before yielding to the winter ice by moving gradually southward to favored wintering grounds.

Can Be Confused With

Although at one time there was a possibility of confusing bowhead and right whales (p. 67), today the right whales are so rare in the North Pacific that probably few venture to the northern limit of their historic range, where they would overlap with bowheads. The characteristics listed below for dead specimens are, in any case, adequate for distinguishing between the two species.

Several of the balaenopterids reach far enough north in summer—even to the edge of pack ice—to overlap in range with bowheads. However, the bowhead can be readily distinguished from them by the absence of a dorsal fin and, on close inspection, by the very different configuration of its mouth and head.

Gray whales (p. 72) are the most common large whales in the Bering and Chukchi Seas in summer, and they are probably the

Figure 79.—A view of a large bowhead killed by Eskimos at Barrow, Alaska. In addition to the characteristic shape of the mouthline and the body size, note the very long baleen plates. (Photo courtesy of NMFS.)

Figure 80.—A fetus taken from a bowhead whale killed at Barrow, Alaska, in 1976. The absence of baleen in this stage of development provides a clear view of the shape of the arching lower lip and the narrow, bowed rostrum. (Photo courtesy of Naval Arctic Research Laboratory, Barrow, Alaska.)

whales most likely to be confused with bowheads. The best character for recognizing gray whales is the knuckled dorsal ridge on the posterior half of the back, usually detected as the whale completes its time on the surface for respiration. Gray whales are generally gray and barnacle-covered, in contrast to the bowhead's general black color and lack of encrustations.

From the air, bowheads are easy to recognize by the rotund black body, which tapers to a narrow tail stock and has no evidence of a dorsal fin. The white chin is often conspicuous, as is the white or light gray band around the tail stock when present. The narrow rostrum, enfolded as it is on either side by the enormously bowed lower lips, is also seen clearly from the air.

Identification of Dead Specimens

In addition to the fact that its range overlaps only slightly with that of the right whale, the bowhead whale may be distinguished from the right whale by differences in coloration, length of longest baleen plates, and callosities.

Bowhead Whale	**Right Whale**
Distribution	
Arctic distribution year-round; south to central Bering Sea in winter.	Baja California north to coasts of Washington and Oregon in winter, historically penetrating the southern Bering Sea in summer.
Coloration	
Black with white patch on front part of lower jaw, sometimes containing a series of	Black, sometimes mottled, with irregular white regions on ventral side; yellowish to pink

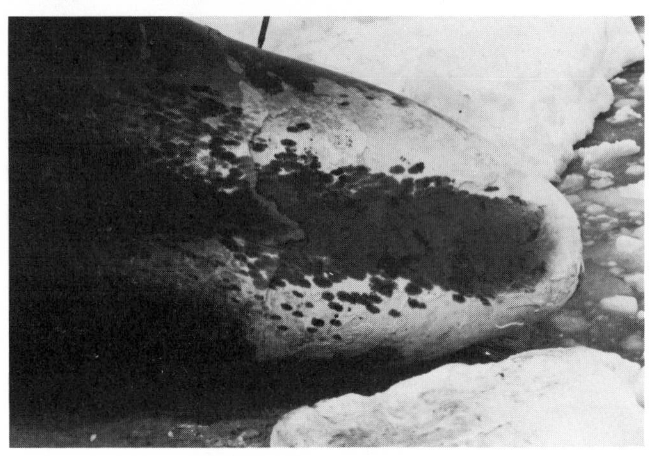

Figure 81.—Detailed views of heads of bowhead whales. Note the high-arching upper jaw. In the right photo, note the white chin, spotted with black. (Photos by D. R. Patten [above]; courtesy of NMFS [right].

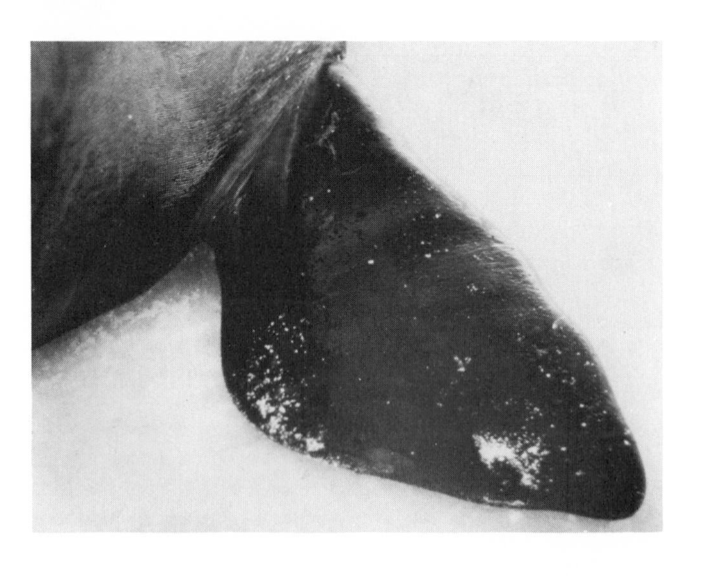

Figure 82.—The bowhead whale's flippers, like those of the right whale, are broad and spatulate, unlike those of other baleen whales. (Photo by W. Marquette, courtesy of NMFS.)

black spots; variable white areas especially on belly.	encrustations (callosities bearing lice) on the head.

Baleen

230–360 per side; plates to 36 cm at base and up to 4.3 m long. Dark gray or black with grayish fringes; anterior margin of some plates whitish, showing green iridescence in sunlight.	250–390 per side; plates to 31 cm at base and up to 2.8 m long. Dirty gray with black fringes; some anterior plates partly or completely white.

Bonnet and Other Callosities

Absent	Present

RIGHT WHALE (B)

Eubalaena glacialis (Borowski, 1781)

Figure 83.—A North Pacific right whale. Note the high arching contour to the mouthline, the scalloped upper edge of the lower lip, and the callosities on the rostrum. (Photo from Japanese Whales Research Institute, courtesy of H. Omura.)

Other Common Names

Black right whale, northwest whale (historical), Nordkaper and Biscayan right whale (applied to North Atlantic right whales, sometimes used by 19th century whalers for North Pacific right whales—not currently in use); ballena franca (Latin America); semi kujira (Japanese); yuzhnyy kit (Russian).

Description

Specimens more than 17 m long have been encountered, but few right whales grow so large. Females are larger than males. Length at birth is about 4.5–6.0 m.

The head, which may be more than a fourth as long as the entire rotund body, has a very distinctive shape, with a narrow arched rostrum and bowed lower jaws. The top of the head has a series of callosities, the largest of which is called the bonnet, in front of the blowholes. Callosities are usually also present above the eyes, on the chin, and elsewhere on the face. Cyamid crustaceans, usually called "whale lice," live on the callosities. The color, which apparently comes mainly from the crustaceans, and extent of these growths varies with individual whales. The paired blowholes are widely separated, resulting in a blow which is distinctly V-shaped.

The right whale has no dorsal fin, and the skin on its broad back is free of callosities and generally free of barnacles. The flippers are widely splayed and relatively long, and the skin is stretched tautly across the arm bones, which can be traced by prominent ridges. The flukes have a smooth, concave rear margin and a deep notch between them.

The body is usually uniformly black, although white splotches are common, especially on the belly, and piebald or white individuals have been observed. Some right whales are mottled.

The baleen distinguishes this species from all others except the bowhead. It is long (up to 2.8 m), narrow, and springy, with dense but fine bristles. Its color varies from dark brownish through dark gray to black; although seen through the water, it often appears light gray to white. There are 206–268 plates per row.

Natural History Notes

It is difficult to comment on the social habits of these whales in the North Pacific population simply because there are so few

Figure 84.—Right whales off Florida. Note the wide V-shaped blow characteristic of right whales. (Photos courtesy of Marineland of Florida [left]; by David K. Caldwell [right].)

Figure 85.—Closeup views of the heads of right whales off northeastern Florida (top) and off Cape Cod, Mass., (bottom) clearly showing the narrow rostrum and the bonnet. In the bottom photo of a feeding whale, note the extremely long baleen plates, characteristic of bowhead and right whales. (Photos by N. Fain, courtesy of Marineland of Florida [top]; W. A. Watkins [bottom].)

animals remaining. Historically, large numbers of right whales may have congregated in protected areas along the west coast for winter calving and in plankton-rich portions of the Gulf of Alaska for summer feeding. Recently they have been sighted singly or in pairs, with groups of up to eight animals seen on occasion.

The reproductive biology of right whales in the eastern North Pacific has never been studied adequately, but it is clear that productivity is very low.

Right whales do not seem to adhere to a rigid migratory schedule or to follow a well-defined route. A tendency for the bulk of the population to move to higher latitudes in summer and to more temperate areas in winter is evident from whaling records and the few sightings in recent years.

Right whales are slow swimmers and are generally not wary of boats, so it is often possible to approach them closely. Like sperm and humpback whales, they frequently throw their flukes high into the air at the beginning of a long dive. They often wave a flipper above the surface and sometimes leap clear of the water, returning with a mighty splash. Right whales are not known to eat fish; their favorite prey are planktonic copepods and euphausiids, which they take by swimming through the patchy swarms, cavernous mouth agape. Killer whales are their only known predator.

Distribution

Nineteenth century whalers hunted right whales intensively on the "Kodiak Grounds," which comprised much of the Gulf of Alaska and the southeastern Bering Sea. Consequently this region is regarded as the primary summer range of right whales in the eastern North Pacific. A few still summer in the Gulf of Alaska, but sightings there are scarce. In April 1959 two pods of eight right whales each were sighted within about 30 km off the Washington and Oregon coasts, and in January 1967, three whales were seen off Cape Flattery, Wash.

Only stragglers seem to venture south of Oregon waters. A total of three whales, each alone, was seen by whalers operating within 61 km of the central California coast between 1956 and 1968. The sightings occurred in April and May. In addition, one was spotted off La Jolla, Calif., at the end of March 1955, and a pair was observed near Punta Abreojos, Baja California (lat.

a

b

c

d

e

f

g

h

Figure 86.—Right whales frequently throw their flukes high into the air and then slip nearly vertically beneath the surface. Note that the rear margin of the flukes in this species are smooth, lacking the frayed or scalloped appearance that so conspicuously denotes the humpback. (Photos from the western North Atlantic by K. C. Balcomb [a–g]; off Florida, courtesy of David Caldwell [h].)

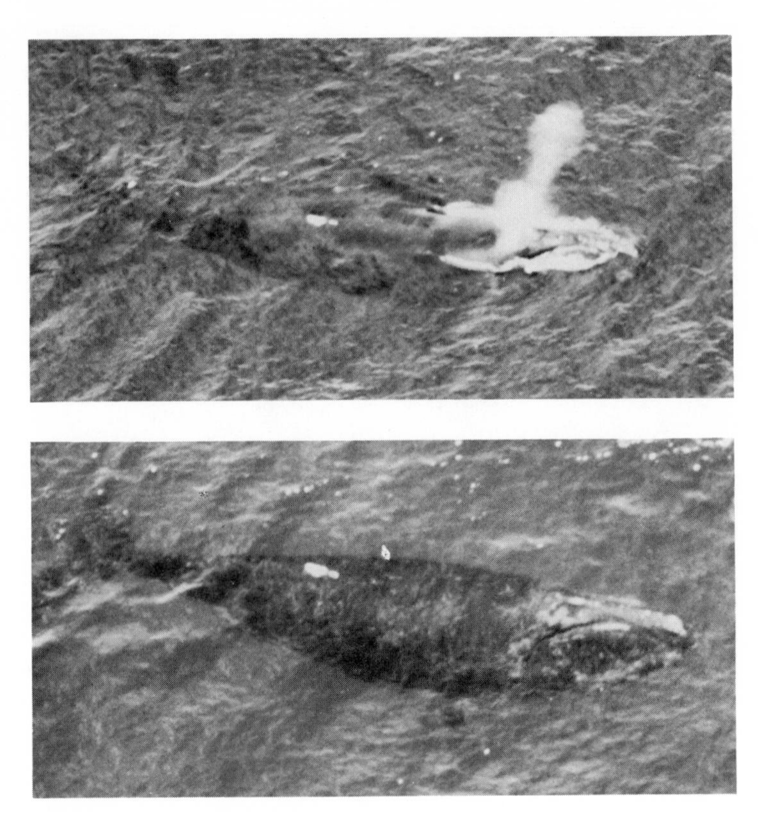

Figure 87.—Three aerial views of a right whale in Hawaii, March 1978, clearly showing the finless back and unmistakably narrow rostrum. (Photos by C. Baker, courtesy of M. Herman.)

26°39′N, long. 113°40′W), in March 1965. There is no historical evidence that right whales were ever present in significant numbers in Hawaiian waters, but one was seen recently in the channel between Maui and Lanai.

No more than several hundred right whales are thought to survive in the entire North Pacific. Since the prospect of seeing them off the west coast of North America is extremely poor, reports of sightings, particularly when documented by photographs, are of great interest to the cetological community.

Figure 88.—Like its Arctic counterpart the bowhead whale, the right whale often breaches. In this ventral view of a whale arching away from the photographer, the large spatulate flippers, in shape unique to the right whales, can be seen clearly. The vertical lines on the whale's belly are caused by splashing water; right whales have no ventral grooves. (Photo by R. M. Gilmore.)

Can Be Confused With

Right whales are only likely to be confused with bowhead whales (p. 60) (in the Bering Sea) and gray whales (p. 72). At sea, there are really only two good methods to distinguish between right and bowhead whales. First, their ranges do not generally overlap, because virtually all bowheads have gone north by the time right whales reach their northernmost summering areas in the southern Bering Sea. However, the discovery of a young bowhead in Osaka Harbor, Japan, (lat. 35°N, similar to the latitude of San Diego) during June, indicates that some overlap occurs. A more reliable key is the right whale's callosities, which bowheads lack entirely. When examined at sufficiently close range to determine the absence of callosities, the white chin of bowheads can usually be seen.

Gray whales usually have a bushy blow, although separate columns of vapor can sometimes be detected. They are generally gray and covered with barnacles, while most right whales have smooth black skin except for the callosities. Gray whales have a knuckled ridge along the spine behind the center of the back, while right whales have nothing resembling a dorsal fin or ridge. The gray whale's head is triangular when viewed dorsally or laterally; the right whale's head is more bulky in both views.

If only the flukes are seen as the animal dives, right (and bowhead) whales can be distinguished from the other four large whales exhibiting this behavior—sperms (p. 51), humpbacks (p. 39), grays (p. 72), and blues (p. 13)—in the following ways: 1) the flukes of the right and bowhead whales are broad, pointed at the tip, concave along the rear margin with a deep median notch, and uniformly dark above and below; 2) those of the sperm whale are more nearly triangular; 3) those of the humpback have a scalloped rear margin and are often variably white underneath; 4) those of the gray whale are similar in shape to

Figure 89.—Pacific right whales on whaling station ramps in Japan (top and right); see Figure 4 for the one from British Columbia. Together these photos clearly illustrate the species' most distinctive features: the arching contour of the mouthline; the extremely long, narrow baleen plates, reaching lengths of 2.8 m; the bonnet (the largest callosity at the front of the rostrum); and the absence of ventral grooves. (Photos by Japanese Whales Research Institute, courtesy of H. Omura.)

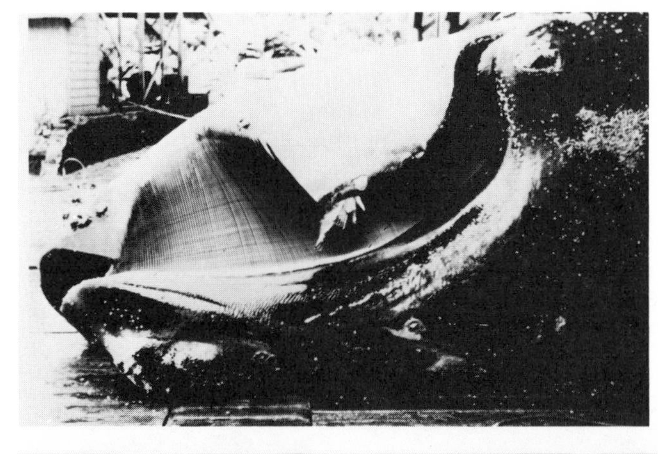

Figure 90.—The head of a North Pacific right whale dead on a whaling station deck, showing the long baleen plates and some of the callosities, including the most extensive one called the bonnet (top). The lower two photos show, in increasing degrees of magnification, the crusty, wartlike bonnet and the tiny crustaceans ("whale lice") that infest it. (Photos by Japanese Whales Research Institute, courtesy of H. Omura.)

the right whale's but are usually broader anteroposteriorly, mottled gray in color, and often encrusted with barnacles; and 5) blue whale flukes are wider, broader, and less deeply notched, and the thick dorsal and ventral keels on the caudal peduncle make the blue whale's tail easy to distinguish from the right whale's surprisingly narrow tail stock.

Right whales seen from the air usually look much less streamlined than other large whales, except possibly the humpback and bowhead, and their lack of a dorsal fin helps make identification easy. From an aerial perspective the impression of a narrow rostrum "pinched" on either side by the lower lips is especially striking. The callosities present on the narrow rostrum usually stand out as stark white interruptions of the otherwise all-black exterior of these whales.

Identification of Dead Specimens

Dead right whales are easy to identify by the arched rostrum and bowed mandibles; the lack of a dorsal fin; the bonnet; the long, springy baleen (only the bowhead's is longer); and the broad spatulate flippers.

GRAY WHALE (B)

Eschrichtius robustus **Lilljeborg, 1861**

Figure 91.—A female gray whale and her calf. (From a drawing by L. Foster, courtesy of General Whale.)

Other Common Names

Summer whale (Arctic only), devilfish, mussel-digger (historical); ballena gris (Latin America); koku kujira (Japanese); angtuchhaq (Alaska Eskimo Yupik); seryy kit (Russian).

Description

Maximum length for gray whales is about 14 m; weight, 33 t. Females grow somewhat larger than males. Sexual maturity in both sexes is attained at 11–12 m. Length at birth averages about 5 m.

The body viewed from above is tapered at both ends, the head appearing narrowly triangular, and the tail stock much attenuated. The long mouthline is arched slightly. There is no head ridge; the rostrum is covered by pits or depressions containing small whiskers. The head viewed from the side slopes steeply downward from the blowholes. The tip of the lower jaw often protrudes beyond the upper.

Instead of ventral grooves, like those found on the throats of balaenopterids, gray whales have two (to five) deep longitudinal creases on the throat.

The back has a low hump about two-thirds of the way from the tip of the snout to the flukes; it is followed by a serrated ridge, marked by 6–12 knobs or bumps along the dorsal midline. These give the top of the tail stock a knuckled appearance when seen from the side. The broad (up to 3 m wide) flukes are separated by a deep median notch. The rear margin of each fluke is generally convex. As gray whales dive at the end of a series of blows, they often raise the flukes high above the surface. The small flippers have rounded margins and pointed tips.

Gray whales have mottled gray skin due to both natural pig-

Figure 92.—Blows of gray whales from the side (top) and the back (bottom). Gray whale blows are bushy, reaching 3-4 m in height. When seen from front or back, the partial separation of the two columns of vapor gives the blow a heart-shaped appearance. (Photos from San Ignacio Lagoon, Baja California, by S. Swartz and M. L. Jones.)

mentation and extensive scarring from defunct barnacle colonies. The darkness of the background and the extent of light blotching vary considerably. When swimming or idling just below the surface, the whale's back may appear uniformly white or slate blue to a surface or aerial observer. Much of the body, the head and tail in particular, is encrusted with barnacles. Clusters of orange whale lice live on these barnacle colonies and even on the skin itself. Orange patches frequently seen on gray whales at a distance are caused by concentrations of "lice." The skin of very young animals is more uniformly dark and barnacle-free. For a period after birth, the skin is wrinkled or pitted, giving it an appearance reminiscent of a waffle iron.

Gray whale baleen is short (to 37 cm) and stiff, with coarse bristles. The plates, of which there are 138–180 per side, are yellowish white to white, and the bristles are yellowish white. An interesting feature of the gray whale's baleen is its uneven wear. The anterior plates on the right side are invariably shorter than those on the left. This condition is believed to result from the whale's "right-handed" approach to grubbing along the bottom for food.

Natural History Notes

Migrating gray whales are encountered alone or in groups of as many as 16 individuals. The composition of these groups, except those with female-calf pairs, fluctuates constantly. On northern feeding grounds gray whales are often solitary, though many animals may be in near proximity in the patchily distributed, food-rich areas. In and around southern wintering lagoons, the whales are extremely concentrated and interaction is frequent. Though nursing females attempt to remain apart from other whales, male suitors persistently attend them. The bond between female and young is extremely strong; it was the vigorous defense of their calves that earned female gray whales the epithet "devilfish" from 19th century whalers.

Most births occur during a 3-month period in winter while the whales are at or en route to their protected assembling areas at low latitudes. Mating activity is intense on these wintering grounds, but most conceptions apparently occur during the southward migration. Females nurse their calves for no more than 9 months, and apparently usually give birth in alternate years.

Figure 93.—Side (top) and rear (left) views of California gray whales just after the blowholes have snapped shut. Gray whales are clearly identifiable by their mottled gray coloration, a mixture of natural pigmentation and areas of scarring where barnacles were once attached, and by the head, which angles steeply downward in front of the blowholes and is triangular in dorsal aspect. (Photos from Laguna Ojo de Liebre [Scammon's Lagoon], Baja California, by S. Leatherwood [top]; from San Ignacio Lagoon, Baja California, by S. Swartz and M. L. Jones [left].)

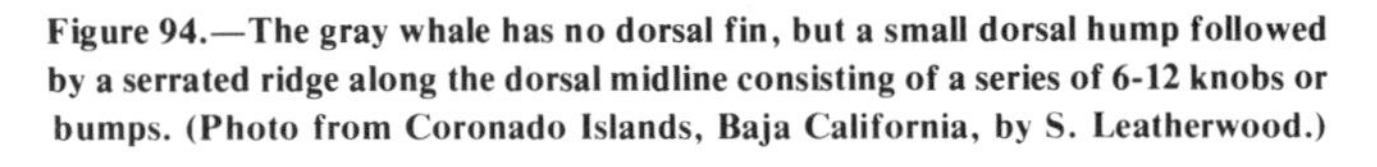

Figure 94.—The gray whale has no dorsal fin, but a small dorsal hump followed by a serrated ridge along the dorsal midline consisting of a series of 6-12 knobs or bumps. (Photo from Coronado Islands, Baja California, by S. Leatherwood.)

Figure 95.—Gray whales habitually raise their flukes following the last blow in a sequence. The peduncle is stocky and sometimes ridged even to the junction with the flukes. The often scarred and barnacle-covered flukes have a deep median notch and are sinuously curved to a sharp pointed tip (left). The flukes sometimes are marred by tooth rakes or are missing large chunks, both probably evidence of encounters with killer whales (below). (Photos from San Ignacio Lagoon, Baja California, by S. Swartz and M. L. Jones [left]; and R. Storro-Patterson [below].)

Figure 96.—Photos of gray whale adult-calf pairs taken in Scammon's Lagoon, Baja California, the best known of the species' southern winter resorts. From the air, gray whales can be identified readily by the uniquely tapered body shape and the mottled gray coloration (top). Note the mud boil stretching behind the adult. As bottom grubbers, gray whales are often seen leaving trails of mud, particularly at high latitudes where most feeding occurs. (Photos by R. Storro-Patterson [top] and S. Leatherwood [bottom].)

Gray whales undertake one of the longest migrations known for any mammal. They parade past the North American west coast, close to shore and on a predictable schedule, supporting a lucrative and growing whale watching tourist industry.

Gray whales are among the most active large whales at the water surface. They breach occasionally during migration, and regularly do so on the wintering grounds. In addition, they often "spyhop" (orient vertically with much of the head above the surface) and "lobtail" (raise the tail and slam it against the surface), allowing the observer a good look at the head and tail. In recent years numerous "friendly" whales have thrilled tourists abroad skiffs in the breeding lagoons. These animals actually solicit the attentions of people, allowing themselves to be patted and stroked.

A gray whale's blow is usually low (less than 3-4 m) and bushy, sometimes described as heart-shaped but also occasionally showing two divergent columns of vapor (i.e., V-shaped).

Migrating gray whales breathe at regular intervals, generally blowing 3-5 times at intervals of 30-50 seconds, then lifting their flukes and submerging for 3-5 minutes. The average swimming speed is about 8 km per hour during southward migration, and 3 km per hour on the trip north in spring. At either end of the migration the whales behave more erratically, sometimes submerging for as long as 15 minutes.

Feeding gray whales are followed by a cloud of mud, stirred up or ejected as they grub along the bottom for gammarid amphipods, which are the staple of their diet. There is some evidence that gray whales feed in one area for a year and then do not return to it for several years, until perhaps it has renewed itself.

Killer whales attack gray whales with surprising frequency, and large sharks may pose a threat to calves in the enclosed breeding lagoons. A newborn gray whale was captured and kept alive for a year in a California oceanarium; its subsequent return to the wild is believed to have been successful.

Distribution

The majority of the gray whale population is concentrated during January to March in three major wintering areas along the outer coast of Baja California: Ojo de Liebre (or Scammon's) Lagoon and adjacent Guerrero Negro Lagoon, San

Figure 97.—Three views—dorsal (left), ventral (top right), lateral (bottom right)—of gray whales spyhopping in the protected waters of the calving lagoons in Mexico. This behavior remains unexplained, but gray whales do it regularly. (Photos by R. Storro-Patterson [left, top right]; S. Swartz and M. L. Jones [bottom right].)

Ignacio Lagoon, and Magdalena Bay and its adjacent protected waters. In past years wintering gray whales have also been found along the mainland Mexican coast south to Yavaros and in small numbers inside the Gulf of California as far north as the Midriff Islands. In early spring the whales stream northward, remaining close to shore except in the California Bight, where many pass seaward of the Channel Islands. A few remain to summer in isolated pockets along the route where productivity is adequate to sustain them (for instance, near the Farallon Islands and Vancouver and Queen Charlotte Islands), but most follow the coastline of British Columbia and southern Alaska northward.

Most of the population of approximately 12,000–17,000 whales funnels through Unimak Pass and into the Bering Sea, pressing close to shore until well inside Bristol Bay. Once in the Port Heiden area the whales fan out in a broad band across Bristol Bay and head for Nunivak Island (or in some cases the Pribilof Islands). After passing Nunivak or St. Matthew Island they continue their dispersal northward, avoiding the shoal areas from Nunivak through Norton and Kotzebue Sounds as well as the deeper waters of the southwestern Bering Sea. Elsewhere throughout the shallow shelf waters of the Bering and Chukchi Seas gray whales are found in spotty concentrations during summer. The eastward limit of their summer distribution is usually not far east of Point Barrow, and few move farther west than Wrangel Island, off the Siberian coast.

As ice begins to form in northern latitudes during the fall, gray whales begin the southbound half of their almost 20,000 km round-trip migration, reversing the pattern outlined above.

Although it was believed to be near extinction early in this century, protection since 1946 from commercial hunting has allowed the gray whale to recover dramatically. It is now believed by some to be near the carrying capacity of its habitat, with a population very near the level that existed before commercial exploitation. A few gray whales are killed by natives of St. Lawrence Island and the northwest coast of Alaska, and Russian government whalers take 140–200 gray whales per year to satisfy subsistence needs of Siberian aborigines.

Figure 98.—In San Ignacio Lagoon certain gray whales have recently shown what can best be interpreted as curiosity toward the humans who come to watch them. Occasionally a gray whale will approach a skiff closely enough to be patted, giving the visitor the thrill of a lifetime. (Photos by S. Swartz and M. L. Jones [top]; D. Cavagnaro, courtesy California Academy of Sciences [bottom].)

Figure 99.—A California gray whale calf was maintained in captivity at Sea World, Inc., San Diego, Calif., in 1972–1973. The study of this animal, the first baleen whale to be kept alive in captivity for more than a few weeks, provided considerable insight into the biology of gray whales. A bottlenose dolphin kept the gray whale company during her year in captivity. (Photo by W. F. Perrin.)

Can Be Confused With

The absence of a dorsal fin makes gray whales easy to distinguish from other large whales except right (p. 67), bowhead (p. 60), and sperm (p. 51) whales, any of which might cause confusion when seen at a distance. However, neither of the former two has a hump or serrated ridge on the dorsal surface, and the skin of both is more smooth and evenly colored than the gray whale's. Right whales have a conspicuous bonnet on the head, and their overall head shape is so distinctive that it should be easy to distinguish from the gray whale's.

Sperm whales have wrinkled skin, are uniformly gray or brown in color, and have a single blowhole set at the front of the head. The blow projects at an angle forward and to the left. Also, the sperm whale's rectangular head is very different from the gray whale's more triangular head. From the air the gray

Figure 100.—Head-on view of a dead gray whale in the surf near Camp Pendleton, Calif. Note the narrow rostrum, lined with lightly pigmented barnacles. (Photo by T. Hoban.)

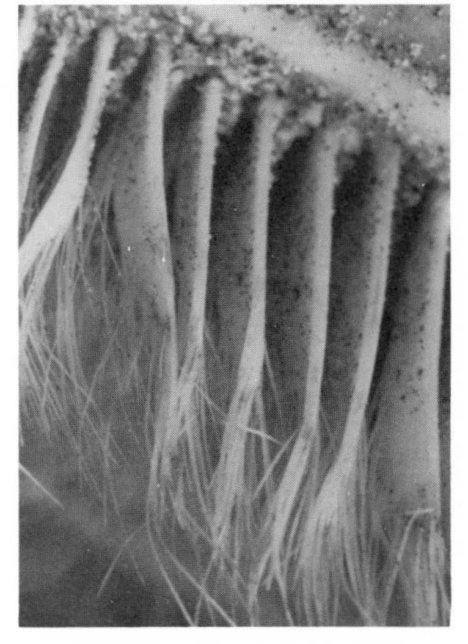

Figure 101.—Closeup view of the baleen of a dead gray whale. Note how straight the mouthline is and how short the bristles of baleen appear (above). The stiff, coarse bristles can be seen particularly well (left). The gray whale's baleen is uniformly cream or ivory in color. (Photos by T. Hoban.)

whale's mottled coloration and generally coastal haunts make mistaken identification highly unlikely.

Identification of Dead Specimens

Only two species have all white or yellowish-white baleen, the minke (p. 80) and the gray. Minkes do not exceed 10 m in length, have numerous ventral grooves, are basically black with white patches on the flippers and several gray areas on the back and head, and have over 280 baleen plates per side. Gray whales may exceed 10 m (maximum of about 14 m) in length, have no ventral grooves but rather two to five creases on the throat, are mottled gray, and have fewer than 280 baleen plates per side (138–180).

Figure 102.—This view of a gray whale's throat shows two deep, nearly parallel furrows. The family Eschrichtidae is, in a sense, intermediate between the Balaenidae (right whales), which lack ventral grooves entirely, and the Balaenopteridae (rorquals), which possess many long, parallel grooves on the throat and chest. (Photo by T. Hoban.)

MEDIUM-SIZED WHALES WITH A DORSAL FIN

(to 13 m maximum length)

There are at least 14 species of medium-sized whales with a dorsal fin known to occur in the eastern North Pacific. These whales range in maximum adult size from about 4 m (Risso's dolphin) to about 13 m (Baird's beaked whale). The group includes such widely distributed and frequently encountered forms as the pilot whale, false killer whale, and minke whale, and such rarely encountered and poorly known species as the various beaked whales.

Aside from their common inclusion within the stated size range and the presence of a dorsal fin in all of them (which ranges from only a small nubbin in some of the beaked whales to a substantial 1.5–1.8 m tall triangle on adult male killer whales), these species have little in common. Therefore, each is discussed in detail and is placed in the text in near proximity to those species with which it is likely to be confused in the field.

MINKE WHALE (B)

Balaenoptera acutorostrata **Lacépède, 1804**

Figure 103.—The North Pacific minke whale. The upward-sweeping white areas vary in intensity. (Drawing by L. Foster, courtesy of General Whale.)

Other Common Names

Little piked whale, sharp-headed finner whale, lesser rorqual, pike whale, Davidson's whale; ballena minke, ballena enana or rorcual pequeño (Latin America); koiwashi kujira or minku (Japanese); qungvughaq (Alaska Eskimo Yupik); malyy polosatik, minke (Russian).

Description

Male and female minke whales in the North Pacific reach sexual maturity at about 7 m in length. Physical maturity in females, which are on average larger than males, is attained at about 8 m, but they can grow to be 10 m long. Newborn minke whales are about 2.8 m long. This is the smallest baleen whale in the North Pacific.

The head is narrow and pointed, with a triangular rostrum bisected by a single ridge beginning in front of the blowholes (see Fig. 11). This ridge resembles that of the fin whale, except that it is much sharper, hence the common name "sharp-headed finner."

The minke's dorsal fin is tall and falcate, placed a bit less than two-thirds of the way back from the tip of the rostrum, in about the same position as that of the sei whale. Normally the fin becomes visible simultaneously with the low, bushy and usually inconspicuous blow.

There are 50–70 thin ventral grooves, the longest of which end slightly anterior to the navel.

Minke whales are black or dark gray on the back and white on the belly and on the undersides of the flippers. Portions of the undersides of the flukes may be bluish gray. The most conspicuous mark is a diagonal band of white on the upper surface of each of the small, pointed flippers. The extent and orientation of the white flipper band varies individually.

Like the fin whale, the minke whale sometimes has a light chevron on the back behind the head and two regions of light gray on each side—one just above and behind the flipper; another just in front of and below the dorsal fin. These may be conspicuous on some individuals and indetectable on others.

The short baleen, which is sometimes visible at close range when the whale is feeding, is mostly yellowish white with fine white bristles. The posterior plates (up to half) may be brown to black. There is sometimes black streaking in the white plates. The longest plates are about 21 cm long (beginning at the gumline and not including the fringes). These plates are about half as wide as they are tall. Minke whales in the eastern North Pacific appear to have fewer baleen plates than those in other parts of the world—about 231–285 on a side.

Figure 104.—A minke whale in the Gulf of California. Note the areas of light gray on the sides of the body, characteristic of most North Pacific minke whales. (Photo by R. S. Wells.)

Natural History Notes

Minke whales are solitary animals, sometimes seen in pairs or trios, but rarely found in large groups outside feeding grounds, where adventitious congregations may be observed in spring and summer.

Breeding activity continues throughout the year but peaks in January and June. The gestation period is believed to be about 10 months, so there are corresponding calving peaks in winter and spring. Although females may be capable of giving birth annually, a 2-year interval is more usual.

The minke whale population as a whole shifts northward in summer and southward in winter, but in some temperate and tropical areas they are present year-round. Pregnant females seem to move farther north in summer than do lactating and immature females.

Minke whales are more likely to be seen closely than their larger relatives—the blue, fin, sei, and Bryde's whales—because they often approach boats, particularly stationary vessels. Charles Scammon (1874), the 19th century whaling captain, remarked on this behavior: "It [the minke] frequently gambols about vessels when under way, darting from one side to the other beneath their bottoms." He also made an interesting observation on the minke's appearance of being at home among the ice floes north of Bering Strait: "Like [bowheads and gray whales] they thread the ice floes, and frequently emerge through the narrow fissures bolt upright, with their heads above the broken ice to blow." This habit of spy hopping in the pack ice has been observed recently in the Bering Sea.

Like fin whales, minkes often arch their tail stock high when beginning a long dive, but they do not raise their flukes clear of the surface. They breach more often than do other finner whales—by leaping clear of the surface and reentering smoothly, headfirst; or with a substantial splash like that created by breaching humpback whales. Minke whales apparently breach most frequently during feeding periods.

Minke whales approach shore and frequently enter bays, inlets, and estuaries. In the North Pacific they prey mainly on euphausiids and copepods, as well as on schooling fishes like sand lances and anchovies. The killer whale preys on minke whales. Also, it is not unusual for these little whales to become trapped in fishing gear, after which they sometimes drown or are shot.

Distribution

Minke whales occur from the Bering and Chukchi Seas south at least to near the equator. Although they have wide distribution, they are not considered abundant in any part of the eastern North Pacific, except perhaps in Alaska waters. Due to their small size, minkes have had no importance to the whaling industry in the eastern North Pacific, and as a result, very little effort has been devoted to mapping their range and assessing their abundance. They now are the mainstay of the Japanese factory-ship operations in the Southern Hemisphere.

As indicated above, minke whales are known to penetrate loose ice during summer, and some venture north of Bering Strait. Eskimos at St. Lawrence Island in the northern Bering Sea take them occasionally. Minke whales are present in Alaska waters and along the Aleutian Islands primarily during summer. Whalers at Port Hobron and Akutan early in this century reported frequent sightings. Recent sightings indicate minkes are abundant near the eastern Aleutians (Fox Island group).

Minke whales are seen or become stranded occasionally in British Columbia and Washington, often in inside waters. Scammon claimed that they could be seen in Juan de Fuca Strait in any season, and more recent evidence supports the idea that they are indeed present in Washington and British Columbia year-round. They are seen fairly frequently in Puget Sound in summer and are common as far south as central California during that season.

Figure 105.—In all these minke whales, the white band on the flippers and the sharply pointed head are evident. Note the gray chevron on the back (top left); the regions of light gray on the sides (top right); and the absence of a conspicuous blow and the appearance of the prominent dorsal fin on the surface while the blowholes are still exposed (bottom). (Photos from off San Diego, Calif., by G. E. Lingle [top left]; from the western Pacific by Japanese Whales Research Institute, courtesy of H. Omura [top right]; from the northern West Indies by J. Hain [bottom].)

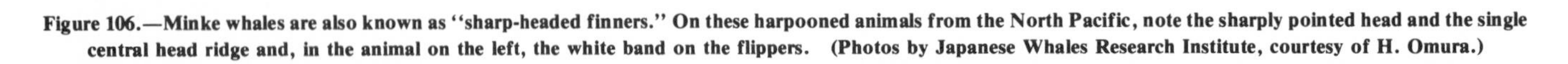

Figure 106.—Minke whales are also known as "sharp-headed finners." On these harpooned animals from the North Pacific, note the sharply pointed head and the single central head ridge and, in the animal on the left, the white band on the flippers. (Photos by Japanese Whales Research Institute, courtesy of H. Omura.)

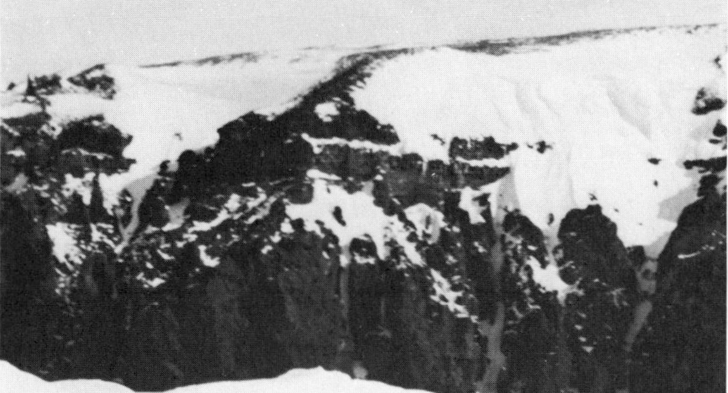

Figure 107.—Two minke whales about to dive under ice at McMurdo Sound, Antarctica (above), and a single animal trapped at Cape Crozier, in the Ross Sea (left). Although minkes do not generally venture as far into the ice in the western Arctic as in the eastern Arctic or the Antarctic, they are the most northerly of the rorqual whales there. (Photos courtesy of Naval Photographic Center, Washington, D.C.)

Figure 108.—A minke whale breaching in Prince William Sound, Alaska. When this much of the animal can be seen, its identity is unmistakable. Minke whales often breach in this dolphinlike manner, reentering headfirst with little splash. (Photo by D. Calkins.)

Figure 109.—Underwater photos of a minke whale off Japan. The animal was harpooned and tethered to the vessel while it was photographed and examined by divers. (Photos by G. Williamson, courtesy of General Whale.)

Figure 110.—Minke whales stranded at Santa Barbara (top) and Arcata (middle, bottom), Calif. Note the dark back, the white-banded flipper, and the narrow ventral grooves ending just behind the flippers. The darker appearance of the Arcata specimen is principally due to postmortem darkening. (Photos by S. Anderson [top]; W. J. Houck [middle, bottom].)

Figure 111.—Minke whales can have as many as 325 short, yellowish-white baleen plates per row (up to half the posteriormost plates may be brown or black), with fine white bristles. (Photos from Santa Barbara, Calif., by S. Anderson [top]; from Arcata, Calif., by W. J. Houck [bottom].)

During the winter, minke whales are present from at least northern Washington south to within 2° of the equator. However, they seem to be most abundant near the California Channel Islands.

Minke have never been reported from the main Hawaiian Islands, but they are sometimes seen near the Leeward Chain.

Can Be Confused With

When seen at relatively close range, minke whales can be readily distinguished from other rorquals that have tall, falcate dorsal fins (fin, p. 23; sei, p. 29; and Bryde's, p. 34) by their much smaller size and by their distinctive white flipper bands. At a distance, however, positive identification may be difficult. Minke whales have a low, inconspicuous blow. Like sei whales, they frequently expose the dorsal fin simultaneously with the blow, but minke whales hump the tail stock higher when beginning a long dive—more like fin whales.

From a distance, the minke whale can also be mistaken for beaked whales if only the back and dorsal fin are seen. Its black, generally unscarred skin might help distinguish it from many beaked whales, whose backs are often heavily scarred. Obviously, if the head is seen, there will be little doubt, since beaked whales have a beak and minke whales have a pointed, triangular head. Though some regional variation in its expression is expected for the eastern Pacific, the white flipper band of the minke whale, when it can be seen, is a diagnostic character. This white flipper band is the best feature for identifying minkes from the air.

Identification of Dead Specimens

Dead minke whales are most readily identified by 1) their small size (usually less than 9 m); 2) the transverse white band on each flipper; 3) the short yellowish-white baleen (up to half the posteriormost plates may be brown or black), 231–285 plates per side, with fine white bristles; and 4) the 50–70 thin ventral grooves, ending well ahead of the navel, often just even with the flipper tips.

BEAKED WHALES (T)

Other Common Names

Ballena con pico (Latin America); klyuvorylye kity (Russian).

Group Characteristics

This interesting and diverse, but very poorly known, group—the family Ziphiidae—poses special problems in the North Pacific. Here at least three genera—*Berardius*, *Ziphius*, and *Mesoplodon*—are represented. The presence of a fourth—*Hyperoodon*—is suspected in tropical areas well offshore. The most varied of the genera is *Mesoplodon*, of which at least five well-defined species are known to inhabit waters off the Pacific coast of North America: *M. densirostris*, *M. carlhubbsi*, *M. stejnegeri*, *M. hectori*, and *M. ginkgodens*. The other three genera are monotypic in the North Pacific.

All North Pacific beaked whales share some very distinctive qualities, including 1) a well-defined beak, with functional teeth in the mandibles only; 2) a single, wide, crescentic blowhole; 3) a triangular or falcate dorsal fin set well behind the middle of the back; 4) small flippers, which in some species fit into slight, differentially pigmented indentations on the sides; 5) a pair of creases on the throat that converge, but usually do not meet, anteriorly; and 6) the lack of a regularly well developed median notch between the flukes. Most appear to remain seaward of the continental shelf, where they seem to subsist on a diet composed primarily of cephalopods. These whales are either very rare in the North Pacific or deliberately avoid frequent contact with people. Most of what we know about them comes from their occasional, usually opportunistic capture by whalers, or from strandings.

Since most external morphological and behavioral differences between living beaked whales are either too subtle or too poorly known to provide ready keys to identification, dentition and skull characteristics provide the most reliable means of distinguishing members of this group. In bottlenose whales and Cuvier's beaked whale, there is a single pair of conical teeth at the tip of the mandibles, which erupt in adult males and remain hidden below the gum in females and young. In Baird's beaked whale, there are two pairs of teeth, both near the tip of the mandibles; they are more flattened (i.e., laterally compressed) than conical, and erupt in adults of both sexes. All forms of *Mesoplodon* have a single pair of laterally compressed teeth that pierce the gum only in adult males. In four recognized North Pacific species, these teeth are positioned behind the apex of the mandibles, but near the point at which the mandibles converge (the mandibular symphysis). In the fifth (*M. hectori*) they are positioned well in front of the symphysis, near the tip of the jaw. *Mesoplodon* teeth are unique in structure. They are flattened and massive, capped by a small, sharp denticle of dentine, which is the tooth that was present at birth.

The species accounts that follow are all too often based on very sketchy data and should be viewed as tentative statements only, particularly with respect to the *Mesoplodon* species. Unfortunately, fine points in the identification of many of the beaked whales remain an esoteric province of museum scientists and taxonomists.

BAIRD'S BEAKED WHALE (T)

Berardius bairdii Stejneger, 1883

Other Common Names

Giant bottlenose whale, North Pacific giant bottlenose whale; ballena nariz de botella, gran calderon (Latin America)[10]; tsuchi kujira, tsuchimbo (Japanese); severnyy plavun (Russian).

Description

This is the largest of the beaked whales, growing to nearly 13 m in length. Females are somewhat larger than males. Length at birth is about 4.6 m.

The prominent, bulging forehead (which is broader and more bulbous in males) slopes gently to a long, cylindrical beak (see Fig. 11). The lower jaw extends slightly beyond the upper jaw, allowing the apical mandibular teeth to be exposed in adults. When they surface to breathe, these whales often bring their heads out of the water at a steep angle, allowing the long beak and forehead to be seen clearly. The paired throat creases characteristic of beaked whales are long in this species—up to about 70 cm—and there may be one or several short, irregular furrows between them.

The long, rotund body has relatively small appendages. The nearly triangular dorsal fin is located more than two-thirds of the way back on the body, and during a normal wheellike surfacing motion it emerges from the water after the head and

[10]Reports of *Hyperoodon* or *Berardius* near the coasts of Mexico or Central America would be exceptional, since both are virtually unknown in tropical or subtropical latitudes. We appreciate the danger in assigning Spanish common names to such species, since it may tend to encourage their imprudent use. Caution is especially necessary when two species have the same or similar common names, as is true of the bottlenose whale and Baird's beaked (or the giant bottlenose) whale.

Figure 112.—Surfacing Baird's beaked whales off Oregon. The rounded, bulbous forehead is clearly seen, set off from the back by a distinct crease in the area of the blowhole. The long cylindrical beak protrudes well in front of the forehead. (Photos by T. R. Wahl.)

Figure 113.—Note the long scars that cover the backs of these Baird's beaked whales. These whales usually surface at a shallow angle, showing a long back with the dorsal fin set far behind its center. The fin generally rises from the back at a low angle, has a blunted peak, and has a straight to slightly concave rear margin. (Photos off Point Conception, Calif., by K. C. Balcomb [top left]; at lat. 29°N by S. Leatherwood [top right]; off Oregon by T. R. Wahl [bottom right].)

Figure 114.—Aerial view of a herd of at least 12 Baird's beaked whales off Japan. Even from the air the bulbous melon and the long beak, tipped by white (marking the positions of the protruding teeth), are clear indications that these large beaked whales are Baird's beaked whales. (Photo courtesy of T. Kasuya.)

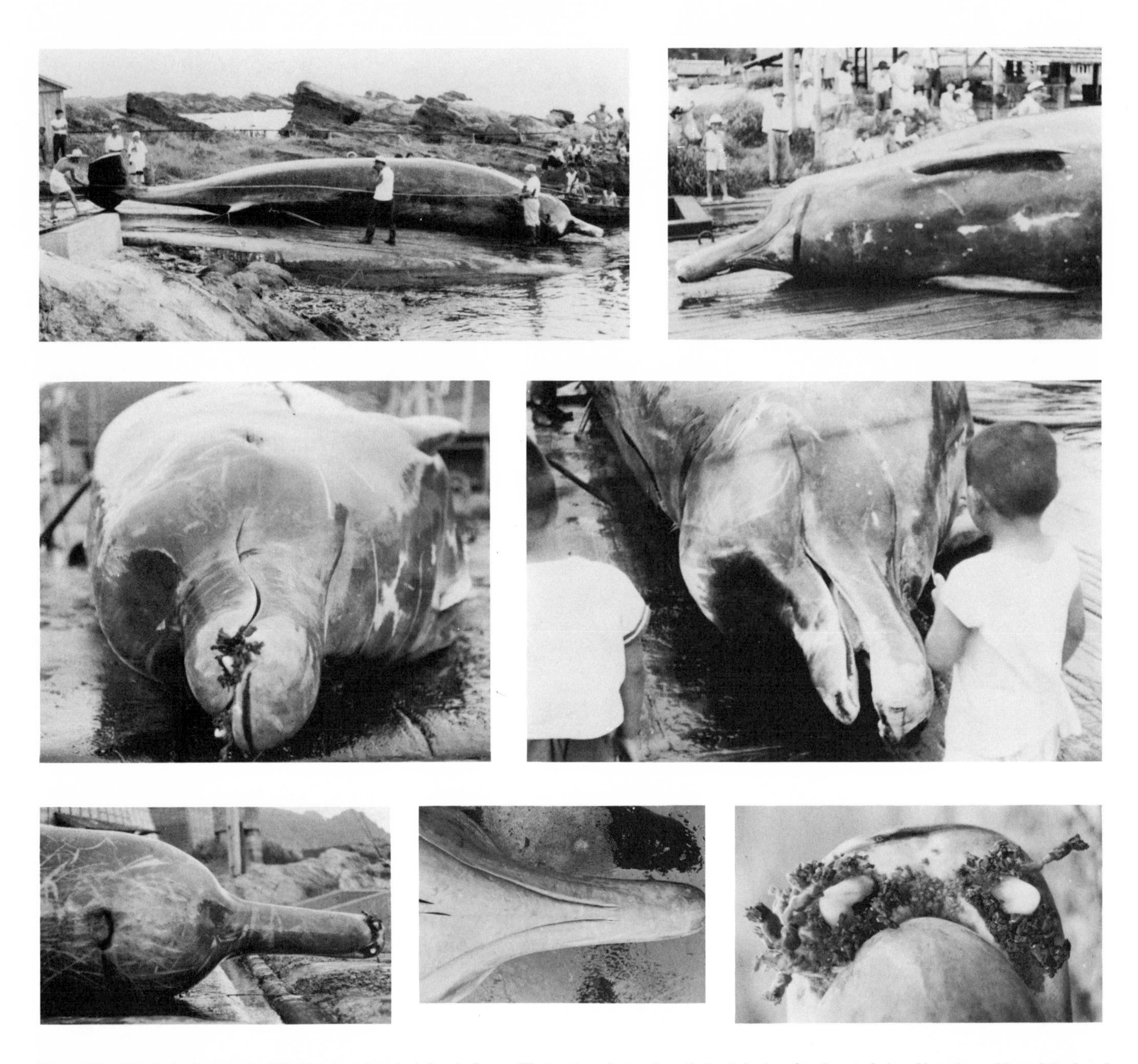

Figure 115.—Baird's beaked whales killed by shore-based whalers in Japan. The top two photos show the body in dorsal and ventral view. Note the position of the dorsal fin, more than two-thirds of the way back from the tip of the beak. Also note the white spots along the ventral midline and how the flippers fold against the body. The middle two photos are front views of two different individuals, one with a conspicuous pair of exposed teeth (definitely an adult) and the other with its teeth unerupted or just beginning to erupt. The lower set of photos show, starting from the left, the head in dorsal profile, the incompletely convergent pair of long throat creases, and a detailed view of the two mandibular teeth, heavily infested with stalked barnacles. Note in the far left photo how the lower jaw extends beyond the upper, leaving the teeth exposed outside the closed mouth, and the shape and position of the blowhole, with the open side oriented posteriorly. (All photos courtesy of H. Omura.)

blowhole are submerged. It varies in shape but is usually neither falcate nor pointed. The flukes, which sometimes are raised as the whale dives, have a nearly straight trailing edge with either a slight prominence or a very slight depression in the middle but usually no actual notch. The flippers are not tapered and have blunt tips.

The color of Baird's beaked whale is slate gray, but may appear army brown, with white blotches on the undersides, particularly on the throat, between the flippers, and around the navel. Both sexes have many linear white scars on the body, some of which occur in parallel pairs. These scars are probably remnants of tooth rakes inflicted during fighting and are usually more numerous on males. When abundant, they cause the animal's dorsal surface to appear lighter than its true color.

Natural History Notes

Records from the largely shore-based whaling operations taking this whale suggest a marked degree of segregation of sexes in the population, the males predominating in the catches. Pod size is generally from 2 to 20 (occasionally up to 30) animals, which surface in tight formation and may respire synchronously while on the move.

The reproductive characteristics of Baird's beaked whale are not well established. The calving interval is probably 3 years. The species is long-lived, with ages of at least 35 years and possibly 70 or more years suggested by tooth layering.

It is not clear whether these whales migrate in the eastern North Pacific, but it can be stated that they generally remain in offshore waters deeper than 1,000 m in all seasons and that there are clear peaks in their occurrence in certain areas. They have been observed in the southern portions of their range, off Baja California, in both winter and summer.

Baird's beaked whales have been reported to be hard to approach, but this is not always the case. They have a low and indistinct blow, and when traveling quickly, roll sharply to the surface, sometimes exposing the flukes as they dive. When resting or traveling slowly they may stretch at the surface to expose head and dorsal fin simultaneously and then not raise the flukes when submerging. On rare occasions they have been known to breach, throwing one-half to three-fourths of the body clear of the water and reentering with a splash.

The main prey of these whales are squid, octopus, and deep-sea fishes, and they also take crustaceans, sea cucumbers, rockfish, mackerel, and sardines. One small group was observed to remain submerged for 42 minutes before resurfacing in almost the exact location where it had dived.

Figure 116.—Flukes of a Baird's beaked whale, showing the slight median notch. Beaked whale flukes are unique in their lack of a consistent notch dividing the flukes. (Photo by G. Pike, courtesy of General Whale.)

Distribution

Baird's beaked whale is native only to the North Pacific, where it is found primarily in offshore waters above the southern temperate zone. Its known southern limit on the eastern side of the North Pacific is about lat. 28°N off Baja California, and it has been known to strand as far north as St. Matthew Island in the Bering Sea (ca. lat. 60°N). Japanese whalers have reported sightings from lat. 25°N to 30°N in the central North Pacific.

Because of its size, Baird's beaked whale has merited the casual attention of whaling crews in the eastern North Pacific, although it never was viewed as a major target species. On the basis of the meager whaling records and the timing and location of strandings, some generalizations can be made about seasonal distribution. There are apparent peaks in abundance off central California in July and October, though the species is certainly present off both central and northern California from June through October. Baird's beaked whales have been either seen or caught off Washington between April and October. They are encountered with some regularity off Vancouver Island, British Columbia, from May through September. There is a peak in abundance there in August.

Can Be Confused With

There is some possibility that a Baird's beaked whale might be mistaken for a minke whale (p. 80) at sea. However, minkes have a much different head shape, an erect, back-curved dorsal fin placed farther forward on the back (and therefore appearing almost simultaneously with the blow), and white flipper bands. Minke whales are frequently found near shore and over the continental borderland, while Baird's beaked whales are found almost exclusively near or seaward of the continental slope. Also, minkes tend to occur singly or in pairs; Baird's beaked whales, in larger groups.

When a group of Baird's beaked whales is encountered at the surface, recuperating from a deep dive, they can be mistaken for sperm whales (p. 51). Their dorsal fin may remain below the surface as they raft during a series of blows. The oblique angle of the sperm whale's blow and its "boxcarlike" head should in most cases prevent confusion, however.

Very young Baird's beaked whales might be small enough to be confused with other species of beaked whales, but they are usually accompanied by adults large enough to make them distinguishable by size alone from other North Pacific beaked whales.

An important consideration is that a form of bottlenose whale, perhaps *Hyperoodon planifrons* (p. 92), may be found in the eastern tropical Pacific. Although the ranges of these two genera probably do not overlap, bottlenose whales could easily be mistaken for Baird's beaked whale at sea if they were found in the same area. The dorsal fin in *Hyperoodon* is proportionately larger, more erect, and pointed at the peak; its forehead is more bulging or bluff than in *Berardius*. Some individuals of *Hyperoodon* have pale heads.

When clearly viewed from the air, Baird's beaked whales are distinctive and easy to identify. The long beak is clearly demarcated from the broad head and body and is itself tipped with white at the locations where the teeth protrude. Though small relative to body size, their teeth are surprisingly evident in dorsal view, perhaps largely because their stark whiteness so vividly contrasts with the animal's body and the surrounding water.

Identification of Dead Specimens

Dead Baird's beaked whales are most likely to be confused with other beaked whales. The best way to distinguish them from North Pacific specimens of species of *Mesoplodon* (p. 98) is by 1) their larger size (maximum length in *Mesoplodon* is less than 7 m); 2) their bulging forehead; 3) their long, cylindrical beak; and 4) the presence of two large teeth at the tip of the lower jaw and a smaller pair (erupted only in older animals) a few centimeters behind the anterior pair. The front pair of teeth can be seen while the mouth is closed. In all five species of *Mesoplodon* in the North Pacific there is only one pair of teeth, which remain unerupted in females; these are situated well behind the tip of the lower jaw in four of the species. Only in Hector's beaked whale (p. 110) is the single pair of teeth found near the tip of the lower jaw.

Cuvier's beaked whale (p. 94) could be confused with Baird's beaked whale, for it has a single pair of teeth located at the tip of the lower jaw. Cuvier's beaked whales are less than 7 m long, however, and generally have a much less pronounced forehead, and much shorter, less well-defined beak than that of Baird's beaked whales. This is particularly true of the older, larger animals that are least easy to distinguish on the basis of body size alone. Cuvier's beaked whales lack the second, posterior pair of teeth possessed by Baird's beaked whales, and their teeth are more nearly conical.

(SOUTHERN ?) BOTTLENOSE WHALE (T)

Hyperoodon sp.

Other Common Names

Ballena nariz de botella, gran calderon (Latin America, see footnote 10); minami tokkuri kujira (Japanese); butylkonos (Russian).

Description

The specific identity of this whale is unkown. No specimens have been measured, but estimated lengths of animals observed at sea are 7–9 m. This is certainly within the size range of the two known species in the genus, the southern bottlenose whale, *H. planifrons*, and the northern bottlenose whale, *H. ampullatus*, the latter confined to the North Atlantic. In both species, males are considerably larger than females, and newborn are about 3 m long at birth.

All that is known about the appearance and behavior of this whale in the eastern Pacific comes from several sightings made by reliable observers in recent years. We are indebted particularly to K. C. Balcomb, who, in his unpublished manuscript, described an encounter with about 25 bottlenose whales in August 1966.

The forehead is extremely bulbous, sloping steeply in adults to a long beak. Although the tip of the lower jaw reaches slightly anterior to that of the upper jaw, this feature is much less pronounced in the bottlenose than in Baird's beaked whale (p. 88). No apical mandibular teeth were observed, so the teeth presumably are small and inconspicuous or concealed within the closed mouth as they are in *H. ampullatus* and *H. planifrons*.

The dorsal fin is strongly falcate and situated behind the middle of the back. The flukes and flippers were not seen, but judging by other beaked whales the flukes are probably unnotched and the flippers relatively small.

Figure 117.—If this is all that were seen of a bottlenose whale, its identification would be uncertain. The falcate dorsal fin, set well back on the body, suggests any species of *Mesoplodon*, and the minke whale and Cuvier's beaked whale could not be ruled out. Fortunately, in recorded encounters to date, tropical bottlenose whales have usually appeared in fairly large groups, and at least a few individuals have shown enough of the head to eliminate confusion with other species. (Photo from near the equator by K. C. Balcomb.)

Balcomb described the body color as flaxen and the forehead as acorn to umber brown on the back, shading to flaxen on the thorax. A darkly pigmented neckline demarcates the forehead pigmentation from that on the back. Some large individuals exhibit puncture scars and scratch marks on the skin.

Natural History Notes

Nothing is known about the biology of these tropical bottlenose whales. Assuming that they are similar to their antitropical congeners, however, one can guess that they are slow to mature and long-lived. They are probably deep and prolonged divers that eat squid and pelagic fish. Elsewhere, bottlenose whales are known to approach ships and to remain near them for long periods. The group observed by Balcomb consisted of approximately 25 individuals and was in company with a herd of about 50 pilot whales. Some of the bottlenoses raised their heads completely clear of the water upon surfacing while being chased, a behavior reminiscent of several other beaked whale species. It appeared as though various age classes and both sexes were represented in this pod of whales.

Distribution

The whales in question have been observed only near the equator in the central Pacific. Since there is no known population of bottlenose whales in the North Pacific, and since the known northern extreme of the southern bottlenose whale's distribution in the Pacific is at about lat. 33°S, there is reason to suspect that the equatorial population is discrete. Balcomb's sighting at lat. 0°, long. 164°46′W was on 11 August, which suggests that these animals do not migrate poleward in the boreal summer. Another sighting occurred on 25 February at lat. 02°18′N, long. 118°36′W. An observation of what might have been this species was reported recently for Hawaiian waters.

Can Be Confused With

If these whales are tropical in distribution, as seems likely, then they are most likely to be confused with minke whales (p. 80) (only at a distance because of their dorsal fin shape and positioning), and perhaps several other beaked whales (e.g., *Mesoplodon ginkgodens*, *M. densirostris*, *M. hectori*, and *M. carlhubbsi*). Adult bottlenose whales are considerably larger than adults of other tropical beaked whales, and a reasonably closeup view of the head contour should obviate confusion between *Hyperoodon* and all forms of *Mesoplodon*. Bottlenose whales have a much more bulbous, steeper forehead, and a more sharply demarcated beak.

Cuvier's beaked whale (p. 94) is perhaps the most problematical lookalike. Only with a good look at the forehead and beak (less steep and less long and distinct, respectively) can the possibility of Cuvier's beaked whale be eliminated.

Identification of Dead Specimens

Based on what is known about the two known species of *Hyperoodon*, dead specimens should be recognizable on the basis of head and beak shape. The single pair of teeth, however, which erupt only in adult males, is positioned at the tip of the lower jaw, so there is a good possibility of confusion with Cuvier's beaked whale and Baird's beaked whale. Examination of the prepared skulls may be necessary for positive identification. Certainly an examined specimen will be necessary before the taxonomic affinities of these tropical bottlenose whales can be determined conclusively.

Figure 118.—This photo of bottlenose whales is more helpful than the previous one. Note the rounded, bulbous head of two of the animals, set off from the rest of the body by a depression near the blowhole and an abrupt lightening of pigmentation. The faint, bushy spout from one individual shows why these and other beaked whales are difficult to detect. In the right of the photo, the short but very distinct beaks of two animals are raised above the surface, showing how bluff the forehead (melon) is in these whales. (Photo from near the equator, 11 August 1966, by K. C. Balcomb.)

CUVIER'S BEAKED WHALE (T)

Ziphius cavirostris **G. Cuvier, 1823**

Figure 119.—An approximately 6 m Cuvier's beaked whale stranded at La Jolla, Calif., on 12 June 1959. (Photo from the Carl L. Hubbs collection, courtesy L. Hubbs.)

Other Common Names

Goosebeak(ed) whale, ziphius; zifios or ballena de Cuvier (Latin America); akabō kujira (Japanese); klyuvoryl (Russian).

Description

Cuvier's beaked whales are not known to grow longer than about 7 m. They become sexually mature at about 5.4 m. Length at birth is 2-3 m.

The head of this robust whale is small relative to body length, with a beak shorter than that of any other beaked whale. The forehead, which can be bulbous or slightly concave, slopes steeply to the abbreviated, poorly demarcated beak, which becomes less distinct with age. The mouthline is upturned near the gape. In profile, head and mouth combine to produce an appearance likened to a goosebeak. There is an indentation on the back behind the blowhole, analogous to a neck crease or nape. It is most apparent in older males.

The single pair of conical teeth are at the tip of the mandibles. They erupt, and can be seen outside the closed mouth, only in adult males. The blowhole is located well forward on the head, and it emits a blow with a slight forward and leftward projection. The blowhole of this and other beaked whales is wide relative to body size, and the blow emanating from it forms a broad short plume, low and inconspicuous compared to those of other similar-sized whales. Though the first blow after a long dive may be more distinct, it is rarely visible for more than a few hundred meters, even under good wind conditions.

On the throat are two long, anteriorly convergent creases like those found in other beaked whales.

The dorsal fin can vary in shape from relatively tall (to at least ⅓ m) and smoothly falcate to low and triangular. It is located well behind the middle of the back. The flukes are normally not divided by a distinct notch; their trailing edge is somewhat concave.

In the eastern North Pacific, at least, coloration appears to be both age and sex related. Calves and juveniles are a tan or light brown color, even reddish in bright sunlight. With age the body becomes marred with scratches and white or cream-colored oval blotches, especially on the abdomen. First the head and neck, then the remainder of the body continue to lighten with age. Older females have lighter heads; older males may appear all white, particularly when seen from above. The area of demarcation between the light head and the darker body is often not well defined and consists of several brushlike intrusions of light into the dark field as a "chin strap" and eye markings. The extent and configuration of the whiteness is extremely variable. The skin darkens immediately after death, so stranded specimens are likely to appear basically gray or black.

Figure 120.—Cuvier's beaked whales near Clipperton Island (top) and the Galapagos, Ecuador (bottom). The head in this species tends to lighten with age and becomes white in large animals, particularly males. The blow, visible in the lower photo, is usually low, inconspicuous, and oriented slightly forward and to the left. (Photos by K. Sexton, courtesy of NMFS [top]; G. Wellington [bottom].)

Figure 121.—Cuvier's beaked whales are rarely seen and recognized at sea. Although any of these photos alone would be inadequate for showing what they look like, the three together give some idea. The body of smaller animals has a brownish cast; there is a noticeable lightening to the anterior part of the back and head as individuals age, particularly males (top). (Photos from Galapagos Islands, by G. Wellington.)

Natural History Notes

Very few at-sea observations of this species have been described, so very little is known about its habits or behavior. Old males apparently are sometimes found alone, but tight groups of 3–10 individuals, including at least one adult male, are usually reported.

These are pelagic creatures whose seasonal movements are not well known. Strandings in winter at relatively high latitudes suggest that a regular north-south pattern of migration may not hold for this species.

Cuvier's beaked whales prey mostly on squid and deepwater fishes and are probably deep divers. When beginning a long dive, the tail flukes are often lifted high above the surface, indicating an almost vertical descent. Similarly, surfacing animals often will be seen deep, heading straight upward toward the surface. In a few protracted observations, groups which were thought to consist of only a few animals expanded from five to eight as other animals, surfacing as described above, joined animals already resting at the surface.

As vigorous swimmers, these whales frequently expose the entire head and chin as they run, rolling high and arching steeply before long dives. Occasionally they will appear unexpectedly near a vessel and seem startled by its presence. After a series of respirations between shallow submergences, the entire pod will sound and not be observed again.

Distribution

Nearly all that we know about the distribution of Cuvier's beaked whale in the eastern North Pacific comes from strandings, of which more than 40 have been documented for the west

Figure 122.—A beaked whale, probably a Cuvier's beaked whale, jumping near a research vessel off northwestern Baja California. The size and position of the dorsal fin are characteristic, as are the head shape and short flippers. Such a high-profile view of this species is rare, since it is wary of boats and may dive for 30 minutes or more. (Photo by S. Leatherwood.)

Figure 123.—An adult male Cuvier's beaked whale stranded in northern California. It has the usual white head and throat blaze and the oval splotches and linear scars on the body that are typical of older individuals. The two teeth, visible at the tip of the lower jaw, erupt only in adult males and may be exposed outside the closed mouth. (Photo by W. J. Houck.)

coast of North America, and from a few dozen reliable sighting reports. Judging by these, the species is continuously distributed from the southern Bering Sea south to the equator, and it may be the most abundant beaked whale in the region.

The northernmost records are from the western Aleutian Islands, and these include both winter and summer occurrences. Strandings have taken place in winter at the Queen Charlotte Islands of British Columbia and in winter and spring on Vancouver Island.

Strandings on the U.S. west coast show no convincing trends, either in terms of their seasonality or the age and sex of individuals involved. There are records for both the Pacific coast of Baja California and inside the Gulf of California. Observers on tuna boats and aboard aircraft have seen Cuvier's beaked whales in the pelagic eastern tropical Pacific, and sightings near the Galapagos demonstrate that their range extends all the way to the equator. Most records are from pelagic waters, and sightings are rare in continental shelf regions of California and Baja California even where survey effort has been extensive. The species is present, but apparently rare, in Hawaiian waters.

Figure 124.—The head (top), throat and lower jaw (bottom) of a female Cuvier's beaked whale stranded in Maryland. Note the upcurved mouthline, the complete absence of teeth, and the coloration. (Photos by J. G. Mead.)

Can Be Confused With

Cuvier's beaked whale grows larger than all other beaked whales in the eastern North Pacific with the exception of Baird's beaked whale (p. 88) [and perhaps the bottlenose whale (p. 92)]. Smaller Cuvier's beaked whales might be confused with any of the whales of the genus *Mesoplodon*; but older individuals are strikingly lighter, at least on the head, grading toward all white in appearance. In general, Cuvier's beaked whales tend to be more active and demonstrative than any species of *Mesoplodon*. There are only two other cetaceans in the eastern North Pacific which are so white—the smaller Risso's dolphin (p. 129) which rarely exceeds 4 m in length and the arctic white whale (p. 134) that rarely exceeds 5 m. One record of a "beluga" from temperate waters off central California was almost certainly of a misidentified Cuvier's beaked whale. From the air, the size, body shape, and coloration of Cuvier's beaked whale permit positive identification.

Identification of Dead Specimens

Of the beaked whales known to occur in the eastern North Pacific, only the largest three (Baird's beaked, p. 88, bottlenose, p. 92, and Cuvier's beaked, p. 94, whales) have teeth at the tip of the lower jaw. The first two have long cylindrical beaks while that of Cuvier's beaked whale is far less distinct. Further, Baird's beaked whale has a second pair of teeth behind the first which may or may not be exposed.

Hector's beaked whale has a pair of mandibular teeth near but slightly behind the tip of the jaw. As in other forms of *Mesoplodon*, the teeth of Hector's beaked whale are flattened rather than conical; when examined closely, they should prevent confusion with Cuvier's beaked whale.

When they are small and superficially toothless, or in an advanced state of decomposition, Cuvier's beaked whales can be difficult to distinguish from other beaked whales. Museum preparation and examination of the skull and teeth may be required. Fresh specimens, particularly larger adult males, may be at least tentatively identified by the features illustrated in the figures.

Figure 125.—A closeup of the flukes of a Cuvier's beaked whale stranded in La Jolla, Calif. Like other beaked whales, this species does not have a distinct median notch on the rear edge of the flukes. (Photo by W. F. Perrin, courtesy of NMFS.)

BEAKED WHALES OF THE GENUS *MESOPLODON* (T)

Mesoplodon spp.

Other Common Names

Mesoplodonts; remnezyby (Russian).

Description

In addition to the Baird's beaked whale (p. 88), the (southern ?) bottlenose whale (p. 92), and Cuvier's beaked whale (p. 94), there are five currently recognized beaked whales of the genus *Mesoplodon* which have been seen in the area covered by this guide. The five whales of this genus about which we know enough to include accounts in this guide are very rarely seen at sea, and most of what we have written comes from descriptions of beached dead specimens. Therefore, statements concerning range should be interpreted with caution, since they are based on little more than inferences from locations of strandings. Information on appearance and habits in the wild is equally suspect, derived as it is from descriptions of a handful of brief encounters.

The infrequency with which these beaked whales are met at sea may reflect their rarity, or it may be simply an artifact of their behavioral characteristics, such as 1) a low inconspicuous blow, 2) avoidance of ships and/or 3) distribution in small groups in offshore areas well outside the normal boating lanes. Experienced observers working in the temperate eastern North Pacific have reported fewer than a dozen confirmed encounters with these animals in over 25 years of research. Observers involved in an extensive seasonal survey program in vast stretches of the eastern tropical Pacific have added about 30 more sightings in about 10 years of research. Though subtle differences in range, habitat preferences, behavior, color patterns, and dorsal fin shape and position may, when better understood, be helpful in narrowing the choices among living animals seen at sea, these whales will probably continue to be extremely difficult to distinguish from one another during the unexpected and always too brief sightings that are typical.

Behaviorally, members of the *Mesoplodon* group are lethargic and sluggish at the surface compared to most cetaceans. If they breach, lobtail, or spyhop, they must do it very infrequently, since no one who has seen them in the wild has noted anything more spectacular than their bobbing to the surface and rolling out of sight.

Although some attempt has been made in the species accounts to describe their coloration, it is probably best not to use color as a key to their identification (except, perhaps, in the case of Hubbs' beaked whale). Variability in lighting conditions,

Figure 126.—Four views of a pair of unidentified beaked whales of the genus *Mesoplodon*, possibly Hector's beaked whales, seen off Catalina Island, Calif. Note the dolphinlike appearance of the beak and melon in profile (a, b) and the small head, the robust body and the barely visible blow (b). The body was mottled brownish gray (c) with numerous long narrow scars (d). (Photos by D. Ljungblad, courtesy of NOSC.)

observer perception, and probably individual markings dictates caution. Robert Pitman (in letter), an observer who has had several encounters with them in the eastern North Pacific, shared the following description with us: "The *Mesoplodon* species are medium brown, but sometimes olive brown or even gray. They sometimes have the large white spots that *Ziphius* often shows, and sometimes scarring is evident but never to the extent of an extremely scarred *Ziphius*. Any white areas seen dorsally are limited to the tip of the rostrum, around the gape, and on or above the melon."

The problem of as-yet-unidentified species adds to the group's inscrutability. Pitman, for instance, related the following: "There is that *Mesoplodon* in the waters off Acapulco (Mexico) that has the big white chevron extending from the melon posterioventrally on each side. The rest of the animal is dark (almost black) so that this pattern is strikingly contrasty. When in schools this pattern occurs only in the larger (male?) animals, while the rest appear to be bronzy-brown."

HUBBS' BEAKED WHALE (T)

***Mesoplodon carlhubbsi* Moore, 1963**

Other Common Names

Ballena de Hubbs (Latin America); Hubbs' oogiha kujira (Japanese); remnezub Hubbsa (Russian).

Description

Although virtually all that is known about the physical appearance of this whale comes from observations of less than a score of stranded individuals, Hubbs' beaked whale is one of the best known forms in its genus. The description herein (as well as those for other *Mesoplodon* species) is largely based on a paper by J. G. Mead, W. A. Walker, and W. J. Houck (in prep.).

Maximum size is about 5.3 m and 1,500 kg. There is no known difference in maximum size between males and females. A rough estimate of size at birth is 2.5 m.

The body is similar to those in other species of *Mesoplodon*, best described as spindle-shaped, with a small head and narrow tail stock. The forehead slopes onto a prominent beak, and there is no crease separating the two. Adult males have a very distinctive elevated prominence on top of the head just anterior to the large, crescentic blowhole; this raised area, which is white, can be likened to a cap or beanie. The mouthline of adult males is interrupted on each side at about midlength by a raised area of the lower jaw, out of which a substantial, laterally compressed tooth protrudes through the gum. The upper portion of the tooth is exposed to a variable degree. It is visible outside the closed mouth and therefore is properly referred to as a tusk. In females and juveniles the teeth are buried in the gum. In females and young males the mouthline forms a noticeable sinusoidal (S-shaped) curve. A pair of long, anteriorly convergent creases is present on the throat.

The dorsal fin, as in other species of *Mesoplodon*, is situated well behind the midpoint of the back. It is falcate and reaches a height of 22–23 cm in adults. The flippers are proportionately small, and they fit into "flipper pockets," slight depressions in the body wall immediately behind the point of their insertion. The flukes are characteristically unnotched.

Hubbs' beaked whale is one of the few of its kind that can be recognized at sea (males only). The key to its identification in the water is the pigmentation pattern on the head. In addition to the white "cap" on the adult male's head, the anterior half of the beak is white. Although the contrast is apparently less vivid on females and juveniles, they too have a relatively pale rostrum and front half of the lower jaw. Elsewhere on the body, males are uniformly dark gray to black, while females have markedly lighter sides and bellies. Adult males are heavily scarred, especially on the flanks. Linear scars up to 2 m long, often in parallel pairs, are believed to be the result of intraspecific fighting, while smaller oval and punctate scars are variously attributed to bites by cookie-cutter sharks or lampreys, attachment by barnacles or parasitic copepods, and punctures by the teeth of other males. Scarring on females and young animals is less extensive.

Natural History Notes

Very little is known about the biology or habits of Hubbs' beaked whale. It is apparently not very gregarious, traveling in groups of perhaps 2–10. Calving is believed to take place in early to midsummer, but this hypothesis is based on very sparse data. Like most other beaked whales, this animal is probably pelagic, shy, deepdiving, and relatively inconspicuous at the surface. As deep divers, these beaked whales apparently dine primarily on mesopelagic fishes and squid.

Distribution

The known distribution of Hubbs' beaked whale is based exclusively on stranding records, which do not necessarily afford a reliable index of either range or abundance. The northernmost stranding occurred on the coast of British Columbia just opposite the northern tip of Vancouver Island at about lat. 51°N. This is believed to be close to the actual northern boundary of the species' range. The southernmost record in the eastern North Pacific is from San Diego, Calif., at about lat. 32°N. It is possible that the whale occurs well south of here and that the absence of records is due more to a lack of observer effort than to a lack of animals, since there are no published *Mesoplodon* stranding records at all from the Mexican or Central American coast between Vizcaino Bay and the equator. However, it has been suggested that *M. carlhubbsi* lives in association with the confluence of the Subarctic and California Current systems, rarely if ever ranging north of the former's

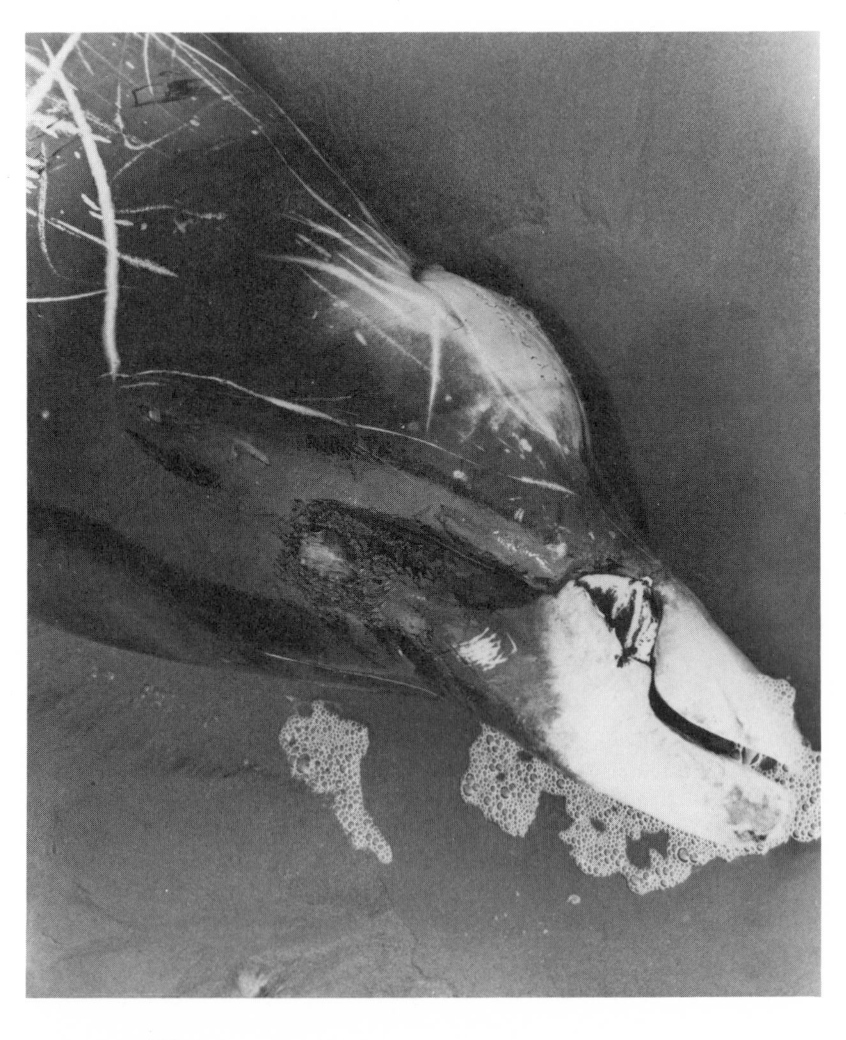

Figure 127.—A dead male Hubbs' beaked whale from central California. Note the extensive linear scarring over much of the body, apparently caused by teeth of other males. The characteristic white convexity immediately in front of the broad, semicircular blowhole, and the white beak with a massive flattened tusk, are also evident. Note that the denticle at the summit of the tusk is situated slightly behind the front edge of the tooth. (Photos by W. Williams, courtesy of R. T. Orr.)

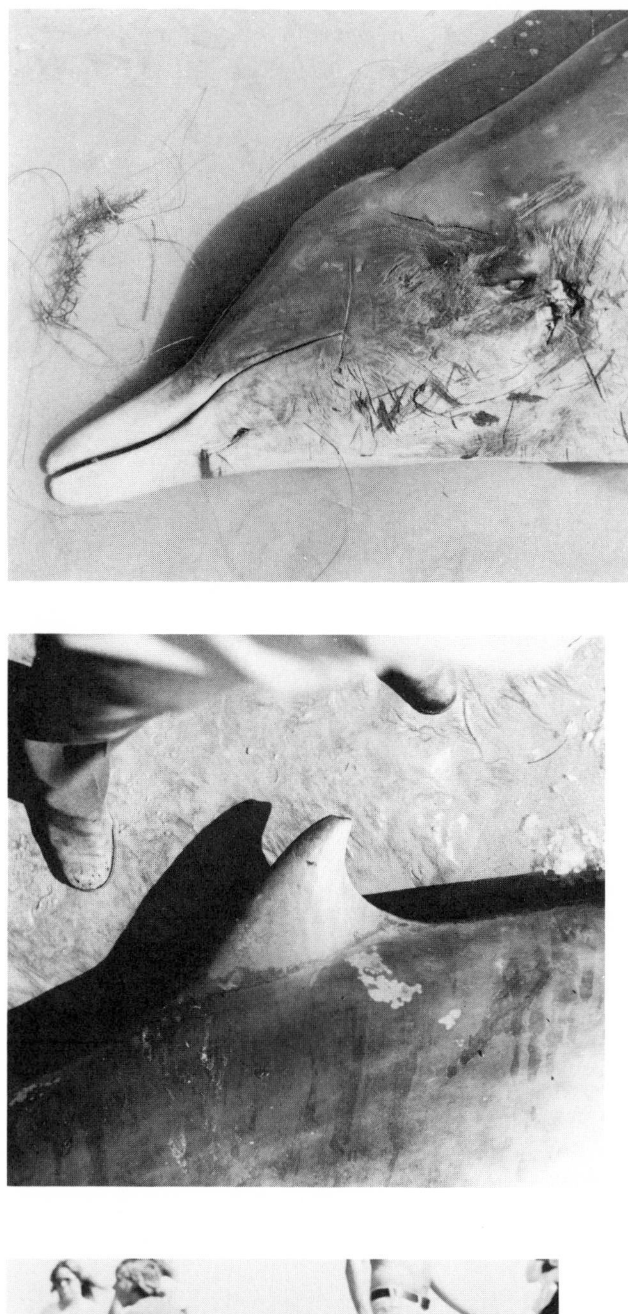

influence or south of the latter's. If this is true, then the pattern of reported strandings may be an accurate representation of the species' distribution.

Can Be Confused With

Four other beaked whales of the genus *Mesoplodon* overlap in range with Hubbs' beaked whale: Stejneger's beaked whale (p. 102), Blainville's beaked whale (p. 103), the ginkgo-toothed beaked whale (p. 107), and Hector's beaked whale (p. 110). Females and young individuals are very difficult or impossible to identify to the species level at sea. Males on the other hand should be relatively easy to distinguish when examined at close range. The raised white "cap" and partly white beak are unique to *M. carlhubbsi*, at least when compared to other North Pacific *Mesoplodon* species.

The two teeth in four species of *Mesoplodon* so far described in the North Pacific rest well behind the tip of the lower jaw, so their positioning in males will not be a particularly useful key to identification at sea. Only in Hector's beaked whale are the teeth near the tip of the lower jaw.

Cuvier's beaked whale (p. 94) often has a good deal of white on the head, but its lack of a long beak and its rather steep forehead, which is sometimes slightly concave in front of the blowhole, should make it fairly easy to tell apart from Hubbs' beaked whale.

The dorsal fin of Hubbs' beaked whale is similar in shape and positioning to the minke whale's (p. 80), so at a distance these two whales might be confused. At closer range, however, they are easy to tell apart. Minkes have a triangular rostrum with a sharp median ridge; their flippers each have a conspicuous white band on them; and their skin has little or none of the scarring characteristic of Hubbs' beaked whales.

Identification of Dead Specimens

In addition to the features mentioned above, with a specimen at hand, the attitude, size and shape of the teeth and their position in the jaw can be useful in separating Hubbs' beaked whale from its North Pacific congeners. The apex of the tooth in *M. carlhubbsi* is placed just behind the tooth's anterior edge. In *M. stejnegeri*, its closest lookalike, the apex is in line with the tooth's front edge. The less massive teeth of *M. ginkgodens* have centrally situated apices, as do the narrower but thicker teeth of *M. densirostris*, whose teeth tilt forward noticeably. The teeth of *M. hectori* are triangular in side view, with a somewhat convex anterior edge, and they are placed well ahead of the posterior boundary of the mandibular symphysis.

Museum preparation is often necessary to make a positive identification of females and juveniles, in which the teeth are concealed beneath the gumline.

Figure 128.—A female Hubbs' bleaked whale stranded in San Diego, Calif. In females, the countour of the mouthline is much less curved than in males, lacking the high prominences which in males house the teeth (top); the dorsal fin is small, located in the latter third of the body and slightly falcate (middle); the flukes are not notched (bottom). (Photos by J. G. Mead.)

STEJNEGER'S BEAKED WHALE (T)

Mesoplodon stejnegeri **True, 1885**

a

b

c

d

e

Other Common Names

Bering Sea beaked whale, sabertoothed whale; ballena de Stejneger (Latin America); oogiha kujira (Japanese); remnezub Stejnegera (Russian).

Description

Maximum size for males and females is probably close to 5.3 m. Newborn length is not known.

In body form Stejneger's beaked whale is little different from others of its genus. It has a long, well-defined beak, a falcate dorsal fin placed well behind midback, usually no median notch between the flukes, small flippers, and a pair of throat creases.

The two mandibular teeth in males erupt well outside the gum and appear, in dorsal view, to pinch or constrict the upper jaw. These teeth are rooted behind the mandibular symphysis; they tilt forward slightly and emerge from very prominent arches which begin well behind the tip of the beak on either side of the lower jaw. The front edges of the flattened teeth are often worn. The denticle on each is very near the anterior edge of the tooth. The arched contour of the lower lip is not nearly so striking in females and juveniles, and their teeth are unerupted.

Few of these whales have been seen and recognized alive, so the color pattern is not well known. Like several other poorly known beaked whales, this species has been described mostly from long-dead specimens which have darkened and lost definition in zones of coloration after death. However, some freshly stranded individuals were grayish brown on the back and lighter on the belly, with striking light brush marks extending up the sides behind the head, at the neck, and around the mouth. Adults generally have many oval white scars on the flanks and in the genital region, and males are covered with linear scars, apparently from fighting.

Figure 129.—Several useful views of a decomposed adult male Stejneger's beaked whale from Homer, Alaska. Note the slightly frayed but otherwise straight trailing edge of the flukes (a), which lack a median notch, and the dorsal fin, placed well behind the center of the back (b). The teeth, one on each side, erupt only in adult males (c). The two large tusklike teeth are oriented slightly forward and slant inward (d). Note that the denticle is on a line with the front edge of the tooth (e). (Photos by F. H. Fay, courtesy of J. G. Mead.)

Natural History Notes

Nothing is known about the natural history of this species.

Distribution

Virtually all that is known about the distribution of Stejneger's beaked whale comes from stranding records. These suggest that it is endemic to the subarctic and cold temperate North Pacific. It inhabits much of the southern Bering Sea, ranging south to the northern Sea of Japan in the west and to Monterey, Calif., in the east. Strandings are most common on the shores of the Aleutian Islands.

Can Be Confused With

The most common ziphiid besides Stejneger's beaked whale in much of its range is Cuvier's beaked whale (p. 94). Its abbreviated beak should distinguish it in the field from Stejneger's beaked whale. In stranded specimens, the long, contoured mouthline, with flattened mandibular teeth exposed far behind the tip of the beak, should also make Stejneger's beaked whale easy to distinguish from Cuvier's beaked whale. The only other *Mesoplodon* species regularly found inside the known range of Stejneger's beaked whale is Hubbs' beaked whale, which ranges as far north as British Columbia. Male Hubbs' beaked whales have a characteristic white "beanie" on the forehead in front of the blowhole. Such a prominence is lacking entirely in Stejneger's beaked whale. Females and juveniles are very difficult to identify prior to museum preparation and examination by a specialist.

BLAINVILLE'S BEAKED WHALE

Mesoplodon densirostris **(Blainville in Desmarest, 1817)**

Other Common Names

Dense-beaked whale, tropical beaked whale; ballena de Blainville (Latin America); kobuha kujira (Japanese); remnezub Blainvillya (Russian).

Description

Fully grown Blainville's beaked whales are 4.5–5.0 m long. Size at birth is unknown.

This spindle-shaped whale has a low, nonbulging forehead that gently slopes onto a long, prominent beak. The area in front of the blowhole is marked by a slight depression, which gives the rostrum a flattened appearance. The long mouthline has a distinctive shape, marked as it is by a prominent arch toward the corners, beginning well before the angle of the gape on each side. These rises, which bear the two laterally compressed teeth, one on each side, give a peculiar high, arching contour to the mouth, particularly in adult males.

The flippers are small (one-eleventh to one-tenth of body length) and originate in the lighter color of the undersides. The dorsal fin's shape varies from small and triangular to moderately falcate and pointed on the tip. It is situated behind the midpoint of the back. The width of the flukes is one-sixth to one-fifth the body length; sometimes there is a slight median convexity on the rear margin but almost never a notch.

Figure 130.—An adult female Blainville's beaked whale stranded at Cape Hatteras, N.C. The bottom photo of the same animal clearly shows the V-shaped throat creases and the flippers fitted snugly against the body. (Photos by J. G. Mead.)

Blainville's beaked whales are gray on the back, lightening toward the abdomen. Males in particular have grayish-white or pink blotches over much of the body, and animals of both sexes are usually scratched and scarred. Males appear to be more heavily scarred than females, and they often have large white or reddish patches on the head. The flippers are lighter than the back. The flukes are dark above and light below.

Natural History Notes

Like its congeners, Blainville's beaked whale probably lives in small bands of less than 10 individuals. It is shy and emits very indistinct blows, which make it difficult to spot and follow. Individuals observed at sea have appeared to be slow-swimming, and they dived for periods longer than 20 minutes. E. W. Shallenberger reported that as Blainville's beaked whales surface to breathe, "they roll gracefully but the rostrum leaves the water first and then slaps down awkwardly." Squid is a known food item. These whales have been known to strand singly, sometimes alive.

Distribution

Although in general more widely distributed than any other member of the genus, from currently available records Blainville's beaked whale appears to be relatively uncommon along the west coast of North America. It has been suggested that it is one of the most thoroughly pelagic beaked whales, since it has stranded as often or more often on oceanic islands than on continental coasts. If true, then a pelagic distribution rather than overall scarcity may account for the paucity of records.

The stranding of a female in mid-December in San Mateo County, northern California (lat. 37°15'N, long. 122°25'W) is the only published record for the North American west coast. Two specimens are known to have stranded on Midway Island in Hawaii's Leeward Chain; small numbers are occasionally sighted in late summer and fall off the Waianae coast of Oahu and in deep waters off Molokai; and animals probably of this species have been seen in February in the Kauai Channel and on Kaula Bank, Hawaii.

Can Be Confused With

Sightings that provide a close look at the head of an adult male may allow field identification. The contour of the mouth and the massive, forward tilting teeth that erupt from the arching prominences near the corners of the mouth, together with the flattened forehead, can aid in identification. There is little hope of recognizing females and young that are unaccompanied by an adult male, since they have no exposed teeth and have less prominent rises at the corners of the mouth.

Blainville's beaked whales are likely to be confused with other whales of the genus *Mesoplodon* (p. 98) and Cuvier's beaked whale (p. 94) throughout their range, and with the bottlenose whale (p. 92) near the equator. The latter should be distinguishable by its steep, more bulging forehead and straight mouthline; and Cuvier's beaked whale by its much more steeply sloping forehead, which appears slightly concave or scooped when viewed laterally, and its shorter beak. Also, in both the bottlenose whale and Cuvier's beaked whale the erupted teeth of adult males are at the tip of the lower jaw.

a

b

c

d

e

Figure 131.—A group of five or six beaked whales, probably Blainville's beaked whales, encountered at Pokai Bay, Oahu, Hawaii. The animals were very shy and had low indistinct blows, making them difficult to spot and follow (a). As they surfaced, they frequently bucked their heads and slapped their chins against the surface (b, upper animal; c). They did not raise their flukes when descending for a long dive. The light lower jaw and arching contour of the mouthline are evident (d,e). (Photos by E. Shallenberger.)

Figure 132.—In this male Blainville's beaked whale that stranded alive in Florida, the broad, symmetrical blowhole is well illustrated, as is the peculiar shape of the mouth. The depression in front of the blowhole and between the raised "cheeks" is helpful in field identification of this species. (Photo by W. A. Huck, courtesy of Marineland of Florida.)

Figure 133.—Four views of a female Blainville's beaked whale stranded in central California. This individual's most striking feature is the polka-dotted appearance of its skin. The oval white scars covering much of the animal's body are believed to be caused by the teeth of "cookie-cutter" sharks (see text) or some other kind of epizoic or parasitic fish. The extent of scarring on this female may be abnormal. (Photos by M. Webber.)

Identification of Dead Specimens

Blainville's beaked whale is identifiable on the basis of the prominences in the lower jaw, the massive, forward-tilting teeth (exposed only in adult males), and the flattened forehead. The two teeth, one of which rests at the summit of each prominence on the sides of the mouth, are concealed throughout life in females. Museum preparation may therefore be necessary to identify females and young males.

GINKGO-TOOTHED BEAKED WHALE (T)

***Mesoplodon ginkgodens* Nishiwaki and Kamiya, 1958**

Other Common Names

Japanese beaked whale; ichōha kujira (Japanese); ginkozubyy remnezub (Russian).

Description

Ginkgo-toothed beaked whales are known to reach at least 5 m in length and about 1,500 kg in weight. The species is too poorly known to say more about size range.

The spindle-shaped body resembles those of other species in the genus. The head is characterized by a smoothly sloping forehead and a prominent beak. There is no crease between beak and head. The mouthline curves abruptly upward about halfway back from the tip of the snout, then continues directly back toward the eye, forming a characteristic raised area in each lower jaw. A single tooth is situated on top and to the front of the raised area. The shape of its two flattened teeth, which erupt through the gumline only in adult males, gave the species its name, for they resemble the leaf of a ginkgo tree. The ginkgo tree is common in Japan, where the first specimens of *M. ginkgodens* were found and described.

The large, symmetrical, crescentic blowhole is situated at the middle of the top of the head, and the convergent pair of throat creases typical of beaked whales is present below.

The appendages are little different from those of other forms of *Mesoplodon*. The flippers are small (only one-ninth to one-tenth of body length). The dorsal fin in all specimens examined to date has been falcate or triangular and placed well behind the middle of the back. The one well-photographed specimen from the west coast of North America, described below, had an extremely hooked falcate fin. The flukes usually have no median notch.

Generally body color has been described as black, although no live specimens have been examined, so perhaps some of the darkness should be attributed to postmortem changes. In any case, the belly is said to be noticeably lighter than the rest of the body and is marked in most cases by many oval white scars that extend onto the sides. The head and lower jaw of one eastern Pacific female specimen was light brownish gray. The side of the head and the area toward the flippers were blotched. Females are said to have rather light-colored heads.

Natural History Notes

Nothing is known about the biology or behavior of this species.

Distribution

The only records of this whale's occurrence, mostly strandings, come from the warm temperate and tropical North Pacific and Indian Oceans. It appears to be more common in the western Pacific than anywhere else. The only published records are for the eastern North Pacific of a female that came ashore at Del Mar, a few kilometers north of San Diego, Calif., in June 1954, and a skull found on Malarrimo Beach near the mouth of Ojo de Liebre (Scammon's) Lagoon, Baja California, in December 1980.

Can Be Confused With

At sea, the ginkgo-toothed beaked whale is likely to be confused with any of its congeners. However, the flattened or depressed area ahead of the blowhole in *M. densirostris* (p. 103) and the white mound on the forehead of *M. carlhubbsi* (p. 99) males should allow them to be distinguished from ginkgo-toothed beaked whales of any age or sex. Also, female and young specimens of Hubbs' beaked whale apparently have whitish, or at least noticeably lightened, beaks. Male ginkgo-toothed beaked whales appear to be less heavily scarred than males of other North Pacific species of *Mesoplodon*, except perhaps *M. densirostris*.

Identification of Dead Specimens

Museum preparation may well be necessary to distinguish dead ginkgo-toothed beaked whales from their congeners, particularly when the specimens are females or juveniles. If an individual's teeth are erupted (i.e., if the animal is an adult male), it may be possible to distinguish it from *M. carlhubbsi* and *M. stejnegeri* in that the apex of its tooth is centrally located, whereas the apex is displaced anteriorly in the other two species. Also, in adult male ginkgo-toothed beaked whales apparently only the very tips of the teeth erupt, while much more of the tooth is exposed in males of the other four North Pacific species of *Mesoplodon*. The teeth in *M. densirostris* are much more massive than in *M. ginkgodens*. In *M. hectori* the triangular teeth occur well in front of the mandibular symphysis.

a
b

c

Figure 134 (opposite page and above).—A male ginkgo-toothed beaked whale on a Japanese beach. Note that the rather small dorsal fin is located well behind the center of the back (a). The teeth, which erupt only in adult males and have barely emerged in this individual, rest at the front upper edge of the raised area of the lower jaw (b). The lower jaw extends beyond the upper. Note the convergent pair of throat creases (c). The white blotching, particularly extensive in the anogenital region, is typical. (Photos by T. Kasuya.)

Figure 135 (below and next page).—A female ginkgo-toothed beaked whale stranded at Del Mar, Calif., in 1954. (Photos courtesy of J. G. Mead, U.S. National Museum.)

Figure 135.—*Continued.*

HECTOR'S BEAKED WHALE (T)

Mesoplodon hectori (Gray, 1871)

Other Common Names

Ballena de Hector (Latin America); remnezub Hectora (Russian).

Description

The occurrence of this species in the North Pacific became known to science as recently as 1980. We are indebted to James G. Mead for allowing us to read his description of Hector's beaked whale prior to its publication and for providing the photographs.

The dimensions of Hector's beaked whale are probably not appreciably different from those of its congeners. A 390 cm male and a 443 cm female stranded on southern Calfornia beaches were physically mature. A 210 cm calf stranded in the same vicinity as and within 2–3 weeks of the adult female.

Several living animals observed at sea and tentatively identified as Hector's beaked whales had relatively short beaks, ''by

Figure 136.—Side view of the adult male Hector's beaked whale that washed onto the beach at Carlsbad, Calif., on 9 September 1978. Note the small flipper and the typical *Mesoplodon* head shape. One of the throat creases is evident despite the poor condition of the carcass. (Photo by J. G. Mead.)

Figure 137.—Three views of the head of the adult male Hector's beaked whale. In side view (left) note that there is no rise in the contour of the mouthline where the tooth erupts and that the tooth is shaped like an equilateral triangle. In dorsal view (middle) the crescentic blowhole is apparent. The material attached to the right tooth, seen in both the dorsal (middle) and ventral (right) views, consists of three stalked barnacles, *Conchoderma auritum*. In the ventral view (right) the throat creases characteristic of all the beaked whales are seen to converge anteriorly. (Photos by J. G. Mead.)

Mesoplodon standards" (Mead in press). The two mandibular teeth, which erupt through the gum only in adult males, are situated near the tip of the jaw. Their exposed portion is, according to Mead, shaped like "an equilateral triangle, with the anterior edge slightly convex." In the 390 cm male mentioned above, the teeth were 23 mm from the tip of the jaw, and the height of the teeth beginning at the gumline was 33 mm.

Coloration, based on the two North American specimens that have been examined soon enough after death to make out any detail, is basically dark above and light below. The living animals mentioned above, tentatively identified as belonging to this species, were, according to Mead, "dark gray-brown above and pale gray on the chin and lower jaw." Adult males have white undersides of the flukes, and there can be a white area around the umbilicus. Mead reported that the adult male he examined had "dark lines radiating out from the tailstock" on the ventral surface of the flukes. Scarring is present on the flanks of adult males, including long linear tooth rakes and oval splotches.

Natural History Notes

The living animals mentioned above were sighted in pairs. In the two instances mentioned by Mead, one member of each pair approached the sighting vessel. Obvious differences in the extent of scarring suggested to Mead that at least one of these pairs consisted of a male and a female.

Figure 138.—This peculiar head-on view of the mouth of the adult male Hector's beaked whale is useful for demonstrating the orientation of the single pair of mandibular teeth. They are situated farther forward in the jaw in this species than they are in any other *Mesoplodon* known to inhabit the North Pacific. (Photo by J. G. Mead.)

Figure 139.—Although the dorsal fin may vary considerably in shape among individual Hector's beaked whales, that of the adult male pictured here is probably typical. (Photo by J. G. Mead.)

The few stomach contents examined to date indicate that Hector's beaked whales eat squid.

Distribution

Hector's beaked whale was known until recently only from specimens stranded in the Southern Hemisphere south of lat. 30°S. The localities of these strandings—New Zealand, Falkland Islands, Tasmania, South Africa, and Tierra del Fuego—suggest a circumpolar distribution for the species.

At present, Northern Hemisphere records exist only for the eastern North Pacific, north of lat. 30°N. There have been four strandings in southern California (during the months of May, September, and December), plus the two sightings (identification tentative)—one near Catalina Island at lat. 33°18′N, long. 117°50′W on 30 July; the other, 50–75 miles west of San Diego on 9 September.

Can Be Confused With

Due to the placement of the teeth near the front of the lower jaw, Hector's beaked whale might be confused with Cuvier's beaked whale (p. 94) as well as with other forms of *Mesoplodon*. The possibility of confusion with Cuvier's beaked whale may be especially good because of the relatively short beak of Hector's beaked whale. Adult Cuvier's beaked whales are noticeably larger (5.4–7 m) than Hector's beaked whales (4.5 m or less).

Mesoplodon hectori is the only member of its genus inhabiting the North Pacific in which the teeth are situated far forward in the lower jaw, well ahead of the mandibular symphysis. This characteristic, evident only in adult males whose teeth have erupted, may in some instances aid in identification at sea.

Identification of Dead Specimens

Female and young specimens should be brought to the attention of a specialist, as it will be very difficult for the layman to make a positive identification. If the erupted teeth of an adult male *Mesoplodon* are found to be near the tip of the jaw, then it is reasonable to suspect *M. hectori*. However, until more is known about how to distinguish the different species in this genus on the basis of external characters, identification of specimens of any age or either sex needs to be confirmed by a specialist.

KILLER WHALE (T)

Orcinus orca (Linnaeus, 1758)

Figure 140.—A killer whale at Sea World, San Diego, Calif. Note the distinctive coloration of the species: white on the throat, belly, and anus, and on both sides above the anus. Note also the distinctive white eye patch often visible on animals at sea. (Photo by R. Reeves.)

Other Common Names

Orca (including Latin America), blackfish, grampus (antiquated); shachi or sakamata (Japanese); mesungesak (Alaska Eskimo Yupik); kosatka (Russian).

Description

Males grow to 9.5 m and at least 8 t. Few are larger than about 8 m. Females are significantly smaller, rarely growing to more than 7 m and 4 t, and they are considerably less robust in form. Newborn are 2.1–2.4 m long and weigh about 180 kg.

The snout is conical, with a blunt, indistinct beak.

The most conspicuous external feature of this whale is the prominent dorsal fin situated in the middle of the back. Although the blow is often seen (and heard) as a single explosive puff of vapor, the dorsal fin can often be seen from as great a distance as the blow. In adult males it is extremely erect and can be as much as 1.8 m tall. It usually is close to being an isosceles triangle, with a height of two or more times the length of the base. Females and juveniles have a much more modest dorsal fin that is often moderately falcate and less than 1 m tall. Even in females and young animals, however, the dorsal fin is taller than in most similar-sized cetaceans.

The large flippers are also distinctive, shaped like broad, rounded paddles. When killer whales breach or spyhop, the flippers are noticeable. The flukes are concave on the rear margin and often pointed on the tips. They are separated by a deep median notch.

The killer whale's coloration is a striking combination of black-and-white, with sharp demarcation between light and dark zones. There is a large, oval white patch on the side of the head just above and behind the eye. The entire chin and throat are white; this white area continues posteriorly along the ventral midline, narrowing as it passes between the flippers. Behind the navel this white stripe branches into three prongs, one extending onto each flank and the other continuing along the ventral midline past the anus. Most animals have a light gray saddle marking just behind the dorsal fin. The size, shape, and intensity of the white zones and the saddle vary among regions. In calves, the white areas are often tan to lemon yellow. The undersides of the flukes are usually white. All-black and all-white individuals have been seen.

Figure 141.—The differences between dorsal fins of adult male killer whales and those of females and immatures are clearly illustrated in these photos from off San Juan Island, Wash. Adult males have an erect dorsal fin that may be more than 1.8 m tall, while the fins of females and immature males are less than 0.9 m tall, falcate, and pointed at the tip. Note the pronounced saddle and the white eye patch. (Photos by K. C. Balcomb [top]; R. Reeves [bottom].)

Natural History Notes

Killer whales travel in pods of a few to 25 or 30 individuals; occasionally several such groups coalesce to form herds of more than 100. Pods of killer whales appear to have integrity over time. They frequently include members of both sexes and members of different age classes. A system for visually recognizing known individuals in repeated encounters has recently been developed, and this technique promises to provide greater insight on what appear to be complex, stable associations. Killer whale populations from five major geographic areas of the world can be readily distinguished on the basis of acoustic characteristics. Dialect differences in sounds produced by killer whales within a given region, suggested by preliminary studies in Puget Sound and off British Columbia, may eventually be used to recognize pods from recordings alone.

The reproductive biology of this species is not well understood. Gestation lasts for 13–16 months, and most calves are born in autumn. The period of calf dependency is prolonged, and the interbirth interval is probably well in excess of 2 years. Calves may remain with their mothers for as much as 10 years.

Figure 142.—Killer whales have 10–12 prominent teeth, curved slightly backward and inward, on each side of each jaw. (Photo from Point Mugu, Calif., by S. Leatherwood.)

In many areas killer whales are present year-round, and local resident pods are recognized. Most of their movements seem to be related to food availability.

Killer whales are extremely fast swimmers, capable of reaching speeds of 25 knots or more. They are also active at the surface, frequently breaching and spyhopping.

Cooperative group hunting by killer whales is perhaps their most spectacular characteristic. In addition to fish of many species and birds, they are known to prey on many kinds of marine mammals in the eastern North Pacific, from harbor porpoises to blue whales. It is probably fair to say that at one time or another killer whales prey on every species of pinniped and

Figure 143.—Killer whales often come very close to shore. In these photos they are shown in two characteristic attitudes—breaching (above, top left) and spyhopping (bottom left). (Photos from Puget Sound by K. C. Balcomb [above, bottom left]; from San Benitos Islands by W. F. Samaras [top left].)

baleen whale in the region.

The killer whale's reputation has been and continues to be a source of controversy. Documented attacks on boats are rare and have usually been provoked (by harpooning or attempts to capture). In some areas fishermen resent the competition they get from killer whales for commercially important fish (e.g., salmon) or marine mammals (e.g., northern fur seals). Their maintenance and training in captivity have given killer whales a sizable following of people who would protect them from any kind of capture. At the same time, their very popularity makes the whales attractive to business interests, whose recent attempts

Figure 144.—A killer whale (top) patrolling very near shore off Punta Norte, Chubut, Argentina, where a pod of southern sea lions huddles, apparently safely out of reach. The sea lion in the bottom photo was not so lucky, being attacked and presumably eaten by a killer whale which nearly beached itself to make the kill. In the eastern North Pacific, killer whales are frequently found near pinniped rookeries. (Photos by B. G. Wursig [top]; courtesy of Hubbs-Sea World Research Institute [bottom left].)

Figure 145.—This dramatic photo leaves little doubt of the killer whale's awesome predatory potential. The young blue whale was corralled for hours and held at the surface by a pack of killer whales, while individual killer whales charged in to tear away chunks of flesh. The incident ended when the killer whales abandoned the badly injured blue whale. (Photos from off Cabo San Lucas, Baja California, Mexico, courtesy of Sea World, Inc.)

to capture killer whales in the inside waters of Washington and British Columbia for display purposes have been frustrated by the whales' passionate defenders.

Whatever one's feelings about killer whales, their power and unpredictability command respect and those who dive with them or attempt close approach in small, unpowered craft are taking an unknown risk.

Distribution

Killer whales are very widely distributed in the eastern North Pacific, from the Chukchi Sea south to the equator. North of Bering Strait they are not common, and most of them probably move south through the Strait ahead of newly forming winter ice, to return only after breakup the following summer. Killer whales range year-round throughout much of the Bering Sea. They are said to be common at the Pribilof Islands during spring and fall, when pinniped prey is easily available, and they are abundant near much of the Aleutian Chain. The Pacific coast of the Alaska Peninsula, Prince William Sound in the Gulf of Alaska, and the Strait of Georgia in British Columbia are areas where killer whales are common. Most of the enclosed waters around Vancouver Island and in and adjacent to Puget Sound are prime killer whale habitat. As two Canadian scientists (Pike and MacAskie 1969) wrote a decade ago: "The killer whale is abundant in coastal waters of British Columbia. By reason of its temerity in frequenting productive sports and commercial salmon fishing areas, it is better known to local residents than is any other species of whale." The same could be said about Washington waters. In both areas they are present year-round, often timing local movements to coincide with major runs of salmon. They are said to be most common in Puget Sound during late summer and in November.

Along the coast of California killer whales are often sighted well out to sea, but they frequently move into the kelp beds and into bays and inlets as well. Along the coast of Baja California, particularly near island seal rookeries, they are abundant, and they are known to enter the Gulf of California. Recent observations from tuna boats in the eastern tropical Pacific indicate that killer whales can be encountered virtually anywhere between Cabo San Lucas and the Galapagos and west to long. 140°W. Records are rare from the vicinity of Hawaii.

Although there may be a seasonal shift to the south in winter, the year-round presence of some killer whales makes it worth looking for them at all seasons throughout their entire range, from the ice edge to the equator.

Can Be Confused With

Because of its very distinctive dorsal fin, body shape, and coloration, the killer whale is not likely to be confused with any other whale when it is examined at close range or when an adult male is present in the group. Pods of females and juveniles, however, can be confused with false killer whales (p. 118) or with Risso's dolphins (p. 129). The killer whale can be distinguished from the false killer whale by the following differences.

Killer Whale	False Killer Whale
Body Shape	
Chunky.	Slender.
Body Color	
Black with white on belly, flank, and head.	All black, with some gray on belly; head perhaps slightly lighter on top.

Figure 146.—Killer whales pursuing (top), herding (bottom left), and later closing in to eat (bottom right) a harbor porpoise off San Juan Island, Wash. The whales apparently played with the porpoise for over 30 minutes, lifting it out of the water and forcing it back and forth among members of the group before finally eating it. Although it is often argued that killer whales prefer fish, virtually no species of marine mammal escapes predation. (Photos by C. A. Goebel.)

Dorsal Fin	
Very tall and erect in adult males; tall and moderately falcate in females and immatures.	Shorter, slender, falcate.
Head Shape	
Broad and conical with a short, blunt beak.	Tapered and slender.
Flipper Shape	
Paddle-shaped; nearly as wide as long.	Moderately long, with characteristic hump near middle of forward edge.
Length	
To at least 9 m.	To at least 5.5 m.

Adult Risso's dolphins have a tall dorsal fin (to 38 cm) which might be suggestive of female and young killer whales. Risso's dolphins, however, have much lighter coloration than do killer whales, from slate gray to nearly white, and larger individuals are covered with scratches and oval scars. On close examination they can be further distinguished from killer whales by a crease on the front of the head that divides the melon into two distinct sections. Finally, Risso's dolphins are much smaller than killer whales, growing to only about 4 m long. Historically, the killer whale has often been called "grampus," and this has generated even more confusion with Risso's dolphin, whose scientific name is *Grampus griseus* and which is itself frequently called "grampus."

The much smaller Dall's porpoise is often identified by untrained observers as a "baby killer whale." Its black and white pigmentation pattern, though arranged differently, is reminiscent of the killer whale's. In addition to its small size (maximum length 2.2 m), Dall's porpoise has a small triangular dorsal fin, and its swimming movements are often quick and jerky.

When viewed from the air, the stark contrasts of white (eye patch, flank patch) and gray (saddle) on black, the body size and the tall distinctive dorsal fin make killer whales unmistakable.

Identification of Dead Specimens

Dead killer whales should be easy to identify by the robust body, the distinctive color markings, and in larger animals the tall dorsal fin. Killer whales have 10–12 large, prominent teeth on each side of the upper and lower jaws.

FALSE KILLER WHALE (T)

Pseudorca crassidens **(Owen, 1846)**

Other Common Names

Orca falsa (Latin America); oki gondō kujira (Japanese); malaya or chornaya kosatka (Russian).

Description

Male false killer whales range up to 6 m long and can weigh 1,360 kg. Females are smaller, not usually exceeding 5 m long. Newborn calves are about 1.8 m long.

The body is long and slender, with a narrow head that tapers gently from the area of the blowhole toward the rounded beak. The mouthline is long and straight; there is no demarcation between head and beak. The dorsal fin, situated slightly behind the midpoint of the back, is tall, falcate, and with either a rounded or a pointed peak. The shape of the fin is extremely variable. The flippers, situated far forward on the sides, are long and have a distinctive broad hump, or crook, resulting in an S-shaped front margin. This flipper configuration is diagnostic for the species. The flukes are pointed at the tips.

These whales are basically all black except for a gray anchor-shaped patch between the flippers. This patch varies from barely visible to light grayish white, similar to but generally fainter than that of the pilot whale (p. 123). The head often appears lighter than the rest of the body.

Figure 147.—This photo of a false killer whale on the bow of a research vessel south of Bermuda demonstrates no less than four key features. The tapered head and the peculiarly shaped flipper, with its crook or hump along the forward edge, are together diagnostic. In addition, the dorsal fin is well behind the midpoint of the back. On this individual there is a chevronlike blaze of light gray or white behind the eye. (Photo by H. E. Winn.)

Figure 148.—In this unusual head-on view, a pod of false killer whales appears to be charging toward the photographer. There is a double neck crease on the middle animal. Note the erect dorsal fin, a feature which should help avoid confusion with pilot whales. (Photo by K. C. Balcomb.)

Figure 149.—Three slow-moving false killer whales in Arikawa Bay, Japan. Notice how far back on the body the dorsal fin is situated, leaving little possibility of mistaking these "blackfish" for pilot whales. Unlike pilot whales, false killer whales lack a saddle of gray behind the fin, and though the head may appear slightly lighter than the rest of the body, these whales usually appear to be uniformly black when observed at sea. (Photo courtesy of T. Kasuya.)

Natural History Notes

False killer whales are highly social, sometimes occurring in herds of well over 500 animals, though smaller herds of a few dozen appear more common. Pairs and small groups are sometimes encountered as well. They are not known to be segregated in any season or area by sex or age.

The reproductive biology has not been studied, but calves appear to be born at any time of the year.

Seasonal movements are not known. One of the most puzzling aspects of this whale's behavior is its proclivity for stranding in very large numbers. One school of at least 835 individuals is known to have stranded en masse. This tendency may have a significant effect on populations, since the animals appear rare to begin with, judging by the infrequency of observations.

False killer whales readily approach vessels to investigate or bow ride, at which time their large prominent teeth can sometimes be seen. They also are known to leap clear of the water, characteristically turning on the side and flexing, to reenter with a huge splash.

False killer whales prey mainly on squid and large pelagic fishes, including dolphinfish, or "mahi-mahi," off Hawaii and yellowfin tuna and bonita off California. They have been observed eating porpoises as the latter are released from tuna purse seines in the eastern tropical Pacific. They are suspected of robbing from tuna longlines, a practice which makes them especially unpopular with the Japanese fishermen. This behavior extends to taking fish from sport fishing lines in numerous areas, and it sometimes results in their being shot by irate anglers.

The species has adapted well to captivity in Japan and the United States, where it is a popular but uncommon display animal.

Figure 150.—Running false killer whales frequently afford the observer a good look at their extremely tapered heads, and sometimes even their distinctive flippers. (Photos from the eastern tropical Pacific by J. Lambert [top] and R. L. Pitman [middle, bottom].)

Figure 151.—In comparison to pilot whales, false killer whales are often vigorous and acrobatic. As this animal in Hawaii's Sea Life Park demonstrates, they frequently perform graceful dolphinlike high leaps; they also leap and slap onto their sides, and taillob upon reentry. (Photos by S. Leatherwood [above]; K. D. Sexton [left].

Figure 152.—False killer whales have 8–11 large, conspicuous teeth in each row. These teeth are sometimes visible in swimming animals, particularly while they are engaged in stealing fish from the lines of fishermen. The teeth are so distinctive that they can be used to identify even badly decomposed stranded specimens. (Photo courtesy of Sea Life Park, Hawaii.)

Distribution

The false killer whale lives primarily in offshore tropical and warm temperate waters. It is generally not abundant north of about lat. 30°N, though it is known to wander occasionally as far north as the Aleutians and Prince William Sound, Alaska. A specimen was once killed in Puget Sound, Wash., in the month of May, and there are records from seamen of sightings in offshore waters west of Oregon, Washington, and California. They are encountered not uncommonly throughout the eastern tropical Pacific tuna fishing grounds. Occasional sightings in offshore waters as far south as the Galapagos and in the Gulf of California indicate that this species is widely distributed. Large herds of false killer whales are seen occasionally near Hawaii.

Can Be Confused With

The false killer whale can be confused with the killer whale (p. 113), the pilot whale (p. 123), or the smaller, poorly known pygmy killer whale (p. 184) and melon-headed whale (p. 188).

Characteristics distinguishing it from the killer whale are tabularized on p. 117-118; from pilot whales on p. 128-129.

← **Figure 153.—Like pilot whales, false killer whales are known to commit what appears to be mass suicide. In the top photo, no less than 10 whales are strewn along a British beach, some recently dead and others moribund. The lower left photo shows a solitary whale stranded in southern Florida. Note the long, straight mouthline and the tapered head. This gaunt individual's ribs are showing, suggesting that it was in poor condition before stranding. The distinctive flippers are clearly evident on the animal in the bottom right photo. (Photos courtesy of A. S. Clarke [top]; Wometco Miami Seaquarium [bottom left]; D. K. Caldwell [bottom right].)**

At sea, false killer whales are distinguishable from pygmy killer whales and melon-headed whales primarily by their large size (the other two are less than 2.7 m long) and subtle pigmentation differences. Pygmy killer whales usually have an extensive white region on the abdomen which may extend onto the sides, and adults of both the pygmy killer whale and melon-headed whale have variable white areas around the lips which are usually lacking on false killer whales. Flippers of false killer whales have an S-shaped forward margin, while the flippers of the other two are continuously convex on the forward margin.

From the air false killer whales appear long, slim, and, in most cases, uniformly black. Juveniles are slightly lighter gray, and adults sometimes appear slightly lighter gray from the dorsal fin forward, accentuated in bright sunlight. The dorsal fin is near midbody, but the flippers appear to be unusually far forward on the body. Traveling false killer whales displace little white water when surfacing, unlike killer or pilot whales. When feeding or fleeing they are often fast and quick to change directions, behavior very different from the slow, lazy movements characteristic of pilot whales.

Identification of Dead Specimens

Dead false killer whales can be positively identified on the basis of their large size (to 6 m); slender body tapering anteriorly to a long, slender head; the markedly long mouth, with 8-11 large, conspicuous teeth in each row, reminiscent of the killer whale's, but circular and not, as in the killer whale, elliptical in cross section; and unusually shaped flippers that bulge conspicuously on the forward edge.

For comparison with the similar-sized short-finned pilot whale, see p. 128-129.

SHORT-FINNED PILOT WHALE (T)

***Globicephala macrorhynchus* Gray, 1846**

Other Common Names

Blackfish (see also p. 125, 184-188), pothead; calderon, ballena piloto (Latin America); kobire gondō kujira (Japanese)[11]; grinda (Russian).

Description

Maximum length is about 7 m for males and 6 m for females. At birth pilot whales in the Pacific are slightly less than 1.8 m long.

The head shape of the pilot whale is distinctive and can be an important visual clue to this animal's identity in some sightings. In fact, it is from the thick bulbous forehead, which sometimes overhangs the rostrum, that the nickname "pothead" originated. It has been speculated but not conclusively shown that this overhang occurs more frequently and is most prominent in adult males, the heads of which may also be flattened or squared off in front. There is generally no distinct beak, although a hint of a beak is evident in some, usually small, individuals.

The pilot whale's dorsal fin is distinctive, set far forward on the body (beginning well ahead of the midpoint of the back) and with a long base and low profile. It is almost always falcate and rounded, rather than pointed, at the tip. The forward margin is believed to be longer and thicker in adult males than in females and young. The profile of the dorsal fin, even when observed at a great distance, is unmistakable.

The body as a whole is robust, somewhat wedge-shaped, and thickened dorsoventrally at the tail stock. This keeled appearance can be observed when an animal lifts its flukes above the surface at the beginning of a long dive. The flukes themselves are notched and slightly concave along the near margin.

[11]Inasmuch as there is continuing controversy over the classification of pilot whales of the northeastern Pacific, the other scientific and Japanese common names frequently used are also included here: *G. melaena*, magondo kujira, and *G. scammonii*, shiogondo kujira.

Figure 154.—An exhaling pilot whale. In adult males, such as this individual proved to be, the head appears more bulbous and the dorsal fin thicker on the leading edge and more strikingly large in all dimensions than in females and juveniles. (Photo from Santa Barbara Island, Calif., by S. Leatherwood.)

Figure 155.—Pilot whales surfacing at lat. 06°55′N, 93°02′W (top), off the Midriff Islands in the Gulf of California (middle), and near Islas Los Coronados, Baja California (bottom). Pilot whales are widely distributed in the warm temperate and tropical eastern Pacific but the questions of how many species occur there and how they can be distinguished at sea remain unanswered. Presence or absence of a saddle behind the dorsal fin or subtle swatches of gray behind the eye, once thought to distinguish tropical from temperate types in the Pacific, now appear to be too variable to be of use. (Photos by R. L. Pitman, courtesy of NMFS [top]; R. S. Wells [middle]; S. Leatherwood [bottom].)

Figure 156.—Pilot whales resting in calm water off the eastern shore of San Clemente Island, Calif. Even from this distance the bulbous head and prominent low-profile dorsal fin, far forward on the back, are unmistakable indications of the whales' identity. Pilot whales are frequently encountered "loafing" at the surface, particularly in the early and midmorning, presumably following a night of feeding. (Photo by S. Leatherwood.)

Figure 157.—Pilot whales are the least acrobatic of the "blackfish." Such signs of apparent exuberance as the breach of this individual are rare and are usually limited to younger animals. (Photo off Santa Barbara Island, Calif., by D. Varoujean, courtesy of BLM.)

Pilot whales have long, sickle-shaped flippers, between one-sixth and one-fifth as long as the body.

Body color in general is black (thus the common name "blackfish") or dark brown. Animals in some portions of the Pacific normally have a light gray saddle behind the dorsal fin, which may be highlighted by bright sunlight. The occurrence and extent of this saddle varies, perhaps among herds or regions. There may also be a faint light blaze from blowhole to eye. A light gray, almost white, anchor-shaped patch marks the throat and chest, and this is often continuous with a lightened zone of variable width that runs along the ventral midline. Adult males can be heavily scarred. Newborn are generally light gray to cream colored, and, though some appear to bear the basic markings of adults, the pattern is muted. Calves appear to begin to darken early in the first year.

Natural History Notes

Pilot whales are extremely gregarious and rarely found alone. Not only do they show an affinity for their own kind, living in herds of a few to several hundred, but they often occur in the company of smaller cetaceans, particularly bottlenose dolphins (p. 173). Herds of pilot whales appear to be highly organized. While hunting or traveling, a herd may be subdivided into closely knit subgroups of adult males, juveniles, or females with young. These groups often travel in long lines of individuals abreast, separated by a few to a few tens of meters, a configuration which is thought to increase food-finding ability by overlap-

Figure 158.—Aerial views of pilot whales off Catalina Island (above) and Santa Barbara Island, Calif. (bottom). Note the long wedge-shaped body, the bulbous head, the placement of the dorsal fin, and, in this herd, the seemingly uniform presence of a saddle behind the dorsal fin. Presence and extent of this saddle vary among individuals and groups of pilot whales. In the bottom figure a bottlenose dolphin (third from the right) accompanies seven pilot whales. The two species are frequently found in close company. Without a careful look, bottlenose dolphins might be recorded as pilot whale calves, which are light brown (see the animal at the right). (Photos by G. E. Lingle.)

ping individuals' effective hunting ranges (prey detection). While feeding, the group's structure apparently relaxes, and individuals go their own way as they become preoccupied with chasing and consuming quantities of squid. In their resting mode, pilot whales generally coalesce into groups of 12 to more than 30 and lie nearly motionless at the surface. Adult males have been reported to patrol, sentrylike, the outer edges of a "loafing" pod.

Reproductive characteristics of short-finned pilot whales in the Pacific are poorly known. However, judging by the results of detailed studies of the long-finned pilot whale, *G. melaena*, in the North Atlantic, they probably have a prolonged breeding season and a gestation period lasting 15–16 months. Since young are nursed for more than a year, the entire reproductive cycle probably takes at least 3 years.

The southern California and northern Baja California pilot whale populations appear to have two components. Some individuals are known to stay year-round in the vicinity of the California Channel Islands and some of the Baja coastal islands, showing a marked affinity for the heads of deep coastal submarine canyons. Others are seen much of the year in deep water, well offshore. In late winter or early spring, when swarms of squid come inshore to spawn, some of these offshore animals appear to move inshore, joining the "residents" to form larger concentrations over the most active squid spawning grounds. In summer or fall, the offshore animals abandon the inshore areas, apparently returning to pelagic waters.

Pilot whales can be playful—spyhopping ("pitch poling"), lobtailing, and occasionally breaching during so-called "loafing" episodes. But more often they are relatively undemonstrative at the surface. Pilot whales do not bow ride, and can be captured only from extended bowsprits or swordfish planks which place the collector well in front of the boat and permit him to be over the whales before they are disturbed by the boat's presence. In captivity they have proven to be highly intelligent and amenable to training.

Pilot whales are notoriously susceptible to mass stranding. The reasons for this tendency are not well known (see Appendix C for discussion), but large herds strand often enough to make this phenomenon a potentially significant mechanism for population regulation. Killer whales and large sharks are suspected predators.

Figure 159.—When seen from aircraft, pilot whales can often be quickly identified by the broad crescent of white water caused by the passage of the bulbous head through the water. (Photo from San Clemente Island, Calif., by S. Leatherwood.)

Figure 160.—Closeup view of the bulbous head and long sickle-shaped flippers of pilot whales in a tank at Marineland of the Pacific. Though the two well-described species of pilot whales in the Atlantic reportedly can be distinguished by the flipper length relative to body length (one-sixth or less in *G. macrorhynchus* and one-fifth or more in *G. melaena*), such a simple formula has not been devised for pilot whales in the Pacific. (Photo by W. J. Houck.)

Distribution

Pilot whales are present, but not at all common, in the Gulf of Alaska and south along the coasts of Washington, Oregon, and northern California. Short-finned pilot whales are believed to prefer warm temperate climates, so their movements north of about lat. 40°N are presumably related to incursions of warm water, the extent and timing of which may vary from year to year.

From Point Conception south to tropical waters off at least Guatemala, pilot whales are abundant. They are known in the Gulf of California and are found both nearshore and offshore throughout their tropical to warm temperate range. Throughout the Hawaiian Chain, pilot whales are seen with some regularity, especially in the channels and in deep areas in the lee of islands.

Taxonomic confusion surrounding the genus *Globicephala* in the Pacific makes a definitive statement about range necessarily tentative. As many as three forms of pilot whale have been suggested in the North Pacific. The name *G. scammonii* is often applied to the animals found off California, but further research is necessary to determine correct taxonomic relationships.

Can Be Confused With

In the tropical portions of its range the pilot whale can be confused with the pygmy killer whale (p. 184) and the melon-headed whale (p. 188). It is distinguishable from both by its larger size, distinctive dorsal fin, and bulbous to squarish head. Confusion is most likely between small pilot whales, in which

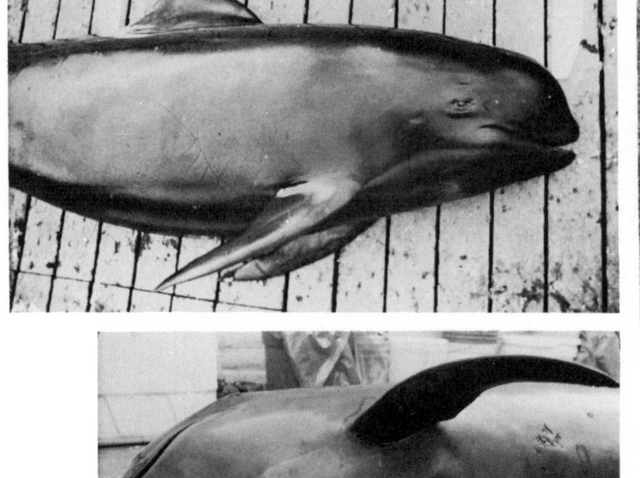

Figure 161.—Dead pilot whales—an adult male on a northern California beach (top, middle right), a calf on the deck of a tuna boat in the eastern tropical Pacific (middle left), and a juvenile killed accidentally in the anchovy fishery off southern California (bottom). Newborn pilot whales are lighter than adults and have a small but noticeable beak. The body darkens during the first few months and the beak disappears gradually as the forehead fills out anteriorly and dorsally. In the younger animals, note the faint hint of an anchor-shaped gray throat patch, consistently present in pilot whales though variable in its intensity. (Photos by W. J. Houck [top, middle right]; courtesy of NMFS [middle left]; courtesy Hubbs Sea World Research Institute [bottom].)

these features are not particularly evident, and adults of the other smaller "blackfish." Both pygmy killer whales and melon-headed whales have dorsal fins that are more erect, slender, and pointed at the peak than is the pilot whale's.

In all parts of its North Pacific range the pilot whale may be confused with the similar-sized false killer whale (p. 118). The two can be distinguished by the following:

Pilot Whale	**False Killer Whale**
Head Shape	
Thick, bulbous, not noticeably tapered.	Longer but slimmer and gently tapered.
Body Shape	
Head, and upper body in particular, robust.	Long and slender.
Flipper shape	
Long, sickle-shaped, smoothly back-curved along leading edge.	Long and tapered, with conspicuous S-shaped leading edge.
Dorsal Fin	
Ahead of midbody; low in profile; broad-based; falcate.	At midbody; more erect; less broad-based; variably shaped;

	from pointed and falcate to rounded and hooked at the peak.
Behavior	
Will not ride bow wave; seldom breaches.	Does ride bow wave; often "porpoises" clear of the water and breaches more frequently.
Coloration	
Black with gray saddle behind dorsal fin; light anchor-shaped patch on throat and along ventral midline.	All black.
Distribution and Abundance	
Common, often over continental shelf, north of lat. 30°N.	Reported only occasionally north of about lat. 25°N, rare above lat. 30°N, increasing toward tropics primarily in pelagic waters.

From the air, pilot whales are readily identifiable by their dark coloration and body and head shape. Because of the broad head they are often first detected by the wave of white-water they push ahead of them when surfacing. The broad-based dorsal fin which is distinctive for this genus can frequently be seen from the air. Though the dorsal surface may be variably gray behind the dorsal fin, the head of larger animals appears uniformly black. Their movements are generally slow in comparison with those of other blackfish.

Identification of Dead Specimens

Dead pilot whales can be confused with any of the species mentioned above. They can be distinguished primarily by 1) the robust body and bulbous head, which is often squared off in front in adult males; and 2) the broad-based, low-profile dorsal fin set far forward on the body. Size alone can rule out the pygmy killer whale and melon-headed whale when the specimen is more than about 2.8 m long. The false killer whale's distinctively shaped flippers can contribute to an identification. Finally, the pilot whale in the North Pacific generally has about seven to nine pairs of teeth above and below, which is significantly fewer than in the other three North Pacific "blackfish."

RISSO'S DOLPHIN (T)

Grampus griseus G. Cuvier, 1812

Other Common Names

Grampus, gray grampus, white-headed grampus, mottled grampus, Risso's grampus; delfín de Risso (Latin America); hana gondō kujira (Japanese); seryy del'fin (Russian).

Description

Risso's dolphins grow to as long as 4 m, and there is no evidence of size differences between sexes. Males become sexually mature at about 3 m. Length at birth is about 1.5 m.

The body is moderately robust, particularly ahead of the dorsal fin. The head has a distinctive shape. There is no clear separation between forehead and beak. Viewed dorsally the head is tapered but with a blunt beak; viewed laterally it is slightly bulbous or almost squarish. The mouthline is fairly long and straight, but points up toward the eye. A conspicuous, shallow, V-shaped crease extends from the blowhole to the tip of the beak. It can be detected only when the animal is viewed head-on or at close range from above.

The flippers are long and pointed. The dorsal fin, located at the middle of the back, is tall (to 38 cm), prominent, falcate, and slightly rounded or pointed. The body tapers markedly behind the dorsal fin, resulting in a narrow tail stock. The flukes are broad, concave along the trailing edge, and deeply notched.

Risso's dolphins are a uniform light gray at birth. During the next few years, their skin darkens through brown to almost black before again beginning to lighten. By adulthood they are largely cream white or silver gray except for the dorsal fin and an adjacent portion of the back, the flukes, and the distal half of the flippers, all of which remain a pale buff to dark ochre. Appreciation of the light brown or black coloration depends very much on lighting conditions. The belly remains dark except for a prominent and continuous light gray pattern on the chest extending posteriorly along the ventral midline, reminiscent of that of the pilot whale. The head becomes almost pure white, though there is usually a dark patch around the eye. The body is usually covered with white oval scars and linear scratch marks, the latter attributed to aggressive intraspecific encounters or to bites from the sharp-beaked squids on which Risso's dolphins prey.

Natural History Notes

Herds of up to several hundred animals have been reported, although groups of a dozen or less are more common. Solitary individuals are sometimes observed. Like pilot whales, Risso's dolphins frequently occur in "chorus lines," groups of nearly evenly spaced individuals swimming in echelon formation. Since no major fishery has exploited the species and since entire herds of Risso's dolphins normally do not strand, the composition of groups is completely unknown. Risso's dolphins are frequently seen in the company of Pacific white-sided dolphins (p. 168), northern right whale dolphins (p. 209), and pilot whales (p. 123).

Figure 162.—A pair of surfacing Risso's dolphins (left) and a single adult male, later captured (right). The high, erect dorsal fin and the flippers remain dark even after much of the body has become white. In the left photo, the individual on the right appears to be a juvenile whose skin is only beginning to lose its pigmentation. (Photos from San Clemente Island, Calif., by L. Hobbs, courtesy of Pacific Search Press [left]; from off San Diego, Calif., by R. Vile, courtesy of Hubbs-Sea World Research Institute [right].)

Figure 163.—A tight group of running Risso's dolphins off Washington State. From a distance they may resemble other small whales with tall, falcate dorsal fins (e.g., female killer whales, bottlenose dolphins, and Pacific white-sided dolphins). However, their blunted, beakless heads and light bodies (in adults) covered by scratches make them fairly easy to identify. (Photo by C. Fiscus.)

Risso's dolphins are regarded as pelagic animals since they are most often encountered seaward of the 100-fathom depth contour. Only in areas where the edge of the continental shelf is relatively near shore are these dolphins likely to be found in coastal waters. Their preference for warmer waters is reflected in their tropical to warm temperate distribution.

Risso's dolphins occasionally ride bow waves or more often stern wakes, but they normally remain indifferent toward powered vessels. They are known to porpoise clear out of the water, slap their sides and tail on the surface, and raise their head as if to survey their surroundings. When an aircraft makes several passes over them they often roll onto their side, seemingly to obtain a clearer view of the intruder.

Risso's dolphins eat cephalopods almost exclusively and fish only exceptionally.

Captive specimens in Japan have survived for over 5 years and have successfully conceived and given birth to young. Life span in the wild is probably at least 20 years.

Distribution

Risso's dolphins are abundant and widely distributed in tropical waters of the eastern North Pacific, where they can be found year-round. They occur as far north as lat. 50°N. Within that range, however, there are apparent gaps in their distribution, one centering at about lat. 20°N and another at about lat. 42°N. Sightings in the northern and inshore portions of the range are most frequent during late spring through early fall, suggesting a relationship between their movements and increases in water temperature. Risso's dolphins are rarely seen near Hawaii.

Can Be Confused With

Risso's dolphin is distinctive in its appearance and when seen at close range is not likely to be confused with other small whales. At a distance, its tall, falcate dorsal fin resembles that of the similar-sized bottlenose dolphin (p. 173). However, the lack

Figure 164.—Performing Risso's dolphin at Marineland of Florida. (The animals at left are bottlenose dolphins.) In young Risso's dolphins, whose back and sides are dark, the two zones of grayish white, one on the chest and one on the belly, are conspicuous. These markings are reminiscent of those on pilot whales. (Photos courtesy of Marineland of Florida.)

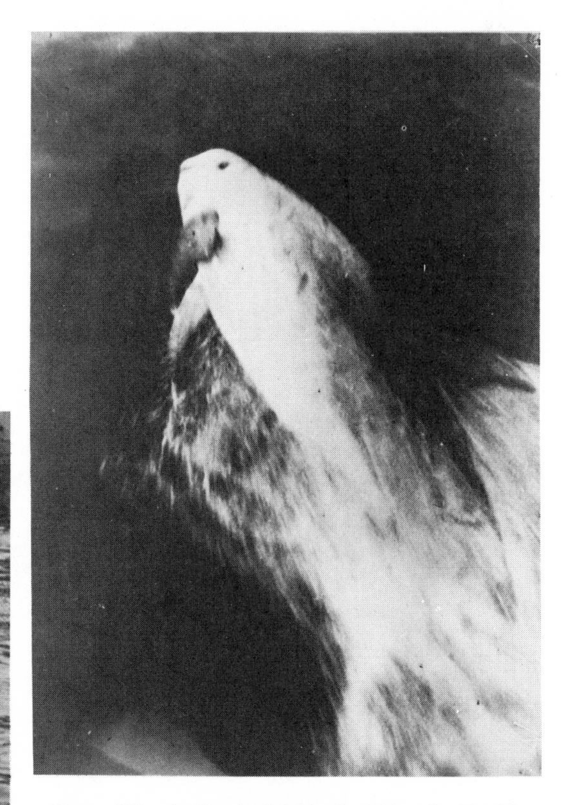

Figure 165.—A Risso's dolphin breaching in Enoshima Aquarium, Japan (left). Note the nearly white adult coloration, interrupted primarily by the dark appendages and the dark eye, the extensive scarring, the long flippers, and the absence of a prominent beak. The photo above, taken in 1907, is of Pelorus Jack, the famous dolphin that accompanied ships through Admiralty Bay, New Zealand, reputedly for 17 years. Discovery and publication of this photo removed all doubt as to the identity of Pelorus Jack. (Photos by W. E. Evans [left]; Capt. C. F. Post, courtesy of. A. N. Baker, Wellington, N.Z. [above].)

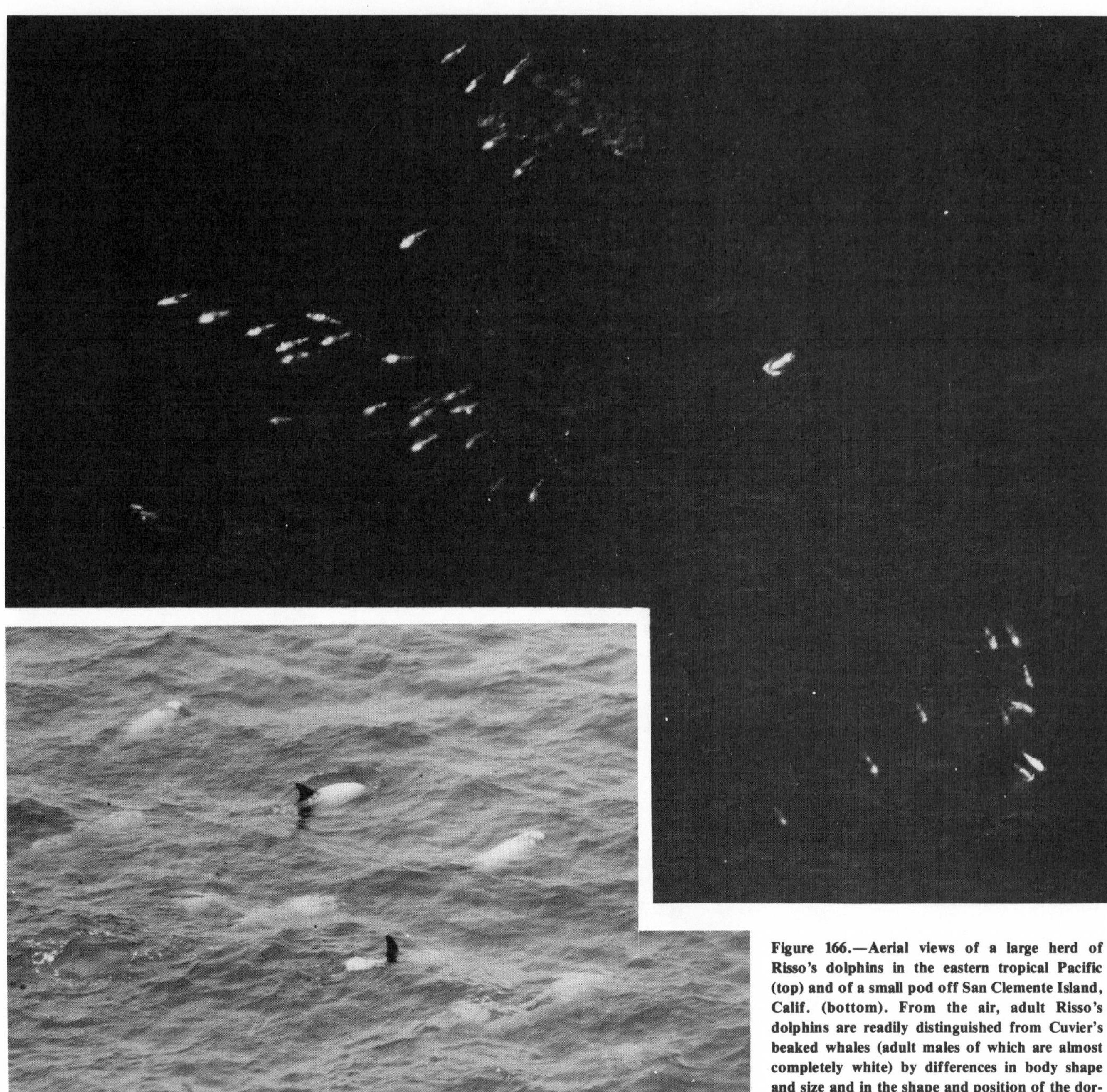

Figure 166.—Aerial views of a large herd of Risso's dolphins in the eastern tropical Pacific (top) and of a small pod off San Clemente Island, Calif. (bottom). From the air, adult Risso's dolphins are readily distinguished from Cuvier's beaked whales (adult males of which are almost completely white) by differences in body shape and size and in the shape and position of the dorsal fin. (Photos courtesy of NMFS [top]; by M. J. White, courtesy of Hubbs-Sea World Research Institute [bottom].)

of a pronounced beak and the scarred white skin of Risso's dolphin contrast with the distinct beak and gray skin of the bottlenose dolphin (although some bottlenoses are themselves heavily scarred).

Large Risso's dolphins have a prominent enough dorsal fin to invite confusion, at a considerable distance at least, with female and juvenile male killer whales (p. 113).

From the air, Risso's dolphins are among the easiest of all cetaceans to identify. In a tight moving herd, the presence of numerous white porpoiselike animals is unmistakable. Viewed from above, adult Risso's dolphins appear white except for the dorsal fin and the area around its base. The evenly brown young contrast sharply with the light adults.

The most likely mistake in a brief encounter from aircraft is that a white animal, seen so briefly that its size and other characteristics cannot be clearly determined, will be summarily logged as a Risso's dolphin when in fact Cuvier's beaked whale (p. 94) is an equally good possibility. Since Risso's dolphins usually occur in larger herds than Cuvier's beaked whales, there is a good chance that at least one individual will be seen well enough to rule out other species. However, as is true of many other pairs or groups of lookalike species, a conservative attitude should be

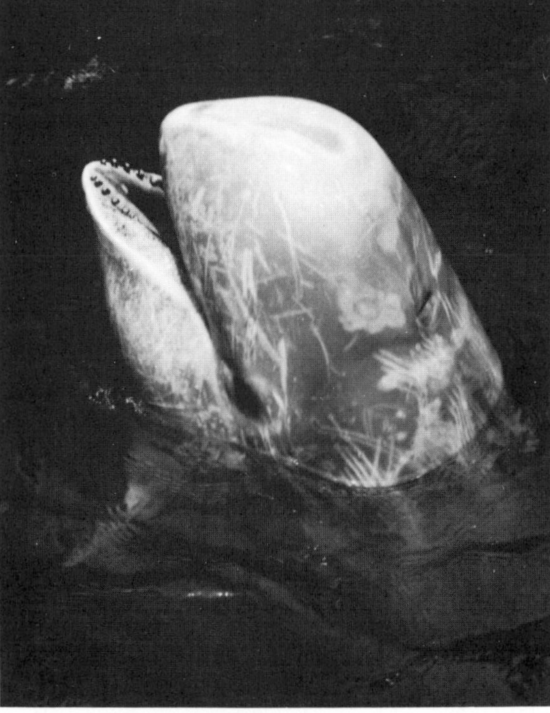

Figure 167.—A dead Risso's dolphin from Florida (top) and a live Risso's dolphin in Enoshima Aquarium, Japan (bottom). Clearly visible in both is the blunt head, marked on the forehead by a deep V-shaped crease with the vertex pointing toward the tip of the snout. Risso's dolphins have seven or fewer teeth in each side of the lower jaw (none in the upper jaw). Many of these teeth may have fallen out in older specimens, and the remaining teeth may be badly worn. (Photos by Marineland of Florida, courtesy of D. K. Caldwell [top]; W. J. Houck [bottom].)

maintained by the observer and positive identifications reserved for cases in which an adequate look at diagnostic field marks has been attained.

Identification of Dead Specimens

Dead Risso's dolphins can be identified most readily by 1) the presence of only seven or fewer pairs of teeth in the lower jaw (many may have fallen out in older individuals and those remaining may be extensively worn) and the absence of teeth in the upper jaw; 2) the presence of a crease or bifurcation in the melon on the extreme front of the head; 3) the presence of numerous scars and scratches all over the body; and 4) the tall, slender, falcate dorsal fin.

MEDIUM-SIZED WHALES WITHOUT A DORSAL FIN

(4–5 m maximum overall length)

Only two species of medium-sized cetaceans without a dorsal fin occur in the area covered by this guide, the white whale (or beluga) and the narwhal. Only the white whale is common, the narwhal being represented only by a few records from the western Arctic. Both species are easily identifiable.

WHITE WHALE (T)

Delphinapterus leucas **(Pallas, 1776)**

Other Common Names

Beluga, belukha; ballena blanca (Latin America); shiro iruka (Japanese); pullzaq or keelaluga (Alaska Eskimo Yupik); belukha (Russian).

Description

Maximum length of adult males is about 4.5 m, but there are marked size differences among geographic stocks. Females are significantly smaller than males. Newborn calves are about 1.6 m long.

White whales are fat animals with proportionately small heads and a somewhat graceless, lumpy body. In fact, the surface of the body often has numerous creases and folds of fat. They have a short, broad beak and a bulbous forehead, which is to the touch like a balloon filled with warm lard. White whales have a very flexible neck, a feature which is reflected in a well-defined crease behind the blowhole.

There is no dorsal fin or hump, although a serrated, often darkened, ridge is detectable along the midline in the middle of the back. The flippers are broad, spatulate, and highly mobile. They are upcurled at the tips, a characteristic that becomes more exaggerated with age. The flukes in adults have a convex trailing edge, distinctly notched near the middle. The convexity increases with age.

The color of white whales makes them very distinctive. At birth they are slate gray to pinkish brown, changing to bluish gray or brownish gray by 1 year of age. Adult white whales are pure white, except for some darker lining on the appendages, especially the rear border of the flukes, and a slight darkening occasionally found along the slight dorsal ridge. The uniform nature of white whale coloration (i.e., the absence of mottling, marking, or countershading) is a distinctive characteristic.

Natural History Notes

These arctic whales are gregarious and rarely found alone. They congregate in large herds of hundreds or thousands around river mouths in summer. Mating occurs mainly in spring, and calves are born in summer after a gestation period of approximately 14.5 months. The calving interval averages 3 years.

White whales are adapted to live in cold water—they are found in ice holes and fissures as well as open water. During spring, animals may be found in small holes seemingly inhospitable to mammals by virtue of their size and distance from other holes and open water. In the Bering and Chukchi Seas, white whales are frequently associated with bowhead whales (p. 60). Ice often forms over resting white whales, and the whales leave impressions or "domes" behind when they swim away. In some areas they ascend rivers to considerable distances; furthermore, they seem capable of living interchangeably in deep or shallow (and turbid) water. Their complex acoustic behavior, including the finest resolution biosonar described to date, may reflect this multienvironment adaptation. Some populations appear to be strongly migratory. The reason for their attraction to river mouths and shallow bays in summer is not clear, but the presence of small calves at these sites suggests that especially favorable conditions for birth or early development (water temperatures of 10°–17°C) are found there.

White whales feed on a wide variety of organisms, including decapod crustaceans, cephalopods, and various schooling fishes. Their habit of preying on salmon smolt in Bristol Bay has prompted efforts by conservation officials to scare them away with recorded killer whale sounds. Killer whales are probably the primary predator of white whales, but polar bears also kill them from time to time. The polar bear lies in wait along a narrow ice crack until a whale surfaces within reach of its powerful paws. In some beluga herds, incidence of claw rakes from unsuccessful polar bear attacks is high. Alaskan aborigines take white whales in small numbers for subsistence, from Bristol Bay northward. Longevity of white whales is at least 25 years. White whales adapt well to captivity and are readily trained to perform.

Distribution

White whales should be looked for only in the coastal waters bordering the northern Gulf of Alaska and throughout the Bering, Chukchi, and Beaufort Seas. A small, apparently isolated population is centered in Cook Inlet and may number no more than several hundred. Recent sightings have been made as far east of Cook Inlet as Yakutat Bay and as far south and west as Kodiak Island, but white whales appear to be absent from the Alaska Peninsula west of Kodiak and from the Aleutians.

Although much of the Bering Sea white whale population is believed to migrate north through Bering Strait, some animals

Figure 168.—White whales surfacing off northwestern Alaska (bottom) and in Vancouver Aquarium (top). In the bottom photo the animal to the right has just begun to exhale, the middle animal is in the midst of inhalation, and the animal on the left has completed its blow and is preparing to dive. Note the all-white coloration on these three and the small dorsal ridge on the animals in the top photo. (Photos by G. C. Ray [bottom] and R. G. Hewlett [top].)

Figure 169.—Note the robust body and the relatively small head of this adult white whale swimming off northwestern Alaska. The white whale has the most versatile and highly sophisticated sonar system of any cetacean studied to date, probably enabling it to occupy varied habitats (from shallow, turbid fresh waters to deep pelagic zones). The shape of the melon, which is to the touch like a balloon filled with warm lard, visibly alters during sound production, probably because of movement of air among the large complicated air sacs behind it. (Photo by G. C. Ray.)

Figure 170.—An adult female white whale, her white body contrasting with the bluish gray of her calf. White whales remain gray until in their sixth or seventh year. (Photo from the St. Lawrence River, by J. Laurin.)

remain in Norton Sound and Bristol Bay for the summer. Some of these latter animals ascend the Yukon, Kuskokwim, Naknek, and Kvichak Rivers. Large numbers are thought to winter along the ice front in the central Bering Sea. They are commonly encountered in the shore lead that opens in spring (late April and May) along the northwest Alaska coast. Upwards of 4,000 white whales congregate in the Mackenzie River Delta of western Canada in summer, most of them probably having migrated from the Bering or Chukchi Sea.

Can Be Confused With

Because of their unique coloration and northern distribution, there is little likelihood of confusing white whales with other cetaceans. Narwhals (p. 137) are extremely rare in the western Arctic of North America, and only in cases of an unusually white animal that either has no tusk or whose tusk is not seen is there a chance of confusion. From an aerial perspective white whales are usually easy to recognize by the white skin, the absence of a dorsal fin, and the distinctly shaped flukes and flippers.

Identification of Dead Specimens

The white body, absence of a dorsal fin, and dental formula (10–11 conical teeth per row with as few as 8 in adults, due to attrition) should be adequate for identifying dead white whales.

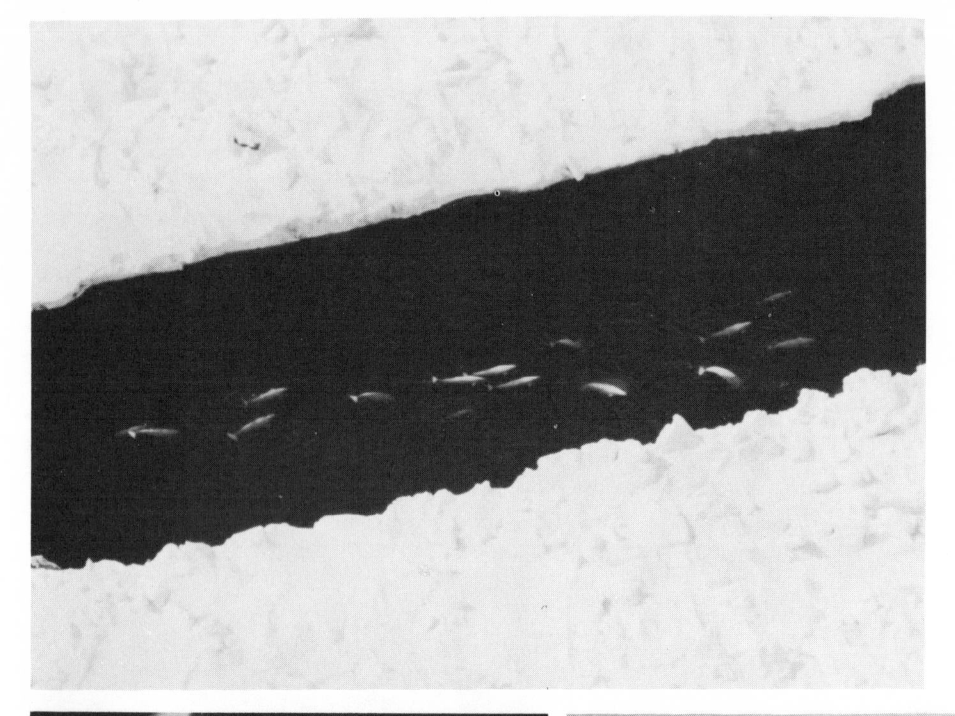

Figure 171.—Aerial views of white whales during spring (top, bottom left) and summer (bottom right). During winter and spring, white whales may be found in surprising locations—deep inside the Arctic pack ice, where they move in chirruping throngs (they have been nicknamed "sea canaries") between openings several kilometers apart. At times, when holes in which they are resting freeze over, departing white whales leave behind small ice domes, molded impressions of the contour of their backs. In summer many venture into shallow river deltas where they feed on salmon smolt and nurse their young. (Photos from Bering Strait by S. Leatherwood [top, bottom left]; from Bristol Bay by D. Lusby, courtesy Sea Library [bottom right].)

Figure 172.—Two white whales in a tank at the Vancouver Public Aquarium. Note the small head, the flexible neck, the fat and wrinkled body (some larger animals even have folds of fat), and the slightly darkened dorsal ridge. (Photo by K. C. Balcomb.)

Figure 173.—An adult white whale killed by Eskimo hunters at Point Hope, Alaska, (top) and a juvenile brought on board a research vessel in the southeastern Bering Sea (bottom photos). Note the narrowness of the tail stock, just in front of the flukes, is accentuated by the robustness of the body. The upturn of the left flipper is not a postmortem artifact but a normal characteristic of this spatulate appendage. (Photos by G. Carroll, courtesy of NMFS.)

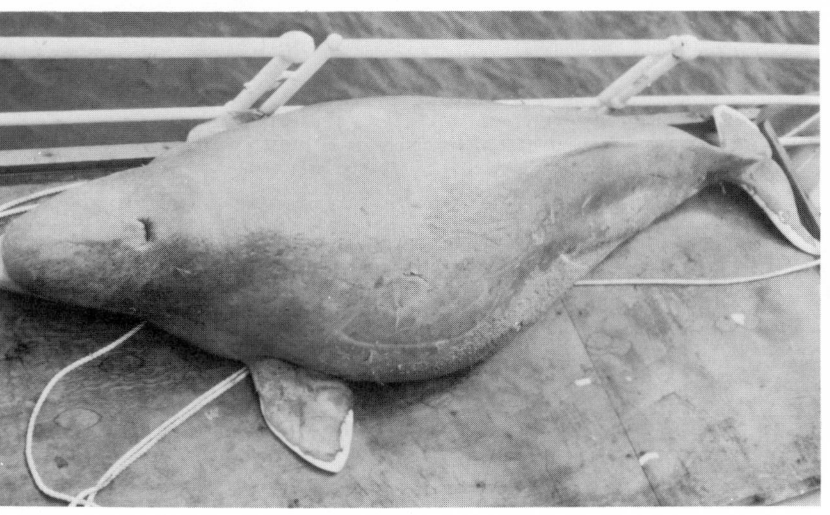

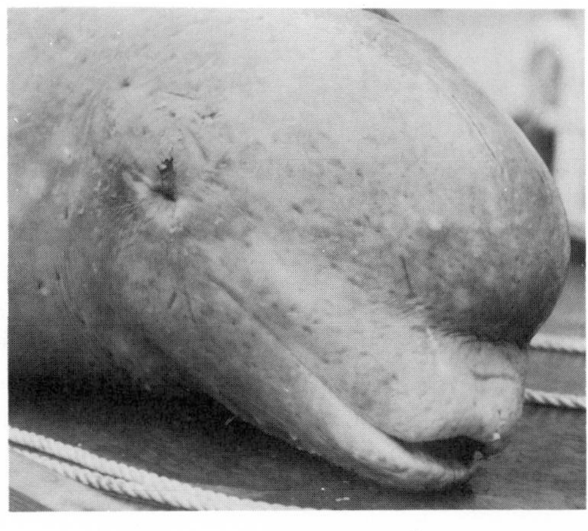

NARWHAL (T)

Monodon monoceros **Linnaeus, 1758**

Other Common Names

Sea unicorn (not currently in use); ikkuka (Japanese); narval (Russian).

Description

Adult male narwhals grow to about 5 m long, with up to an additional 3 m of tusk. Females are smaller than males of the same age and only rarely possess an external tusk. Newborn narwhals are 1.5–1.7 m long.

The narwhal has a bulbous forehead and only a hint of a beak. The head is proportionally small, with little evidence of a neck crease. A straight, spiraled tusk erupts through the left upper lip of males early in life and becomes the whale's most prominent feature.

The back is smooth and finless, though there is a bumpy ridge along the midline in the posterior half of the back. The flukes, as in the white whale, have a pronounced convexity to the trailing edge, especially in adults. The flippers are small and upcurled distally in adults.

The color pattern of narwhals alters with age. As newborns they are a blotchy gray. They become purplish black before irregular white areas begin to develop on the ventral surface and around the head. By adulthood, narwhals have white bellies and mottled flanks and backs. Very old animals are mostly white,

Figure 174.—In this photo of narwhals, the origin of the name "unicorn whale" is apparent. The animal at right, probably an adult male, exposes its tusk as it surfaces. Even when this feature is not observed, however, the narwhal's coloration, ranging from a blotchy gray at birth, through a bluish-black juvenile stage, to almost completely white except for a dark dorsum, makes it easy to distinguish from the white whale. Note also the dorsal ridge on the animal to the left. (Photo by D. Lusby, courtesy of Sea Library.)

except on the back, where some black spotting remains.

Narwhal dentition is so bizarre that it merits special note. The mouth is effectively toothless—the two adult teeth remaining embedded in the upper jaw. The left one normally pierces the upper lip in the male and elongates to become an impressive spear matching the spiraled horn of the fabled unicorn. Occa-

Figure 175.—An adult female narwhal and her newborn calf in Admiralty Inlet, eastern Canadian Arctic. Calves, which are born in summer, are an uneven gray at birth but soon darken to a shiny black or blue-black. Adults are white ventrally and mottled on the back and sides. In this view note that the trailing edge of the flukes of the calf is flat; as the animal ages that margin will become increasingly convex. The dark dorsal ridge of the adult is clearly visible. The white mark on the neck of the female is probably a healed bullet wound, common on narwhals in Canada. (Photo by R. Reeves.)

Figure 176.—A young narwhal caught by fast-moving ice in a natural trap off the northeast coast of Newfoundland. Along with several humpback whales, it apparently survived the trauma of entrapment and was able to return to its more northern home when the ice barrier cleared. Not all narwhals are so lucky—hundreds are sometimes forced to share a single narrow crevice for weeks, becoming vulnerable to starvation, suffocation, or predation by polar bears and Eskimo hunters. Note the blunt head and the emerging tusk, only a few centimeters long. (Photo courtesy of NMFS.)

Figure 177.—An aerial view of eight narwhals in the eastern Arctic of Canada. From the air, tusked males and heavily mottled adult females should be clearly distinguishable from white whales. (Photo by W. Hoek.)

sionally both teeth will develop into external tusks, but the right one generally is less well developed than the left. Females with single tusks and double tusks have been observed.

Natural History Notes

Although narwhals are at times gregarious in areas where they are abundant, solitary animals or very small groups of less than 10 are most likely to be seen in the area covered by this guide.

Narwhals are believed to have a reproductive regime similar to that of white whales, with most conceptions in spring, and births in summer following about 14–15 months of gestation.

Narwhals' lives are closely associated with pack ice, and they are rarely found far from it. They are known to undertake predictable migrations in some areas, and such movements coincide with major changes in ice conditions. Because narwhals are essentially strays in Alaska waters, no generalizations can be made about their patterns of movement there.

In most areas narwhals subsist on squid, polar cod, and various benthic fishes and invertebrates. They show a marked preference for deep water. Killer whales probably account for some natural mortality, and ice entrapment and consequent starvation, suffocation, or polar bear predation appears to be significant in some areas. In areas where they concentrate near human population centers, narwhals are hunted for their ivory and muktuk (skin with a thin layer of attached blubber). Recent observations indicate that the tusk may be used in dominance combat among adult males.

Distribution

Narwhals are extremely uncommon in the western Arctic of North America. There are no records south of the Bering Sea, and there is only one from south of Bering Strait—a specimen stranded at the mouth of the Caribou River in Nelson Lagoon on the Alaska Peninsula, April 1957. Although this is the only published Bering Sea record, the Eskimos on St. Lawrence Island have in their language a name for the narwhal, suggesting its previous presence and the current possibility of its chance occurrence there. There are a few records from Point Hope on the Chukchi Sea north and eastward to the Canadian border, primarily of solitary stranded or shot specimens. Narwhals do not become abundant until one moves east of Cornwallis Island in the central Arctic of Canada.

Can Be Confused With

Because of its lack of a dorsal fin and extreme northern distribution, the narhwal is unlikely to be confused with anything other than the white whale (p. 134). Adult male narwhals have the conspicuous tusk, which sometimes breaks the surface of the water. Coloration is the best aid to distinguish females and young narwhals from white whales. Their spotted or mottled skin is unlike any stage in the uniformly colored white whale's development. From the air, the narwhal's coloration and tusk, when present, should distinguish it from white whales or any other arctic whales.

Identification of Dead Specimens

Dead narwhals should be easy to identify by their dentition. There are no teeth or alveoli in the mouth. Coloration and absence of a dorsal fin should help identify fresh specimens.

Figure 178.—Adult male narwhals killed by Eskimo hunters of eastern Canada. The long spiraling tusk is one of two teeth, the other normally remaining buried in the gum; both teeth of females are normally concealed throughout life. Note the low but conspicuous dorsal ridge, appearing as a dark longitudinal line. (Photos by D. Lusby, courtesy of Sea Library.)

Figure 179.—An immature male narwhal killed in the local native fishery at Arctic Bay, Northwest Territories. In the left photo note the rounded, almost beakless head, and the small upturned mouth. The tusk of this young animal is just emerging in the lightly pigmented area in the left upper lip. The animal to the left has no erupted teeth; narwhals are functionally toothless except for the tusk. In the right view, note the white mottling, which has begun to encroach up the sides and will become more extensive with age. Note also the convexity of the rear margin of the deeply notched flukes and their rounded tips. (Photos by R. Reeves.)

SMALL WHALES, DOLPHINS, AND PORPOISES WITH A DORSAL FIN

(less than 4 m maximum length)

The 15 species in this group are not discussed in order of length. Instead, the species of the genus *Stenella* are treated together and then they and other species are placed in near proximity to those animals with which they are likely to be confused in the field.

SPOTTED DOLPHIN (T)

Stenella attenuata **(Gray, 1846)**

Other Common Names

Spotter, spotted porpoise; delfín machado, delfín pintado or tonino pintado (Latin America); arari iruka (Japanese); kiko (Hawaiian); pyatnistyy del'fin (Russian).

Description

In overall body shape, this animal is very much like the common dolphin (p. 160) and striped dolphin (p. 155). Adults range from 1.6 to 2.6 m long, and weigh up to 100 kg or more, depending on the geographic race involved (see section on Distribution below). Spotted dolphins are about 80 cm long at birth and are unspotted. Dark spots begin to appear ventrally when the animals reach about 1.5 m in length, followed by light spots appearing on the dark gray dorsal surface. In adults the ventral spots have fused and lightened, giving the animal a uniform gray appearance below. The light spots above persist and are on the average largest and most numerous in the relatively large-bodied, large-toothed, and robust "coastal" spotted dolphin. The "northern offshore" and "southern offshore" forms are relatively smaller, more lightly built, have smaller teeth, and on the average are less spotted. Spotted dolphins around Hawaii are still less spotted than the offshore forms in the eastern tropical Pacific, but are similar to them in size and shape.

The northern and southern offshore forms differ from each other in average values of some external and skull measurements, and specimens are assigned to the two stocks based on where they are captured or seen.

Natural History Notes

Most of what is known about spotted dolphins comes from studies of the offshore race, which is the cetacean most heavily involved in the eastern tropical Pacific tuna fishery. These dolphins are regularly found in an as-yet-unexplained association with yellowfin tuna. Fishermen spot, chase, and encircle large schools of spotted (and other) dolphins with purse seines, then attempt to release the dolphins before hauling aboard the catch of tuna that remains beneath the mammals during the chase and capture operation. The release procedure is not always successful, and in the early 1970's 100,000 or more spotted dolphins died in tuna nets each year. Dolphin-release techniques have improved, and kills in recent years have been in the tens of thousands. Release-technology research continues.

Spotted dolphins are extremely gregarious and are often found in offshore aggregations of more than 1,000 animals, frequently in mixed herds with spinner dolphins. The coastal form is usually encountered in herds of less than 100.

The life history of the northern offshore race has been studied intensively. Breeding takes place during prolonged spring and fall seasons; little of it occurs in winter, but there may be a third peak in summer. Gestation lasts for about 11.5 months, nursing for about 11.2 months. Since most females "rest" for a few months following lactation, the average calving interval is greater than 2 years.

Spotted dolphins are very active animals at the surface, and herds can be sighted at a great distance because of the froth caused by their porpoising and leaping. In some areas they still ride bow waves, but in the offshore eastern tropical Pacific, years of harassment by tuna boats appear to have discouraged this behavior, and they now usually flee from powered vessels. Although they do not adapt well to captivity, a few spotted dolphins have been maintained successfully in Hawaiian oceanaria.

Mesopelagic and epipelagic fishes and squids form the diet of spotted dolphins. They are preyed on by large sharks, killer whales, false killer whales, and possibly other small whales.

Distribution (see map, Fig. 185)

Spotted dolphins have not been recorded off the North American coast north of the United States-Mexican border and are clearly a tropical species. The coastal form ranges into the Gulf of California to about lat. 28°N. This coastal race is normally confined to waters within 50 km of the coast. It occurs continuously along the Mexican, Central American, and South American coasts to well south of the equator. Frequently it is seen around the Trés Marías Islands and on the way in and out of Panama, Punta Arenas, and Costa Rica.

The offshore forms are found from south of Cabo San Lucas to below the equator and west to about long. 145°W. They have been seen as far inshore as 20 km from the coast but are generally distributed farther offshore. Two populations were recently defined, north and south of lat. 1°S. The Hawaiian race inhabits the waters around the Hawaiian archipelago and may extend westward and southward from there. The populations of the

Figure 180.—Three types of spotted dolphins occurring in the eastern tropical Pacific. Coastal spotters, restricted in distribution to within 60 nm of the coast, are larger and more robust and exhibit more spotting in all age groups (top). The spotting on adults is so extensive that they are sometimes called "silver-backs." This spotting aids immeasurably in making aerial identifications. Slightly smaller, slimmer, and less spotted, offshore spotted dolphins occupy the bulk of the species range in the eastern tropical Pacific (middle). Hawaiian spotted dolphins are often nearly unspotted as adults (bottom). (Photos from the Gulf of Panama by K. D. Sexton [top left], from the Gulf of Tehuantepec [top right] and from lat. 17°23'N, long. 103°00'W [middle left] by R. L. Pitman, and from near Clipperton Island by R. Garvie [middle right], all courtesy of NMFS; from Pokai Bay, Oahu, Hawaii, by E. W. Shallenberger [bottom].)

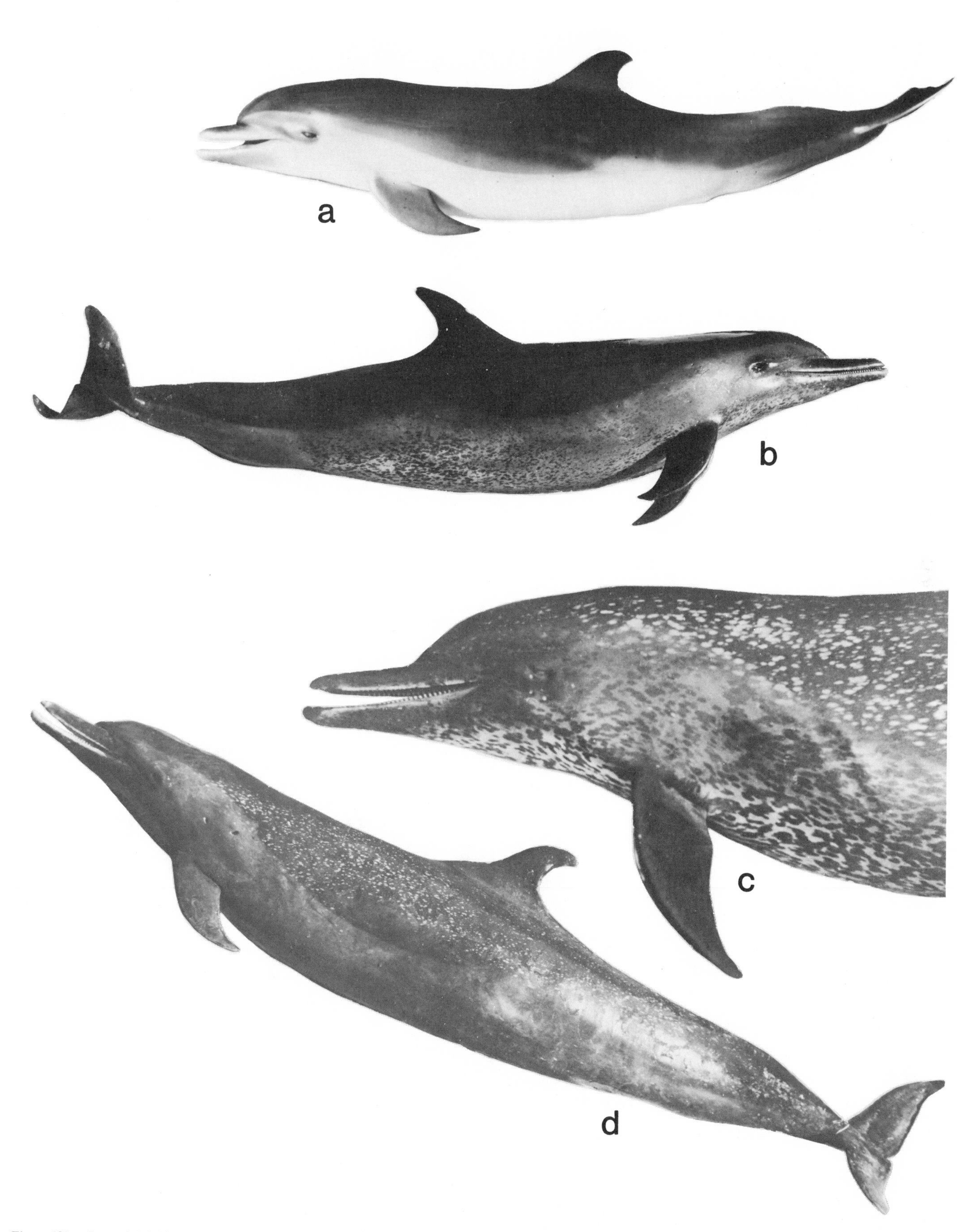

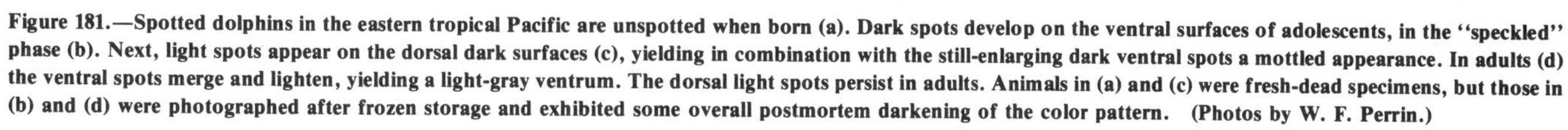

Figure 181.—Spotted dolphins in the eastern tropical Pacific are unspotted when born (a). Dark spots develop on the ventral surfaces of adolescents, in the ''speckled'' phase (b). Next, light spots appear on the dorsal dark surfaces (c), yielding in combination with the still-enlarging dark ventral spots a mottled appearance. In adults (d) the ventral spots merge and lighten, yielding a light-gray ventrum. The dorsal light spots persist in adults. Animals in (a) and (c) were fresh-dead specimens, but those in (b) and (d) were photographed after frozen storage and exhibited some overall postmortem darkening of the color pattern. (Photos by W. F. Perrin.)

Figure 182.—Even though markedly less spotted than their more easterly counterparts, Hawaiian spotted dolphins are readily identifiable by the white lips and the white tipped beak—the light "mark"—and the dark cape (left). Juvenile spotted dolphins are known for their frequent high leaps in the wild (right). (Photos by E. Shallenberger.)

Figure 184 (opposite page).—Spotted dolphins awaiting release from tuna seines. In addition to affording excellent views of body shape and proportions, these photos clearly show the structure of the cape pattern, details of the coloration of the head, including the light mouth and darker flipper stripe, and the pointed flippers. The bulging keel is usually most pronounced in adult males. (Photos by W. High, courtesy of NMFS.)

Figure 183.—Spotted dolphins rarely strike the pose in this photo taken at lat. 17°23'N, long. 102°46'W. This is a juvenile in late "speckled" phase. Note the well-defined cape pattern, the dark flecking on the white throat, and the characteristic white-tipped beak. (Photo by R. L. Pitman.)

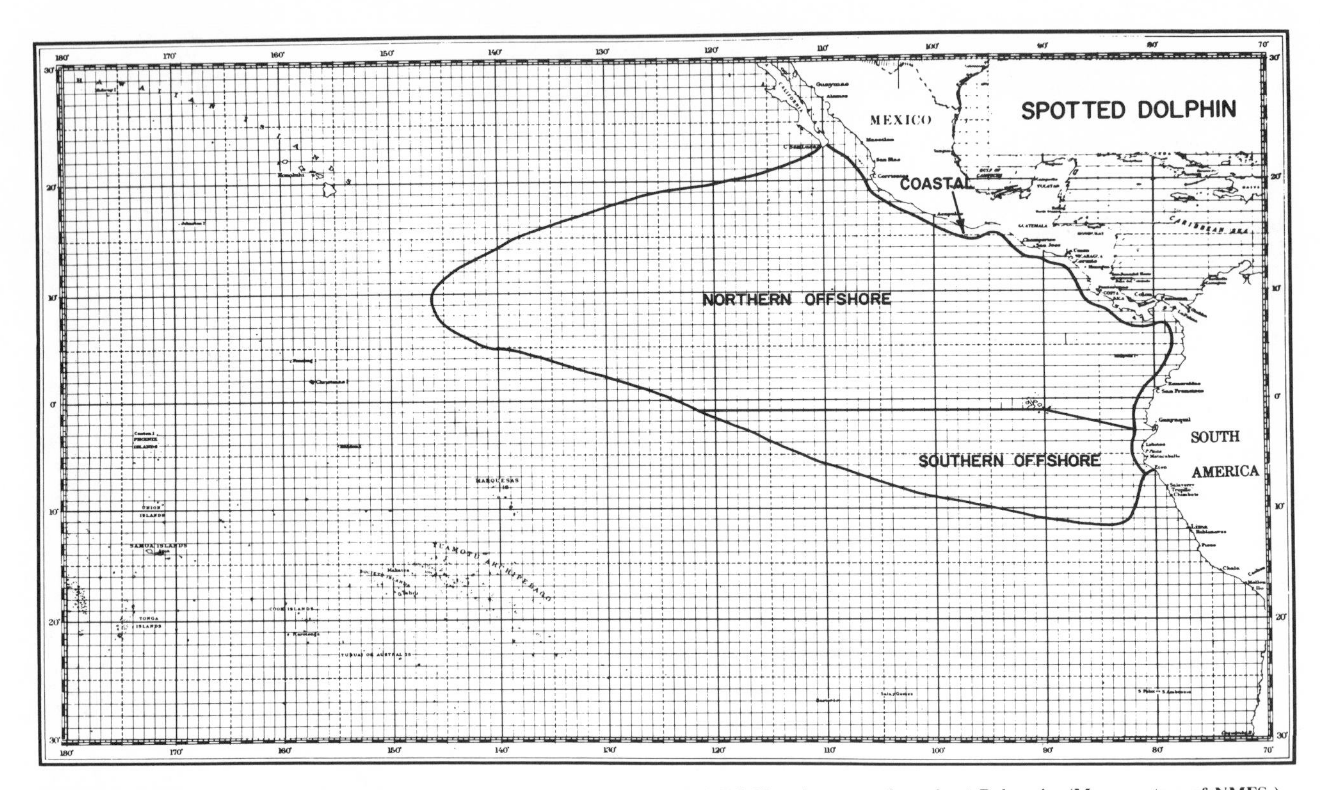

Figure 185.—Distribution of races of spotted dolphins in the eastern Pacific. Spotted dolphins also occur throughout Polynesia. (Map courtesy of NMFS.)

Figure 186.—An adult male spotted dolphin killed in the eastern tropical Pacific tuna fishery. This animal was taken in the far offshore part of the eastern Pacific range and resembles Hawaiian spotted dolphins in being relatively unspotted. Spotted dolphins have about 35–50 teeth in each row. (Photo by W. F. Perrin, NMFS.)

Figure 187.—Spotted and spinner dolphins are frequent companions throughout much of their common range in the tropical eastern Pacific, often occurring with large numbers of seabirds. They are often killed together in tuna purse seines. When they can be examined closely, there is little basis for confusion in identity of adults, since the spinners are unspotted and have triangular dorsal fins and black-tipped beaks. There are two spotted dolphins (one adult and one unspotted juvenile) and three whitebelly spinner dolphins (two juveniles) in this photo. (Photo by C. J. Orange, NMFS.)

offshore races have been estimated at more than 2 million animals in the aggregate.

Can Be Confused With

Young spotted dolphins are superficially almost indistinguishable from small bottlenose dolphins (p. 173). However, they are usually seen in the company of spotted adults. Common dolphins (p. 160) and striped dolphins (p. 155) behave much like spotted dolphins around a boat, frequently jumping clear of the water and darting back and forth erratically when they ride the bow wave. Both, however, have white bellies that stand out sharply against their variously colored and patterned sides, while the spotted dolphin has a gray belly and spotting that is entirely absent in the other two species.

Because of their spotting, rough-toothed dolphins (p. 178) may also be confused with spotters. However, there is no crease to demarcate the beak from the forehead of the rough-toothed dolphin, and its spotting or mottling is generally not as extensive as that of the spotted dolphin.

Particularly since they occur in mixed herds, spotted and spinner dolphins (p. 148) can be confused. Spinners have a triangular or even slightly forward-curved dorsal fin. Other differences between spotters and spinners are described in Figure 187.

Identification of Dead Specimens

The combination of spots, sharply demarcated rostrum, 34–48 teeth in each row, and no strongly marked pattern of stripes makes this animal easy to identify. Since the various geographical forms vary from each other only in average character state, individual specimens often cannot be identified to race on the basis of morphology alone.

SPINNER DOLPHIN (T)

Stenella longirostris (Gray, 1828)

Figure 188.—Spinners off Puerto la Cruz, Venezuela. The long, slim dark-tipped beak and the erect dorsal fin are characteristics of spinners. (Photo by G. di Sciara, courtesy of Hubbs-Sea World Research Institute.)

Other Common Names in Current Use

Spinner, spinner porpoise; delfín tornillon or delfín churumbelo (Latin America); hashinaga iruka (Japanese); dlinnonosyy or vertyashchiysya del'fin (Russian).

Description

Adult spinner dolphins are about 1.5–2.2 m long, with females on the average about 4 cm shorter than males. Size varies among the several geographical races (see section on Distribution below). The Costa Rican spinner is the longest, adults reaching 2 m or more, while the immediately adjacent "eastern" form is the smallest (one pregnant female weighed only 39 kg (85 lb)).

The races also differ widely from each other in body shape and in color pattern. The Costa Rican and "eastern" spinners differ in length and in relative length of the beak (longer in the Costa Rican) but are otherwise similar. Both are dark gray except for light areas on the throat, in the axilla (behind the flipper), and in the genital region (Fig. 190). Sizes of the light areas vary among individuals. In calves they are confluent, making the animal basically dark above and white below. Older juveniles are intermediate. The Costa Rican and eastern spinners also share a peculiar sexual dimorphism in body shape. In adult males the dorsal fin is erectly triangular; in some large males it even is canted forward, appearing to be "on backwards." Degree of forward cant of the fin is correlated with size of the postanal ventral hump composed largely of connective tissue. The combination of forward-leaning dorsal fin and large ventral hump give large males an appearance unique among the dolphins. The function of the anomalous features is unknown.

The more offshore northern and southern "whitebelly" spinners and spinners around Hawaii and in other parts of Polynesia are more like spinners in other tropical waters around the world. The color pattern consists of a dark gray dorsal cape, a lighter gray lateral area, and a white belly. The three elements of the pattern vary geographically in contrast and definition. In the "northern" whitebelly spinner, the cape is relatively indistinct and the margin between lateral field and white underside is more or less ragged. In "southern" whitebelly spinners the cape is more visible, and the lateral field darkens ventrally, giving the animal a striped appearance at a distance. In spinners around Hawaii, all three zones of the pattern are well defined and contrast sharply with each other. The Hawaiian spinner has the most falcate fin among the races, but it is still erectly subtriangular. The ventral hump is nearly absent. The whitebelly spinners are again intermediate, having a highly variable degree of erectness of dorsal fin and size of ventral hump. These, of course, are average differences, and some individuals in any large herd or sample can be expected to exhibit the "wrong" color pattern or shape. The whitebelly spinners are especially variable.

Natural History Notes

Spinners often occur in very large herds, and it is not unusual to find them mixed with spotted dolphins. Both species experience significant mortality in the eastern tropical Pacific as a result of tuna purse seine operations (see p. 141). The two forms most involved are the eastern and whitebelly spinners. Harassment by tuna boats appears to have affected the behavior of these dolphins. On the tuna grounds most herds now begin "running," swimming very rapidly near the surface with long flat jumps, whenever a motor vessel approaches. This is less true of animals of the Costa Rican and Hawaiian races, which still appear relatively unafraid and approach vessels to ride the bow.

The spinner's common name is derived from its habit of leaping clear of the water and spinning on its longitudinal axis, rotating as many as 7 times in one leap.

Distribution (see map, Fig. 195)

The spinner is a tropical animal, its range in the eastern tropical Pacific coinciding roughly with that of the spotted dolphin. In the rest of the Indo-Pacific, it is not found on the high seas but stays close to islands and banks. The reason for the high-seas distribution in the eastern tropical Pacific is not known but probably has something to do with the fact that the region is peculiar in having a very shallow mixed layer (50–100 m) underlaid by a sharp thermocline (region of rapidly changing temperature with depth) and a thick oxygen-minimum layer. These oceanographic features define a shallow, sharply bounded habitat that may in some way approximate the habitat around islands and over banks.

Can Be Confused With

Among the small dolphins with long beaks, the spinner is unique in having an erect triangular dorsal fin, the best field character to look for. The spinning behavior (as distinguished from other kinds of high leaps, somersaults, etc.) is also diagnostic. These two features, in combination with the long beak, reliably separate spinners from common dolphins (p. 160), striped dolphins (p. 155), spotted dolphins (p. 141), Fraser's dolphins (p. 166), and bottlenose dolphins (p. 173)

Identification of Dead Specimens

Again, the long beak and triangular dorsal fin are diagnostic. The spinners also have relatively high tooth counts (45–61 in the eastern tropical Pacific), although the lower end of the range overlaps those of some of the other long-beaked dolphins. If the tripartite color pattern is intact, it also is diagnostic.

Figure 189 (opposite page).—A spinner dolphin just breaking the surface, its blowhole open. Note the gentle angle formed between the melon and the long slim beak, the distinctive black edges of the lips, and the black rostrum tip. The photos show variation in beak length among spinner dolphins. (Photos courtesy of NMFS and by W. F. Perrin [right].)

a
b
c
d

Figure 190 (opposite page and above).—Spinner dolphins of four races described from the eastern North Pacific: eastern (a), northern whitebelly (b), southern whitebelly (very much like Hawaiian in color pattern) (c, d), and Hawaiian (e). (Photos by R. L. Pitman [a], R. J. Olsen [b], F. L. Fredenheim [c, d], and K. C. Balcomb [e], all courtesy of NMFS.)

Figure 191.—Adult male eastern spinners have their dorsal fin on backwards. Development of the forward-canted fin is correlated with a pronounced postanal hump of unknown function. Although eastern spinners are largely gray all over, these animals appear darker than they really are, because of postmortem darkening (above) and silhouetting (below). (Photos by W. F. Perrin.)

Figure 192.—Eastern spinners on the bow of a research vessel off southern Mexico (top) and Atlantic spinners (very much like Hawaiian spinners) on the bow of a vessel in the Caribbean, illustrating the range of dorsal appearance among races of spinners. Note the eastern spinner's lack of a visible cape and its triangular dorsal fin (as compared to the slightly falcate fin of the Atlantic spinners). (Photos by R. Green, courtesy NMFS [top]; A. Taruski, courtesy of H. E. Winn [bottom].)

Figure 193 (opposite page).—This sequence, the order of which is indicated by the numbers, illustrates the unique spinning behavior (repeated rotations along the longitudinal axis) from which the spinner dolphin derives its common name. Spinner dolphins may make seven or more revolutions in a single leap. The meaning of this behavior is not known. (Photos from 16 mm movie footage by F. S. Hester, courtesy of NMFS.)

1 2 3

4

5

6

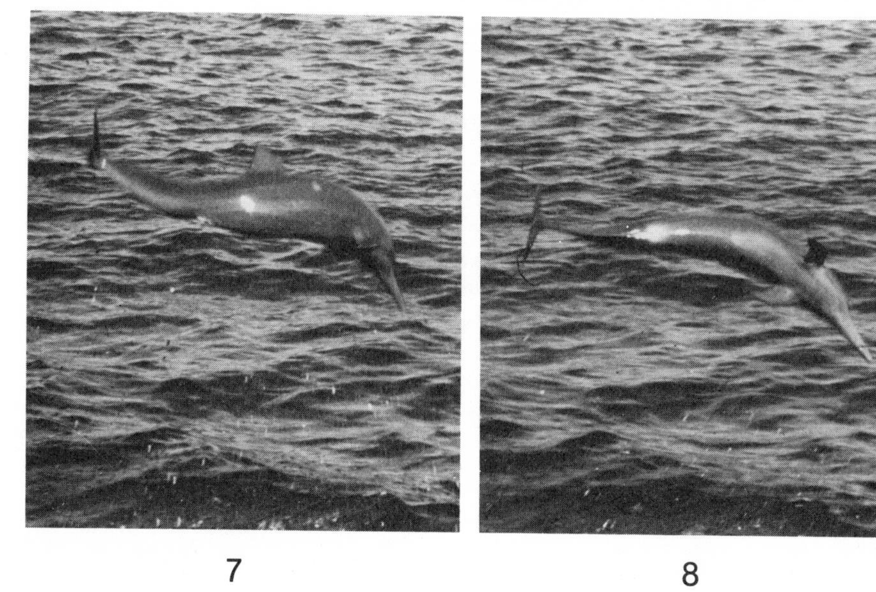

7 8

9

Figure 194.—Aerial view of a large herd of eastern spinners off southern Mexico (top), with a close-up of some running animals (bottom). Spinners are slim of body with strikingly long beaks. Eastern spinners are uniformly battleship gray with erect, even forward canting dorsal fins. Of the dolphins in the eastern North Pacific, spinners are perhaps the easiest to recognize from the air. Of the spinners, eastern spinners are easiest to identify positively. (Photos courtesy of NMFS.)

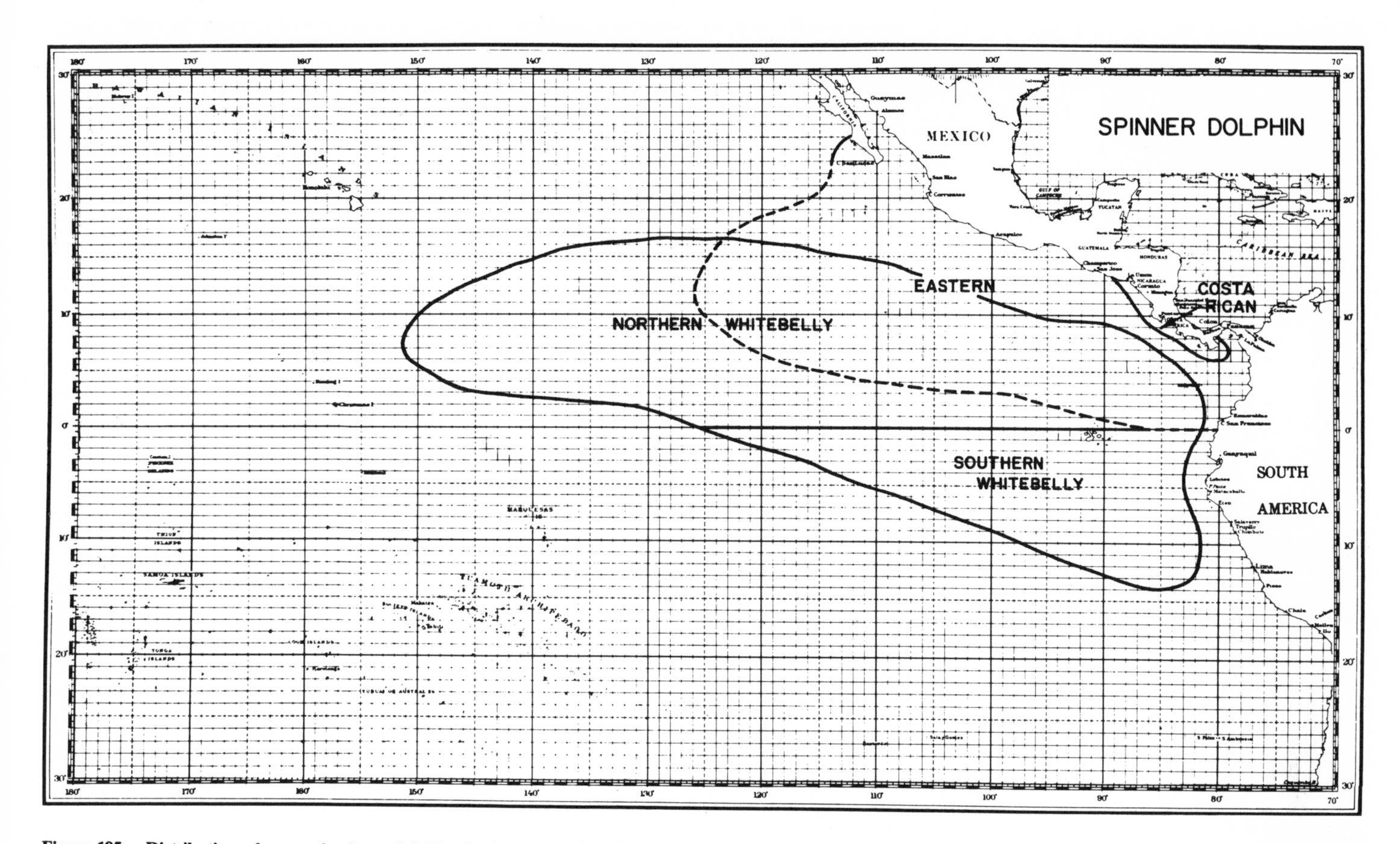

Figure 195.—Distribution of races of spinner dolphins in the eastern Pacific. Spinner dolphins also occur throughout Polynesia. (Figure courtesy of K. Raymond, NMFS.)

STRIPED DOLPHIN (T)

Stenella coeruleoalba **(Meyen, 1833)**

Other Common Names

Streaker porpoise, whitebelly (applied by fishermen to this species and to *Delphinus delphis* and *Lagenodelphis hosei*); delfín listado (Latin America); suji iruka (Japanese); polosatyy del'fin or stenella (Russian).

Description

This dolphin is closely related to the common dolphin, *Delphinus delphis*, and the spotted dolphin, *Stenella attenuata*, and is very much like them in size and shape, having a long, sharply defined beak, pointed flippers, and a falcate dorsal fin. Adults in the eastern tropical Pacific range from about 1.9 to 2.3 m. Adult males are on the average about 6 cm longer than adult females. Calves are about 1 m long when born and possess the full adult color pattern.

The color pattern of the striped dolphin is distinctive. In general, the top of the head and the back are dark gray to bluish gray, the sides lighter gray, and the belly and throat white. In living animals, the belly can appear bright pink. The dorsal fin, flukes, and flippers are all dark. There are two black stripes on the lower half of each side—one from eye to anus, one from eye to flipper. The eye-to-anus "flank" stripe generally has a short, inferior branch that ends above and somewhat behind the flipper. The eye-to-flipper stripe is often double. A black patch around each eye is connected to the black beak. A distinctive light blaze extends up and back from the lateral field into the cape toward the dorsal fin. It is conspicuous against the dark gray of the cape. The blaze is the best feature for identifying animals that are bow riding or leaping clear of the water.

Natural History Notes

Like the other pelagic dolphins, the striped dolphin is gregarious and usually encountered in herds of several hundred animals. Its biology has been studied off Japan, where the population has been depleted by driving large numbers ashore, but little work has been done on those living in the eastern North Pacific.

Off Japan, there is a protracted breeding season, with peaks

Figure 196.—Running striped dolphins, just south of the equator (top) and off Clipperton Island (bottom). At a distance striped dolphins might be confused with the smaller but similarly built common dolphin, or with the more robust but similarly striped Fraser's dolphin. (Photos from lat. 01°21′S, long. 88°38′W [top] by R. L. Pitman, courtesy NMFS; from near Revillagigedo Islands by S. Leatherwood [bottom].)

Figure 197.—Upon close examination, striped dolphins can be readily distinguished from common dolphins, which bear an hourglass or crisscross pattern on the side, by the distinctive lateral striping. They can also be distinguished from the more robust, nearly beakless Fraser's dolphin by differences in the striping pattern and by the striped dolphin's larger flippers and more substantial falcate dorsal fin. (Photo from lat. 01°21′N, long. 88°38′W by R. L. Pitman, courtesy of NMFS.)

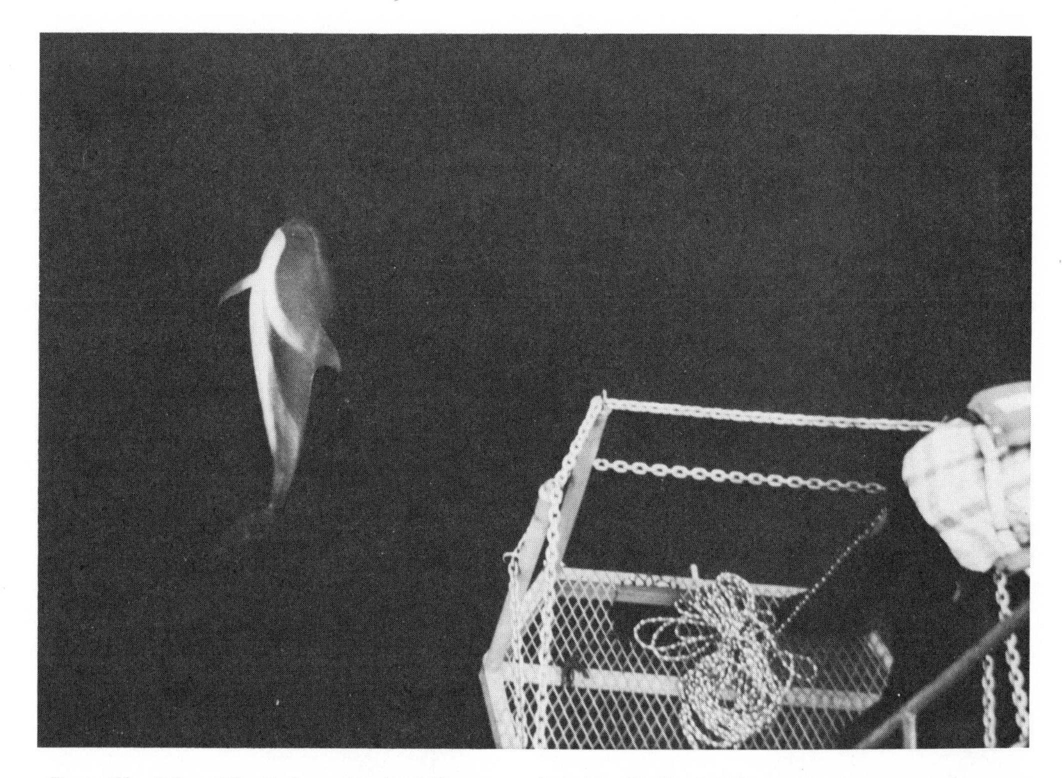

Figure 198.—When riding the bow, striped dolphins can usually be identified by the light shoulder blaze extending back and up from the light lateral field. This blaze is variably expressed and sometimes absent, however, and the dolphin may sometimes appear uniformly pale gray from a distance. In a given herd of striped dolphins, the spinal blaze or the distinctive lateral stripes will usually be detectable on at least some individuals and will serve as the primary basis for positive identification. (Photo from the tropical Atlantic, courtesy of H. E. Winn.)

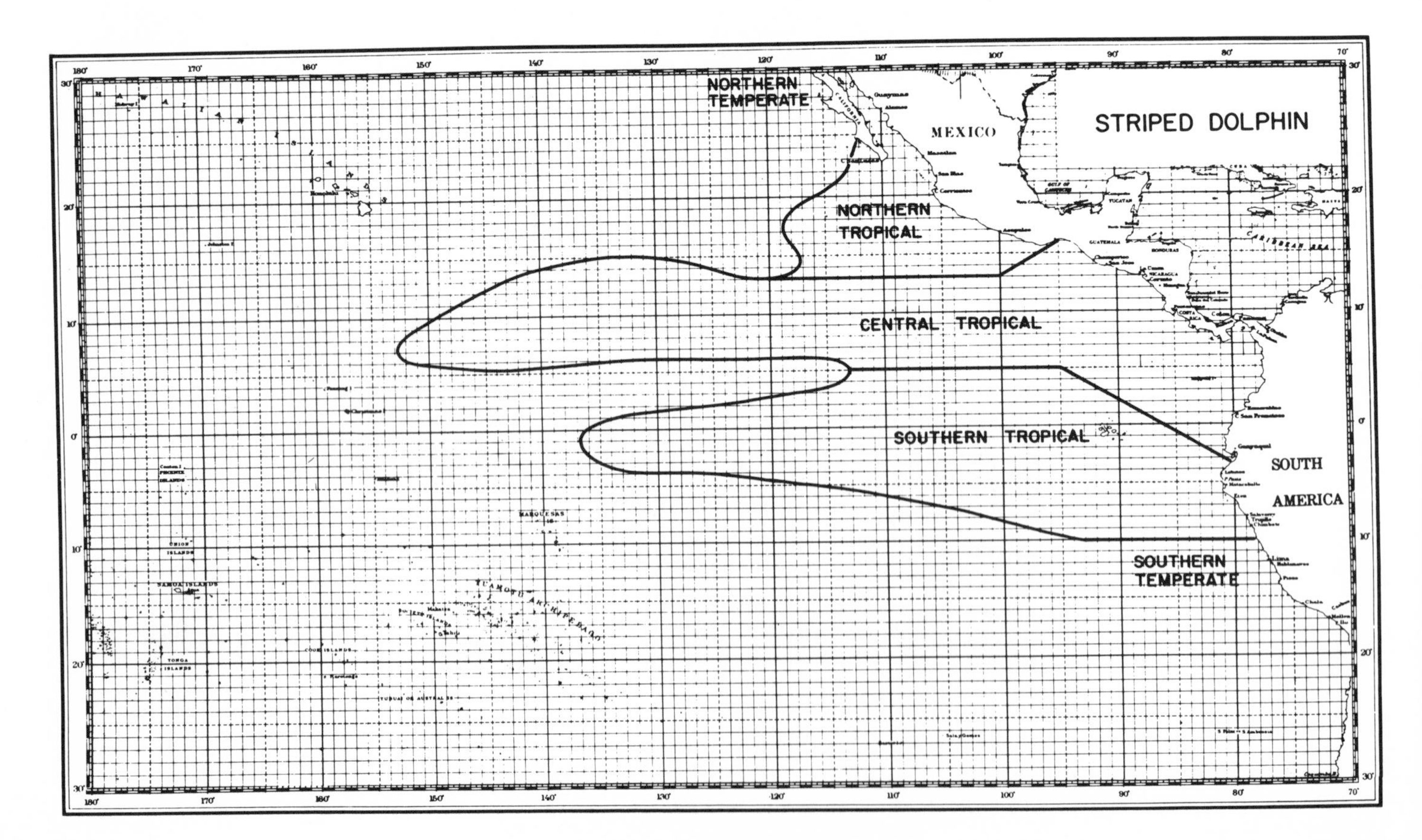
STRIPED DOLPHIN
NORTHERN TEMPERATE
NORTHERN TROPICAL
CENTRAL TROPICAL
SOUTHERN TROPICAL
SOUTHERN TEMPERATE
MEXICO
SOUTH AMERICA

Figure 199.—Dead striped dolphins from Japan. Note the distinctive black stripes from eye to flipper and from eye to anus and the shoulder blaze. (Photo by W. E. Schevill.)

of reproductive activity in winter, spring, and possibly late summer. The gestation period is thought to be about a year, and calves appear to remain dependent for more than a year after birth. The calving interval probably averages 3 years.

A seasonal north-south migration has been noted off Japan, but a comparable pattern has not been recognized off the Americas.

Striped dolphins are not known to ride bow waves in the eastern Pacific, although they are said to in some areas. They are capable of high leaps (6–7 m) and are sometimes given to amazing aerobatics. Backward cartwheels, upside-down "porpoising," and "roto-tailing" (furious tailspins accomplished while leaping from the water) are among their antics.

Striped dolphins feed on various mesopelagic fishes (especially myctophids), squids, and crustaceans. They sometimes associate with yellowfin tuna in the eastern tropical Pacific and are consequently killed in purse seines. Striped dolphins, common dolphins, and Fraser's dolphins are all called "whitebellies" by the tuna fishermen.

Distribution (see map, Fig. 200)

A few striped dolphins have been found stranded in British Columbia, Washington, Oregon, and southern California. However, they are certainly not common on the continental shelf of western North America. A sighting 1,000 km due west of Los Angeles suggests that they may be more abundant far offshore in warm temperate waters.

From about lat. 20°S to the equator, the striped dolphin is much more common, especially off the Mexican mainland and off southwestern Central America and northwestern South America. It occurs in the Gulf of California at least as far north as La Paz and Espiritu Santo Island. Low-density gaps in distribution indicate that several geographical stocks may exist in the eastern tropical Pacific, although definitive morphological comparisons have not yet been done.

Figure 200.—Distribution of striped dolphins in the eastern Pacific. Striped dolphins also occur in Polynesian waters. (Map courtesy of K. Raymond, NMFS.)

Can Be Confused With

The striped dolphin is most likely to be confused with the common dolphin (p. 160). The two may be distinguished by the following characteristics:

Striped Dolphin	Common Dolphin
Distinctive black lateral striping 1) from eye to anus (flank stripe), 2) from eye to flipper, and 3) the shoulder blaze.	Hourglass or crisscross pattern on sides resulting in downward pointing dark apex just below the dorsal fin; gray thoracic patch; distinct black stripe from eye to middle of lower jaw.

The striped dolphin can also be confused with Fraser's dolphin (p. 166), because both animals possess a dark flank stripe, and some Fraser's dolphins may also have a shoulder blaze. Before they were known to be part of the cetacean fauna off Durban, South Africa, Fraser's dolphins there were identified as striped dolphins. Fraser's dolphin, however, has a very short beak, is heavier in build and has a smaller, triangular dorsal fin. If a good look at the beak is not attained, identification should be tentative.

The shoulder blaze is the best characteristic for recognizing striped dolphins from the air. When a large herd of animals is encountered, it is usually possible to catch sight of this bold mark. The striping pattern on the sides can rarely be seen from the air. It is important to note that not all individuals have a vivid shoulder blaze, and this can make aerial identification extremely difficult.

Identification of Dead Specimens

Dead striped dolphins that are not badly decomposed are identifiable from their lateral striping pattern described above. If the color pattern has been lost, identification should be made on the basis of skull characters.

COMMON DOLPHIN

Delphinus delphis **Linnaeus, 1758**

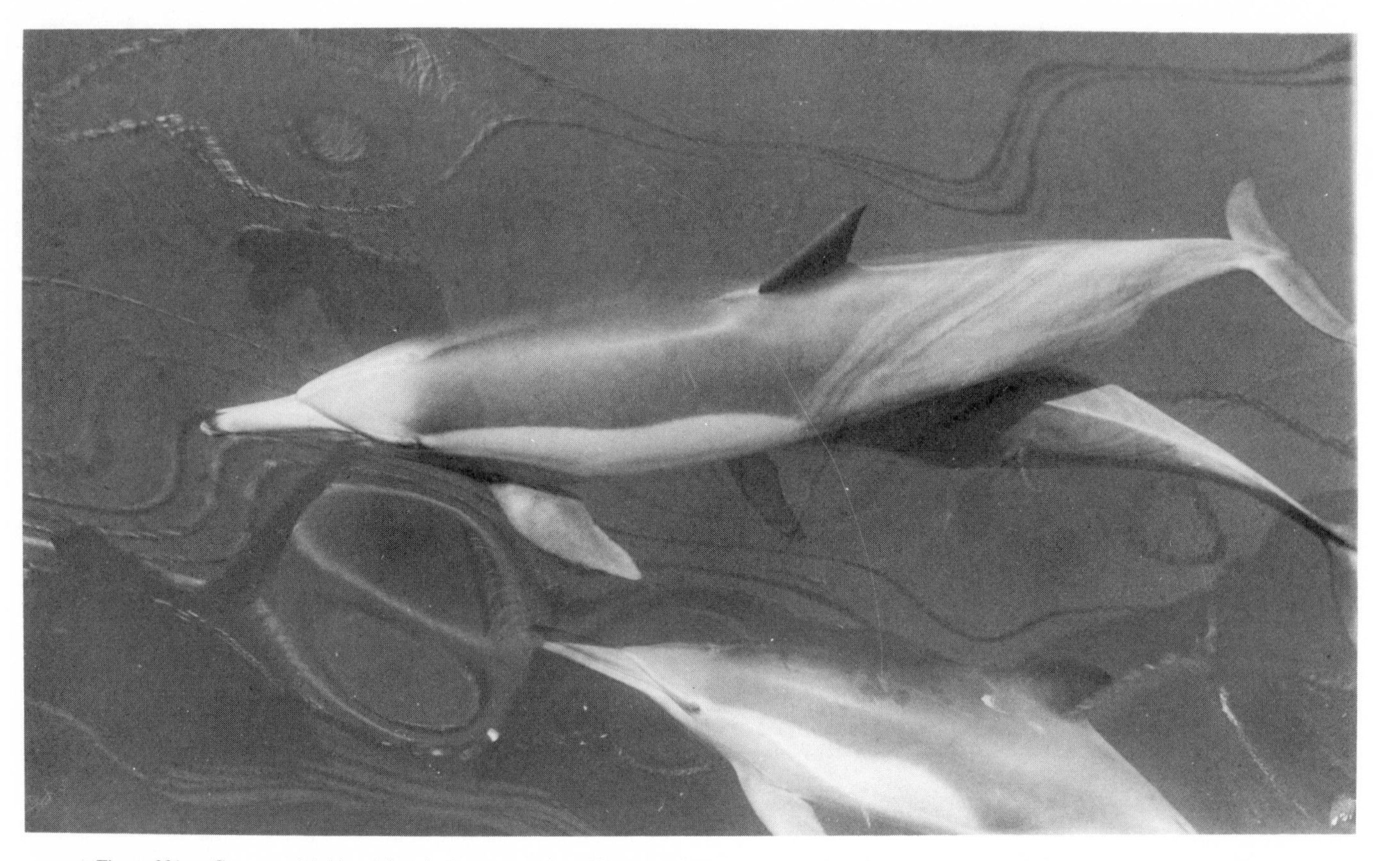

Figure 201 .—Common dolphins riding the bow wave of a sailing vessel 35 km south of Magdalena Bay, Baja California. (Photo by B. Würsig.)

Other Common Names

White-bellied porpoise, saddleback dolphin, crisscross dolphin, hourglass dolphin; delfín común (Latin America); tobi iruka (adults), ma iruka (juveniles) (Japanese); obyknovennyy or del'fin belobochka (Russian).

Description

Maximum body length is about 2.5 m, though most individuals are less than 2.3 m long. Males are slightly larger than females of the same age. Length at birth is about 80 cm.

The beak of this dolphin is well defined, and it is often black with a white tip. The dark eyepatch is confluent with a dark stripe (or pair of stripes) running to the corner of the mouth.

In body shape the common dolphin closely resembles the striped dolphin (p. 155). The tall dorsal fin situated near the middle of the back varies from nearly triangular to distinctly falcate, and it is pointed. It ranges from all black to light gray with a black border. A black stripe that attenuates anteriorly connects each flipper with the lower jaw.

The most distinctive external feature is the color pattern on the sides. The light ventral field extends up into the cape, yielding a four-part pattern defined by a crisscross. The back is black, the belly white, the overlap of cape by ventral field tan or yellowish tan, and the area behind the cape gray. These dolphins

Figure 202.—Perhaps the most certain clue to the identity of the common dolphin, when little of the body and back can be seen, is the deep "V" of dark coloration on each side below the dorsal fin. This "V" marks the confluence of the major elements of the crisscross pattern. Note the high but falcate dorsal fin, which often is dark on the border and lighter near the center. Some adult male common dolphins in the eastern tropical Pacific have erect triangular fins like that of the spinner dolphin. (Photo by S. Leatherwood.)

Figure 203.—These recognizably different animals are all common dolphins and are thought to belong to the single species *Delphinus delphis*. The long-beaked "Baja neritic form" (top) inhabits only waters inside the 100-fathom curve north of lat. 20°N and including the Gulf of California. Several smaller short-beaked races (bottom) occur from southern California south to warm temperate South American waters (see map, Fig. 208). The long-beaked form usually has a more muted color pattern than do the others. (Photos from northern Gulf of California by R. S. Wells [top left]; from Magdalena Bay, Baja California, by K. C. Balcomb [top right]; from Baja California by R. L. Pitman [bottom left] and W. F. Perrin [bottom right].)

Figure 204.—Their habit of assembling in large herds, which often travel with much jumping and splashing, makes some common dolphins visible from considerable distances. When stressed, herds bunch tightly together, like the group in this photo, and run. The light-colored thoracic patch, extending high onto the sides in front of the dorsal fin, clearly marks these animals as common dolphins. (Photo from off San Diego, Calif., by S. Leatherwood.)

can be positively identified even at a considerable distance from this unique pigmentation pattern. In southern California, at least, the color of the posterior flank blaze is often subdued, disrupting the crisscross effect.

Natural History Notes

Common dolphins are frequently encountered in herds of a thouand or more, and they are often very active, with many leaping clear of the water at a given time. Like Pacific white-sided dolphins, they are active and willing bow riders and may approach a vessel from a considerable distance. Once on the bow, they may ride for long periods.

The peak seasons for calving in the eastern North Pacific are spring and fall, after a gestation period of 10–11 months. Lactating and near-term pregnant females may segregate themselves from the rest of the population. Gestation and lactation have been tentatively reported as 10–11 months and 5–6 months. Females are capable of bearing calves in successive years, but usually give birth at intervals greater than a year.

Clear seasonal shifts in distribution are observed off southern California, where some common dolphins are present year-round with peaks of abundance in June, September–October, and January. The species appears to prefer water temperatures ranging from 10° to 28 °C.

In southern California waters, common dolphins move along major features of bottom relief, such as seamounts and escarpments, remaining generally outside the 183 m (100-fathom) curve. After sunset they dive through the vertically migrating deep scattering layer to prey on lanternfishes and squids. They are known to dive to depths of at least 280 m and to remain submerged for as long as 8 minutes. Their fall and winter staples off southern California are anchovies and squid; in spring and summer they consume more deep-sea smelt and lanternfishes. Hake are also eaten.

Distribution

The northernmost stranding record in the eastern North Pacific is from Victoria, British Columbia, but the common dolphin's occurrence that far north must be regarded as exceptional. The few sightings north of Point Conception have generally occurred in spring and summer when fingers of warm water extend northward.

The known range of the species is from lat. 36 °N to well south of the equator and offshore to long. 132 °W. There are known gaps between lat. 13 °N and 20 °N, and between lat. 27 °N and 32 °N, where common dolphins are absent or rare.

At least two forms inhabit eastern North Pacific waters. The smaller, short-beaked form occurs in three apparently separate populations—one north of lat. 32 °N off southern California, one between lat. 28 °N and 30 °N off Baja California, and one south of lat. 15 °N. A long-beaked form inhabits only waters inside the 100-fathom curve north of lat. 20 °N, including the Gulf of California. Where both forms are found in the same geographic range, they apparently do not mix.

The total number of common dolphins living off central and southern California and Baja California has been estimated conservatively to be about 10,000–15,000. Since the common dolphin is found in association with schools of tuna in the eastern tropical Pacific, it has experienced a significant annual mortality as a result of purse seining operations there.

Can Be Confused With

Common dolphins can easily be confused with striped dolphins (p. 155) because of their similarity in build and behavior. The larger striped dolphin has two distinctive black stripes on each side, both of which originate near the eye. One ends in the anal region, the other at the forward insertion of the flipper. There is a striking light shoulder blaze. The common dolphin also has two black stripes on each side, but one extends from the eye to the forehead crease and the other from the insertion of the flipper to the lower jaw. The crisscross flank pattern or the V-shaped saddle of the common dolphin is a reliable way to distinguish it from the striped dolphin.

From a distance, common dolphins may also be confused with spinner dolphins (p. 148) and Pacific white-sided dolphins (p. 168), both of which form large, frolicsome herds and ride bow waves. However, spinners in the Pacific usually have a tall erect triangular dorsal fin, a long narrow beak, and no striking coloration pattern on the sides. Pacific white-sided dolphins have a taller, more falcate dorsal fin and a much shorter beak than common dolphins. Also, they lack the crisscross pattern or saddle on the sides that is characteristic of common dolphins.

Identification of Dead Specimens

Common dolphins have 40-50 small, sharply pointed teeth in each side of the upper and lower jaws. This tooth count overlaps those of striped dolphins (43-50) and spinner dolphins (46-65).

Figure 205.—Aerial view of a herd of common dolphins in the Gulf of California (bottom). Small dolphins of many species assemble into large herds, but when they are seen up close (top), common dolphins can generally be distinguished from the others by the extent to which the light color of the thoracic patch extends up the sides. In all other species of "white bellies" found in the eastern North Pacific, the patch is more limited in the degree to which it intrudes into the dark dorsal field. (Photos by S. Leatherwood.)

Figure 206.—A group of common dolphins awaiting release from a tuna purse seine set off Costa Rica in the eastern tropical Pacific. Most of the common dolphin's distinctive features are apparent in one or more members of the group. (Photo by W. High, courtesy of NMFS.)

Figure 207 (below and opposite page, top).—A stranded short-beaked common dolphin. Note the highly distinctive crisscross or hourglass pattern, creating a tan or yellowish-tan thoracic patch (c); the essentially dark back, dorsal fin, and flukes, the more complicated pattern of the beak, and the extension of the brushed gray of the sides onto the top of the tail stock (b); and the light tip of the beak and the dark line from the center of the lower jaw to the flipper (a). In the Baja neritic common dolphin, the flipper stripe begins at the corner of the mouth. (Photos from northern California by L. Ullberg, courtesy of California Academy of Sciences.)

Figure 208.—Distribution of races of common dolphins in the eastern Pacific. (Map courtesy of K. Raymond, NMFS.)

FRASER'S DOLPHIN (T)

Lagenodelphis hosei **Fraser, 1956**

Other Common Names

Fraser's porpoise, Sarawak dolphin, Bornean dolphin (not currently in use), whitebelly (applied by fishermen to this species and to *Delphinus delphis* and *Stenella coeruleoalba*); Sarawaku iruka (Japanese); saravakskiy or del'fin Frasera (Russian).

Description

Adults are about 2.5 m long, and males probably are somewhat larger than females. Length at birth is about 1 m.

Fraser's dolphin is a robust animal with a very short beak and proportionately small dorsal fin and flippers. The slender dorsal fin is usually falcate to a slight degree, although the rear margin can be vertical or even convex in some individuals. The flippers are pointed.

The color pattern is complex. The back is bluish gray, the undersides pinkish white. There is a wide flank stripe that varies in definition. The dark stripe is bordered above and below by parallel cream-white stripes. The appendages and the upper side of the beak are dark.

Natural History Notes

This dolphin was named in 1956 and only very recently has been observed and recognized at sea. Herds numbering 100 to 1,000 have been reported. These dolphins are sometimes found among or near schools of spotted dolphins, false killer whales, sperm whales, striped dolphins, and spinner dolphins.

Fraser's dolphins are probably deep divers; they feed on deep-living fish, squid, and crustaceans. They are very fast swimmers and often throw up spray from their heads as they break the surface to breathe. They leap clear of the water but are not as acrobatic as some other pelagic dolphins. In the Pacific, they are generally shy and hard to approach.

Distribution

Fraser's dolphin is poorly known but pantropical; its range in the eastern Pacific probably coincides roughly with that of the spinner dolphin (p. 148). It has not yet been recorded from Polynesia but can be expected to occur there.

Can Be Confused With

Because of its lateral striping pattern and offshore tropical distribution, this dolphin is most likely to be confused with the striped dolphin (p. 155). The two species can be distinguished at sea by the following characteristics:

Fraser's Dolphin	Striped Dolphin
Coloration	
Single, broad, dark flank stripe from beak and eye to area of anus; faint stripe from lower jaw to flipper. Shoulder blaze may be present.	Narrow black stripes, shoulder blaze usually present.
Beak	
Extremely short and almost unnoticeable.	Long.
Body Shape	
Robust, particularly ahead of the dorsal fin.	Slender.
Flippers	
Small, dark, and originating in light color of sides.	Long, sometimes lighter on upper surface.
Dorsal Fin	
Small, slender, usually weakly falcate, and usually pointed.	Taller, longer at base, and falcate.

Many of the same features can be used to distinguish the common dolphin (p. 160) from Fraser's dolphin. In addition, the former's crisscross lateral pattern makes it easy to recognize. Although the range of Fraser's dolphin is unlikely to overlap that of the similarly shaped and strikingly patterned Pacific white-sided dolphin, the two dolphins are easily separable on the basis of dorsal fin size and shape; that of the white-sided dolphin is very large and strongly falcate (see p. 169).

Identification of Dead Specimens

A dead Fraser's dolphin can be identified by its coloration, short but well-defined beak, very small appendages, and robust form. Fraser's dolphin has 34–44 teeth in each row of the upper and lower jaws.

Figure 209.—Even when none of the coloration is clearly visible, Fraser's dolphins are readily identifiable by the short beak, robust body, and very small appendages. (Photo from near the Phoenix Islands by K. C. Balcomb.)

Figure 210.—Running Fraser's dolphins. This dolphin, which appears limited in distribution to a rather narrow belt of equatorial water, is identifiable within its range by the short beak, the dark flank stripe (variable in degree of expression) and the small appendages. Fraser's dolphins reach at least 2.5 m in length and occur in herds of 500 or more, sometimes mixed with spinner and spotted dolphins. When frightened they bunch tightly and begin dramatic runs with much surface commotion. They are most likely to be confused with the longer beaked, less robust striped dolphin. Note the pronounced variation in expression of the flank stripe (lighter in juveniles and females). **(Photos from lat. 00°37′S, long. 136°52′W by G. L. Friedrichsen [top]; from lat. 4°06′S, long. 90°42′W by P. L. Ritchie [middle]; from lat. 00°22′N, long. 95°45′W by P. L. Ritchie [bottom]; all courtesy of NMFS.)**

Figure 211.—The external appearance of Fraser's dolphin was unknown until 1971, when several were captured in a tuna seine. The species has since been reported from all tropical seas. (Photos by J. La Grange, courtesy of NMFS.)

Figure 212.—A very young Fraser's dolphin (captured in a purse seine). Note the light density and unclear definition of the flank stripe of this and the specimen in Figure 211 (an immature male) as compared to the bolder stripes of some of the animals in Figure 210. In its boldest expression, this stripe widens at the face to form a "bandit-mask." (Photo by L. Ford, courtesy of NMFS.)

PACIFIC WHITE-SIDED DOLPHIN (T)

Lagenorhynchus obliquidens **Gill, 1865**

Other Common Names

Lag, white-striped dolphin (see also p. 155), hookfin porpoise; delfín lagenorringo (Latin America); kama iruka (Japanese); tikhookaenskiy belobokiy del'fin (Russian).

Description

The Pacific white-sided dolphin reaches lengths of at least 2.3 m. Large individuals may weigh close to 150 kg. Sexual maturity is reached by males at 1.7–1.8 m and by females at 1.8–1.9 m. Length at birth is about 80–95 cm.

The head tapers continuously and smoothly and has only a very abbreviated beak.

The dorsal fin is tall and strongly recurved, with a long base. It is situated near the middle of the back. Because of its extremely falcate dorsal fin, this dolphin is referred to by some Pacific fishermen as the "hookfin porpoise." The flukes have a concave trailing edge and a median notch. The flippers are long and tapered to a blunt tip.

The Pacific white-sided dolphin's color pattern is complex but usually distinctive. The back is black, the sides light gray, and the belly white. The black of the back is interrupted on each side of the dorsal fin by a white or light gray stripe, which begins in the light color of the forehead and face, curves upward over the top of the head, continues along the back to the area of the dorsal fin, and then widens and curves toward the anus, forming a prominent light gray patch on the flank. These light "suspenders" on the back are clearly visible when animals ride the bow wave, permitting easy identification. The short beak is dark, and

Figure 213.—A group of Pacific white-sided dolphins running beside a fishing vessel off northern California. Even from this distance the dolphins are easy to identify by the prominent dorsal fin, dark on front, light gray on the back. When they are running in this manner Pacific white-sided dolphins may create a "rooster tail" of spray, similar to that produced by the fast-swimming Dall's porpoise. But the dorsal fin alone, the character which prompted the fisherman's nickname "hook-finned porpoise," clearly distinguishes this dolphin from the Dall's porpoise and all other small cetaceans in the eastern North Pacific. (Photo from lat. 41°45′N, long. 134°10′W by W. C. Flerx, courtesy of NMFS.)

Figure 214.—Side views of fast-swimming Pacific white-sided dolphins near San Clemente Island (left) and in Monterey Bay (right), Calif. Even when very little of the animal can be seen, as in these two photographs, Pacific white-sided dolphins are positively identifiable by the bicolored, hooked dorsal fin. (Photos by G. E. Lingle [left]; G. A. Antonelis [right].)

a narrow stripe between the corner of the mouth and the flipper is continuous with the dark pigmentation of the lips. A light gray zone on each side begins below the dorsal fin and extends forward, encompassing much of the forehead. A dark line begins in the axilla and connects the gray flippers with the dark area on the flank. The dorsal fin is bicolored—dark on the forward third and light gray on the rear two-thirds. The flukes are dark.

Some variations have been observed in the color pattern, particularly of more northerly groups, manifested in the complexity of the lateral pattern and the bridle. The extent of this variability and its meaning in separating local forms is unknown.

Natural History Notes

Pacific white-sided dolphins are extremely gregarious, occurring in herds of up to several thousand, although groups of less than 200 are more common. These dolphins are frequently found in the company of other dolphins (especially common dolphins) as well as seabirds and California sea lions. On several occasions they have been seen forcing common dolphins to abandon the preferred riding position on the bow of a moving vessel.

Most calving apparently takes place in summer, but little else is known with certainty about the reproductive cycle.

Although resident in some areas, Pacific white-sided dolphins appear to shift seasonally northward and southward, or in some cases inshore and offshore, according to changes in water temperature. The species is basically a temperate-region one, found north of the tropics and south of the colder waters influenced by arctic currents. In some places these animals approach shore closely, particularly at the coastal heads of deep submarine canyons, but they can be found anywhere at or inside the edge of the continental shelf.

Figure 215.—A Pacific white-sided dolphin on the bow of a research vessel off Baja California. Even from this perspective, the animal is easy to identify. Note the small but distinct beak and the striking markings, dominated from this perspective by the ''suspender'' markings from behind the head onto the side above the anus. (Photo by R. L. Pitman, courtesy of NMFS.)

Figure 216.—Pacific white-sided dolphins frequently jump well clear of the water. When they do so, the striking markings (highlighted by the complex brush strokes of light on dark), the distinctive dorsal fin, and the short but distinct beak are ready clues to their identity. Leaping, sometimes somersaulting, and often charging to the bow of a vessel to ride in its pressure wave, these are frolicsome dolphins. (Photo from off Santa Rosa Island, Calif., by K. C. Balcomb.)

White-sided dolphins are vigorous swimmers and often leap clear of the water. Jumping animals often land on their sides or belly, hitting the water with a resounding smack that can be heard at a great distance. They sometimes make complete aerial somersaults.

Pacific white-sided dolphins prey on a wide variety of fishes and squids. Small numbers have been maintained in captivity, where they become adept performers. One individual survived in captivity for just over 10 years.

Figure 217.—Pacific white-sided dolphins, circling the underwater viewing bubble on the RV *Sea See* off Catalina Island, Calif., (top) and in the tank at Marineland of California (right). They seem extremely curious about boats, often approaching them even when they are idling or dead in the water. (Photos courtesy of NOSC.)

Figure 218.—Pacific white-sided dolphins are often seen in mixed groups with common dolphins (upper left and lower background). (Photo from underwater viewing chamber of RV *Sea See* by W. E. Evans.)

Distribution

Pacific white-sided dolphins have been reported as far north as Amchitka Island in the Aleutians, and they are known to be present throughout the Gulf of Alaska. Records from the northern portion of the Gulf (to Kodiak Island) appear to be seasonal and could be associated with periods of exceptional warming there. Large groups (over 200) seem to be the rule rather than the exception in the Gulf of Alaska during summer.

The species' range extends southward at least to the southern tip of Baja California, thence northward in the Gulf to at least Cabo Pulmo. Small numbers can be found from Monterey, Calif., south to Gordo Bank off Baja California at any time of year. The year-round stocks near Cedros Island, Natividad

Figure 219.—A Pacific white-sided dolphin stranded at La Jolla, Calif. Although emaciated, this animal illustrates the dolphin's distinctive features, by which even badly decomposed specimens can be positively identified—the short but distinct beak and the tall strongly falcate dorsal fin. White-sided dolphins of the Pacific usually have 23–32 teeth in each upper jaw and 24–31 in each lower jaw. (Photo by W. F. Perrin, courtesy of NMFS.)

Island, and several of the California Channel Islands are augmented by an influx of animals in the period October through February. Apparently these dolphins are retreating southward and inshore as the water cools. By the end of May a marked decrease in abundance occurs off southern California, presumably because the animals disperse west and northward for the summer. This pattern is not evident in years when unseasonably warm water temperatures persist north of Monterey.

Can Be Confused With

Two species found within the range of the Pacific white-sided dolphin may cause confusion. The prominent, sickle-shaped dorsal fin slicing through the water can cause a splash resembling the "rooster tail" of spray characteristic of surfacing Dall's porpoises (p. 200). The surface disturbance caused by a large herd of frolicking "lags" can be mistaken at a great distance for an active herd of common dolphins (p. 160). Key differences among the three species are tabularized below:

Pacific White-Sided Dolphin	Common Dolphin	Dall's Porpoise
	Dorsal Fin	
Very tall; strongly falcate; bicolored with dark front two-thirds and lighter rear third.	Prominent and erect; only slightly falcate; dark, often with a lightened zone in the middle.	Relatively low; triangular; bicolored, with white upper half, black lower half.
	Head	
Conical; short, indistinct but well-demarcated beak that is darkly pigmented.	Moderately long, well-demarcated beak; lips dark; white tip on beak.	Disproportionately small head; no beak; all black.
	Body Color	
Black dorsally and white ventrally; white or light gray "suspenders"; light gray zone on side extending onto rostrum.	Characteristic dark dorsal saddle; white belly, hourglass or crisscross effect on sides, with tan tinge.	Black and white; large white patch on each side; flukes with white rear border.
	Behavior	
Acrobatic in air, splashes when breaking surface to breathe.	Gregarious and frolicsome; often leaps clear of water.	Does not leap clear of water; splashes characteristically when surfacing.
	Range	
Temperate region north of southern Baja California; throughout Gulf of Alaska.	Warm water; uncommon north of Point Conception.	Cold waters from southern Bering Sea to California; seasonally south to Baja California.

From the air, Pacific white-sided dolphins appear chunky, like the Dall's porpoise, and obviously lack a distinct beak. The most distinctive features of the otherwise dark body are the white belly and suspender marks. When seen in profile the very large dorsal fin is unmistakable.

Identification of Dead Specimens

Dead Pacific white-sided dolphins should be easy to recognize by the distinctive features mentioned above. In addition, the upper jaw has 23-32 pairs of teeth; the lower jaw, 24-31. This is considerably fewer than in the common dolphin (40-50 pairs per jaw) but overlaps the numbers in the Dall's porpoise (19-28/20-28). The latter's teeth are shaped differently, however; they are flattened at the crown rather than pointed.

BOTTLENOSE DOLPHIN (T)

Tursiops truncatus **(Montagu, 1821)**

Other Common Names

Bottlenosed dolphin or porpoise, black porpoise (tuna fishermen), gray porpoise, common porpoise; delfín naríz de botella (Latin America); taiseiyo bandō iruka (Japanese); afalina (Russian).

Description

Bottlenose dolphins in the Pacific reach lengths of 3-4 m. Males are generally larger than females of the same age. At birth these dolphins are about 1-1.3 m long.

Figure 220.—Bottlenose dolphins at Clipperton Island (top) and at lat. 12°30′N, long. 89°44′W (bottom). Oceanic islands often have small resident populations that come out to greet passing ships. Note the short, thick beak, clearly demarcated from the melon, and the tall falcate dorsal fin. Although they appear in these photos to be almost uniformly dark, bottlenose dolphins have complex color patterns. (Photos by R. L. Pitman [top] and K. D. Sexton [bottom], courtesy of NMFS.)

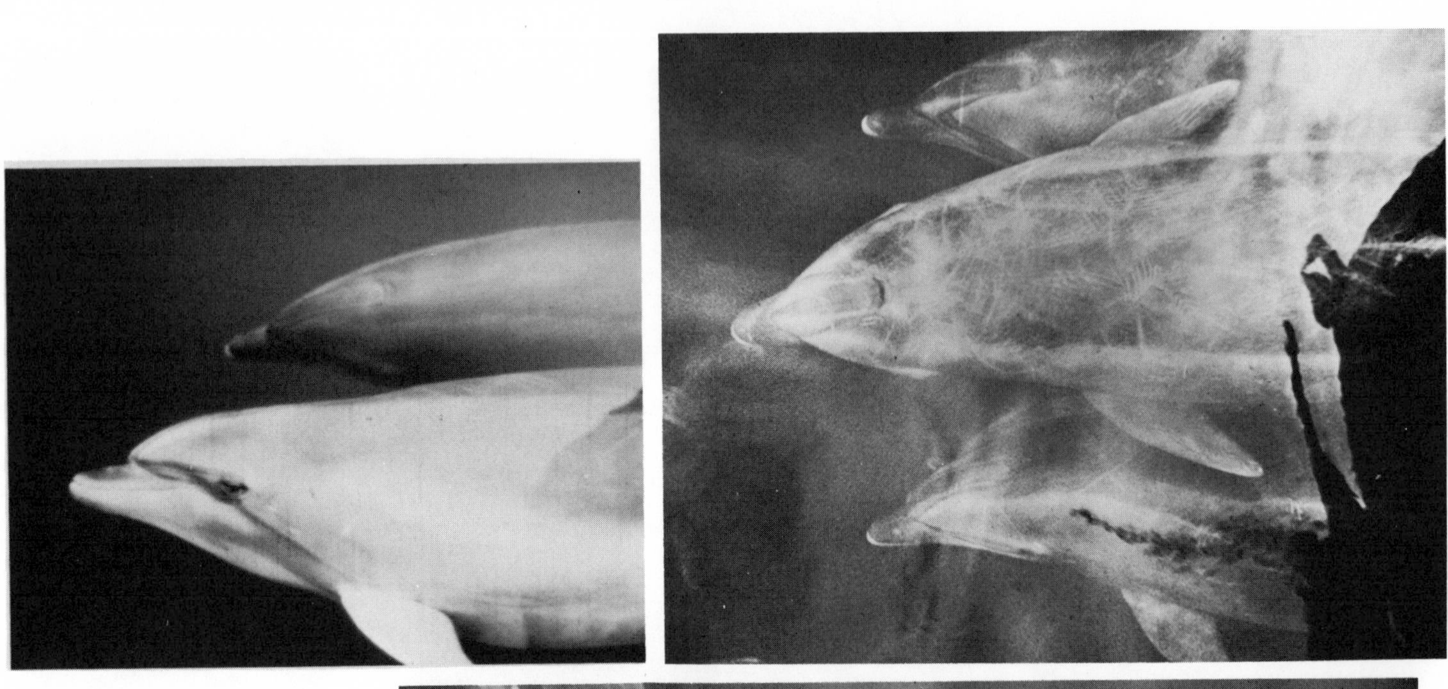

Figure 221.—Throughout their range, bottlenose dolphins are active bow riders, sometimes coming from considerable distances to catch a ride and often turning on their sides (top left) once in the wave. In the other two photos, the dorsal cape can be seen. Extensive tooth rakings can be seen on one of the animals in the top right photo. In the lateral photo, note the flipper stripe to the corner of the mouth. There are clearly two forms of bottlenose dolphins in the eastern North Pacific, though at present they are only tentatively separable by differences in skull characters and not by external field marks. (Photos from off the Galapagos, Ecuador, by G. M. Wellington [top left]; the Gulf of Guayaquil, Ecuador, by R. Olson, courtesy of NMFS [top right]; off Acapulco, Mexico, by C. W. Oliver courtesy of NMFS [bottom].)

The physical appearance of this dolphin is familiar to nearly everyone, because most performing dolphins in oceanaria are bottlenoses (although these are usually the Atlantic variety). The well-defined beak ranges from relatively short (less than 16 cm long) and stubby to nearly nonexistent. The body is robust.

The prominent dorsal fin is centrally positioned on the back, strongly falcate and erect, and pointed. The flippers are moderate in size and taper to a point. The flukes are notched and have a smooth, concave rear margin.

There is a great deal of variety in coloration among bottlenose dolphins in the eastern North Pacific. Some are nearly black all over, while others have a gray body that lightens gradually toward the sides and belly. Some forms have a well-defined dark cape set off from the light gray sides and an almost white belly.

There are two forms of bottlenose dolphin postulated for the North Pacific—a coastal form and an offshore form—though there currently are no reliable means for differentiating them.

Natural History Notes

The coastal form of bottlenose dolphin is rarely seen in groups of more than 50 animals, while the offshore variety is sometimes found in herds numbering several hundred. Bottlenose dolphins are frequently found near herds of pilot whales, and they sometimes appear to associate with migrating gray whales, riding their pressure waves as if they were the bow waves of small vessels. This behavior may be the natural precursor of bow riding. In Hawaii, during the winter, they are often similarly associated with humpback whales.

The reproductive characteristics of bottlenose dolphins in the Pacific have mostly been inferred from what is known about the Atlantic bottlenoses, which mature at lengths of 2.2-2.4 m for females and 2.5-2.6 m for males. There appear to be two peaks of reproductive activity—one in spring and another in fall. Gestation lasts about a year; lactation, 12-18 months.

Movements of some *Tursiops* populations have been shown to be local, the animals being confined to limited home ranges. Seasonal movements of the stocks off western North and Central America have not been well mapped, but may not be very extensive. Some offshore islands (e.g., Clipperton and Galapagos) appear to have their own local populations.

Bottlenose dolphins are versatile feeders, eating a wide variety of fishes, crustaceans, and cephalopods. They are attracted to a variety of fishing activities, feeding behind shrimp boats and near many kinds of nets. In some areas they have incurred the wrath of fishermen because of their bold competition with them for hooked or netted fish.

The behavior of bottlenose dolphins often appears clownish and acrobatic. They come readily to the bow of a vessel underway, playfully veering in and out of its path, sometimes falling back to frolic in the stern wake. While on the bow they often turn on their sides and peer searchingly at observers aboard the vessel, occasionally spinning around their longitudinal axis while doing so. They are expert body surfers. It is not unusual for wild bottlenose dolphins to jump several meters clear of the water, a feat on which oceanaria have capitalized.

Figure 222.—Although many dolphins leap clear of the water, none appears to do so from sheer exuberance more frequently than does the bottlenose dolphin. Their leaps may take many forms, as with the two animals which repeatedly jumped over one another, leap-frog style (top), the high acrobatic bursts in a stern wake (bottom left), and the slow-motion jump reminiscent of those seen in captive animal shows (bottom right). (Photos from lat. 12°26′N, long. 89°44′W by R. L. Pitman, courtesy NMFS [top]; from the eastern tropical Pacific by K. Sexton, courtesy NMFS [bottom left]; from near the Midriff Islands, Gulf of California, by R. Storro-Patterson [bottom right].)

Figure 223.—A pair of bottlenose dolphins just entering (top) and bodysurfing in the curl (bottom) of a wave off La Jolla, Calif. Though most dolphins have been reported to ride ground swells at sea and many are known to ride pressure waves created by vessels and the heads of large whales, the only dolphin known to surf routinely is the bottlenose. Along much of their coastal range, bottlenose dolphins can be seen frolicking in the waves, leaping dramatically out of them just before they break. (Photos by W. F. Perrin.)

Captive bottlenose dolphins have lived for as long as 40 years. In the wild, predation by killer whales and sharks is not known to be a major mortality factor but probably occurs occasionally.

Distribution

The neritic (coastal) form of the bottlenose dolphin is continuously distributed from the southern border of Los Angeles County south to the tropics, including the entire Gulf of California and Baja California; it frequents harbors, bays, lagoons, estuaries, and other shallow coastal regions.

The offshore form ranges farther from the mainland, around the islands of California and Baja California, at least as far north as Point Conception and in the open sea out to and along the 183 m (100-fathom) curve. It is also found throughout the pelagic zone in the eastern tropical Pacific and in waters around all the Hawaiian Islands, including the Leeward Chain.

Bottlenose dolphins probably have a more extensive distribution than any other small cetacean in the temperate to tropical eastern North Pacific, and they can be considered very abundant in the aggregate.

Can Be Confused With

Bottlenose dolphins can be confused at sea with several other dolphins, including Risso's dolphin (p. 129) at a distance, the rough-toothed dolphin (p. 178), especially in offshore subtropical and tropical areas, and young spotted dolphins (p. 141), south of lat. 30°N. The first of these can best be distinguished from the bottlenose by its lack of a prominent beak and its white and extensively scarred skin. The distinguishing features of the bottlenose dolphin, rough-toothed dolphin, and spotted dolphin are tabularized below:

Bottlenose Dolphin	Rough-Toothed Dolphin	Spotted Dolphin
	Maximum Size	
2.4-4 m	At least 2.4 m	Up to 2.5 m

Figure 224.—Bottlenose dolphins have 20-26 teeth in each side of the upper jaw and 18-24 in each side of the lower jaw. The teeth are sharply pointed in young animals but may wear substantially as the animal ages. (Photo by G. E. Lingle, courtesy of NOSC.)

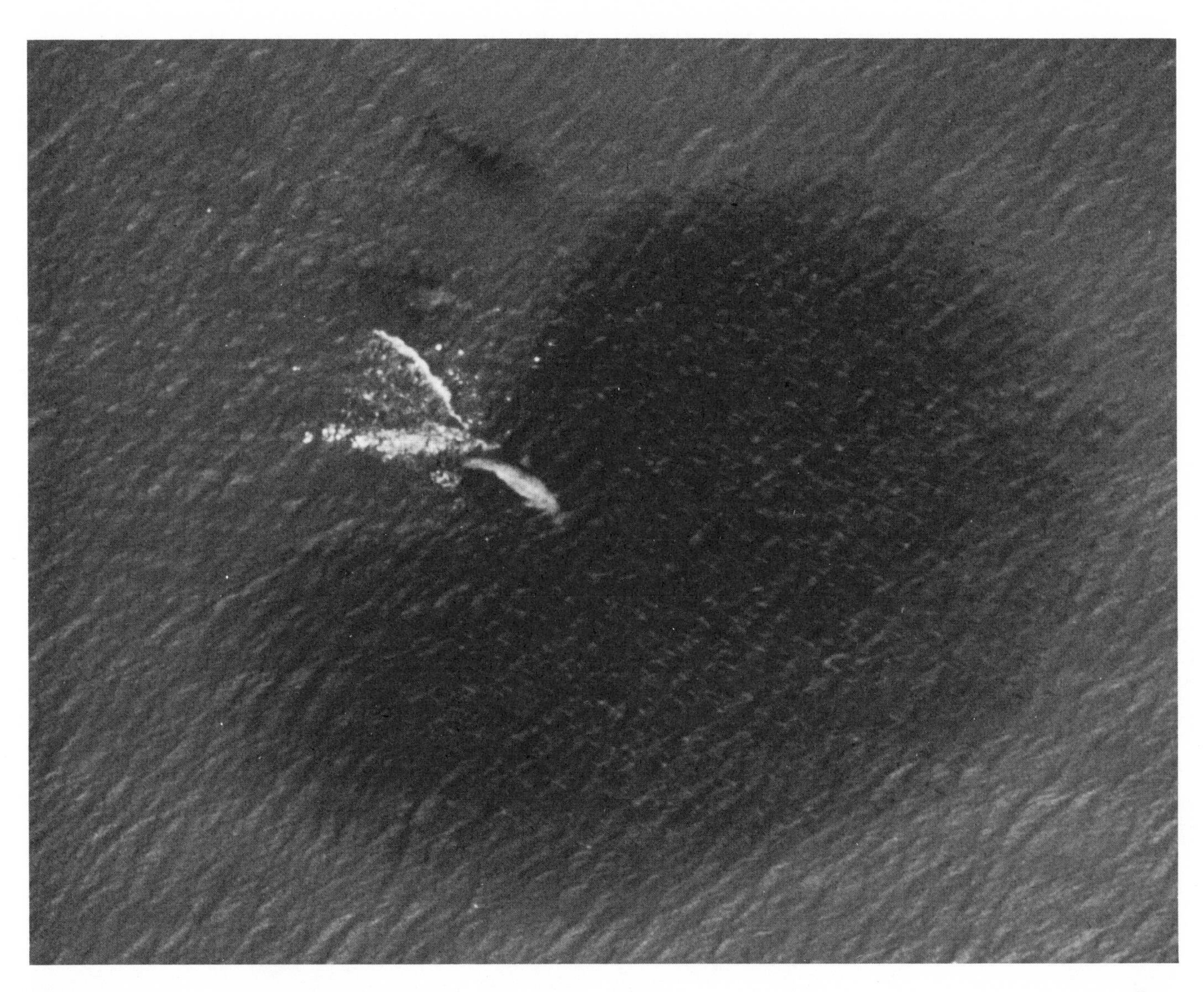

Figure 225.—A bottlenose dolphin feeding on mullet off Cat Island, Miss. Bottlenose dolphins are easy to identify from the air when they are seen clearly under good light conditions. However, since many dolphins may appear drab and colorless under low light conditions, aerial observers are cautioned against simply classifying groups of gray animals as bottlenose dolphins. Note the individual on its side. Bottlenose dolphins frequently feed on their sides or backs, possibly to improve returns from echolocation signals in the shallow environment. (Photo by S. Leatherwood.)

	Body Coloration	
Gray to black (old females may have spots on belly); dark dorsal cape, with gradual lightening on sides and belly in most cases.	Dark gray, almost purplish with yellow spots; lighter on belly.	Dark gray dorsal cape with lighter zones on flanks and belly; adults often heavily spotted but young unspotted.
	Head and Beak	
Head robust; beak relatively short but defined by a crease; usually all gray; some older individuals have white-tipped beaks and/or white lips.	Long and slender; beak not clearly demarcated from forehead; lower jaw and lips speckled white.	Head relatively slender; beak moderately long; well demarcated from forehead by transverse crease.

Bottlenose dolphins can be difficult to identify positively when seen from the air. The color pattern is so generalized and nondescriptive that one is often uncertain of whether lack of pattern and color in an animal seen is real or an artifact of lighting conditions. The best clues are the short stubby beak, the broad head and body, and the falcate dorsal fin. In coastal haunts in the tropics one must be particularly wary of confusing bottlenose dolphins and coastal spotted dolphins.

Identification of Dead Specimens

In addition to the characteristics mentioned above, dead bottlenose dolphins can be distinguished from spotters by their relatively low tooth count: 20–26 in each upper jaw and 18–24 in each lower jaw. The rough-toothed dolphin has close to the same number of teeth as the bottlenose but can readily be distinguished on close examination by the absence of a crease dividing the beak from the forehead and by its relatively long and slender beak.

ROUGH-TOOTHED DOLPHIN (T)

Steno bredanensis **(G. Cuvier in Lesson, 1828)**

Other Common Names

Black porpoise (applied by fishermen to this species and to bottlenose dolphins) and "steno"; delfín de pico largo (Latin America); shiwaha iruka (Japanese); grebnezubyy del'fin (Russian).

Description

Rough-toothed dolphins have not been well studied, but they are known to reach lengths of at least 2.4 m in this area, almost 2.8 m elsewhere.

The most distinctive external feature is the beak, which is long and slender and grades into the melon with no sharp demarcation. It may be white or pinkish white along both sides, including one or both lips and the tip of the beak. Because the forehead and sides of the head slope smoothly onto the rostrum, the entire head appears very long and nearly conical when viewed from above or from the side. The eyes are unusually large.

The high dorsal fin is variable in shape but usually falcate. It has a long base. The flippers are large and taper to a blunt point.

Coloration is quite variable. The back is often dark gray to

Figure 226.—The highly distinctive head of a rough-toothed dolphin, showing the white lips and the lack of a clear demarcation between the beak and the melon (hence the nickname "slopehead"). (Photos from Sea Life Park, Hawaii, by K. C. Balcomb [top]; S. Leatherwood [bottom].)

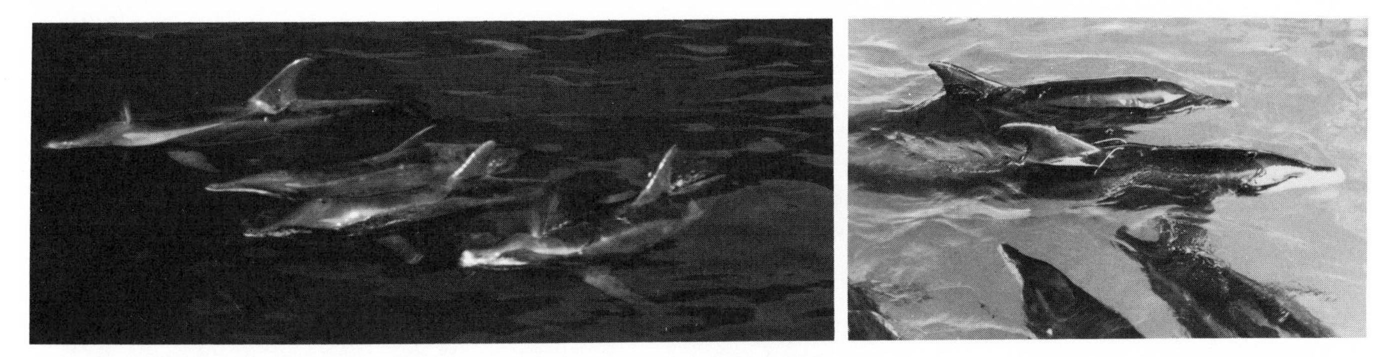

Figure 227.—Captive rough-toothed dolphins. Note the prominent falcate dorsal fin, the smoothly tapering head (appearing cone-shaped in dorsal and lateral views), and the white coloration on the lips and the beak tip. Rough-toothed dolphins are present, albeit in relatively low densities, throughout the eastern tropical Pacific, with extralimital records as far north as Marin County, Calif. (Photos courtesy of Japanese Whales Research Institute.)

Figure 228.—A tightly packed group of rough-toothed dolphins approaching a research vessel at approximately lat. 04°30′N, long. 91°30′W in February 1979. As they skim along the surface, a characteristic swimming pattern for the species, the pink/white lips and lower jaws are clearly visible (bottom). (Photos by R. L. Pitman, courtesy of NMFS.)

dark purplish gray, and there may be yellowish or pinkish white blotches on the sides and belly. The flippers are dark and the belly is white. Some animals are scarred with numerous white streaks and oval scars. The lips are often white, a feature which appears age related.

Natural History Notes

Herds of up to 50 have been reported, but smaller groups of 10–20 seem more usual. They have most often been encountered rafting at the surface. When approached by a vessel, these dolphins sometimes ride the bow wave, but more often simply "squirt" out of the way. They occasionally leap half-heartedly out of the water. Rough-toothed dolphins are often mixed in herds of other species, such as pilot whales, bottlenose dolphins, spotted dolphins, and spinner dolphins. They have a remarkable affinity for flotsam and are commonly associated with floating logs in the eastern tropical Pacific.

Rough-toothed dolphins are known to prey on pelagic fishes and squid, but very little is known about their food habits or reproductive biology. There was a mass stranding in Maui, Hawaii.

These animals have been successfully maintained and trained at Sea Life Park in Hawaii and at oceanaria in Japan. A female at Sea Life Park bred with a bottlenose dolphin and produced an apparently healthy hybrid offspring that lived for almost 5 years.

Distribution

Before American tuna fishermen began to catch and identify this species in purse seines set in the eastern tropical Pacific, only two records existed for the eastern Pacific—a weathered skull had washed ashore in Marin County, Calif., and some hard parts of a specimen had been recovered from the Galapagos. Although a few more specimens have been collected on California beaches, it still is assumed that these records represent extralimital occurrences and that rough-toothed dolphins do not

Figure 229.—Two views of rough-toothed dolphins on the bow of a research vessel at approximately lat. 15°30′N, long. 99°45′W (top) and approximately lat. 14°49′N, long. 97°42′W (bottom). Together, these photos clearly illustrate the distinctive head shape, the large flippers, the long, almost cone-shaped, head, and the extremely narrow cape. (Photos by R. L. Pitman, courtesy of NMFS.)

Figure 230.—When one is fortunate enough to have a clear view of them from the air, rough-toothed dolphins can be positively identified. Although larger than any of the spinners, they appear spinnerlike, i.e., slim in dorsal aspect. The primary clues distinguishing them from spinners and others are the elongated cone-shaped appearance of the front part of the body and the very slim cape. Even such small-scale features as the partially to all-white lips are sometimes visible from the air. (Photo by Peter Herring, February 1968.)

Figure 231.—A rough-toothed dolphin nursing her newborn calf, a hybrid resulting from her mating with a male bottlenose dolphin. The bottom photo shows the hybrid as a yearling, in the company of a bottlenose dolphin. Note that the hybrid has a hint of a crease separating the rostrum from the melon, a state clearly intermediate between the cone-shaped head of the mother and the short beak and well-defined melon of the bottlenose dolphin. (Photos courtesy of Sea Life Park, Hawaii [top]; by S. Leatherwood [bottom].)

regularly inhabit nearshore waters of the western United States. It is now well established, however, that rough-toothed dolphins are present, albeit in relatively low densities, throughout the eastern tropical Pacific. They also occur in Polynesian waters and around Hawaii. Sea surface temperatures, when recorded, have always been above 25 °C when these dolphins were encountered. *Steno bredanensis* seems quite clearly to be a warmwater pelagic species.

Can Be Confused With

In the offshore waters where they live, rough-toothed dolphins are most likely to be confused with bottlenose dolphins (p. 173), spotted dolphins (p. 141), and spinner dolphins (p. 148). All three have a distinct transverse crease, or depression, that demarcates the beak from the forehead. In addition, the bottlenose dolphin has a much shorter, stubbier beak and does not have the speckled or blotchy appearance around the beak and on the sides and belly that is characteristic of the rough-toothed dolphin. The spotted dolphin has a somewhat shorter, more massive beak and, in adults at least, many light spots on the dark back and sides. The spinner dolphin has a tall, erect, nearly triangular dorsal fin and a fairly even coloration pattern—gray on the back and sides, white on the undersides. See Tables (p. 176, 177) for further comparison with the bottlenose and spotted dolphins.

Even at some distance, the blotched coloration of the sides and the white coloration of the lips of rough-toothed dolphins may be visible. If closer examination is possible, the distinctive shape and coloration of the beak should make positive identification possible. The long-based dorsal fin may contribute to an identification as well.

With a good vertical view one can identify rough-toothed dolphins from the air. The principal cues are the rather slim body, almost spinnerlike in appearance, and the dark narrow cape, which barely covers the midline on the tail stock, broadens briefly at the dorsal fin, and then constricts to a narrow zone from the front of the dorsal fin to the head. Because of the shape of the beak (no apex to the melon) the body in front of the flippers appears as a long cone; under good light conditions white is visible on the mouth of some, usually larger, animals.

Identification of Dead Specimens

In addition to the characteristics listed above for distinguishing living animals, dead rough-toothed dolphins can be identified by noting the texture of their tooth crowns. These possess a series of fine vertical wrinkles, from which the species gets its common name. Unfortunately, the wrinkles are often difficult to detect. The number of teeth (20–27 per row) is fewer than for spinner and spotted dolphins but about the same as for bottlenose dolphins.

Figure 232.—A rough-toothed dolphin, captive at Sea Life Park, Hawaii, for many years, voluntarily out of water during a performance and performing a flip (right). Researchers have found rough-toothed dolphins to be easily trained and highly inventive. (Photos courtesy of Sea Life Park, Hawaii [top]; K. D. Sexton [right].)

Figure 233.—Underwater photograph of a free-ranging rough-toothed dolphin investigating a diver off the west coast of Oahu, Hawaii. The species' principal markings, including the narrow cape, speckling on the belly, white lips, and dark eye are all visible. (Photo by E. Shallenberger, Sea Life Park, Hawaii.)

Figure 234.—A rough-toothed dolphin stranded at Cape Hatteras, N.C., illustrating the white splotches and polka dots (scars) often seen on large specimens. The round scars are probably caused by the "cookie-cutter" shark. (Photos by J. G. Mead.)

PYGMY KILLER WHALE (T)

Feresa attenuata **Gray, 1874**

Other Common Names

Slender blackfish, slender pilot whale, blackfish (applied by some fishermen to all the small, dark, blunt-headed whales); orca pigméo (Latin America); yume gondō kujira (Japanese); karlikovaya kasatka (Russian).

Description

This uncommon cetacean grows to lengths of about 2.4–2.7 m. Length at birth is not known, although it is probably about 1 m.

The body is slender and in general resembles that of the false killer whale (p. 118). The head is rounded, and there is no beak. The mouthline is straight.

The pygmy killer whale has a prominent, falcate dorsal fin, located at about midback, with the peak varying in shape from broadly rounded to bluntly pointed. It is usually 20–30 cm high. The flippers are moderate in length (about one-eighth of body length) and have rounded tips.

Most of the pygmy killer whale's body is black or dark gray. An indistinct cape similar to that of the spinner dolphin (p. 148) is present, with its maximum width below the dorsal fin. A pale, anchor-shaped patch is present on the chest between the flippers, similar to that found on pilot whales (p. 123) and Risso's dolphins (p. 129), and there is usually a variable white area on the belly posterior to the navel. The area around the mouth is marked with varying amounts of white; sometimes the lips and entire chin are white. The white "goatee" on the chin is clearly visible on swimming animals.

Natural History Notes

Virtually nothing is known about the habits or biology of this species. It is generally seen in groups of a few to about 50 (rarely to a few hundred) and is not easily approached. Though the head may sometimes clear the water as the animals run near the surface, they are not acrobatic. They occasionally ride bow waves. Several individuals have been kept for a few months in captivity. They proved to be surprisingly aggressive, so there is reason to believe they prey on mammals as well as fish.

Distribution

This is a tropical species, and its range is limited to low latitudes worldwide. There are no records of its presence along the west coast of North America, but it is occasionally caught in tuna purse seines in the eastern tropical Pacific. In Hawaiian waters small herds are seen with some regularity, and it occurs elsewhere in Polynesia.

Figure 235.—A slow-swimming group of "blackfish" encountered at lat. 15°16′N, long. 99°58′W during a February 1979 research cruise. When they were later approached and observed more closely, they were positively identified as pygmy killer whales. Because the differences between this species and the melonheaded whale are so subtle, very close examination is often necessary before a positive identification can be made. The bottom photo shows a pygmy killer whale 5 miles off Kaena Point, Oahu, Hawaii. The animal was dark on the back with varying degrees of lighter coloration on the sides, the cape extending high onto the sides in front of the dorsal fin. In subsequent encounters with the species throughout its range the intensity of the cape pattern has appeared to be one of the most useful means of distinguishing pygmy killer whales from melon-headed whales. When the cape is apparently absent, however, it cannot be assumed that what is seen is a melon-headed whale. (Photos by R. L. Pitman, courtesy of NMFS [top]; E. Shallenberger, courtesy of Sea Life Park, Hawaii [bottom].)

Figure 236.—When stressed, pygmy killer whales behave much like the similar melon-headed whale and must be approached closely before positive identification is possible. Pygmy killer whales are often seen swimming in perfectly coordinated "chorus lines" (bottom). (Photos from the eastern tropical Pacific, by R. L. Pitman [top]; W. H. Brinkerhoss [bottom].)

Can Be Confused With

The pygmy killer whale most closely resembles the false killer whale (p. 118) and the melon-headed whale (p. 188). It is much smaller than the false killer whale, and the zones of white coloration help distinguish it at close range. False killer whales grow to at least 5.5 m and are all black. The pygmy killer whale's white belly patch sometimes extends high enough onto the sides to be seen as the animal surfaces. The light areas below the cape on the sides ahead of the dorsal fin can also help in identification. The pygmy killer whale's head is more rounded, i.e., less tapered, than that of the false killer whale.

The melon-headed whale is even more difficult to distinguish from the pygmy killer whale because it is similar in size. Only experienced observers are likely to be able to separate the two at sea. The melon-headed whale is not thought to have the extensive white and light gray zones characteristic of the pygmy killer whale, although its lips are often white and it can have a white spot near the anus. One character apparently separates the two animals consistently: the melon-headed whale has pointed flippers. The flippers, however, are difficult to see in the wild. Observations to date suggest that the melon-headed whale is more likely to be encountered in large herds than is the pygmy killer whale and is more likely to run from oncoming vessels.

Identification of Dead Specimens

Dead specimens of the three small "blackfish"—false killer, pygmy killer, and melon-headed whales—can be readily distinguished. In addition to the characteristics mentioned above, the following are key differences between false and pygmy killer whales:

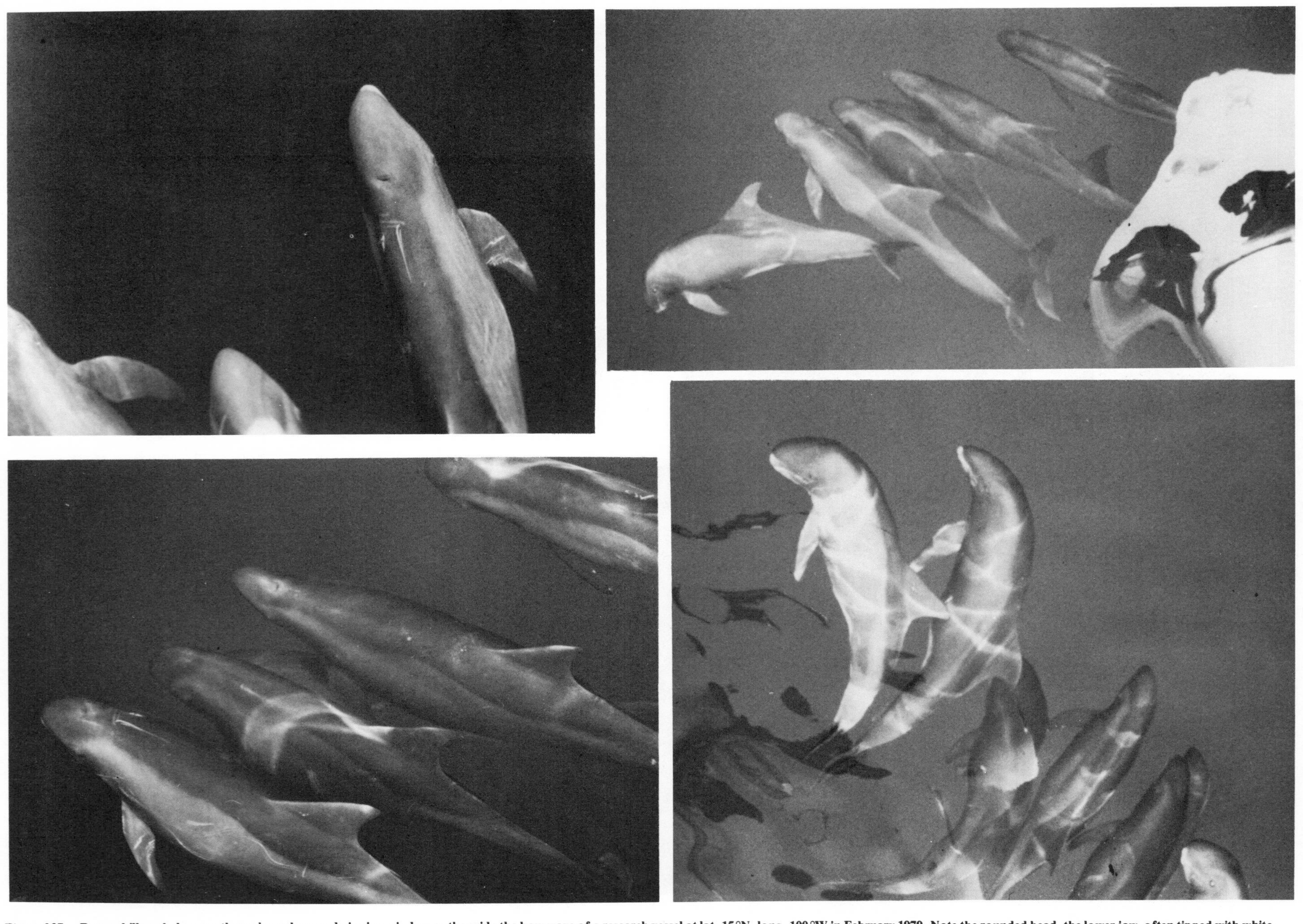

Figure 237.—Pygmy killer whales seen through a submerged viewing window as they ride the bow wave of a research vessel at lat. 15°N, long. 100°W in February 1979. Note the rounded head, the lower jaw, often tipped with white, the generally rounded tips of the flippers, and the distinctive dark cape, with lighter sides and belly. The mobility of the head apparent in these photos is not artifactual. (Photos by R. L. Pitman and by P. L. Ritchie [lower left], courtesy of NMFS.)

Figure 238.—Stranded pygmy killer whales from South Africa (a, b, c) and Florida (d). Note the variation in white coloration of the lower jaw, the white region on the ventral surface (extending up onto the sides just below the dorsal fin), and the falcate, sharply pointed dorsal fin. Note also that the flippers lack the hump on the forward margin characteristic of the false killer whale and are slightly rounded on the tips, in contrast to the sharply pointed flippers of the melon-headed whale. Pygmy killer whales have 8–11 teeth in each side of the upper jaw and 11–13 in each side of the lower jaw. (Photos courtesy of P. B. Best [a, b, c] and Miami Seaquarium [d].)

Pygmy Killer Whale	False Killer Whale
Teeth	
10–13 in each row above and below; lower teeth smaller.	8–11 per row; larger and more prominent.
Ventral Coloration	
White area behind the navel, may reach onto the sides.	Normally dark behind the navel.
Flippers	
Smoothly rounded on front edge.	Characteristic S-shaped front margin.

Pygmy killer whales can be distinguished from melon-headed whales by the latter's larger number of teeth. Melon-headed whales have at least 22–25 teeth per side in the upper jaw and 21–24 teeth per side in the lower jaw.

MELON-HEADED WHALE (T)

***Peponocephala electra* (Gray, 1846)**

Other Common Names

Many-toothed blackfish, Hawaiian blackfish, blackfish (applied by some fishermen to all small, dark, blunt-headed whales); kazuha gondō kujira (Japanese); shirokoklyuvyy del'fin (Russian).

Description

The melon-headed whale is poorly known. Since only a few individuals have been examined closely, and since it appears to be difficult to distinguish from the pygmy killer whale (p. 184) at sea, what is said in this section about the appearance and habits of the melon-headed whale should be taken as tentative and in need of revision as more is learned.

The melon-headed whale's body shape is similar to those of the larger false killer whale (p. 118) and the similar-sized pygmy killer whale (p. 184). Maximum length is at least 2.7 m. It is elongated and slim, with a narrow tail stock. The head is generally shaped like that of the false killer whale, but has a sharper appearance and tapers to a blunt point. There is an indistinct beak. The mouthline is long and straight.

The high dorsal fin is usually at least slightly falcate, with either a rounded or a pointed tip. The relatively long flippers are pointed. The melon-headed whale is black on the back and slightly lighter on the belly. There is a faint, brownish cape on the back. There are white regions on the lips and around the anal and genital openings. As in several other small dark whales, there is an anchor-shaped gray patch on the throat.

Natural History Notes

The melon-headed whale is a gregarious, pelagic animal that occurs in herds of several hundred, often in tightly packed association. These herds occasionally show interest in riding bow waves but are often difficult to approach. They reportedly respond to motor vessels by running and creating considerable disturbance, much like Fraser's dolphins (p. 166).

Nothing is known about the melon-headed whale's reproductive biology or seasonal movements. Mass strandings involving hundreds of individuals are known to occur.

Distribution

The melon-headed whale is not known to be common anywhere. It appears to be confined to tropical waters, where it is known to prey on squid. Its distribution in the eastern North Pacific appears to be limited to offshore tropical waters. It occurs in Hawaiian waters and elsewhere in Polynesia.

Can Be Confused With

The melon-headed whale is easily confused with the false killer whale (p. 118) and the pygmy killer whale (p. 184). It is considerably smaller than the false killer whale, has a slightly more pointed head, and lacks the S-shaped, humped forward margin on the flippers which is characteristic of *Pseudorca*. Unfortunately, none of these characters, except size, is likely to be evident during sightings made at sea.

The melon-headed whale and the pygmy killer whale are about the same size and are generally black. In general, the melon-headed whale appears to occur in larger herds than does the pygmy killer whale. The white area on the pygmy killer whale's abdomen may extend higher onto the sides than the melon-headed whale's, and the former often has a white "goatee" on the chin and lower jaw. The pygmy killer whale's flippers are less tapered and have rounded rather than pointed ends. Its dorsal fin is often larger and more erect than that of the melon-headed whale. The head of the melon-headed whale is slightly more pointed than that of the pygmy killer whale. None of these differences is striking enough to ensure that these two small whales can be distinguished from each other by inexperienced observers.

Identification of Dead Specimens

There is an easy way of distinguishing dead melon-headed whales from their two lookalikes. Melon-headed whales have more than 15 teeth per row (more than 60 total), while both false and pygmy killer whales have less than 15 teeth per row.

Figure 239.—Melon-headed whales at lat. 02°34′N, long. 140°48′W in November 1977. Note the slight beak on some animals, the dark face, and the absence of a well-defined cape. When seen closely, as on the bow of a vessel, the head appears triangular in dorsal aspect, less so in lateral aspect. (Photos by D. Au and W. Perryman, courtesy of NMFS.)

Figure 240.—A herd of melon-headed whales in the eastern tropical Pacific seen from a research ship. Like many small cetaceans in that part of the world where tuna boats chase dolphins, melon-headed whales seem wary of vessels and run from them, often forming broad "chorus lines" which work the sea into a froth. While pygmy killer whales have rounded heads with a subterminal mouth, melon-headed whales more often have a terminally opening mouth and short but distinct beaks, particularly in juveniles and immatures. (Photo by R. L. Pitman, courtesy of NMFS.)

c

Figure 241.—Juvenile melon-headed whales stranded in Hawaii (opposite page—a, b, this page—c, d) and killed in a purse seine in the eastern tropical Pacific (e). This whale is smaller than the false killer whale and can be positively identified by the large number of teeth, more than in any other "blackfish." Melon-headed whales have 21-25 teeth per side in both the upper and lower jaws. Other blackfish have fewer than 15. (Photos courtesy of T. Dohl [a-d] and W. F. Perrin [e].)

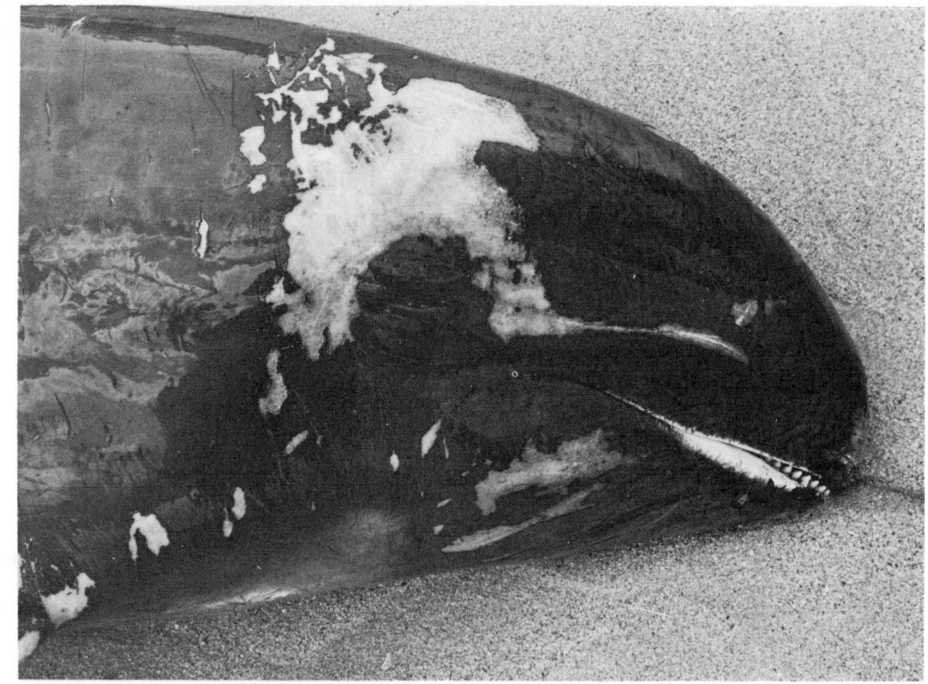

d

e

Figure 243 (above and opposite page).—Melon-headed whales driven ashore in Japan; above photos show the pointed flippers characteristic of the species. Melon-headed whales are not known to be common anywhere and have thus far been reported only in widely scattered locations in deeper offshore tropical waters. (Photos courtesy of T. Kasuya.)

Figure 242.—Stranded melon-headed whales. Of particular interest in these views are the sharply pointed flippers and the head shape, appearing on both bottom animals to be triangular in dorsal and ventral aspect. (Photos courtesy of U.S. National Museum.)

PYGMY SPERM WHALE (T)

Kogia breviceps **(Blainville, 1838)**

Other Common Names

Cachalote pigméo (Latin America); komakkō kujira (Japanese); karlikovyy kashalot (Russian).

Description

This little whale grows to lengths of at least 3.7 m and weighs 408 kg. No sexual dimorphism is known. Length at birth is a little over 1 m.

The pygmy sperm whale has a robust body with a small but distinctively shaped head and a narrow tail stock. The forehead overhangs to a noticeable extent the tip of the underslung lower jaw. This lower jaw is small, narrow, and superficially similar to a shark's jaw in its position. The head is conical viewed from above; when viewed in profile, it varies in shape from conical in juveniles to squared off or slightly bulbous in adults.

The dorsal fin is usually small, falcate, and positioned behind midback. The flippers, which are smoothly curved on the forward margin and reach lengths of ½ m or more in adults, are located well forward on the body, just below and behind the "false gills" (see below). The notched flukes have a concave rear margin.

Pygmy sperm whales are dark steel gray to bluish gray on the back, shading to lighter gray on the belly. A conspicuous feature is the white, crescent-shaped bracket mark on each side of the head. Because of its location behind the eye and ear, this strange mark superficially resembles a fish's gill slit and is sometimes called a "false gill." The outer surface of the flippers and upper surface of the flukes are steel gray.

Natural History Notes

Since the pygmy sperm whale is hardly ever seen and recognized at sea, little is known about its social relationships. Apparently it is not particularly gregarious, being found in small pods of 3-6 individuals. Strandings generally are of solitary animals or of females with calves.

All that is known about the pygmy sperm whale's reproductive biology is that females, which are sometimes simultaneously lactating and pregnant, appear to be capable of bearing young in successive years. Females off South Africa are believed to become sexually mature at lengths of 2.7–2.8 m; males at 2.7–3.0 m.

Based on the few accounts that exist of at-sea observations, the following remarks can be made about behavior of pygmy sperm whales. They rise to the surface slowly, produce an inconspicuous blow, and normally do not roll sharply at the surface like many small cetaceans. They have been reported to lie motionless in the water ("loglike"), with the back of the head exposed and the tail hanging loosely in the water. (A similar habit of sperm whales has made them a minor hazard to shipping, since it has resulted in some collisions with ships.) When startled in this posture, they may defecate, issuing a cloud of reddish-brown to rust-colored feces.

The main prey appears to be squid, but they also eat pelagic crustaceans and some fishes. Judging by what was found in the stomachs of stranded specimens, a South African cetologist has suggested that pygmy sperm whales live in deep water beyond the edge of the continental shelf. This seems consistent with the fact that sightings are extremely rare. Pygmy sperm whales often

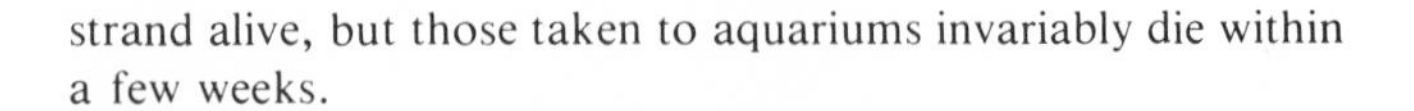
strand alive, but those taken to aquariums invariably die within a few weeks.

Distribution

There are two unfortunate obstacles to our understanding of this species' distribution. First, most records are of stranded animals, and these may not provide a very accurate picture of the distribution of living animals. Second, the pygmy sperm whale was not distinguished from the dwarf sperm whale (p. 198) until recently, so it is difficult to determine how much the ranges of the two species overlap. In general, the pygmy sperm whale is thought to have a more antitropical distribution than the dwarf sperm whale in most areas.

The northernmost record of the pygmy sperm whale in the eastern North Pacific is from a stranding in May of a young male just south of Gray's Harbor, Wash. This whale may be sparsely distributed, then, from Washington south to Baja California, where it is known to enter the Gulf of California. It is also present in Hawaiian waters.

Can Be Confused With

Pygmy sperm whales are so distinctive that, when seen at close range, they are not likely to be confused with anything other than dwarf sperm whales (p. 198). The two very closely

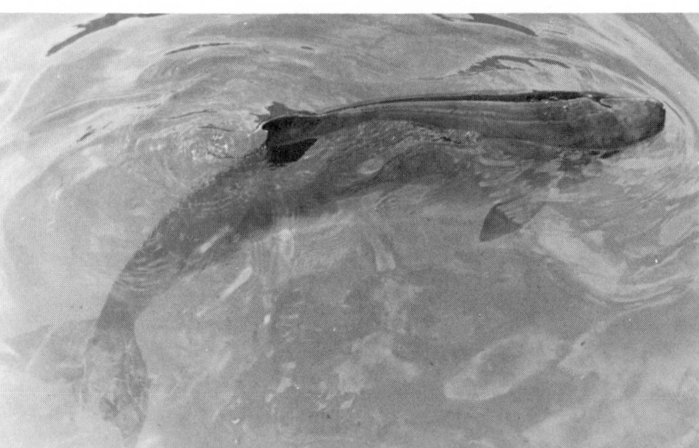

Figure 244.—A young pygmy sperm whale (top) and a female pygmy sperm whale and her calf (bottom) swimming in a tank at the New York Aquarium after being recovered from New York beaches where they stranded. In all three animals, note the shape and position of the dorsal fin, smaller and more posteriorly placed than that of the dwarf sperm whale. Note also the oddly shaped head, triangular in dorsal profile, bluff in the front, and entirely beakless. The white scrapes on the adult in the lower photo probably resulted from stranding. (Photos by H. E. Winn [top]; courtesy of N. Y. *Post* [bottom].)

related whales cannot be reliably distinguished from each other at sea based on current knowledge. At a distance, they might be confused with any of the smaller beaked whales (p. 98) that also have a relatively small falcate dorsal fin set far back on the body. Closer examination should permit easy separation, however, since the pygmy sperm whale has no beak, while the beaked whales have prominent, dolphinlike beaks. Adult beaked whales are all larger than adult pygmy sperm whales. The features by which to distinguish between pygmy and dwarf sperm whales are summarized below (see section on Identification of Dead Specimens).

Seen from the air in bright sunlight, the color ranges from greenish brown to grayish brown. Some lighter coloration is visible approximately adjacent to the blowhole (thought to be the bracket marks). The head is very rounded, almost spade-shaped; the flippers, tail stock, and flukes are small relative to body size. The body contours are lumpy in contrast to the smooth lines of most small whales.

Identification of Dead Specimens

Stranded pygmy and dwarf sperm whales are not likely to be confused with any other cetaceans, but their narrow, underslung jaw and blunt head could result in their casual dismissal by some beach walkers as stranded sharks. Specimens of the two species of *Kogia* can be separated by the following characteristics:

Pygmy Sperm Whale	**Dwarf Sperm Whale**
Teeth	
12–16 (rarely 10–11) in each lower jaw; no teeth in upper jaw; teeth longer (to 40 mm) and thicker (to 9 mm in diameter).	7–12 (rarely 13), small and sharply pointed teeth in each lower jaw; sometimes up to 3 in each upper jaw; teeth less than 30 mm long and less than 4.5 mm in diameter.
Throat	
No creases on throat.	Several short irregular creases on throat.
Maximum length	
To 3.7 m.	To 2.7 m.
Dorsal Fin	
Small (height normally less than 5% of body length); falcate; usually located behind midback.	Taller (height normally greater than 5% of body length); more like that of bottlenose dolphin; usually located near midback.

Figure 245.—Pygmy sperm whales at lat. 31°27′N, long. 120°04′W, 10 October 1979. The species is most often seen in flat calm water when groups containing calves are rafting at the surface (top left). When alarmed, they whirl slowly forward and submerge (top right). The ridge behind the dorsal fin is creased into subtle crenulations, reminiscent of those on the sperm whale (bottom). The body behind the dorsal fin is also sometimes wrinkled. (Photos by M. R. Graybill [top] and G. L. Friedrichsen [bottom], courtesy of NMFS.)

Figure 246.—A pygmy sperm whale stranded at La Jolla, Calif. In particular, note the position and shape of the sharklike mouth, the position of the flippers (low on the body), the abrupt tapering of the body at the narrow tail stock, and the posterior position of the dorsal fin. (Photos by K. Benirschke.)

Figure 247.—A pygmy sperm whale from northeastern Florida showing the lightly pigmented bracket mark, sometimes referred to as a "false gill." Apparently present in both species, these marks have been visible in the few confirmed sightings at sea in which observers had clear looks at the side of the head. (Photo by F. G. Wood.)

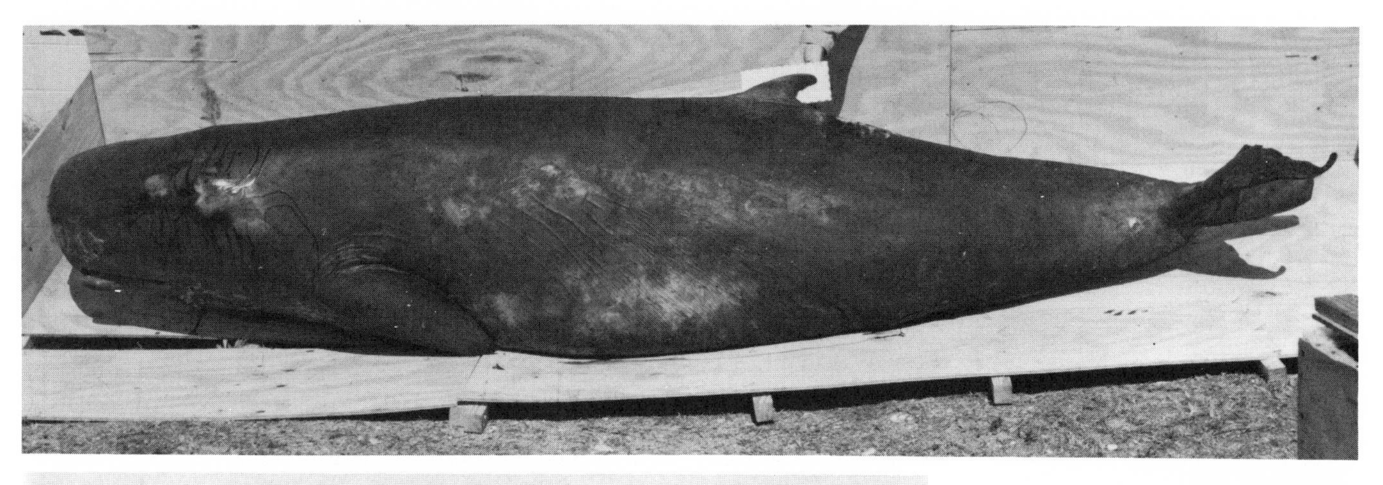

Figure 248.—When beached, specimens of the two species of *Kogia* can be distinguished with some confidence. The pygmy sperm whale, *K. breviceps,* (top) reaches a length of about 3.7 m; its dorsal fin is a small nubbin located in the posterior half of the back. The dwarf sperm whale, *K. simus,* (left) reaches only about 2.7 m; its dorsal fin, much taller and more dolphinlike, is located near the middle of the back. Coloration of fresh specimens is probably similar for both species—the lightened areas in the lower photograph are the result of decomposition. (Photos from Jekyll Island, Ga., by D. K. Caldwell [top]; and San Luis Obispo County, Calif., A. Roest [left].)

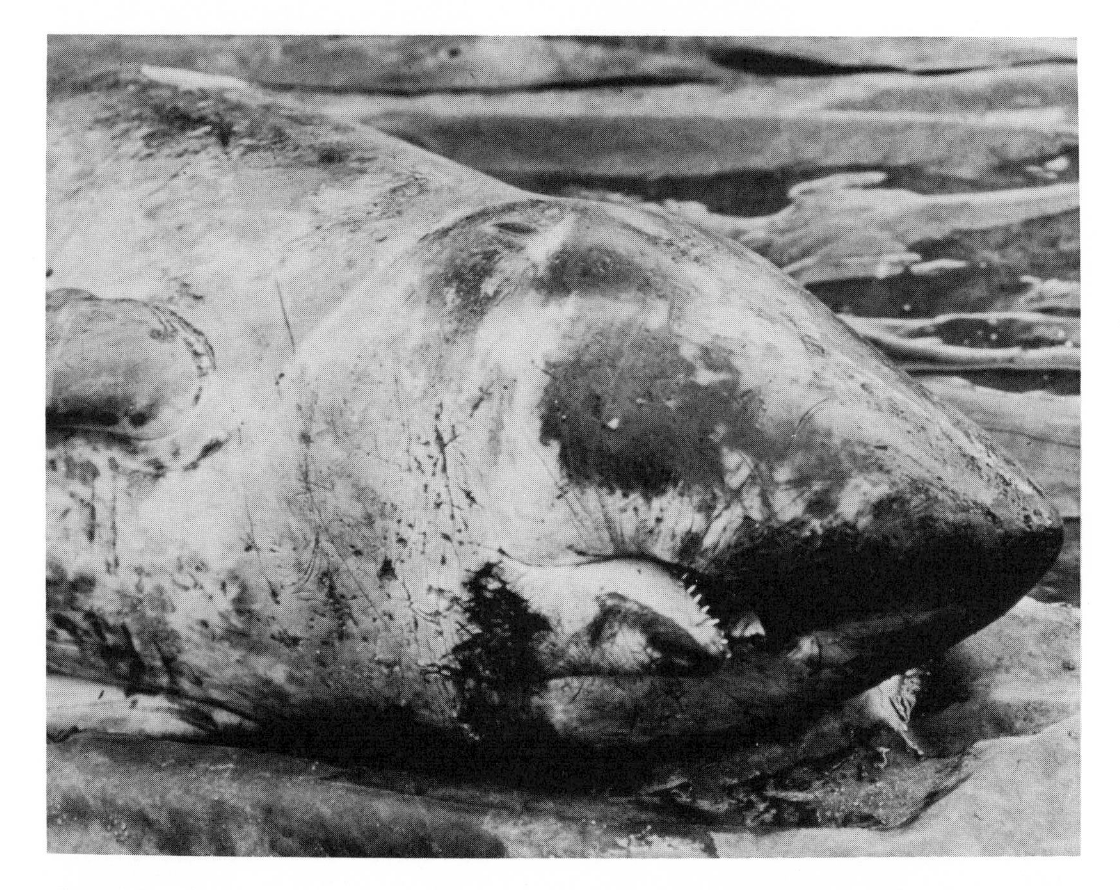

Figure 249. — Mouth of a pygmy sperm whale from Monterey County, Calif. In both species of *Kogia,* these long, curved, needle-sharp teeth, found principally in the lower jaw, fit into sockets in the upper jaw. Pygmy sperm whales have 12–16 (rarely 10 or 11) pairs of teeth; dwarf sperm whales have 8–11 (rarely 13) pairs. (Photo by G. V. Morejohn.)

DWARF SPERM WHALE (T)

Kogia simus **(Owen, 1866)**

Other Common Names

Ogawa komakkō kujira (Japanese); malyy karlikovyy kashalot (Russian).

Description

Adult dwarf sperm whales are 2.1–2.7 m long and weigh 136–276 kg. Length at birth is unknown but is probably close to 1 m.

In general this animal is similar to the pygmy sperm whale, but it is smaller. It has a squarish head and a robust body that tapers rapidly near the tail. The lower jaw is underslung and sharklike. A lightly colored line, called a "false gill" or bracket mark, is present on each side behind the eye.

In contrast to the pygmy sperm whale's small dorsal fin set well back on the body, the dwarf sperm whale's dorsal fin is generally tall and falcate, resembling that of the bottlenose dolphin. It is placed near the middle of the back. There are often several short, irregular creases on the throat similar to those found on the throat of the sperm whale (p. 51).

Dwarf sperm whales are dark bluish gray on the back, grading to lighter gray on the sides, and fading to dull white on the belly.

Natural History Notes

Data on any aspect of the natural history of the little sperm whales are very sparse, so any generalization about them should be viewed as extremely tentative. Dwarf sperm whales probably travel in small groups of less than 10, and these groups may consist of juveniles only, of females accompanied by calves, or of sexually mature males and females. Females and calves sometimes strand together, and in one instance a group of four juveniles ran aground along the same short stretch of beach. It is not unusual for these animals to become beached while still alive.

Little is known about the reproductive characteristics of dwarf sperm whales. Both males and females are believed to become sexually mature at lengths of 2.1–2.2 m. Calves nurse until they are more than 1.5 m long. As is true of the pygmy sperm, the dwarf sperm may give birth in successive years, since a high proportion of females stranded with suckling calves are pregnant. Japanese investigators, who have had experience with pygmy and dwarf sperm whales captured at sea, have remarked that they are often found floating ("loglike"), or basking at the surface, at which time they are easy to approach.

Stomach content analyses have shown that dwarf sperm whales primarily eat cephalopods, although a fairly broad assortment of deepwater fishes and crustaceans is also eaten. The assumption generated by these data is that *K. simus* is a slightly more inshore species than *K. breviceps*, occupying waters over the continental shelf and slope.

Distribution

In the eastern North Pacific the dwarf sperm whale has been recorded from only two localities: San Luis Obispo County in central California and Cabo San Lucas in southwestern Baja California. There is also a record from Hawaii. To what extent these occurrences reflect the actual range of the species is a matter of speculation. Since *K. simus* has only recently been accord-

Figure 250.—Three progressively closer views of a pygmy or dwarf sperm whale, most likely the latter, at lat. 8°30′N, long. 87°17′W in January 1979. In the few confirmed sightings of pygmy and dwarf sperm whales at sea, the animals were moving slowly, not normally rising abruptly to the surface like most other small whales, and their blows were low and inconspicuous. The best view of the head and body shown here (bottom right) leaves little doubt that the animal is a specimen of *Kogia*. The strongest clue that it is a dwarf rather than a pygmy sperm whale is the prominent dorsal fin positioned near midbody. Both species, like their larger relative the sperm whale, apparently often lie motionless at the surface. (Photos by R. L. Pitman [top, bottom left] and P. L. Ritchie [bottom right], courtesy of NMFS.)

Figure 251.—A dwarf sperm whale swimming in the tank at Marineland of Florida. It was recovered after stranding near St. Augustine, Fla. In this species the dorsal fin is generally taller than that of the pygmy sperm whale and located near the midpoint of the back. (Photo courtesy of Marineland of Florida.)

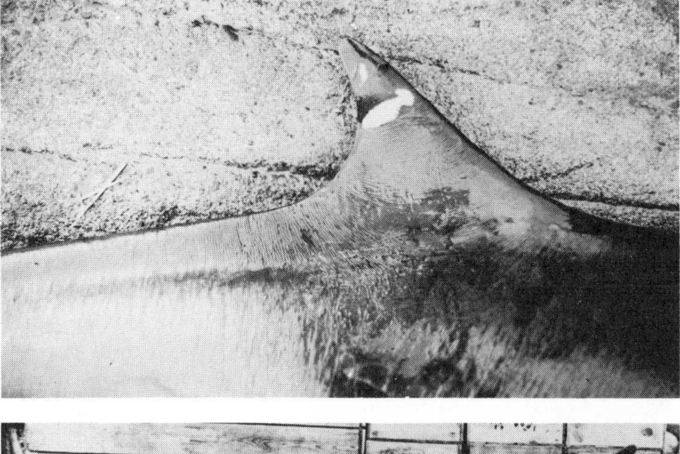

Figure 252.—A dwarf sperm whale taken at Taiji, Japan. Note the prominent dorsal fin, situated near midbody, the underslung lower jaw, the extension of the keel far back nearly to the fluke notch, and the bracket mark on the side of the head. (Photos by R. L. Brownell, Jr.)

Figure 253.—Dwarf sperm whales can have several short creases on the throat, similar to those found on the sperm whale; pygmy sperm whales lack these creases. (Photo from Pokai Bay, Hawaii, by D. Bryant.)

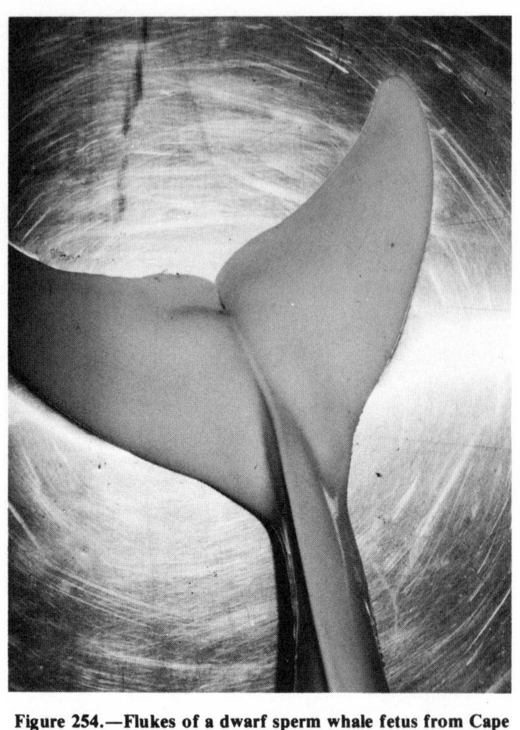

Figure 254.—Flukes of a dwarf sperm whale fetus from Cape Hatteras, N.C. Note that the dorsal ridge extends almost to the notch in the flukes, a characteristic of both species of *Kogia*. (Photo courtesy of J. G. Mead.)

ed the status of a species distinct from *K. breviceps*, and even more recently given a common name, records of the dwarf sperm whale may have been confused in the past with those of its close relative.

Can Be Confused With

Because of the tall, falcate, centrally situated dorsal fin, dwarf sperm whales may be confused at a distance with any of the small dolphins that have this feature. The all black or dark steel-gray coloration and blunt head increase the likelihood of confusion with pygmy killer whales (p. 184) and melon-headed whales (p. 188). So far, the ranges of pygmy killer whales and melon-headed whales have not been found to overlap that of the dwarf sperm whale. The dwarf sperm whale has been reported only north of lat. 20°N; the pigmy killer whale and melon-headed whales are only in tropical waters south of lat. 20°N. The record is sketchy, however, and distribution alone should not be used as a basis for identification. From what is known about its behavior the dwarf sperm whale appears to be much less gregarious and to swim more slowly and less aggressively than pygmy killer whales and melon-headed whales. To be certain with these three species, examination of head shape and coloration at close range may be necessary.

The important differences between dwarf and pygmy sperm whales are tabularized on p. 195.

Identification of Dead Specimens

On the beach, dead dwarf sperm whales are easy to identify to the generic level due to their peculiar head shape and jaw configuration, i.e., the broad head dominating the body shape and the narrow underslung jaw. They have 8–11, rarely 13, pairs of mandibular teeth (fine, needlelike, and hooked) and usually, in contrast to the pygmy sperm whale, 1–3 pairs of functional maxillary teeth. Differences between the two species are tabularized on p. 195.

DALL'S PORPOISE (T)

Phocoenoides dalli **(True, 1885)**

Other Common Names

True's porpoise, Dall porpoise; delfín de Dall (Latin America); ishi iruka—Dall, rikuzen iruka—True (Japanese); belokrylaya morskaya svin'ya (Russian).

Description

Maximum size of this stocky porpoise is 2.2 m and about 200 kg. Sexual maturity is reached at about 1.9 m in males and 1.7 m in females. Males are much thicker bodied than females. Newborn calves are about 1 m long.

Figure 255.—Dall's porpoises may be easily identified when seen on the bow wave of a moving vessel (left) or swimming leisurely at the surface, which they are rarely seen doing outside the Alaskan coastal waters (right). The most prominent characteristics are the white side patch, the white markings on the dorsal fin and the trailing edge of the flukes, and the robust body tapering to a small head. (Photos from lat. 34°N, long. 121°W by K. C. Balcomb [left]; in a tank at Point Mugu, Calif., by S. Leatherwood [right].)

The body shape alone distinguishes Dall's porpoise from all other small cetaceans in the eastern North Pacific. It is extremely robust, making the tiny head and small flukes look inappropriate. The forehead slopes steeply to a short, poorly defined beak. The mouth is small and narrow, the eye located far forward on the head.

The dorsal fin is variable in shape but basically triangular, with a long base. The flippers are small, slightly tapered toward the tips, not pointed, and located far forward on the body. The tail stock has a pronounced keel, both dorsally and ventrally, and this character is most exaggerated in adult males. The small flukes have a nearly straight trailing edge with only a shallow median notch.

In addition to its peculiar body shape, Dall's porpoise has a striking black-and-white color pattern that helps make it easy to identify. The body is basically shiny black (entirely black, gray, and brownish gray animals have been observed), with a large, conspicuous oval patch of white (sometimes containing faint dark speckling) on each side, at about midbody (in True's porpoise the patch extends further anteriorly). The two patches meet at the midriff ventrally but end well below the dorsal fin. The dorsal fin is usually bicolored—the upper half being white, the lower portion black. The upper rear border of the flukes is also white. There is wide variation in pigmentation among these animals.

Natural History Notes

In the eastern North Pacific, Dall's porpoises are usually encountered in small bands of 2–20, although on feeding banks off Alaska several hundred may be seen in the same small area. In at least one area (Monterey Bay), the consistency with which juveniles were found closer inshore than adults is the basis for speculation that there may be some degree of age segregation within the population. Dall's porpoises have been observed frequently in mixed herds, most often running with Pacific white-sided dolphins (p. 168) and pilot whales (p. 123).

Scant data from the eastern North Pacific are interpreted to indicate that there are twin calving peaks; winter-early spring and another in summer, but births apparently occur year-round. In other parts of its range, where details of life history are more complete, calving occurs between July and September.

Although they are present year-round in much of their range, there is some seasonal north-south and inshore-offshore movement by these porpoises off central and southern California. They seem to prefer colder waters between 36° and 62°F, and this preference probably influences significantly the southern limit of their occurrence in particular. Incursions inshore have been equated to the movements of squid, a principal prey of these porpoises.

Dall's porpoises bow ride, moving quickly and jerkily, darting in and out of the bow wave. They are extremely fast swimmers, however, and often show impatience with vessels traveling at less than 9 knots. In some areas of Alaska, where Dall's porpoises frequently pass portions of their days cruising slowly and creating little surface disturbance, one must examine animals carefully before finally settling on an identification.

Even when these usually highly animated porpoises do not come to the bow, they are a thrill to see and easy to identify. During high speed runs, while feeding or attempting to overtake or avoid a boat, the entire body may be obscured by the "rooster tail" of spray caused by the animal's lunge to the surface for air. Since the spray is often all that can be seen, these creatures are difficult to photograph. Dall's porpoises almost never leap clear out of the water.

Dall's porpoises feed on squid, crustaceans, and many kinds of fish, including myctophids, saury, hake, herring, and jack mackerel as well as other mesopelagic, bathypelagic, and deep-water benthic species. Killer whales and sharks are known to prey on Dall's porpoises. Attempts to maintain these high-strung porpoises in captivity have not been particularly successful.

Distribution

The Dall's porpoise is one of the most common small cetaceans in the northern North Pacific. Its normal distribution appears to extend north at least to the Pribilofs and possibly

Figure 256.—Until they arrive at the bow of a moving vessel, Dall's porpoises are rarely seen clearly. What is more usually seen is shown in these three views from off Anacapa Island (top left), San Clemente Island (bottom left), and San Francisco (right), Calif. These vigorous swimmers frequently create a "rooster tail" of spray as they surface. In rough seas, their splashes blend with white caps, making them difficult to detect. (Photos by K. D. Sexton [top left]; S. Leatherwood [bottom left]; M. Webber [right].)

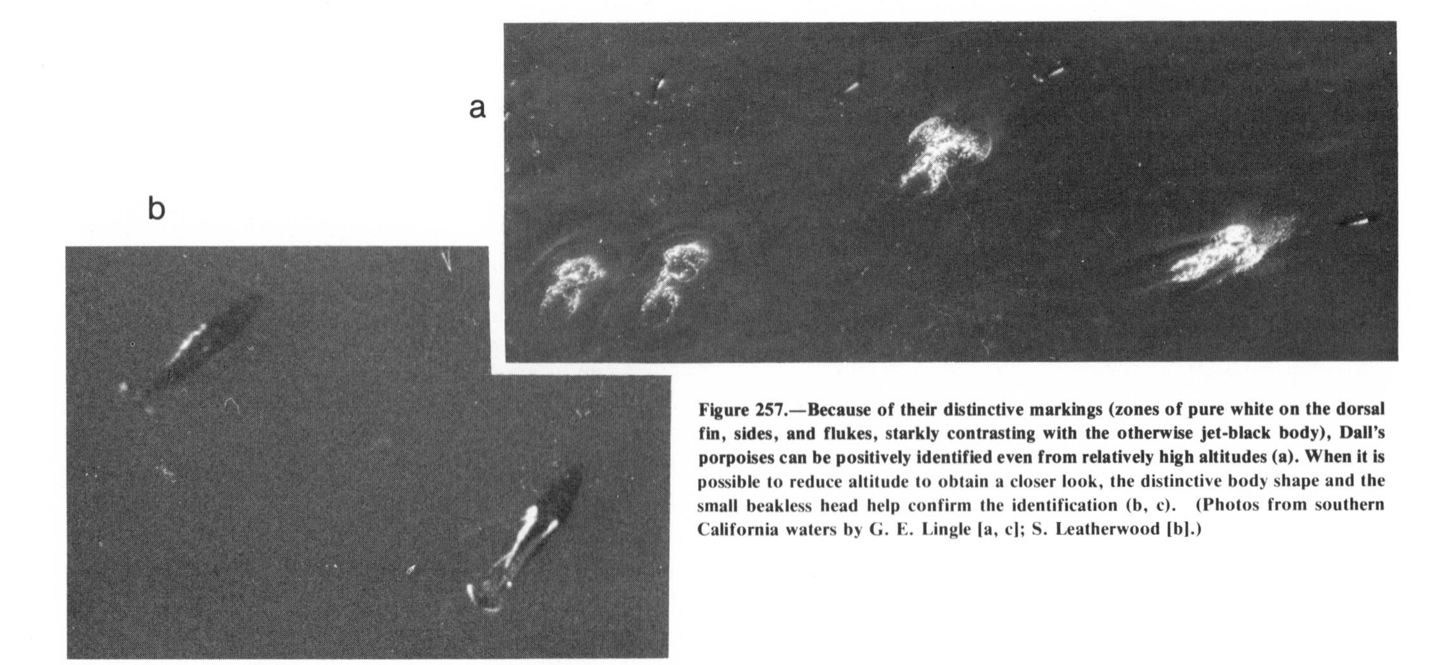

Figure 257.—Because of their distinctive markings (zones of pure white on the dorsal fin, sides, and flukes, starkly contrasting with the otherwise jet-black body), Dall's porpoises can be positively identified even from relatively high altitudes (a). When it is possible to reduce altitude to obtain a closer look, the distinctive body shape and the small beakless head help confirm the identification (b, c). (Photos from southern California waters by G. E. Lingle [a, c]; S. Leatherwood [b].)

even to Bering Strait in summer. It is abundant in outer Bristol Bay and throughout the southern Bering Sea and the Gulf of Alaska. The continental shelf waters of the northern Gulf of Alaska between Kodiak Island and Icy Straits are particularly well populated. During any season it can be seen in the deep fjords along the coast of southern and southeastern Alaska, notably in Prince William Sound and Glacier Bay, as well as in waters far offshore. It frequently is encountered year-round in deep inside waters of British Columbia and Washington, and along the coast as far south as the California Channel Islands, where it generally remains well offshore and outside the 100-fathom curve.

In winter and spring from about late October to late May, Dall's porpoises penetrate south and move inshore along the coasts of California and Baja California (to Cedros and Guadalupe Islands). The extent of and numbers involved in this penetration appear tied to water temperatures, being greatest south of Point Conception in colder water years.

A major conservation problem may exist in the western and far northern North Pacific, where Japanese fishermen kill several thousands of Dall's porpoises each year, intentionally with harpoons and accidentally with drifting salmon gill nets. Stocks in the eastern North Pacific, at least some of which are probably distinct from those fished off Japan, are relatively unmolested.

Figure 258.—A Dall's porpoise in a tank at Marineland of the Pacific, showing the small head, the sharply defined white-on-black color pattern, the small flippers, and the odd shape of the body. In the lateral view, note that the thickening of the peduncular keel is quite exaggerated, due partly to the emaciated condition of this individual, though dorsoventral keeling is very prominent in some healthy Dall's porpoises. (Photos by S. Leatherwood.)

Can Be Confused With

In calm open water, or in protected inland waters, Dall's porpoises often swim in a manner very much like the harbor porpoise. Experienced observers have at first mistaken the slow roll of a Dall's porpoise for that of a harbor porpoise; their dorsal fins are shaped very similarly and their sizes are roughly comparable. The two species overlap in distribution to a significant degree, although harbor porpoises are generally regarded as inhabitants of more inshore and shallower water. Harbor porpoises on the

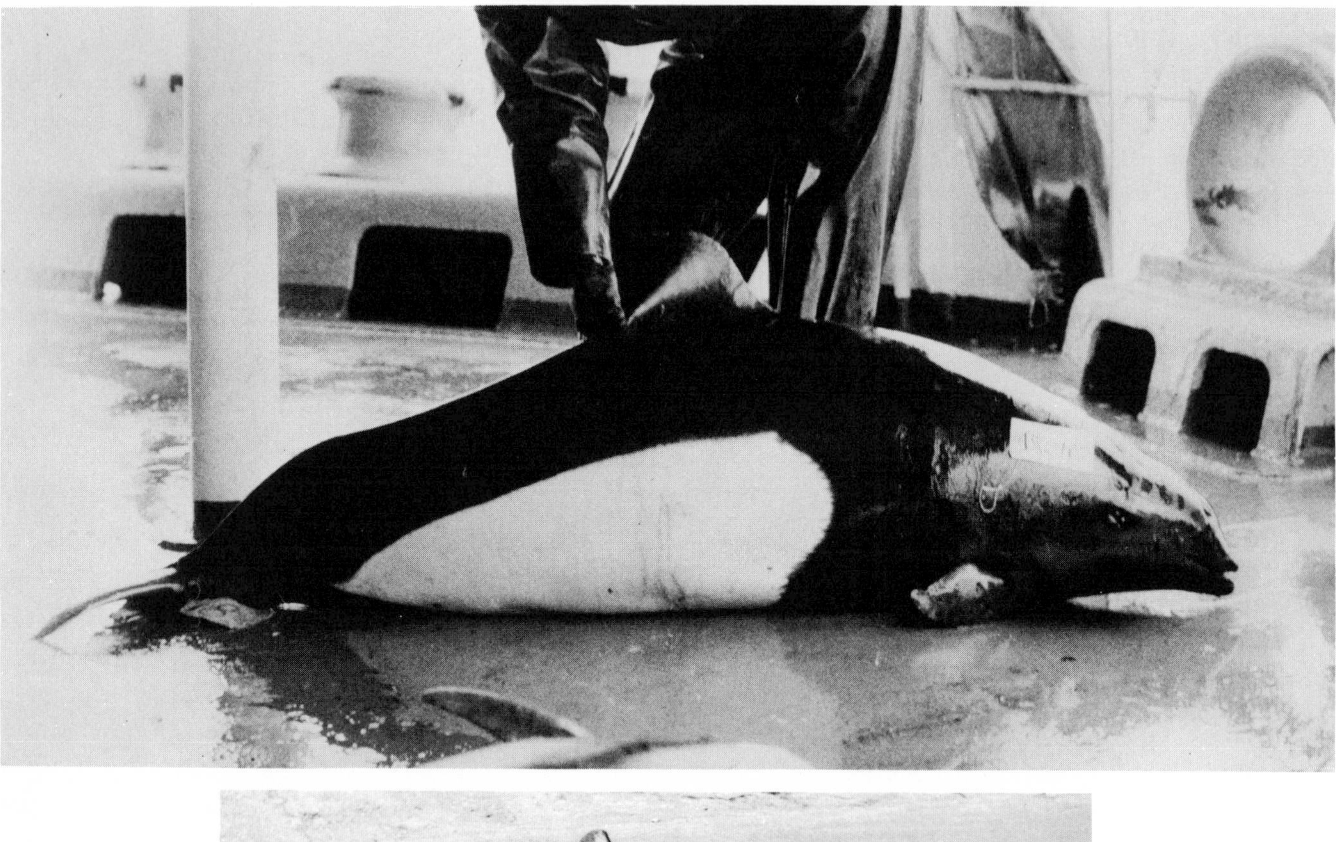

Figure 259.—Dall's porpoise (top) differs externally from True's porpoise, another form of *P. dalli* (bottom), primarily in the extent of white coloration. Though highly variable in both forms, in Dall's porpoise the white patch begins about midbelly and ends about even with the keel; in True's porpoise it begins farther forward, sweeps upward above the flipper toward the eye, then encompasses most of the lower lateral surface to the vicinity of the keel. Both forms have a bicolored dorsal fin and white-edged flukes. True's porpoises occur in abundance only off the east coast of Japan and in the southern Sea of Okhotsk, and apparently rarely overlap with Dall's porpoise in the eastern Pacific. Both forms are taken for food off northern Honshu, Japan. (Photos from the Aleutian Islands by R. Beach [top]; from northern Japan, by W. J. Houck [bottom].)

whole are less gregarious and less boisterous in the way they swim. However, since harbor porpoises sometimes do make a spray as they surface and since Dall's porpoises sometimes do not, it is well to note the striking differences in coloration between the two species. Harbor porpoises have subdued, even drab markings, comprised mainly of shades of brown and gray. The prominent white trim of the Dall's porpoise's tail and dorsal fin, as well as the large white patches on the sides, contrast abruptly with the otherwise black body.

Dall's porpoises can also be confused with Pacific white-sided dolphins, which sometimes make a similar splash as they break the surface to breathe. Differences are tabularized on p. 172.

From the air, Dall's porpoises can be most readily identified by the stark white zone on the ventrum, sides, and belly, and by the white or light gray triangular zones on the posterior and lateral portions of the flukes—both white zones contrast starkly with the otherwise black body.

Identification of Dead Specimens

Dead Dall's porpoises are easy to identify from their peculiar body shape and color pattern. In addition they have 19–28 teeth per side in each jaw. The teeth are small and spade-shaped like those of the harbor porpoise, rather than pointed or conical as in most other small cetaceans.

HARBOR PORPOISE (T)

Phocoena phocoena **(Linnaeus, 1758)**

Other Common Names

Common porpoise, herring hog, puffing pig; nezumi iruka (Japanese); morskaya svin'ya (Russian).

Description

The harbor porpoises (this species and the cochito [p. 208]) are the smallest cetaceans in the eastern North Pacific. Maximum length is about 1.8 m and maximum weight about 90 kg, though most adults do not approach these dimensions. Adult females are slightly larger than adult males. Newborn harbor porpoises are 70–90 cm long and, except for slightly duller expression of coloration elements, resemble adults.

These small, chunky animals have no prominent forehead and only a very short and indistinct beak. The mouthline is abbreviated and straight, angled upward toward the eye.

The dorsal fin is usually low and triangular with a blunt tip. Occasionally the rear margin is slightly concave. The small flippers taper to blunt points. The flukes have a slightly concave trailing edge and a shallow median notch.

The harbor porpoise is basically dark brown or gray above and light gray to white below. The upper jaw and lower lip are dark, but the ventral white extends onto the chin. It also intrudes onto the sides in front of the dorsal fin, forming a lighter gray zone which is often conspicuous when the animal surfaces. There is often speckling in the transition zone between ventral light and dorsal dark. A dark stripe of variable width connects the corner of the mouth with the flipper.

Natural History Notes

Harbor porpoises are usually seen in pairs or in small groups of up to 10 animals.

Figure 260.—Harbor porpoises frequent inshore areas, shallow bays, estuaries, and harbors (a) from about Morro Bay, Calif., (there are a handful of records from south of Point Conception) along the entire Alaska coast to the Canadian border, though they are only chance visitors in the Chukchi and Beaufort Seas and are uncommon north of Bristol Bay. Photos of harbor porposes just offshore from Rio del Mar, Seaside, Calif. (b), off southeast New Brunswick (c), and near the British Isles (d). Note the small size (usually less than 1.5 m), the small triangular dorsal fin, the dark brown to gray color of the back, and the lighter color of the sides and belly, extending onto the sides anterior to the dorsal fin. (Photos by J. D. Hall [a, b]; D. Yurick [c]; J. Matthews, courtesy of H. Pepper [d].)

Figure 261.— A trained captive harbor porpoise in the Copenhagen Zoo. Although breaching is commonly seen in many other small cetaceans, wild harbor porpoises apparently rarely indulge in aerobatics of this sort. While feeding, they sometimes clear the water in a rapid, arcuate leap. (Photo courtesy of Copenhagen Zoo.)

Most calves are born during summer (May–July) after a gestation period of perhaps 11 months. They probably remain dependent for at least 6 months. The calving interval is probably 2 years, although occasionally females may give birth in successive years. Harbor porpoises are found almost exclusively shoreward of the 183 m (100-fathom) curve, with the vast majority inside the 18 m (10-fathom) curve. The seasonal movements of harbor porpoises in the eastern North Pacific are poorly understood, but they are present year-round in some areas. If there are major seasonal shifts in distribution, they are as likely to be inshore-offshore as north-south. The animal is most often seen, as its common name implies, in inshore waters, including bays, harbors, and river mouths.

The harbor porpoise is usually shy and difficult to approach. Since it shows little of itself while surfacing, it is difficult to photograph. It almost never rides bow waves and does not normally leap clear of the water or lift its flukes above the surface when diving. Harbor porpoises have been caught in nets set for bottom fish at 73 m (40 fathoms) or deeper.

There is little use looking for harbor porpoises on rough days, but when the water is calm their presence can often be detected by the sharp puffing sound of their exhalation. The appearance of their surface rolls at a distance has been described as "the passage of the triangular dorsal fins up, over and down (as if mounted on revolving wheels thrust briefly above the surface and withdrawn)" (Scheffer and Slipp 1948). While feeding they often take 3–4 breaths at 2- or 3-minute intervals; in passage, they breathe at shorter intervals. Maximum swimming speed is said to be about 12 knots. The only times harbor porpoises create much commotion in the water is when they attain these speeds in bursts, during feeding or flight.

Harbor porpoises prey on a wide variety of cephalopods and fishes, but seem particularly fond of schooling, nonspiny fish like shad, herring, mackerel, sardines, pollock, and whiting. They are themselves preyed on by large sharks and killer whales.

Distribution

The harbor porpoise is a cold-temperate, subarctic species found only as a stray south of Point Conception, Calif. (strandings have occurred in Santa Barbara and Los Angeles). From Morro Bay, Calif., northward it is one of the most common inshore cetaceans. It can be seen in outer San Francisco Bay, Puget Sound, Juan de Fuca Strait, and along much of the open coast within 38.5 km (20 nmi) of shore. There is evidence that some harbor porpoises are year-round residents in certain areas.

Harbor porpoises are fairly common along much of the shoreline bordering the Gulf of Alaska and along at least the eastern Aleutian chain. Prince William Sound may be more densely populated in winter than any other part of the eastern Pacific. There are harbor porpoises in the eastern Bering Sea, and they are occasionally found near the Pribilof Islands.

Infrequent occurrences along the northern coast of Alaska and into northwestern Canadian waters are difficult to explain. Most records from northern Alaska are for August and September, so perhaps these are summer migrants from south of Bering Strait. In any case, the harbor porpoise is but a chance visitor to the Chukchi and Beaufort Seas, and it is apparently uncommon north of Bristol Bay.

Figure 262.—A harbor porpoise recovered from a Connecticut beach where it had stranded alive. This is the most coastal of the small cetaceans in the eastern North Pacific. (Photo courtesy of Mystic Marinelife Aquarium.)

Figure 263A.—Harbor porpoises killed in the Japanese North Pacific gill net fishery for salmon (top) and live-stranded on the central California coast (bottom). In both specimens note the robust body, the triangular dorsal fin, the irregular border between the light ventral and the darker lateral and dorsal coloration, separated more by a zone of intergraded flecking than by a distinct line. In both photos note the dark lower lips, the dark mouth-to-flipper stripe, the all-dark flipper, and the absence of a beak. (Photos by B. Long, courtesy of NMFS [top]; M. Webber [bottom].)

As inshore animals, harbor porpoises are particularly vulnerable to the impact of human activities. Native peoples of the Pacific Northwest traditionally hunted them for food and oil. They now have come to be regarded as nuisances by some fishermen because they get tangled in nets or lodged in fish traps. The impact on harbor porpoises of incidental mortality in fishing gear has not been evaluated but could be serious in certain areas, as could the effects of coastal development.

Can Be Confused With

The small cetacean most likely to be confused with the harbor porpoise is Dall's porpoise (p. 200). The latter has very conspicuous black-and-white coloration, with a white patch on the upper half of the dorsal fin and a white flank patch as well as white trim on the flukes. Such sharply defined pigmentation should distinguish it from the more nondescript harbor porpoise. Dall's porpoises usually make a "rooster tail" of spray as they surface, and this should also help distinguish them from the usually less flamboyant harbor porpoises.

Viewed from the air, harbor porpoises appear rotund and uniformly brownish to rust in color on the back. When they are running near the surface, they often roll onto their sides enough to provide glimpses of their white undersides.

Identification of Dead Specimens

Harbor porpoises can be readily identified by their small, spade-shaped (rather than conical) teeth, of which there are 23–28 in each upper jaw and 22–26 in each lower jaw. Head shape and the size and shape of the dorsal fin also aid in identification.

VAQUITA

Phocoena sinus **Norris and McFarland, 1958**

Other Common Names

Gulf of California harbor porpoise; cochito (Latin American); kogashira nezumi iruka (Japanese); kaliforniyskaya morskaya svin'ya (Russian).

Description

Females attain body lengths of up to 150 cm; males, 140 cm. Length at birth is about 70 cm.

The vaquita's dorsal fin is proportionally much higher than those of the other species of *Phocoena.* It is roughly triangular, with the front edge convex and the rear edge almost straight or somewhat concave. The details of its shape can vary between individuals.

The overall color pattern is complex but subdued, consisting of interacting components of different shades of gray. The belly is grayish white. There is a bold, dark eye patch and a well-defined dark lip patch which continues onto the chin. The flipper stripe is present but varies in intensity and form among individuals. At sea, calves appear slate gray and darker than adults, which can appear to be more olive or tawny brown than gray.

Natural History Notes

Very little is known about the natural history of this species.

Remains of grunt, Gulf croakers, and squid were found in the stomach of one specimen.

Distribution

From what little is known about the vaquita's current distribution, it appears to be confined to the upper quarter of the Gulf of California, where the majority of records are from the shallower waters produced by siltation from the mouth of the Colorado River and the narrow coastal margins of the mainland and islands. There is some uncertain historical evidence suggesting that it may have occurred along the Mexican mainland south to the Tres Marías Islands and Banderas Bay at one time. The current restricted range effectively isolates this species from its near relative, the harbor porpoise, whose nearest occurrence is over 900 km north and separated from the Gulf by the Baja California Peninsula. Another near relative, Burmeister's porpoise, *P. spinipinnis,* inhabits coastal waters of Peru, more than 3,500 km to the south, and areas farther south.

Incidental mortality resulting from entanglement in shrimp trawls and fishing nets appears to have had a serious impact on the vaquita. It is also possible that reduced productivity in the Gulf of California due to damming of the Colorado River and heavy pesticide contamination have affected the porpoise population.

Can Be Confused With

Only two dolphins, the bottlenose dolphin (p. 173) and the common dolphin (p. 160), are known to occur regularly in the portions of the Gulf of California frequented by the vaquita. The common dolphin is a vividly marked dolphin which usually travels in large herds, primarily over deep water, and leaps frequently. Herds often leave a long V-shaped wake on the water surface. Bottlenose dolphins, occurring in smaller groups and often close to the mainland and islands, are somewhat less frolicsome than common dolphins but are still far more demonstrative than vaquitas. The vaquita's small size, dull color and lack of a beak should make it fairly easy to distinguish. There are no Dall's porpoises (p. 200) or harbor porpoises (p. 205) in the Gulf of California.

Identification of Dead Specimens

Like the harbor porpoise, the vaquita has spade-shaped, rather than conical, teeth. Specimens examined so far have had 17–21 pairs in the upper jaw and 17–20 pairs in the lower.

Figure 263B.—This adult and calf vaquita were encountered in late March 1986 near the Baja California Coast between San Felipe and Rocas Consag in the northern Sea of Cortez. Note the relatively prominent dorsal fin, which distinguishes this small porpoise from other species of *Phocoena.* (Photo by G. Silber, West Coast Whale Research Foundation.)

Figure 263C.—Vaquitas from El Golfo de Santa Clara, Sonora, Gulf of California, Mexico. The individual in the foreground is a 70-cm calf. (Photo by A. Robles.)

SMALL WHALES, DOLPHINS, AND PORPOISES WITHOUT A DORSAL FIN

(less than 4 m maximum length)

There is only one small cetacean in the area covered by this guide which has no dorsal fin, the northern right whale dolphin, *Lissodelphis borealis*.

NORTHERN RIGHT WHALE DOLPHIN (T)

***Lissodelphis borealis* (Peale, 1848)**

Figure 264.—Northern right whale dolphins are often wary of boats and attempt to avoid them by sneaking away slowly with little surface disturbance or by running as in these photos off Santa Rosa Island (top) and off Point Conception (middle), Calif. When large herds run in series of low-angle leaps, they may work the sea into a froth (middle). Running right whale dolphins are known to reach burst speeds of at least 35 km per hour and sustained speeds (for nearly a half hour) of 26 km per hour. Care must be taken not to dismiss sightings of smooth-backed animals as sea lions (bottom) or fur seals, which may also "porpoise." (Photos by K. C. Balcomb [top]; R. L. Pitman [middle]; R. R. Reeves [bottom].)

Figure 265.—Normally wary of boats, northern right whale dolphins tend to come more readily to the bows of vessels when they are in the company of Pacific white-sided dolphins (top), with which they often travel. The two share the same approximate distribution from about lat. 50°N southward, though the white-sided dolphin routinely ventures nearly 1,000 km further south. Once on the bow, the two dolphins are almost impossible to confuse. (Photos from off San Francisco, Calif., by S. Stansbury [top]; off northern California by R. K. Fountain [bottom], courtesy of NMFS.)

Other Common Names

Delfin de liso (Latin America); kiti demi iruka (Japanese); severnyy kitovidnyy del'fin (Russian).

Description

Maximum known length in the eastern North Pacific is about 3 m. Females are not known to grow longer than 2.3 m, and they may in general be somewhat smaller than males. Both sexes appear to mature sexually at lengths of just over 2.0 m. Length at birth has been estimated to be about 80–100 cm.

This dolphin's body is long and slender, tapering to an extremely narrow tail stock with no keel. The animal's appearance is eellike. There is virtually no forehead or chin; the short beak is very indistinctly set off by a faint crease above the mouth. The mouthline is long and straight.

The complete absence of either a dorsal fin or a dorsal ridge is the right whale dolphin's most distinguishing feature. The narrow flukes have a deeply concave trailing edge and a shallow median notch.

The body is mainly black, though the back can have a brownish sheen under some light conditions. The ventral surface has a variable white pattern with a sharp border between black and white. A narrow band of white begins far back on the tail stock and continues forward along the ventral midline, widening abruptly just behind the flippers and forming a prominent thoracic patch. A small white mark is usually present at the tip of the lower jaw. The flukes are light gray dorsally and partly white ventrally. Calves are much lighter—from cream to light gray.

Figure 266.—An aerial view of a portion of a herd of northern right whale dolphins, including a calf, off southern California. When seen from the air this sleek finless dolphin can be easily identified by the all-black dorsal surface and the occasional flash of white as an animal rolls (left). The upper surface of the flukes is consistently light gray near the tips (right). Newborn are lighter dorsally than are adults, varying from almost cream color to light gray (upper inset). Juveniles apparently acquire adult coloration some time in the first year. (Photos by C. A. Hui [left]; D. K. Ljungblad, [inset] courtesy of NOSC; S. Leatherwood [right].)

Natural History Notes

The right whale dolphin is a gregarious animal. It is frequently seen in herds of more than 100 individuals. The frequency with which it is found in the company of the Pacific white-sided dolphin (p. 168) suggests that the two species mix freely and share much of the same habitat.

Except for minimum sizes at sexual maturity, nothing is known about the reproductive biology of the northern right whale dolphin. Newborns are seen most frequently in early spring.

Seasonal shifts in distribution appear to be related to water temperature and movements of prey. Right whale dolphins are not usually found in waters warmer than 19°C. They tend to move southward and inshore in late fall and northward and offshore in spring. Their appearance inshore generally coincides with peaks in abundance of squid, a major prey item.

Right whale dolphins are fast swimmers; they have been clocked at speeds of more than 18 knots. They often run from approaching vessels, either by sneaking just below the surface and barely coming up for breath, or by making low-angle leaps. Much of the herd may be airborne at the same time, but, unlike Pacific white-sided dolphins, they leap on an even keel and seldom engage in aerobatics. Some belly flop, side slap, or lobtail as they run. Occasionally right whale dolphins ride bow waves, particularly while in the company of Pacific white-sided dolphins. They have been seen riding the pressure waves of large whales, notably fin whales and gray whales.

The diet of northern right whale dolphins consists mainly of squid and lanternfish (myctophids). Some other mesopelagic fishes are also eaten. Strandings of individuals are not infrequent on the California coast.

Distribution

In the eastern North Pacific northern right whale dolphins are normally confined to temperate waters between lat. 30°N and 50°N. They apparently move south of lat. 30°N only during periods of intrusion of unseasonably cold waters. Right whale dolphins are present at all seasons seaward of the continental shelf off central and northern California, but they are seen off southern California and in shelf waters farther north primarily in winter and spring. They are relatively abundant from Point Sur south to Point Conception and around the California Channel Islands. They are less common off Oregon, Washington, and British Columbia.

Can Be Confused With

At times, when they are moving through the water slowly, barely exposing the head and back, or when they are alarmed and swimming very rapidly in a series of low-profile leaps across the surface, these animals may resemble a moving herd of sea lions or fur seals. At close range, however, these uniquely marked animals are unlikely to be confused with any other species of dolphin or whale.

Identification of Dead Specimens

In addition to the features listed above, northern right whale dolphins have 37–49 sharply pointed, peglike teeth in each row.

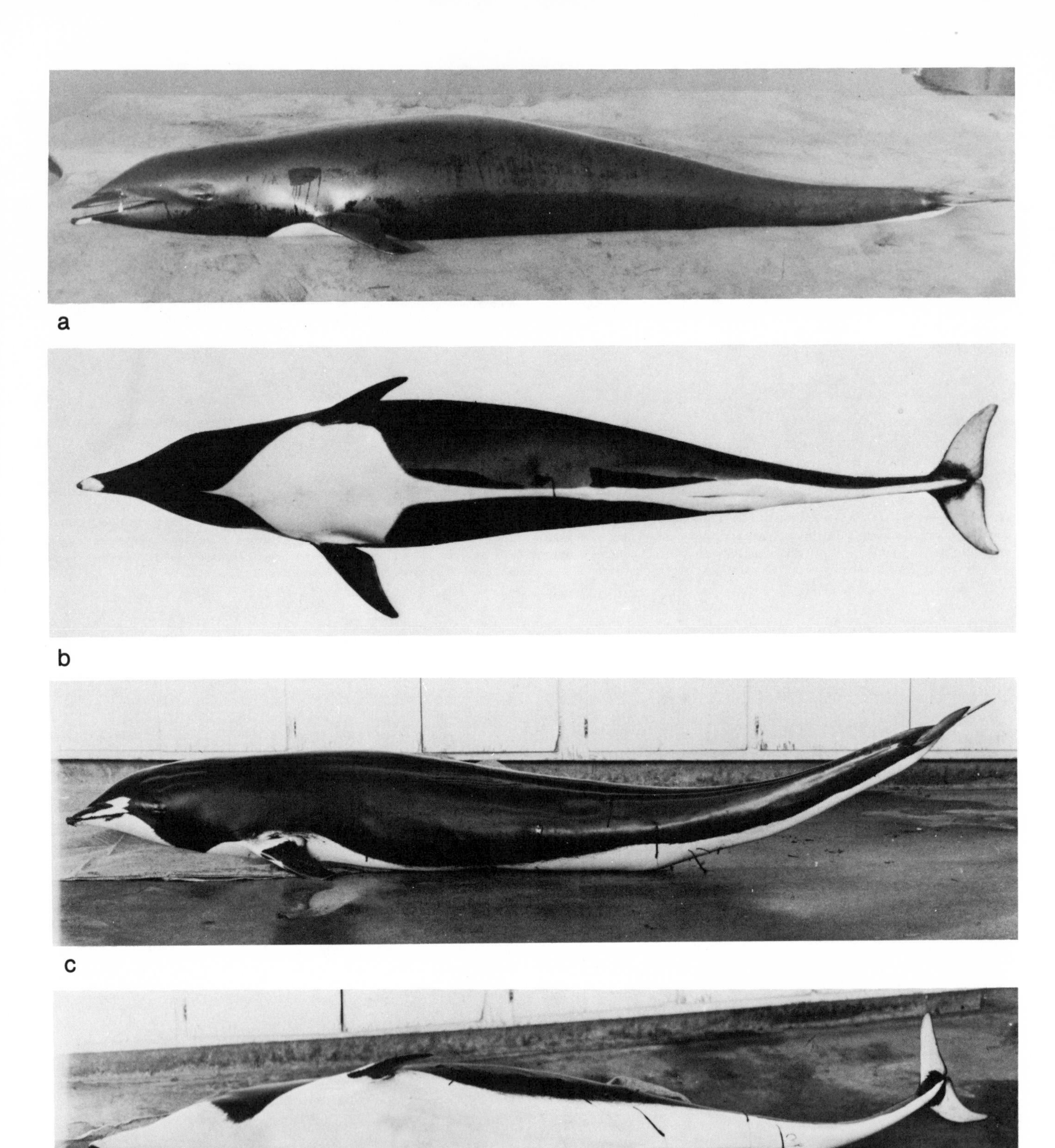

Figure 267.—A male northern right whale dolphin captured off Santa Rosa Island, Calif., in December 1968 (a, b) and an anomalously colored northern right whale dolphin stranded at Santa Monica, Calif. (c, d). Such color pattern variants are not uncommon among herds of otherwise normally colored northern right whale dolphins. Ectoparasites are *Penella* sp. The tuxedoed appearance created by the white ventrum is typical for the species, though the band of white tends to be broader in the urogenital area of females than of males. Northern right whale dolphins have 37–49 extremely fine, sharp, peglike teeth in each jaw. (Photos by F. G. Wood, courtesy of NOSC [a, b]; W. A. Walker [c, d].)

ACKNOWLEDGMENTS

It is clear with this revision as it was with the original Pacific guide that such documents could not have been produced without the generosity and cooperation of many people. Following the publication of the first Pacific guide in 1972 and the Atlantic guide in 1976, colleagues have been extremely helpful in making suggestions for improvement. Such a cooperative spirit has special significance in a field which is advancing as rapidly as the branch of natural history we sometimes call cetology. Our understanding of the lives of many of the cetaceans is growing at a rate with which journals are sometimes unable to keep pace. For that reason, at any given time, much of the best available information has not reached press, and any review like this one that restricts itself to published data will present but a fraction of what is really known. We, therefore, heartily thank our many colleagues who have contributed unpublished data to this book. In particular we are grateful to James G. Mead, U.S. National Museum, Washington, D.C.; R. L. Brownell, Jr., National Fish and Wildlife Laboratory, Smithsonian Institution, Washington, D.C.; Larry Hobbs, Marine Mammal Tagging Office, Northwest and Alaska Fisheries Center National Marine Mammal Laboratory, Seattle; Kenneth C. Balcomb, Orca Survey, San Juan Islands, Wash.; John D. Hall, Alaska Offshore, Inc.; Warren J. Houck, Humboldt State College, Arcata, Calif.; William A. Walker, Los Angeles County Museum of Natural History; Raymond M. Gilmore, San Diego Natural History Museum; Edward W. Shallenberger, Sea Life Park, Hawaii; Ronn Storro-Patterson, the Whale Center, Oakland, Calif.; Robert L. Pitman, NMFS; Larry Foster, General Whale, Oakland, Calif.; Giuseppe di Sciara, Hubbs/Sea World Research Institute, San Diego; and the late Carl L. Hubbs.

Although photo credits follow each figure, we particularly cite the generosity of the Northwest and Alaska Fisheries Center National Marine Mammal Laboratory (NWAFC), NMFS, NOAA, Seattle; Toshio Kasuya, Ocean Research Institute, Tokyo; Seiji Ohsumi, Far Seas Fisheries Research Laboratory, Shimizu; Hideo Omura, The Whales Research Institute, Tokyo; J. G. Mead, U.S. National Museum; Francis H. Fay, University of Alaska, Fairbanks; Lloyd Lowry, Alaska Department of Fish and Game, Fairbanks; K. C. Balcomb, Orca Survey; Naval Ocean Systems Center (NOSC); Southwest Fisheries Center (SWFC) La Jolla Laboratory, NMFS, NOAA; Enforcement Division, NMFS, NOAA, B Street Pier, San Diego; and Hubbs/Sea World Research Institute.

By the quality of their photography, such colleagues as Ken Balcomb and Bob Pitman are making it almost unnecessary for the rest of us to take our cameras into the field for marine mammal photos; we greatly respect their skills.

The illustrations were prepared by Larry Foster, courtesy of General Whale (Figs. 7, 10, 11, 12, 69, 91, 103); Ken Raymond, SWFC, La Jolla (Figs. 8, 9, 185, 195, 200, 208); and Debbie Dukelow Young, Sea World, Inc. (Figs. 1, 2).

Spanish names used in this guide were provided by the Inter-American Tropical Tuna Commission and reviewed by R. Clarke and A. Aguayo. Common names in Russian were generously added to the text by Alexey Yablokov, A. S. Sokolov, and Vladimir S. Gurevich; transliterations were provided by the U.S. Joint Publications Research Service. Common names in Japanese with transliterations were provided by Larry Tsunoda, Northwest and Alaska Fisheries Center, NMFS, NOAA, Seattle. Phonetic spellings of common names of cetaceans occurring in the northern Bering Sea and known by Eskimos speaking Siberian Yupik dialect were obtained by S. Leatherwood from Conrad Ozeeva, Gambell Village, St. Lawrence Island, Alaska.

The extensive and often tedious job of preparing black and white photographs of suitable format from the vast array of black and white and color negatives and prints and from color transparencies was accomplished by the Sea World Photo Laboratory (Cay McDonald, Bob French, and Jerry Roberts), by Wallace A. Sneathen (Photic of San Diego), and by Mark Towner (NWAFC, Seattle).

Elizabeth Mooney and Derrith Bartley assisted us in many phases of manuscript preparation; their boundless energy and helpful spirits made completion possible when it would have been easier to quit altogether.

Various drafts of the manuscript were typed by Leola Hietala and Joanne Hultgren, NWAFC, Seattle; Karie Wright, Yvonne Moreno, and Diane Baldwin of Hubbs/Sea World Research Institute; and Lorraine Prescott, SWFC, La Jolla. Suzanne Bond and Elizabeth Mooney performed careful proofreadings of the several typed drafts.

A partial list of materials consulted, each a good source of reference material on cetaceans in general or on cetaceans of the eastern North Pacific in particular, is provided in the following section, "Selected Bibliography." We have tried to list at least one monograph or paper for each species covered in this guide.

The following colleagues read all or part of the manuscript and made useful suggestions for its improvement: K. C. Balcomb, R. L. Brownell, Jr., L. Consiglieri, D. W. Doidge, C. Fiscus, G. Friedrichsen, J. D. Hall, L. Hobbs, J. G. Jennings, M. L. Jones, L. Jones, J. G. Mead, R. L. Pitman, D. W. Rice, S. Swartz, G. di Sciara, and W. A. Walker.

Funds for this revision were provided by a grant through Lew Consiglieri, National Marine Mammal Laboratory, to Randall R. Reeves.

SELECTED BIBLIOGRAPHY

ANDERSEN, H. T. (editor).
1969. The biology of marine mammals. Acad. Press, New York, 511 p.

ANONYMOUS.
1977. Report of the Special Meeting of the Scientific Committee on Sei and Bryde's whales, La Jolla, California, December 1974. Rep. Int. Whaling Comm., Spec. Issue 1, 150 p.
1978. Alaska whales and whaling. Alaska Geogr. 5(4):1-144.

BEST, P. B.
1979. Social organization in sperm whales, *Physeter macrocephalus*. *In* H. E. Winn and B. L. Olla (editors), Behavior of marine animals: current perspectives in research, Vol. 3 Cetaceans, p. 227-289. Plenum Press, New York and London.

BRAHAM, H. W., W. M. MARQUETTE, T. BRAY, and S. LEATHERWOOD (editors).
1980. The bowhead whale: Whaling and biological research. Mar. Fish. Rev. 42(9-10):1.

BROWNELL, R. L.
1986. Distribution of the vaquita, *Phocoena sinus*, in Mexican waters. Marine Mammal Science 2(4): 299-304.

BROWNELL, R. L., JR., L. T. FINDLEY, O. VIDAL, A. ROBLES, and S. MANZANILLA N.
1987. External morphology and pigmentation of the vaquita, *Phocoena sinus* (Cetacea: Mammalia). Marine Mammal Science 3(1): 22-30.

BRYDEN, M. M., R. J. HARRISON, and R. J. LEAR.
1977. Some aspects of the biology of *Peponocephala electra* (Cetacea: Delphinidae) I. General and reproductive biology. Aust. J. Mar. Freshwater Res. 28:703-715.

CALDWELL, D. K., and M. C. CALDWELL.
1971. The pygmy killer whale, *Feresa attenuata*, in the western Atlantic, with a summary of world records. J. Mammal. 52:206-209.
1972. The world of the bottlenosed dolphin. J. B. Lippincott, Philadelphia and New York, 157 p.

DAUGHERTY, A. E.
1972. Order Cetacea. *In* Marine mammals of California, p. 10-55. Calif. Dep. Fish Game, 2d rev., 86 p.

EVANS, W. E.
1975. Distribution, differentiation of populations, and other aspects of the natural history of *Delphinus delphis* Linnaeus in the northeastern Pacific. Ph.D. Thesis, Univ. California, Los Angeles, 164 p. (Diss. Abstr. Int. 36(10):4893-B.)

EVANS, W. E. (editor).
1974. The California gray whale. Mar. Fish. Rev. 36(4):1-64.

FRASER, F. C., and B. A. NOBLE.
1970. Variation of pigmentation pattern in Meyen's dolphin. *In* G. Pilleri (editor), Investigations on Cetacea, 2:147-163.

GASKIN, D. E., P. W. ARNOLD, and B. A. BLAIR.
1974. *Phocoena phocoena*. Am. Soc. Mammal., Mammal. Species 42, p. 1-8.

HALEY, D. (editor).
1978. Marine mammals of eastern North Pacific and Arctic waters. Pacific Search Press, Seattle, 256 p.

HERSHKOVITZ, P.
1966. Catalog of living whales. Bull. U.S. Natl. Mus. 246, 259 p.

HUBBS, C. L.
1951. Eastern Pacific records and general distribution of the pygmy sperm whale. J. Mammal. 32:403-410.

HUBBS, C. L., W. F. PERRIN, and K. C. BALCOMB.
1973. *Stenella coeruleoalba* in the eastern and central tropical Pacific. J. Mammal. 54:549-552.

KLEINENBERG, S. E., A. V. YABLOKOV, B. M. BEL'KOVICH, and M. N. TARASEVICH.
1969. Beluga (*Delphinapterus leucas*): investigation of the species. Isr. Program Sci. Transl., Jerusalem, 376 p. (First published in Russian in 1964.)

LEATHERWOOD, S., W. F. PERRIN, V. L. KIRBY, C. L. HUBBS, and M. DAHLHEIM.
1980. Distribution and movement of Risso's dolphin, *Grampus griseus*, in the Eastern North Pacific. Fish. Bull., U.S. 77:951-963.

LEATHERWOOD, S., and R. R. REEVES.
In press. Bottlenose dolphins, *Tursiops* cf. *T. truncatus*, and other toothed cetaceans. *In* J. Chapman and G. Feldhamer (editors), Wild mammals of North America: Biology, management and economics, Chapter 18. Johns Hopkins Press, Baltimore.

LEATHERWOOD, S., AND W. A. WALKER.
1979. The northern right whale dolphin, *Lissodelphis borealis* Peale in the Eastern North Pacific. *In* H. E. Winn and B. L. Olla (editors), Behavior of marine animals, Vol. 3 Cetaceans, p. 85-141. Plenum Press, New York and London.

MEAD, J. G.
1981. First records of *Mesoplodon hectori* (Ziphidae) from the Northern Hemisphere and a description of the adult male. J. Mammal. 62(2):430-432.

MITCHELL, E.
1965. Evidence for mass strandings of the false killer whale (*Pseudorca crassidens*) in the eastern North Pacific Ocean. Norsk Hvalfangst. Tid. 54(8):172-177.

MITCHELL, E. D.
1968. Northeast Pacific stranding distribution and seasonality of Cuvier's beaked whale, *Ziphius cavirostris*. Can. J. Zool. 46:265-279.
1970. Pigmentation pattern evolution in delphinid cetaceans: an essay in adaptive coloration. Can. J. Zool. 48:717-740.
1975. Porpoise, dolphin, and small whale fisheries of the world: status and problems. Morges, Switzerland: International Union for Conservation of Nature and Natural Resources. IUCN Monograph 3, 129 p.

MITCHELL, E. D. (editor).
1975. Review of biology and fisheries for smaller cetaceans: Report on the Meeting of Smaller Cetaceans. Montreal, April 1-11, 1974. J. Fish. Res. Board Can. 32:889-983.

MOREJOHN, G. V.
1979. The natural history of Dall's porpoise in the North Pacific Ocean. *In* H. E. Winn and B. L. Olla (editors), Behavior of marine animals, Vol. 3 Cetaceans, p. 45-83. Plenum Press, New York and London.

NORRIS, K. S. (editor).
1966. Whales, dolphins, and porpoises. Univ. California Press, Berkeley, 789 p.

NORRIS, K. S.
1974. The porpoise watcher: a naturalist's experiences with porpoises and whales. W. W. Norton and Co., New York, 250 p.

NORRIS, K. S., and W. N. McFARLAND.
1958. A new harbor porpoise of the genus *Phocoena* from the Gulf of California. J. Mammal. 39:22-39.

NORRIS, K. S., and J. H. PRESCOTT.
1961. Observations on Pacific cetaceans in California and Mexican waters. Univ. Calif. Publ. Zool. 63:291-402.

NORRIS, K. S., and R. R. REEVES (editors).
1977. Report on a workshop on problems related to humpback whales (*Megaptera novaeangliae*) in Hawaii. Final report, U.S. Marine Mammal Commission, National Technical Information Service, PB 280 794, Arlington, Va., 90 p.

ORR, R. T.
1972. Marine mammals of California. Univ. California Press, Berkeley, Los Angeles, London, 64 p.

PERRIN, W. F.
1972. Color patterns of spinner porpoises (*Stenella* cf. *S. longirostris*) of the Eastern Pacific and Hawaii, with comments on delphinid pigmentation. Fish. Bull., U.S. 70:983-1003.
1975. Variation of spotter and spinner porpoise (genus *Stenella*) in the eastern Pacific and Hawaii. Bull. Scripps Inst. 21, 206 p.
1976. First record of the melon-headed whale, *Peponocephala electra*, in the eastern Pacific, with a summary of world distribution. Fish. Bull., U.S. 74:457-458.

PERRIN, W. F., P. B. BEST, W. H. DAWBIN, K. C. BALCOMB, R. GAMBELL, and G. J. B. ROSS.
1973. Rediscovery of Fraser's dolphin, *Lagenodelphis hosei*. Nature 241:345-350.

PERRIN, W. F., and C. L. HUBBS.
1969. Observations on a young pygmy killer whale (*Feresa attenuata* Gray) from the eastern tropical Pacific Ocean. Trans. San Diego Soc. Nat. Hist. 15:297-308.

PERRIN, W. F., and W. A. WALKER.
1975. The rough-toothed porpoise, *Steno bredanensis*, in the eastern tropical Pacific. J. Mammal. 56:905-907.

PIKE, G. C., and I. B. MacASKIE.
1969. Marine mammals of British Columbia. Fish. Res. Board Can., Bull. 171, 54 p.

PRYOR, K.
1975. Lads before the wind; adventures in porpoise training. Harper and Row, New York, 278 p.
REEVES, R. R., and R. L. BROWNELL, JR.
In press. Right whale, *Eubalaena glacialis*, and other baleen whales. *In* J. Chapman and G. Feldhamer (editors), Wild mammals of North America: Biology, management and economics, Chapter 19. Johns Hopkins Press, Baltimore.
REEVES, R., and S. TRACEY.
1980. *Monodon monoceros*. Am. Soc. Mammal., Mammal. Species 127, 7 p.
REILLY, S. B.
1977. The distribution of pilot whales, *Globicephala macrorhynchus* Gray, 1846, in the eastern tropical Pacific. M.S. Thesis, California Polytechnic State Univ., San Luis Obispo, 79 p.
RICE, D. W.
1967. Cetaceans. *In* S. Anderson and J. K. Jones (editors), Rècent mammals of the world; a synopsis of families, p. 291-324. The Ronald Press, New York.
1977. A list of the marine mammals of the world. NOAA Tech. Rep. NMFS SSRF-711, 15 p.
RICE, D. W., and A. A. WOLMAN.
1971. The life history and ecology of the gray whale (*Eschrichtius robustus*). Am. Soc. Mammal., Spec. Publ. 3, 142 p.
RIDGWAY, S. H. (editor).
1972. Mammals of the sea; biology and medicine. Charles C Thomas, Springfield, Ill., 812 p.
ROEST, A. I.
1970. *Kogia simus* and other cetaceans from San Luis Obispo County, California. J. Mammal. 51:410-417.
ROSS, G. J. B.
1979. Records of pygmy and dwarf sperm whales, genus *Kogia*, from southern Africa, with biological notes and some comparisons. Ann. Cape Prov. Mus. (Nat. Hist.) 11:259-327.
SCAMMON, C. M.
1874. The marine mammals of the north-western coast of North America: together with an account of the American whale fishery. John Carmany and Co., San Francisco, 319 p. (Reprinted 1968 in paperback, New York: Dover.)
SCHEFFER, V. B.
1973. Marine mammals of the Gulf of Alaska. *In* D. H. Rosenburg (editor), A review of the oceanography and renewable resources of the northern Gulf of Alaska. Inst. Mar. Sci., Univ. Alaska, p. 175-207.
SCHEFFER, V. B., and J. W. SLIPP.
1948. The whales and dolphins of Washington State with a key to the cetaceans of the west coast of North America. Am. Midland Nat. 39:257-337.
SCHEVILL, W. E. (editor).
1974. The whale problem. A status report. Harvard Univ. Press, Cambridge, Mass., 419 p.
SHALLENBERGER, E. W.
1980. The status of Hawaiian cetaceans. Draft report for the U.S. Marine Mammal Commission, Contract MM7ACO28, Washington, D.C., 79 p.
TOMILIN, A. G.
1967. Mammals of the U.S.S.R. and adjacent countries. Vol. IX: Cetacea. Isr. Program Sci. Transl., Jerusalem, 717 p. (Originally published in Russian in 1957.)
TOWNSEND, C. H.
1935. The distribution of certain whales as shown by logbook records of American whaleships. Zoologica (N.Y.) 19:1-50.
YABLOKOV, A. V., V. M. BEL'KOVICH, and V. I. BORISOV.
1974. Whales and dolphins. 2 parts. Joint Publications Research Service, JPRS-62150-1 and 2, National Technical Information Service, Arlington, Va., 528 p. (Originally published in Russian in 1971.)

Table 1.—Ranges in number of teeth in each side of upper and lower jaws of eastern North Pacific odontocetes.

Common name	Scientific name	Page of species account	Ranges in tooth count per row[1]		Remarks
			Upper	Lower	
Sperm whale	*Physeter macrocephalus*	51	18-25	10-16	Upper teeth rarely emerge. Lower teeth fit into sockets in upper jaw.
Baird's beaked whale	*Berardius bairdii*	88	0	1 or 2	At tip of lower jaw; sometimes 2d pair behind the first in older animals.
(Southern ?) bottlenose whale	*Hyperoodon* sp.	92	0	[2]1	At tip of lower jaw.[3]
Cuvier's beaked whale	*Ziphius cavirostris*	94	0	[2]1	At tip of lower jaw.[3]
Stejneger's beaked whale	*Mesoplodon stejnegeri*	102	0	[2]1	Teeth emerge from prominent arches behind tip of snout on either side of lower jaw.
Hubbs' beaked whale	*Mesoplodon carlhubbsi*	99	0	[2]1	On raised area midlength along lower jaw.
Blainville's beaked whale	*Mesoplodon densirostris*	103	0	[2]1	On prominences near corner of mouth. Forward tilting.
Ginkgo-toothed beaked whale	*Mesoplodon ginkgodens*	107	0	[2]1	About ½ way from tip of snout to gape.[3]
Hector's beaked whale	*Mesoplodon hectori*	110	0	[2]1	Near tip of lower jaw.
Killer whale	*Orcinus orca*	113	10-12	10-12	Prominent; curved and oriented backward and inward; pointed.
False killer whale	*Pseudorca crassidens*	118	8-11	8-11	Prominent; pointed and curved.
Short-finned pilot whale	*Globicephala macrorhynchus*	123	7-9	7-9	
Risso's dolphin	*Grampus griseus*	129	0	0-7	Near front of jaw; may have fallen out in older specimens; sometimes teeth in upper jaw.
White whale	*Delphinapterus leucas*	134	10-11	10-11	As few as 8 in older adults due to attrition.
Narwhal	*Monodon monoceros*	137	1	0	One (rarely both) pierce gum to become straight, spiraled external tusk, to 3 m long.[3]
Spotted dolphin	*Stenella attenuata*	141	34-48	34-48	
Spinner dolphin	*Stenella longirostris*	148	46-59	46-59	
Striped dolphin	*Stenella coeruleoalba*	155	43-50	43-50	
Common dolphin	*Delphinus delphis*	160	40-50	40-50	
Fraser's dolphin	*Lagenodelphis hosei*	166	34-44	34-44	
Pacific white-sided dolphin	*Lagenorhynchus obliquidens*	168	23-32	24-31	
Bottlenose dolphin	*Tursiops truncatus*	173	20-26	18-24	
Rough-toothed dolphin	*Steno bredanensis*	178	20-27	20-27	Tooth crown is sometimes marked by many fine vertical wrinkles.
Pygmy killer whale	*Feresa attenuata*	184	10-13	10-13	Lower teeth smaller. Many specimens have fewer teeth on right side than on left.
Melon-headed whale	*Peponocephala electra*	188	22-25	21-24	
Pygmy sperm whale	*Kogia breviceps*	193	0	12-16	Rarely 10-11; curved inward and backward, fit into sockets of upper jaw.
Dwarf sperm whale	*Kogia simus*	198	0-3	7-12	Rarely 13 on lower jaw; curved backward and inward, fit into sockets in upper jaw.
Dall's porpoise (including True's porpoise)	*Phocoenoides dalli*	200	19-28	20-28	
Harbor porpoise	*Phocoena phocoena*	205	23-28	22-26	Spade-shaped and relatively small.
Vaquita	*Phocoena sinus*	208	17-21	17-20	Spade-shaped.
Northern right whale dolphin	*Lissodelphis borealis*	209	37-49	37-49	Peglike teeth, extremely fine and sharp.

[1]See text footnote 5.

[2]Usually erupted from gums only in adult males.

[3]May have additional vestigial teeth in either jaw.

Table 2.—Body size; numbers, maximum dimensions and descriptions of baleen plates; and numbers and relative lengths of ventral grooves of eastern North Pacific mysticetes (see test footnote 5).

Common name	Scientific name	Page of species account	Maximum body size (m)	No of baleen plates per side	Maximum dimension of plates (cm)		Color of baleen	Mean number of bristles (per cm²)	Number of ventral grooves	Length of ventral grooves
					Length	Width base				
Blue whale	*Balaenoptera musculus*	13	26	270–395	84	30	All black with black bristles.	10–30	55–88	At least to umbilicus.
Fin whale	*Balaenoptera physalus*	23	24	262–473	70	30	Bluish gray with yellowish white stripes. Front 1/5–1/3 on right side all white.	10–35	56–100	At least to umbilicus.
Sei whale	*Balaenoptera borealis*	29	15.6	219–402	75–80	39	Ash black with blue tinge and fine light bristles; some near front may be light.	35–60	32–60	Ends about ½ way between flippers and umbilicus.
Bryde's whale	*Balaenoptera edeni*	34	14	255–365	42	24	Slate gray with lighter gray bristles.	15–35	40–50	At least to umbilicus.
Humpback whale	*Megaptera novaeangliae*	39	16	270–400	80	13	Black to olive brown, sometimes whitish. Bristles generally olive brown, sometimes whitish.	10–35	14–22	At least to umbilicus.
Bowhead whale	*Balaena mysticetus*	60	18	230–360	430	36.5	Dark gray to black; fringes slightly lighter.		None	xx
Right whale	*Eubalaena glacialis*	67	17	206–268	280	30.5	Dirty or yellowish gray; black fringes, some anterior plates partly or all white.	35–70	None	xx
Gray whale	*Eschrichtius robustus*	72	14	138–180	37	18	Yellowish white to white.		None	2 to 5 deep longitudinal creases on chin and throat.
Minke whale	*Balaenoptera acutorostrata*	80	10	231–285 (in other areas reported as up to 325).	21	10	White to yellowish white. Posterior plates may be brown or black.	15–25	50–70	End short of umbilicus, often just behind flippers.

APPENDIX A

Tags on Whales, Dolphins, and Porpoises

LARRY HOBBS[1]

Whether one's interest is the preservation of individual whales and porpoises, the conservation of a species, or the rational exploitation of a stock, it is important to have basic biological information about the lives of cetaceans. What, for example, are the limits of a given population's range, and how does its distribution within that range vary seasonally and from year to year? What is the population's size? What are its natural rates of reproduction and mortality? If there are identifiable subpopulations within the population, what is the extent of intermixing among them?

In seeking answers to these questions, we are hindered from the outset by the fact that most of the vital activities of cetaceans (e.g., feeding, reproduction, social interactions, and defense against natural enemies) occur primarily below the surface, well out of view to a surface observer. Some dolphins leap clear of the water as they travel or frolic, and certain whales are known to breach occasionally. But for the most part, individual cetaceans are visible to a surface observer only during brief moments when they break the air-water interface to breathe.

Some of our disadvantages in working with these animals are overcome when we can recognize individuals or groups in repeated encounters over time. It is toward this end that most marking and tagging techniques have been developed. Tagging and other marking have been carried out in the eastern North Pacific, making it desirable for readers of this book to become acquainted with various kinds of tags and marks, to be on the lookout for recognizable individuals, and to report observations of those animals to appropriate offices.

Natural Markings

For centuries people have been able to identify individual animals by their unique markings. Early whalers, for example, knew of distinctively marked or anomalously colored whales, such as the famous all-white bull sperm whale ("Mocha

[1]Marine Mammal Tagging Office, Northwest and Alaska Fisheries Center National Marine Mammal Laboratory, National Marine Fisheries Service, NOAA, 7600 Sand Point Way N.E., Bldg. 32, Seattle, WA 98115.

Appendix Figure A-1.—Humpback flukes are often so distinctively shaped, scarred, and pigmented that they can be used to identify individuals in repeated encounters. Similarly, barnacle patterns (in gray whales) and callosity patterns (in right whales), dorsal fin shapes (in bottlenose dolphins and killer whales), saddle patterns (in pilot whales and killer whales), and combinations of these have been used as "natural tags" in studies of cetaceans. (Photo from Hawaii, by D. McSweeney.)

Appendix Figure A-2.—A herd of short-finned pilot whales off Catalina Island, Calif., including an animal with a truncated dorsal fin which made it recognizable for nearly 7 years in repeated encounters around the Channel Islands. Note the light gray saddle behind the dorsal fin in the two animals at the rear. Saddles are absent in some groups of eastern North Pacific pilot whales. (Photo by G. E. Lingle.)

Appendix Figure A-3.—Some gaping wounds, such as the hole in the left side of this gray whale, may never heal. Other lesser injuries, however, may heal, leaving scars and/or unpigmented areas by which individual whales can be identified. (Photo from San Ignacio Lagoon, Baja California, by L. Hobbs.)

Dick") after which the novel *Moby Dick* was patterned. Similarly, researchers today can often use natural markings and unusual appearances to identify individuals and monitor their behavior and movement. Investigators have compiled pictorial catalogues of markings of gray whales, shapes and color patterns of humpback whale flukes, and dorsal fin shapes and body markings of killer whales and bottlenose dolphins. Using these catalogues, a great deal has been learned about social behavior, herd structure, migration routes, and short-term movements of these species. Records of other cetaceans with anomalous marking, unusual coloration, or disfigured dorsal fins have been used in studies of various aspects of cetacean life history and behavior.

Static Tags

Whalers before the turn of the 20th century occasionally found old harpoons embedded in the tissue of freshly killed whales, evidence of a previous unsuccessful hunt. From reports of these harpoons, cetologists conceived of marking whales with labeled harpoons as a means of gathering information from killed whales on migrations, sizes of their stocks, and effects of exploitation by the whaling industry. Following a successful experimental tagging cruise in 1932–33, an extensive tagging program was undertaken by the British Discovery Investigations using standardized 23 cm long metal tubes fitted with a ballistic head. These marks, which became known as Discovery tags, are fired from a 12-gauge shotgun into the flesh of the whale. Later, marks were also made for smaller whales and were shot from a 410-gauge shotgun. Each tag is labeled with a serial number and an address for return. A reward is offered for receipt of the tag along with pertinent information concerning the animal and its taking. Although the Discovery Committee discontinued its involvement in this marking effort in 1939, marking of whales with Discovery-type tags has continued by agencies in many whaling countries.

It was not until the 1960's, when interest in cetacean studies greatly increased, that investigators began to experiment with

Appendix Figure A-4.—Although color patterns of many species of cetaceans change with age, individuals occasionally assume radically anomalous adult coloration. For example, in the waters off San Francisco, Calif., a "normally" colored Pacific white-sided dolphin (upper animal) is seen in the close company of an anomalously pigmented individual (lower animal). (Photos by R. L. Brownell, Jr.)

methods of tagging and marking which did not depend for their success on killing the animal. As a consequence, a variety of externally visible tags and marks were developed to give the investigator a record of the identity of individual cetaceans.

Because some porpoises and dolphins often ride the bow pressure wave of boats and ships, they are relatively easily captured or tagged from a moving vessel. In recent years, many types of spaghetti streamers and dorsal fin tags or marks have been placed on small cetaceans of the eastern North Pacific.

The spaghetti streamers are generally placed immediately in front of the dorsal fin, slightly to either side of the midline of the back. These tags can be attached to free-ranging animals with a pole applicator or crossbow, not requiring capture. The tag consists of a stainless steel barb which penetrates through the blubber just into the muscle; a stainless steel or monofilament leader which is attached to the barb and passes out through the skin; and an attached streamer which may be a color-coded extension of the leader or a wide, flat strip of tough plastic which ideally trails along the animal's body. Spaghetti tags are numbered and often labeled with an address for return. Because of their small size, the labels cannot be seen clearly on a free-ranging dolphin, even at close range, and specific information can only be obtained when a tag is examined closely on a captured animal or extracted from an animal, usually postmortem. Color coding, however, can often be recognized from a distance and may provide critical information concerning the date and location of tag placement and subsequent movement of the animal.

When investigators need more specific and longer term information about the dolphins being studied, they may need to capture the animal and apply more readily visible tags and marks with individual coding. The dorsal fin is generally chosen as the site for tag/mark placement as it is the most prominent and easily observed portion of a surfacing small cetacean and is thought to be more durable than other potential sites. Small triangular wedges clipped out of the tough connective tissue on the trailing edge of the dorsal fin have facilitated identification of individual cetaceans in some studies. Alternatively, button or disc tags are placed near the center of the dorsal fin and are held on both surfaces by a central bolt which passes through the fin. The smaller jumbo rototags, a type of cattle ear tag, pivot from a single forward stud which passes through the trailing edge of the dorsal fin. Finally, "flag" tags, which also are attached at their leading edge, have been tested in captivity, but these larger tags have not, at this writing, been used in the field. The three tags mentioned above have characteristic symbols or alphanumeric designations that allow individual identification at ranges varying according to the size of the symbols.

Freeze brands—symbols or alphanumeric designations applied to skin tissue with irons that have been cooled in liquid nitrogen, Freon-22,[2] or dry ice and alcohol—have proven effective as permanent marks which are highly visible at moderate ranges. These marks have been placed on the back of animals (for aerial observers) or on the dorsal fin (for surface observers) causing no apparent long-term discomfort to the animal.

All methods described above have been utilized on a variety of smaller cetaceans. However, due to the obvious difficulties of handling the larger whales, only remote application of tags and

[2]Reference to trade names does not imply endorsement by the National Marine Fisheries Service, NOAA.

Appendix Figure A-5.—Discovery tags, named after the British Discovery Expeditions for which they were developed, have been used for half a century in studies of cetaceans. Shot into the flesh of large whales (bottom) and smaller whales (top) by 12-gauge of 410-gauge shotguns, these numbered darts provide information on movements and growth rates. Unfortunately, they can be recovered only by killing the tagged animal (in whale fisheries). (Photo courtesy of D. W. Rice.)

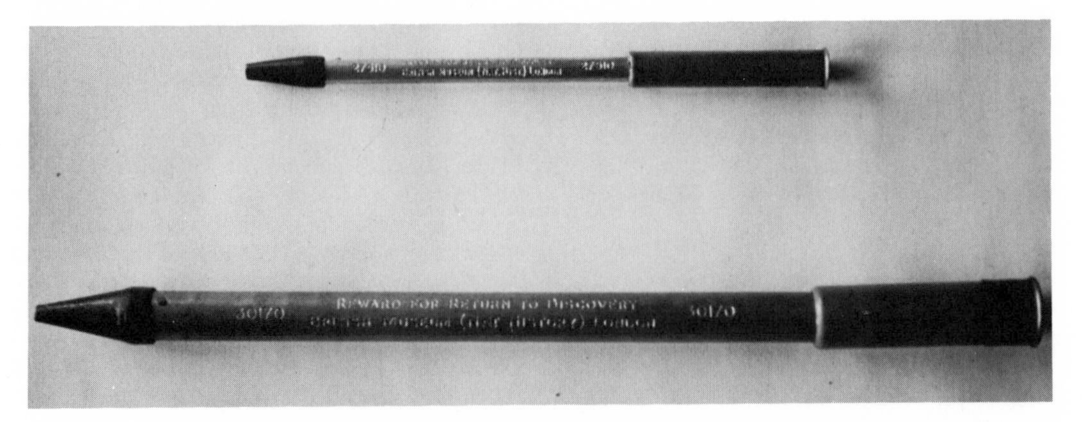

Appendix Figure A-6.—Some small or medium-sized whales have been captured, marked with patterns of notches carved from the rear margins of the dorsal fin, and released. Sometimes naturally frayed and marred dorsal fins bearing patterned notches, such as on this male killer whale, can facilitate identification of individuals. Note the postdorsal saddle characteristic of some killer whale groups. (Photo by K. C. Balcomb.)

marks is practical for them. To date, only spaghetti streamer tags have been used in external marking of larger whales. Some researchers feel that life expectancy of these tags is so short and the probability of resighting so poor, that such programs are not worthwhile. Nonetheless, spaghetti streamers shot from crossbows have been placed in numerous whales in the eastern North Pacific, and we request the cooperation of readers in reporting sightings of these tagged animals.

Radio tags

Since cetaceans spend the majority of their life under water, move during the night as well as the day, and often vanish from the watchful eye of an observer even though they may be clearly marked or tagged, the development of radio transmitters for whales and dolphins has greatly aided investigators. Early radio-tracking systems for dolphins consisted of a simple radio beacon on the animal and a directional antenna and receiving system on an aircraft or surface vessel. Each time the instrumented animal surfaced, a pulsed signal was broadcasted from the transmitter and the direction of the signal was determined by rotating the antenna. Because of the inherent problems in localizing such a short signal, an automatic direction finder (ADF) was developed which would indicate instantaneous relative bearing of the tagged animal. At about the time this ADF became available, sensors were added to the basic transmitter to encode and transmit parameters such as depth of dive (as pressure) and ambient temperature. This allowed scientists to begin to understand the relationship between certain environmental parameters and cetacean behavior. In addition to their transmitting function, radio packages are highly visible and can serve as identifiers, especially when a xenon flasher or a colorful streamer is attached.

Techniques for attaching radio transmitters continue to pose the major problem for the full utilization of this valuable tool. Various attachments have been tested over the years in an attempt to reduce the effect of transmitters on the behavior of the animals and to increase their retention time. Toward this end, the early dorsal fin saddles and transmitters used on free-ranging dolphins and pilot whales have been modified to reduce their weight and mass and thus their drag through the water. Several larger whales have been restrained and transmitters attached to them with varying degrees of success. Elastic harnesses and surgical attachment using sutures have been tested on juvenile gray whales, a cross-pinning attachment through the dorsal fin has been tried on a killer whale, and dorsal fin packages have been placed on humpback whales temporarily trapped in gill nets or fish traps in the North Atlantic. Recently a transmitter shot from a modified 12-gauge shotgun and designed to imbed in the blubber of a free-ranging whale was tested on humpback and fin whales. This method of remotely administering the transmitter to unrestrained whales may, with further modification, prove valuable for shorter term telemetry studies. Another recent approach uses two "barnacle" anchors implanted by small explosive charges. So far, each attachment method employed has its own drawbacks, and the ultimate attachment devices, which will vary from species to species, have yet to be developed.

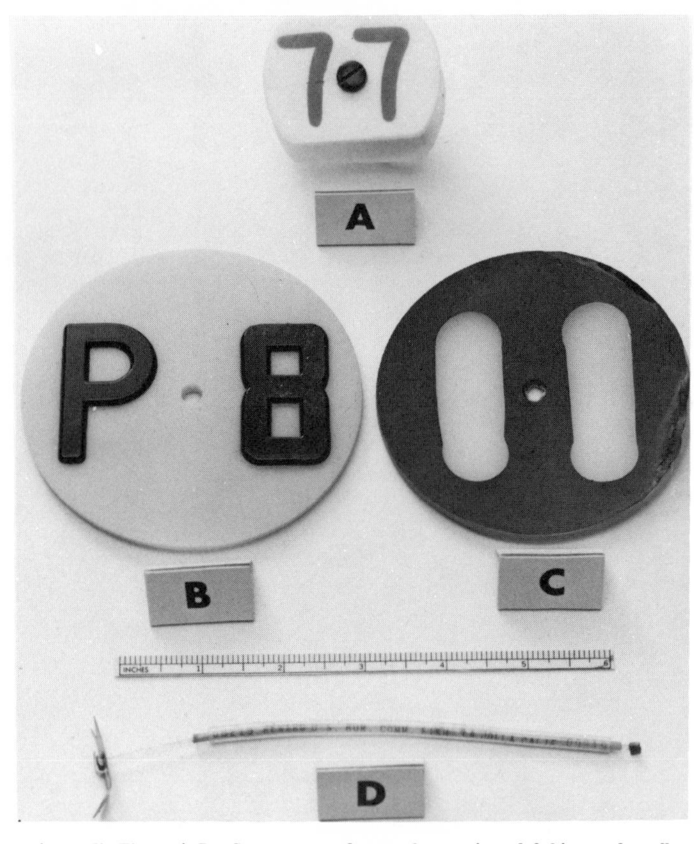

Appendix Figure A-7.—Some tags used to mark porpoises, dolphins, and small whales. A, B, and C are nylon button tags, which are placed in the dorsal fin and may be clearly visible as an animal surfaces to breathe; D is a vinyl spaghetti tag. (Photo courtesy of NOSC.)

Present and Future Research

There is a great deal of interest in and research directed toward improving tags and marks, especially for use in population estimation. Proposed devices are tested in captivity and in the wild, when practical, to determine if there are any harmful effects to the animal, if the materials and design are adequate for the prescribed task, and if the tag or mark will last a sufficient length of time under field conditions. Methods under investigation which show promise for the future include laser marking, satellite-linked telemetry, improved spaghetti streamer tags, methods of attachment similar to those of parasites or symbionts occurring naturally on free-ranging cetaceans, and cross-pinned dorsal fin attachments.

This discussion of cetacean tagging and marking is by no means exhaustive and will quickly become outdated as new materials and methodologies evolve. This appendix is intended to impress upon the reader that even after the techniques are perfected, tagging and natural-marking programs depend for their success on the resighting of tagged or marked animals or the recovery of tags. We therefore appeal to readers to be careful and critical observers at sea, to photograph tagged or marked animals, and to forward the information (including: date, time, location, observer, ambient conditions, description of observation, photograph, number of animals in herd, direction of movement, etc.) to one of the authors or the National Marine Mammal Laboratory, National Marine Fisheries Service, NOAA, 7600 Sand Point Way N.E., Bldg. 32, Seattle, WA 98115. Your reported resightings may play a critical role in resolving the mysteries surrounding the natural history of porpoises, dolphins, and whales.

Appendix Figure A-8.—A spaghetti tag in the right side of a short-finned pilot whale off Santa Catalina Island, Calif. (Photo by L. Hobbs.)

Appendix Figure A-9.—Examples of dorsal fin tags used on small cetaceans: a button tag on a free-swimming common dolphin off Palos Verdes, Calif. (left); a double-bolted dorsal fin tag (no. 61) and a cattle ear tag (no. 46) on a bottlenose dolphin off Sarasota, Fla. (top right); a modified disc tag or "sand dollar tag" designed for closer adherence to the fin (middle right); and a "flag" tag on the dorsal fin of a spinner dolphin in Sea Life Park, Hawaii (bottom). Dorsal fin tags have enjoyed limited success,but there is still no version adequate for long-term studies of cetaceans. (Photos by B. Noble, courtesy of Marineland of the Pacific [top left]; A. B. Irvine [top right]; courtesy of NMFS [middle right, bottom].)

Appendix Figure A-10.—Freeze-branding is an apparently painless method of applying a long lasting identifying mark to the body of a cetacean, as illustrated by these two photos of freeze-branded bottlenose dolphins. Some systems are alphanumeric codes (left), while others use angular marks in combination having numeric translations. (Photos by A. B. Irvine [left]; S. Leatherwood [right].)

Appendix Figure A-11.—Freeze-branded bottlenose dolphins at liberty off Sarasota, Fla. Though many subtle details remain to be tested and refined, freeze brands appear to offer great promise. In the right animal, note the disfigured dorsal fin. In the left animal, note the cattle ear tag placed near the top of the fin. (Photo by A. B. Irvine.)

Appendix Figure A-12.—A common dolphin wearing a radio tag transmitter surfaces to breathe off southern California. (Photo courtesy of W. E. Evans.)

Appendix Figure A-13.—Wild tagged dolphins. Dolphin in foreground has a radio transmitter above a freeze brand (#18). Dolphin to the left has a behavioral observation tag (#22) with a freeze brand (#80) below it. The three nearest dolphins all have Rototags trailing from their dorsal fins. (Photo by M. D. Scott.)

Appendix Figure A-14.—A killer whale in Puget Sound, Wash., wearing a radio tag (painted with the number 1) which provided tracking signals to aircraft and small boats outfitted with special antenna arrays. (Photo by J. O. Sneddon, courtesy of University of Washington, Seattle.)

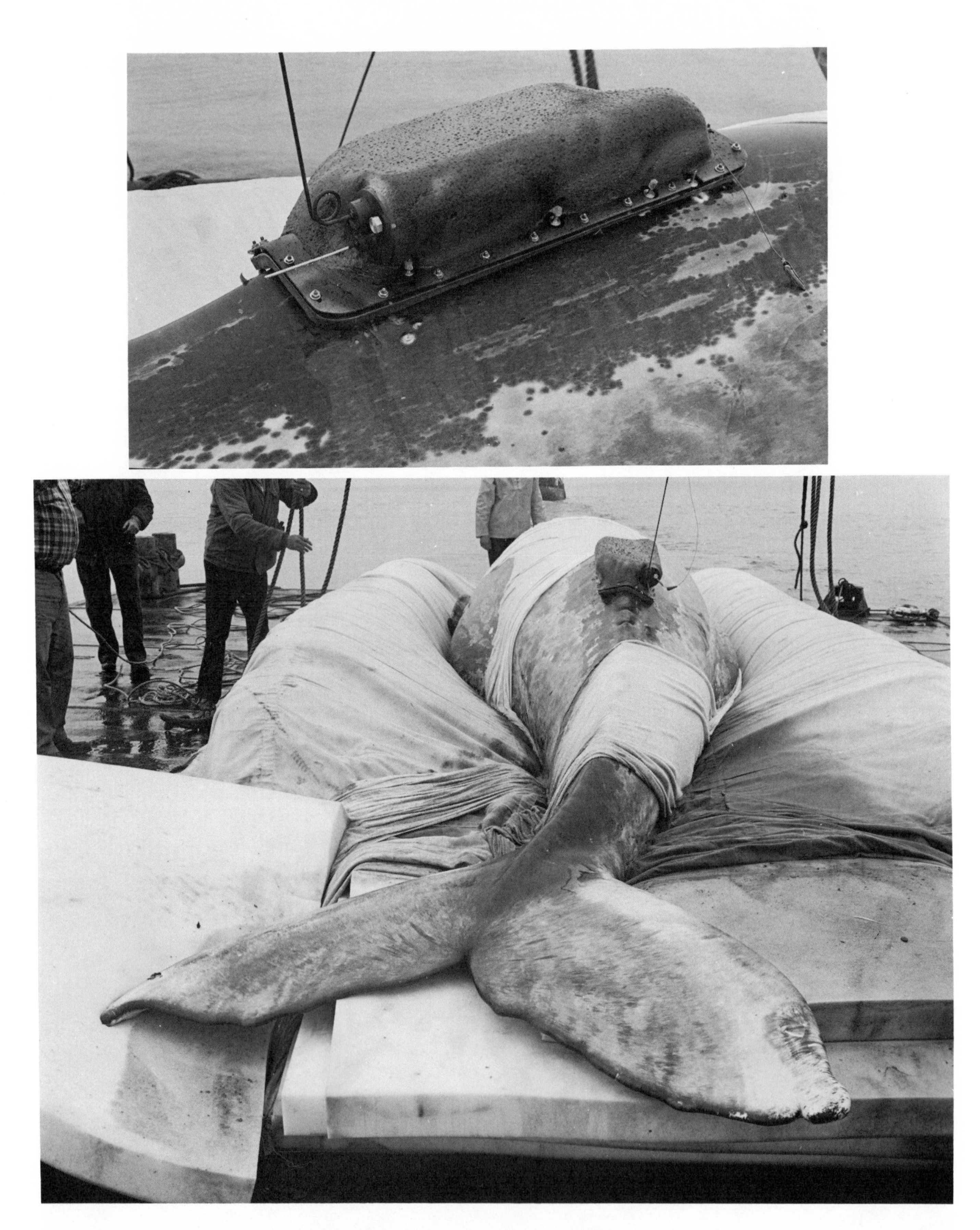

Appendix Figure A-15.—A radio transmitter package surgically attached to the dorsal ridge of a California gray whale. This yearling animal, captive for most of the first year of its life, was released into the ocean off San Diego, Calif., in March 1972 and was subsequently tracked from shipboard and aircraft for over 30 days. The sensor-transmitter package, shown in detail (top), was designed to measure the maximum depth of the animal's dive and the water temperature at that depth. (Photos by S. Leatherwood.)

Appendix Figure A-16.—This "friendly" California gray whale was approached in San Ignacio Lagoon, Baja California, close enough to allow pole application of a "barnacle" tag developed by Bruce Mate. This gray whale was successfully tracked over nearly its entire migration route from the Mexican lagoon to Unimak Pass, Alaska. (Photo by L. Hobbs.)

Appendix Figure A-17.—Many recent efforts have concentrated on remotely attaching radio transmitters to large whales and then tracking them. Here (left), a researcher fires a radiotag at a fin whale in Prince William Sound, Alaska (the line can be seen unfurling to his left); the nearer of the two fin whales wears the implanted tag (bottom). Though tags so applied have resulted in successful short-term tracks and subsequent relocations and show tremendous promise, there continue to be technical problems requiring systematic attention. (Photos courtesy of NMFS.)

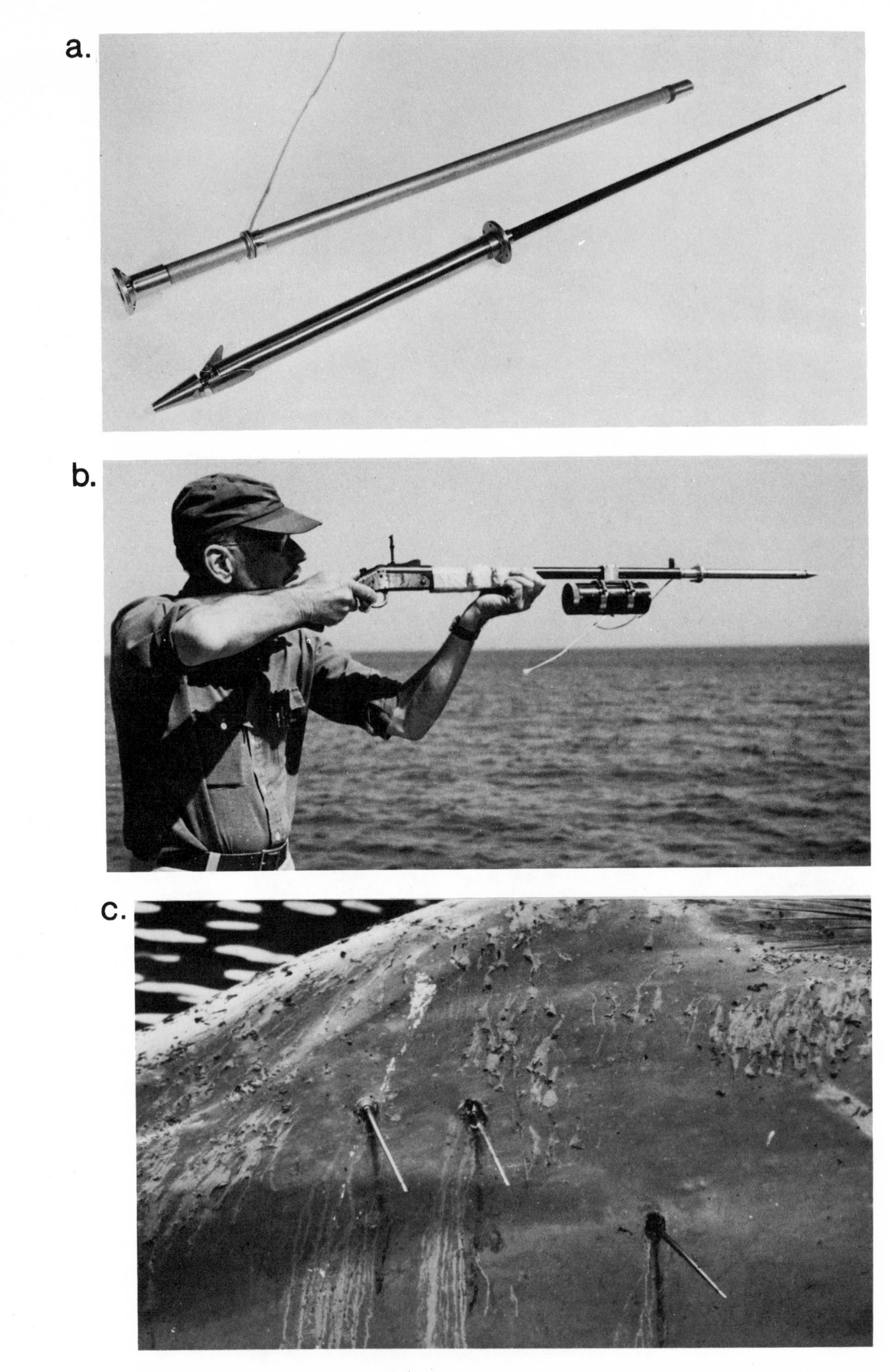
a.
b.
c.

Appendix Figure A-18.—Remotely implantable tags (top) in the firing gun (middle) and in the flesh of a fin whale carcass (bottom). (Photos courtesy of W. E. Schevill and W. A. Watkins.)

Appendix Figure A-19.—A satellite linked radiotag recently developed for attachment to small whales and dolphins. (Photo by J. Jennings, courtesy of NMFS.)

Appendix Figure A-20.—A tag-reward poster. (Photo by J. Jennings, courtesy of NMFS.) →

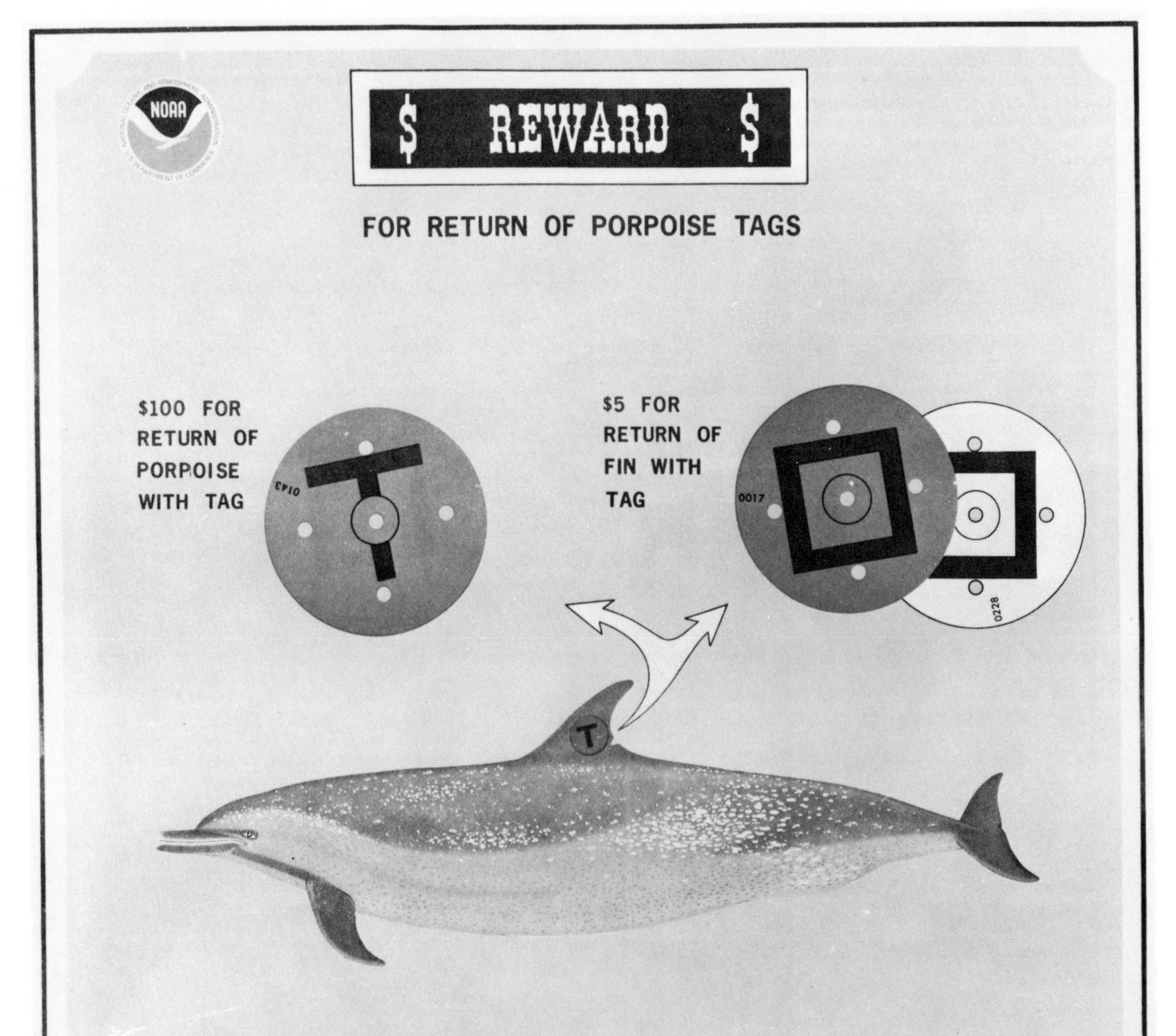

The U.S. National Marine Fisheries Service conducted an experimental tagging study in the area to the east of Clipperton Island in October - November, 1978. Orange and yellow disc tags were attached to the dorsal fins of 656 porpoise. Of these, 331 were tagged with special orange "T" tags indicating tetracycline injections for an age determination study. All fins were notched to serve as permanent marks.

It is essential that the bodies of any accidentally killed porpoise involved in the age determination study, as indicated by the "T" tag, be returned so that the teeth and bones can be examined. Only the fins with the tags in place need to be returned from any dead porpoise with other types of disc tags, so the tags can be evaluated. The location and date of tag recovery must be indicated. Reports of sightings of tagged porpoise will be appreciated.

When an observer is on board, the reward will go to the vessel.

TO COLLECT REWARD: Send fin with tag or entire porpoise if a "T" tag. Tell where and when tag was collected.

MAIL TO:
U.S. National Marine Fisheries Service
Southwest Fisheries Center
P.O. Box 271
La Jolla, California 92038
PHONE:
(714) 453-2820

WARNING: NO PORPOISE ARE TO BE INTENTIONALLY KILLED – IN ACCORDANCE WITH THE MARINE MAMMAL PROTECTION ACT OF 1972.

APPENDIX B

RECORDING AND REPORTING OBSERVATIONS OF CETACEANS AT SEA

To increase reliability of identifications, observers should train themselves to ask the following kinds of questions each time a cetacean is encountered:

1. How large was the animal?
2. Did it have a dorsal fin? If so, what was its size, shape, and position?
3. Was the animal's blow visible? If so, how tall did it appear? What was its shape? How frequently did the animal blow?
4. What was the animal's color and color pattern?
5. Did the animal have any distinctive markings?
6. If it was a large or medium-sized animal, did it show its tail flukes?
7. If it was a medium-sized or small animal, did it approach, avoid, or ignore the vessel? Did it ride the bow or stern wave?
8. What was the animal's behavior? Did it jump from the water? If so, did it make a smooth graceful arching jump, or did it spin, somersault, or reenter with a splash?

One characteristic alone is rarely sufficient. The more relevant evidence the observer obtains, the greater the likelihood of a reliable identification. Even the most experienced cetologists are often unable to make a positive identification. Therefore, even if you cannot positively identify an animal or make a good guess as to its identity, do not hesitate to fill out the rest of the sighting record form and submit it to an appropriate office. A listing of observed characters and a partially completed form may enable a cetologist to make an identification based on those characters and his knowledge of the distribution, movements, and behavior of cetaceans. A sketch made as soon as possible after the encounter and photographs taken from as many angles as possible will aid in the identification. **If you identify the species, state the basis for the identification (features seen)!**

A sample sighting report is provided here to demonstrate the proper recording of observations. A blank copy, which may be photocopied for field use, is included at the end of the guide.

Reliable, intermittent reports of cetaceans are of interest. It is also useful to have a record of an entire cruise track and of the

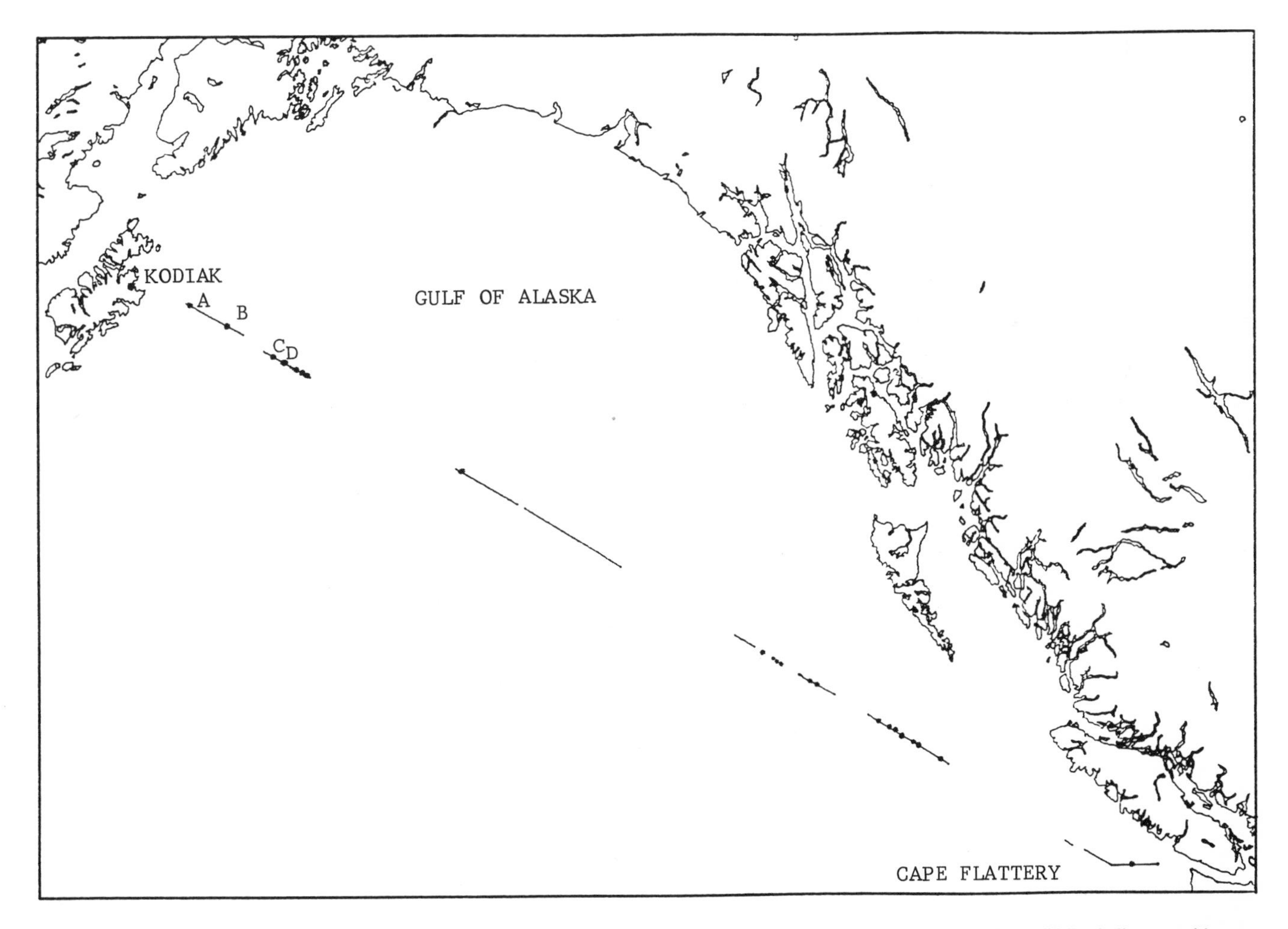

Appendix Figure B-1.—A map of a portion of the temperate eastern North Pacific, showing the cruise track of a research vessel. The solid line indicates positions over which observer(s) maintained watches for marine mammals. Dots indicate locations of sightings of marine mammals (note that several sightings occurred while there was no official watch). Consult the text of this appendix for sample journal entries for sightings at locations indicated by the letters. (Computer plot and sample data courtesy NMFS.)

zones in which vigilance was maintained but no cetaceans were observed. Such data can be used to determine relative density and seasonal changes in distribution.

To be useful, effort records should include the following minimum information: time and location of beginning and ending of each continuous cetacean watch, weather conditions as they affect visibility, sea state, ship's speed, height of the observer(s) above the water, number of persons on watch, and details of each sighting, particularly the relative bearing and distance of the animals from the ship at the time of the initial sighting.

The following report is a sample of the sighting log of an observer cruise. Although there were 12 watch periods and 29 separate sightings made during the cruise, only the first two legs and four sightings are listed as examples. The data were collected on special forms developed by NMFS, and the plot is derived from a computer program developed for graphic analysis of sighting data. Over 25,000 sightings made in the eastern North Pacific since 1958 have been coded in a special format and are analyzed on an ongoing basis under the NMFS Marine Mammal Platforms of Opportunity Program. Sighting forms which include effort data are available from the Platforms of Opportunity Program, National Marine Mammal Laboratory, National Marine Fisheries Service, NOAA, 7600 Sand Point Way N.E., Bldg. 32, Seattle, WA 98115.

GENERAL INFORMATION

NOAA Ship DISCOVERER (303 foot research vessel)
U.S. Department of Commerce
National Ocean Survey

Kodiak, Alaska to Cape Flattery, Washington

8–11 June 1978

Observers: T. Crawford and R. Beach, NMFS, Dall Porpoise Program
National Marine Mammal Laboratory, NMFS, NOAA
7600 Sand Point Way N.E., Bldg. 32
Seattle, Washington 98115

Eye level of observers: 36 feet above water

Average ship speed: 15 knots

Continuous watch information (Fig. B-1):

Leg	Date	Start time	End time	Start position	End position	Weather-Visibility
1-2	6/8	1300	1630	57-24N	56-59N	Beaufort II
				151-01W	149-36W	vis. 12 miles
3-4	6/8	1800	21u1	56-45N	56-22N	Beaufort I
				149-04W	147-50W	vis. 15 miles

Cetacean observations (Fig. B-2):

A - 6/8 1305 — 42 Dall's porpoise (*Phocoenoides dalli*) bearing 270° relative at 200 yards. Headed SW. In small groups. Ten in largest group. No bow riding. Roostertails. Surface temp. 8 °C. Identified by shape of head, color pattern, and dorsal fin (half white).

B - 6/8 1527 — 27 Dall's porpoise bearing 045° at 150 yards. Headed NW. Roostertails. 2 groups - 1 rode bow for a few minutes. Surface temp. 8 °C.

C - 6/8 1839 — 1 humpback whale (*Megaptera novaeangliae*) bearing 290° at 300 yards. Saw dorsal fin or hump and long knobby flipper. Headed NW. Surface temp. 9 °C.

D - 6/8 1915 — 4 Dall's porpoise bearing 045° at 300 yards. Headed SE. Slow abbreviated rolling, then roostertails as ship approached. No bow riding. Surface temp. 9 °C.

SIGHTING INFORMATION — Alitak Bay, Kodiak Is.

DATE AND LOCAL TIME: 2 July 1978, 1753 — POSITION[1]: 56° 45'N × 154° 15'W

WEATHER CONDITIONS: Foggy w/light rain; vis. 3 miles. Beaufort II.

OCEANOGRAPHIC CONDITIONS[2]: Sea surface temp. 8°C. Strong scattering layer on fathometer at 30-40 ft.

SPECIES[3]: Humpback whales (Megaptera noveangliae) — NUMBER OF ANIMAL(S): 8 ± 2

HEADING OF ANIMAL(S) (TRUE): Milling (enclosed bay) — SPEED OF ANIMAL(S) (KNOTS): —

ASSOCIATED ORGANISMS: 1 Harbor porpoise (Phocoena phocoena) seen briefly. Thousands of sooty shearwaters feeding at surface.

TAGS OR UNUSUAL MARKINGS[4]: Observed one humpback with distinctive white pattern on underside of flukes. (See photo KDE-7).

CHARACTERISTICS OBSERVED WHICH RESULTED IN SPECIES IDENTIFICATION: Mushroom shaped blow, greyish-black color, back strongly arched & flukes shown on dives, small hooked dorsal fin. 40 ft.

BEHAVIOR OF ANIMAL(S) - INCLUDE CLOSEST APPROACH: Diving repeatedly - several breaching within 300 yards of ship.

SKETCHES

Humpback - beginning dive

Harbor porpoise

PHOTOS AVAILABLE: YES ✓ NO

ADDITIONAL REMARKS: Observed whales (apparently feeding) for over 4 hours before we departed area. Harbor porpoise surfaced near ship, then moved quickly out of sight.

NAME AND ADDRESS OF OBSERVER (SHIP OR A/C): Kathleen Edwards
NOAA Ship SURVEYOR
FPO Seattle, WA. 98799

[1]If latitude and longitude are not available, record best estimate of position, e.g., 5 hours at 10 knots, SE of Kodiak.

[2]Any oceanographic or bathymetric information obtainable at the time of sighting may be significant. Such measurements as water depth, presence of large fish schools or deep scattering layer, organisms characteristic of the bottom (e.g., flat sand plain, sea mount, submarine cliff), surface temperature, depth of thermocline, and salinity should be included if available. In the Pacific, similar data have been used to demonstrate reliable associations between common dolphins and significant features of bottom relief and relationships between the onset of their nighttime deep diving (feeding) patterns and the upward migration of the scattering layers.

[3]Sometimes cetaceans of two or more species are found together. If more than one type is sighted, try to identify each. Give both common and scientific names of each, and even if you cannot identify the animal(s), describe, sketch, and if possible, photograph them and fill out the rest of the sighting report.

[4]Describe any tags seen (see Appendix A), including their size, shape, color, and position on the animal's body and any symbols or numbers they contain.

Appendix Figure B-2.—A sample sighting form resulting from an encounter with 6–10 humpback whales and a single harbor porpoise. It cannot be emphasized too strongly that the value of a sighting report is directly proportional to the amount of quality information it contains. A sighting report is far more valuable if it describes the animal(s) and the encounter in detail than if it simply reports the observer's decision about species identity, with no supporting documentation. Use form, following page 245.

APPENDIX C

STRANDED WHALES, DOLPHINS, AND PORPOISES

Appendix Figure C-1.—Whales and dolphins sometimes strand themselves individually or as entire herds, for reasons still incompletely understood. Mass strandings are not limited to the smaller whales and dolphins. Though no large group of baleen whales has been reported to have stranded en masse, pods of sperm whales, such as this group in Florence, Oreg., in June 1979, show up with surprising frequency along beaches of the world. (Photo by R. Pitman, courtesy of NMFS.)

As we discussed briefly in the introduction, whales, dolphins, and porpoises sometimes strand or beach themselves, individually or in entire herds. Stranded individuals are often sick or injured. Mass strandings, involving from several to several hundred individuals, appear to have more complex causes. They may result from fear reactions, bad weather conditions, herd-wide disease or malfunctioning of the echolocation system. Whatever their causes, cetacean strandings usually attract crowds and elicit much public interest and sympathy. There are frequently attempts to save the lives of the animals involved.

Individually stranded cetaceans rarely survive, even if they are found soon after stranding and are transported to adequate holding facilities. However, in mass strandings, some individuals may be completely healthy. If they are found soon enough after stranding, properly protected and transported, and correctly cared for in the initial few days after collection, they may survive for long periods in captivity. Attempts to rescue all the animals in a mass stranding by towing them out to sea are frustrating because the animals usually swim back onto the beach.

If you discover a stranding, before you become involved in an attempt to save a live stranded animal or to collect data from a dead one, be aware of the following:

Marine mammals, alive or dead, are currently protected by law in U.S. waters and on U.S. beaches. Under provisions of the Marine Mammal Protection Act of 1972, it is unlawful for persons without a permit to handle, harass, or possess any marine mammal or possess any part of a marine mammal. It is within the authority of the State officials and the National Marine Fisheries Service employees to arrange for the care of live

Appendix Figure C-2.—Strandings of individual cetaceans, such as this Cuvier's beaked whale in La Jolla, Calif., have been most often related to disease or injury. Though some stranded small cetaceans may be easy to retrieve and transport, the problems clearly increase with the size of the animal. (Photo by W. F. Perrin, courtesy of NMFS.)

Appendix Figure C-3.—While waiting for help to arrive to collect a live-stranded cetacean, such as this common dolphin at Point Mugu, Calif., one should endeavor to keep it as comfortable as possible. In the absence of a pool of water sufficiently deep for the animal to submerge itself, one might cover much of the body (being careful to leave the blowhole clear) with wet towels. In particular, dorsal fin, flippers, and flukes should be kept wet. (Photo by S. Leatherwood.)

animals through certified institutions, such as many of those listed in Appendix E. (Even if the animals were not protected by law, any impulse to take them to backyard swimming pools, for instance, should be tempered by the knowledge that their chances of survival are far greater in an institution with the facilities and expertise to care for them properly.) The best general rule is to notify the nearest State fish and game agency or National Marine Fisheries Service Office. If you prefer, however, you may contact one of the institutions listed in Appendix E and ask it to handle the situation. Some will already have permits to investigate strandings. Most will be anxious to help.

Although you cannot remove the animal from the beach without a permit, you can help keep it alive until it is removed. While waiting for help to arrive, endeavor to keep the animal as comfortable as possible. If it is not too large and surf conditions permit, it should be removed to shallow water where it is barely afloat. The bouyancy of the water will reduce the stress to the animal and will help prevent overheating—a real danger to stranded cetaceans.

Whether or not the animal can be floated, care should be taken to protect it from sunburn, drying out, and overheating. If it is afloat, exposed parts should be splashed down frequently. If it is high and dry, it should be covered with damp cloth, particularly on the dorsal fin, flippers, and flukes, and the body and the terrain should be watered frequently to prevent the animal from overheating in the areas of contact with the sand or rock.

Be careful to leave the blowhole free so that the animal can breathe. Note also that the eyes are particularly sensitive and susceptible to injury; they should be covered with a wet cloth and treated with special care.

With luck, this handling will be rewarded by the animal's timely removal to an aquarium, where it can receive proper attention. Even if the animal cannot be kept alive, collection and examination of the carcass can provide valuable information for studies of cetacean biology, disease, or reaction to environmental pollutants.

Dead stranded cetaceans, even when badly decomposed, are an important source of materials for museum study and display. Therefore, every attempt should be made to get the carcass into the best hands. Dead cetaceans, like the live ones, are protected by law and may not be removed without a permit. The procedure for obtaining permission to collect them is the same as that outlined for live strandings. The majority of the listed institutions along the Pacific coast will respond to calls about live or dead strandings. Even if you are unable to contact an appropriate official, you can still collect some valuable information by identifying and photographing the specimen and by taking measurements (see Appendix D).

APPENDIX D

RECORDING AND REPORTING DATA ON STRANDED CETACEANS

So that measurements of cetaceans taken at different times and locations can be compared, the methods of taking them have been standardized, although there is still some disagreement about which of the measurements are most important. The data form located at the end of this guide, usable for both baleen and toothed whales, includes all the measurements routinely made by cetologists plus a few new ones the authors consider important. The form and the directions for taking measurements are synthesized from those currently in use by the Naval Ocean Systems Center, San Diego; the Fisheries Research Board of Canada; Hubbs/Sea World Research Institute; the Los Angeles County Museum; the U.S. National Museum, Washington, D.C.; and the National Marine Fisheries Service, Southwest Fisheries Center, La Jolla, Calif.

Data on stranded cetaceans should be collected by someone experienced in handling and measuring cetaceans. The legal problems associated with collection of a specimen are discussed in Appendix C. In addition to having a permit or knowing how to obtain permission to collect the specimen, persons active in cetacean research will usually have access to laboratory facilities where in-depth studies, including postmortem examinations and collection of tissues for specialized laboratory examinations, can be conducted. Furthermore, specialized equipment, and the number of steps required to do a complete examination of the specimen, make the procedure prohibitive for most noncetologists. Diligent attempts should be made to contact one of the institutions listed in Appendix E. If no one is available and no permit or approval is obtainable, you are limited to photographing, sketching, and measuring the specimen without removing the carcass or any part of it from the beach.

Any person taking data on stranded cetaceans should follow the instructions itemized below, being careful to take measurements in the manner prescribed and to record data in as much detail as possible.

1. Specimens should be preserved in 10% buffered Formalin[1] except for the stomach contents, which should be kept in 70% ethyl or 40% isopropyl alcohol, or frozen. Commercial rubbing alcohol (isopropyl) will suffice. As a minimum, the head, flippers, and reproductive tract should be preserved. If no other method of handling the specimen is available, and only as a last resort, it may be buried in the sand well above the high tide line and carefully marked so it can be recovered later. Burying usually results in the loss of at least some parts of the skeleton.

2. The carcass should be examined for external parasites, particularly in such areas as the blowhole(s), the eyes, any wounds, and on the trailing edges of the dorsal fin, flippers, and flukes. Occasionally barnacles will be found on teeth or baleen plates. Like the stomach contents, parasites should be preserved in alcohol.

3. Photographs and sketches are a valuable part of data collection—views of the animal(s) from as many angles as possible, and detailed shots of such features as baleen plates, mouth and teeth, ventral grooves, flippers, flukes, and unusual scars or coloration should be included. Including a ruler or other object of known size is helpful for reference.

4. Although scientific data are usually expressed in metric units, measurements should be taken in whatever units are readily available. All measurements should be taken in a straight line, as shown in the diagram, unless otherwise noted. Measurements which refer to the rostrum are taken from the tip of the upper jaw. The external auditory meatus (ear) is a small, inconspicuous opening located just below and behind the eye. To locate the ear the observer must sometimes scrape away some of the skin to expose the pigmented ear canal beneath it.

5. Throat creases are found on the throat of beaked whales, sperm whales, and dwarf sperm whales. Ventral grooves are found only on balaenopterid whales. Ventral grooves should be counted between the flippers.

6. Numbers of teeth or baleen plates are often conclusive indicators of species, and they should be counted and described in as much detail as possible.

It is difficult to overstress the importance of data from stranded cetaceans. For some species, the only data available have come from stranded individuals. By carefully gleaning from each specimen all the data that can be collected, you will make a valuable contribution.

[1]Reference to trade names does not imply endorsement by the National Marine Fisheries Service, NOAA.

CONVERSION FACTORS

To change	Into	Multiply by:
Centimeters	Inches	0.3937
Meters	Feet	3.282
Meters	Yards	1.094
Kilometers	Statute miles	0.6214
Kilometers	Nautical miles	0.5396
Fathoms	Feet	6.0
Fathoms	Meters	1.829
Kilograms	Pounds	2.205
Centigrade (C)	Farenheit (F)	(C × 9/5) + 32

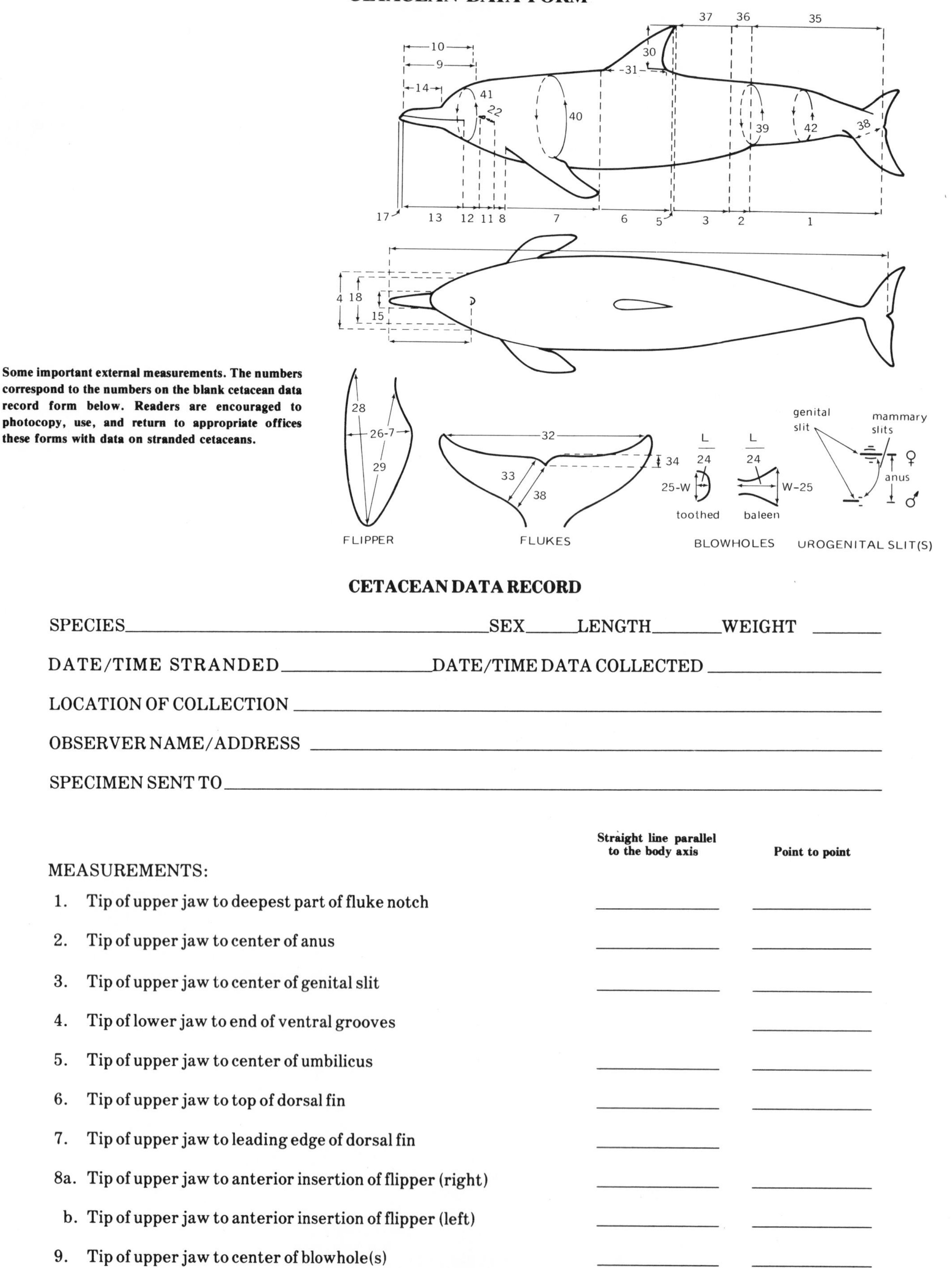

CETACEAN DATA FORM

Some important external measurements. The numbers correspond to the numbers on the blank cetacean data record form below. Readers are encouraged to photocopy, use, and return to appropriate offices these forms with data on stranded cetaceans.

CETACEAN DATA RECORD

SPECIES____________________ SEX_____ LENGTH_______ WEIGHT _______

DATE/TIME STRANDED______________ DATE/TIME DATA COLLECTED ______________

LOCATION OF COLLECTION ____________________

OBSERVER NAME/ADDRESS ____________________

SPECIMEN SENT TO____________________

MEASUREMENTS:	Straight line parallel to the body axis	Point to point
1. Tip of upper jaw to deepest part of fluke notch	________	________
2. Tip of upper jaw to center of anus	________	________
3. Tip of upper jaw to center of genital slit	________	________
4. Tip of lower jaw to end of ventral grooves		________
5. Tip of upper jaw to center of umbilicus	________	________
6. Tip of upper jaw to top of dorsal fin	________	________
7. Tip of upper jaw to leading edge of dorsal fin	________	
8a. Tip of upper jaw to anterior insertion of flipper (right)	________	________
b. Tip of upper jaw to anterior insertion of flipper (left)	________	________
9. Tip of upper jaw to center of blowhole(s)	________	________

	Straight line parallel to the body axis	Point to point
10. Tip of upper jaw to anterior edge of blowhole(s)	________	________
11a. Tip of upper jaw to auditory meatus (right)	________	________
b. Tip of upper jaw to auditory meatus (left)	________	________
12a. Tip of upper jaw to center of eye (right)	________	________
b. Tip of upper jaw to center of eye (left)	________	________
13. Tip of upper jaw to angle of gape		________
14. Tip of upper jaw to apex of melon	________	
15. Rostrum - maximum width		________
16. Throat grooves - length	________	________
17. Projection of lower jaw beyond upper (if reverse, so state)	________	
18. Center of eye to center of eye		________
19a. Height of eye (right)	________	
b. Height of eye (left)	________	
20a. Length of eye (right)	________	
b. Length of eye (left)	________	
21a. Center of eye to angle of gape (right)	________	________
b. Center of eye to angle of gape (left)	________	________
22a. Center of eye to external auditory meatus (right)	________	________
b. Center of eye to external auditory meatus (left)	________	________
23a. Center of eye to center of blowhole (right)	________	________
b. Center of eye to center of blowhole (left)	________	________
24. Blowhole length	________	
25. Blowhole width	________	
26. Flipper width (right)		________
27. Flipper width (left)		________
28a. Flipper length - tip to anterior insertion (right)	________	
b. Flipper length - tip to anterior insertion (left)	________	
29a. Flipper length - tip to axilla (right)	________	
b. Flipper length - tip to axilla (left)	________	

	Straight line parallel to the body axis	Point to point
30. Dorsal fin height	______	
31. Dorsal fin base	______	
32. Fluke span	______	
33. Fluke width	______	
34. Fluke depth of notch	______	
35. Notch of flukes to center of anus	______	
36. Notch of flukes to center of genital aperture	______	______
37. Notch of flukes to umbilicus	______	
38. Notch of flukes to nearest point on leading edge of flukes	______	
39. Girth at anus		______
40. Girth at axilla		______
41. Girth at eye		______
42. Girth ______ cm in front of notch of flukes		______
43a. Blubber thickness (middorsal)		______
b. Blubber thickness (lateral)		______
c. Blubber thickness (midventral)		______
44. Width of head at post-orbital process of frontals	______	
45. Tooth counts: right upper ______		
right lower ______		
left upper ______		
left lower ______		
46. Baleen counts: right upper ______		
left upper ______		
47. Baleen plates, length longest		______
48. Baleen plates, no. bristles/cm over 5 cm	______	
49a. Mammary slit length (right)		______
b. Mammary slit length (left)	______	
50. Genital slit length	______	
51. Anal slit length	______	

APPENDIX E

LIST OF INSTITUTIONS TO CONTACT REGARDING STRANDED CETACEANS

The following list includes many of the institutions in the area covered by this guide which are likely to respond to calls about stranded cetaceans. Those on the mainland are listed roughly in order from north to south. Several Hawaiian island institutions are also included.

As a rule of thumb, anyone finding a stranded cetacean in United States or Canadian waters might be best advised to contact the following organizations: Alaska—the Alaska Department of Fish and Game or U.S. Department of Commerce, National Marine Fisheries Service (NMFS); British Columbia, Canada—The Department of Fisheries and Oceans; Washington and Oregon—The State Patrol; California—The California Department of Fish and Game or NMFS; Mexico—The Institute of Fisheries. Each of these organizations has some responsibility for dealing with strandings and will be informed on procedures and other, perhaps nearby, organizations to contact.

In addition to those listed, almost any university biology or zoology department, State or Federal conservation agency or marine laboratory, or local natural history museum or society can recommend an interested biologist if no staff member is interested. Such organizations are widely distributed along the coast and are usually adequately listed in local telephone directories.

Oceanaria are likely to be most helpful in caring for live animals on an emergency basis. They also often cooperate with biologists by picking up dead animals. Museums are most interested in dead animals, as they have no facilities for handling live ones. They often cooperate with oceanaria and will usually help make arrangements for picking up live animals. Stranding networks, intended to ensure this sort of cooperation, are being organized or implemented in several areas. Therefore, rather than the finder's making a decision about which institution can best respond to a given stranding, we would urge that the nearest organization in the following list be contacted under any circumstances.

Space is provided at the end of the list for addition of contacts inadvertently overlooked by us, or of institutions which come into being after its publication. Institutions marked with an asterisk have some responsibility for responding to strandings and should be contacted promptly for advice and assistance.

ALASKA

University of Alaska
Institute of Marine Sciences
Fairbanks, Alaska 99701

U.S. Department of the Interior
U.S. Fish and Wildlife Service
4454 Business Park Blvd.
Anchorage, Alaska 99503

*Alaska Department of Fish and Game
333 Raspberry Road
Anchorage, Alaska 99502
(also field offices in Barrow, Kotzebue, Nome, Kodiak, Juneau and Ketchikan)

*Auke Bay Laboratory
National Marine Fisheries Service, NOAA
P.O. Box 155
Auke Bay, Alaska 99821

National Park Service
Glacier Bay National Park
Auke Bay, Alaska 99821

*National Marine Mammal Laboratory
National Marine Fisheries Service, NOAA
7600 Sand Point Way N.E., Bldg. 32
Seattle, Washington 98115

BRITISH COLUMBIA

*Environment Canada
Department of Fisheries and Oceans
Pacific Biological Station
Nanaimo, British Columbia V9K 5K6

Curator of Vertebrate Zoology
Provincial Museum
Parliament Building
Victoria, British Columbia V8V 1X4

Department of Zoology
University of British Columbia
Vancouver, British Columbia V6T 1W5

Sealand of the Pacific
Oak Bay
Victoria, British Columbia V8S 2N4

Vancouver Public Aquarium
Stanley Park
Vancouver, British Columbia V6B 3X8

WASHINGTON

*National Marine Mammal Laboratory
National Marine Fisheries Service, NOAA
7600 Sand Point Way N.E., Bldg. 32
Seattle, Washington 98115

Marine Animal Resource Center
4002 West Prosper
Seattle, Washington 98199

The Whale Museum
Moclips Cetological Society
Friday Harbor, Washington 98250

Orca Survey
Center for Whale Research
Friday Harbor, Washington 98250

University of Puget Sound Museum
Tacoma, Washington 98416

Seattle Aquarium
Pier 59
Waterfront Park
Seattle, Washington 98101

OREGON

Oregon State University
Marine Science Center
Newport, Oregon 97365

CALIFORNIA

*California Department of Fish and Game
(contracted by NMFS to report and handle all strandings).

California Department of Fish and Game
1416 Ninth Street
Sacramento, California 95814

California Department of Fish and Game
350 Golden Shore
Long Beach, California 90802

California Department of Fish and Game
411 Burgess Drive
Menlo Park, California 94025

Department of Zoology
Humboldt State University
Arcata, California 95521

California Marine Mammal Center
Marine Headlands Ranger Station
Building 1050
Fort Cronkite, California 94965

Bodega Bay Marine Laboratory
University of California
Bodega Bay, California 94293

Pt. Reyes Bird Observatory
4990 Shoreline Highway
Stinson Beach, California 94970

Museum of Vertebrate Zoology
University of California
Berkeley, California 94720

Steinhart Aquarium or Division of Birds and Mammals
California Academy of Sciences
Golden Gate Park
San Francisco, California 94418

Western Regional Office
National Park Service
450 Golden Gate Avenue
San Francisco, California 94102

Coastal Marine Laboratory
University of California
Santa Cruz, California 95064

Moss Landing Marine Laboratory
Moss Landing, California 95039

Hopkins Marine Station
Stanford University
Cabrillo Point
Pacific Grove, California 93950

Point Lobos State Preserve
c/o Monterey SHP
210 Oliver Street
Monterey, California 93940

Department of Biological Sciences
California Polytechnic State University
San Luis Obispo, California 93407

Santa Barbara Museum of Natural History
2559 Puesta Del Sol Road
Santa Barbara, California 93105

Channel Islands National Marine Sanctuary
c/o The Sea Center
211 Stearns Wharf
Santa Barbara, California 93101

Department of Mammalogy
Los Angeles County Museum of Natural History
900 Exposition Blvd.
Los Angeles, California 90007

*National Marine Fisheries Service
Southwest Fisheries Center
La Jolla Shores Drive
La Jolla, California 92038

Naval Ocean Systems Center
Marine Mammal Research Group
Catalina Blvd.
San Diego, California 92152

Sea World, Inc.
1720 South Shore Road
San Diego, California 92109

Sea World Research Institute
Hubbs Marine Research Center
1700 South Shores Road
San Diego, California 92109

Scripps Institution of Oceanography
La Jolla, California 92037

San Diego Natural History Museum
P.O. Box 1390
San Diego, California 92112

HAWAII

Sea Life Park
Waimanalo
Oahu, Hawaii 96734

MEXICO

Baja California

Unidad de Ciencias Marinas
Universidad Autónoma de Baja California
Apartado Postal 453
Ensenada, BCN

Centro de Investigaciones Biológicas de Baja California Sur
Jalisco y Madero, Apartado Postal 128
23060 La Paz, BCS

Depto. de Ciencias Marinas (Biología Marina)
Universidad Autónoma de Baja California Sur
Km 5, Carretera al sur
Apartado Postal 219-B
23000 La Paz, BCS

Centro Regional de Investigación Pesquera (CRIP)
Instituto Nacional de Pesca
Km 1, Carretera a Pichilingue
23000 La Paz, BCS

Mainland Mexico

*Instituto Nacional de Pesca
Londres 259, Esquina con Sevilla
Col. Juárez
06600 México, D.F.

Laboratorio de Mastozoología—UNAM
Instituto de Biología
Apartado Postal 70-153
04510 México, D.F.

Centro para Estudios de Desiertos y Océanos (CEDO)
Edifício Agustín Cortés
Las Conchas
Apartado Postal 53
83550 Puerto Peñasco, Sonora

Programa de Observación y Estudio de Mamíferos Marinos (POEMM)
Instituto Tecnológico y de Estudios Superiores de Monterrey (ITESM)—Campus Guaymas
Bahía de Bacochibampo
Apartado Postal 484
85400 Guaymas, Sonora

Centro Regional de Investigación Pesquera (CRIP)
Instituto Nacional de Pesca
Calle 20 No. 605 Sur
85400 Guaymas, Sonora

Depto. de Hidrobiología
Universidad de Occidente
Benito Juárez No. 434 Pte.
Los Mochis, Sinaloa

Instituto de Ciencias del Mar y Limnología—UNAM
Estación Mazatlán
Península del Farro
Apartado Postal 811
82000 Mazatlán, Sinaloa

Instituto Oceanográfico de Manzanillo
Secretaría de Marina
Apartado Postal 458
Manzanillo, Colima

Laboratorio de Vertebrados, Depto. de Biología
Facultad de Ciencias—UNAM
Ciudad Universitaria
Apartado Postal 70-572
04510 México, D.F.

GENERAL

Inter-American Tropical Tuna Commission
c/o Southwest Fisheries Center
P.O. Box 271
La Jolla, California 92038
U.S.A.

Appendix F

List of cetacean names in Japanese and Russian[1]

Species	Japanese[2]		Russian[3]	
Baird's beaked whale	ツチクジラ	(tsuchi kujira)	Северный плавун	(severnyy plavun)
Beaked whales	アカボウクジラ科	(akabo kujra ka)	Клюворылые киты	(klyuvorylye kity)
Blainville's beaked whale	コブハクジラ	(kobuha kujira)	Ремнезуб Вленвилля	(remnezub Blainvillya)
Blue whale	シロナガスクジラ	(shiro nagasu kujira)	Блювал или Голубой кит	(blyuval *or* goluboy kit)
Bottlenose dolphin	バンドウイルカ	(bando iruka)	Афалина	(afalina)
Bowhead whale	ホッキョククジラ	(hokkyoku kujira)	Гренландский или Полярный кит	(grendlandskiy *or* polyarnyy kit)
Bryde's whale	ニタリクジラ	(nitari kujira)	Полосатик Брайда	(polosatik Brayda)
Common dolphin	マイルカ	(ma iruka)	Обыкновенный дельфин или дельфин белобочка	(obyknovennyy del'fin *or* del'fin belobochka)
Cuvier's beaked whale	アカボークジラ	(akabo kujira)	Настоящии клюворыл или кювьеров клюворыл	(nastoyashchiy klyuvoryl *or* kyuv'erov klyuvoryl)
Dall's porpoise	リクゼンイルカ	(rikuzen iruka)	Белокрылая морская свинья	(belokrylaya morskaya svin'ya)
Dwarf sperm whale	オガワコマッコウクジラ	(ogawa komakko kujira)	Малый карликовый кашалот	(maly karlikovyy kashalot)
False killer whale	オキゴンドウクジラ	(oki gondo kujira)	Малая или черная косатка	(malaya *or* chornaya kosatka)
Fin whale	ナガスクジラ	(nagasu kujira)	Финвал	(finval)
Fraser's dolphin	サラワクイルカ	(Sarawaku iruka)	Саравакский дельфин или дельфин Фразера	(saravakskiy del'fin *or* del'fin Frasera)
Gray whale	コククジラ	(koku kujira)	Серый кит	(seryy kit)
Gingko-toothed beaked whale	イチョウハクジラ	(ichoha kujira)	Гинкозубый ремнезуб	(ginkozubyy remnezub)
Harbor porpoise	ネズミイルカ	(nezumi iruka)	Морская свинья	(morskaya svin'ya)
Hector's beaked whale	ニュージーランドオオギハクジラ	(nu zerando oogiha kujira)	Ремнезуб Хектора	(remnezub Hectora)
Hubbs' beaked whale	ハッブスオオギハクジラ	(Hubbs' oogiha kujira)	Ремнезуб Хаббса	(remnezub Hubbsa)
Humpback whale	ザトウクジラ	(zato kujira)	Горбач	(gorbach)
Killer whale	シャチサカマタ	(shachi; sakamata)	Косатка	(kosatka)
Minke whale	コイワシクジラ; ミンク	(koiwashi kujira; minku)	Малый полосатик или минке	(malyy polosatik *or* minke)
Melon-headed whale	カズハゴンドウクジラ	(kazuha gondo kujira)	Ширококлювый дельфин	(shirokoklyuvyy del'fin)
Narwhal	イッカク	(ikkaku)	Нарвал	(narval)
Northern bottlenose whale	キタトックリクジラ	(kita tokkuri kujira)	Северный Бутылконос	(severnyy butylkonos)
Northern right whale dolphin	キタセミイルカ	(kita semi iruka)	Северный китовидный дельфин	(severnyy kitovidnyy del'fin)
Pacific white-sided dolphin	カマイルカ	(kama iruka)	Тихоокеанский белобокий дельфин	(tikhookeanskiy belobokiy del'fin)
Pygmy killer whale	ユメゴンドウクジラ	(yume gondo kujira)	Карликовая косатка	(karlikovaya kosatka)
Pygmy sperm whale	コマッコウクジラ	(komakko kujira)	Карликовый кашалот	(karlikovyy kashalot)
Right whale	セミクジラ	(semi kujira)	Южный кит	(yuzhnyy kit)
Risso's dolphin	ハナゴンドウクジラ	(hana gondo kujira)	Серый дельфин	(seryy del'fin)
Rough-toothed dolphin	シワハイルカ	(shiwaha iruka)	Гребнезубый дельфин	(grebnezubyy del'fin)
Sei whale	イワシクジラ	(iwashi kujira)	Сейвал	(seyval)
Short-finned pilot whale	コビレゴンドウクジラ	(kobire gondo kujira)	Гринда	(grinda)
Southern bottlenose whale	ミナミトックリクジラ	(minami tokkuri kujira)	Южный бутылконос	(yuzhnyy butylkonos)
Sperm whale	マッコウクジラ	(makko kujira)	Кашалот	(kashalot)
Spinner dolphin	ハシナガイルカ	(hashinaga iruka)	Длинноносый или вертящийся дельфин	dlinnonosyy *or* vertyashchiysya del'fin)
Spotted dolphin	アラリイルカ	(arari iruka)	Пятнистый дельфин	(pyatnistyy del'fin)
Stejnegers' beaked whale	オオギハクジラ	(oogiha kujira)	Ремнезуб Стейнегера	(remnezub Stejnegera)
Striped dolphin	スジイルカ	(suji iruka)	Полосатый дельфин или стенелла	(polosatyy del'fin *or* stenella)
Vaquita	コガシラネズミイルカ	(kogashira nezumi iruka)	Калифорнийская морская свинья	(kaliforniyskaya morskaya svin'ya)
White whale	シロイルカ	(shiro iruka)	Белуха	(belukha)

[1]Common names in Spanish and, when available, in Alaska Yupik are listed with "Other Common Names" under each species. They were provideded by the Inter-American Tropical Tuna Commission and reviewed by R. Clarke and A. Aguayo and by Conrad Ozeeva, Gambell Village, St. Lawrence Island, Alaska, respectively.

[2]Provided by Larry Tsunoda, National Marine Mammal Laboratory, NMFS, NOAA.

[3]Provided by A. V. Yablokov, A. S. Sokolov, and V. S. Gurevich with transliterations standardized by U.S. Joint Publications Research Service.

MARINE MAMMAL SIGHTING INFORMATION

DATE AND LOCAL TIME ________________________ POSITION[1] ____________

WEATHER CONDITIONS ____

OCEANOGRAPHIC CONDITIONS[2] ____

____

SPECIES[3] ________________________ NUMBER OF ANIMAL(S) ________

IN DEGREES TRUE HEADING OF ANIMAL(S) ____________________________

ASSOCIATED ORGANISMS ____

____

TAGS OR UNUSUAL MARKINGS[4] ____

____

CHARACTERISTICS WHICH RESULTED IN SPECIES IDENTIFICATION ____________

____

____

BEHAVIOR OF ANIMAL(S)-INCLUDE CLOSEST APPROACH ____________________

____

SKETCHES

PHOTOS AVAILABLE YES______ NO______

ADDITIONAL REMARKS ____

____

____

NAME AND ADDRESS OF OBSERVER (SHIP OR AIRCRAFT) ____________________

____

____

____